TOP 50 hits

Arranged by Dan Coates

Copyright © MMIX by Alfred Music Publishing Co., Inc.
All Rights Reserved   Printed in USA
ISBN-10: 0-7390-5917-3
ISBN-13: 978-0-7390-5917-3

TABLE OF CONTENTS

Amazed	4
Angel Eyes	11
As Time Goes By	14
At Last	17
Beautiful (As You)	20
Beauty and the Beast	24
Because You Loved Me	28
Can You Feel the Love Tonight	33
Can You Read My Mind?	36
A Certain Smile	8
Come Rain or Come Shine	40
Endless Love	43
The Gift	48
Hold Me, Thrill Me, Kiss Me	52
How Could I Ever Know	56
How Deep Is Your Love	59
How Do I Live	62
I Believe in You and Me	72
I Don't Want to Miss a Thing	76
I Get a Kick out of You	67
I Only Have Eyes for You	80
I've Grown Accustomed to Her Face	84
Killing Me Softly with His Song	90
La vie en rose	87
Laura	92

Let's Do It (Let's Fall in Love)	95
Love Is a Many Splendored Thing	98
Misty	101
Moonlight Serenade	104
My Funny Valentine	107
The Prayer	110
The Rose	115
Somewhere, My Love	118
Take My Breath Away	122
Taking a Chance on Love	126
This I Promise You	129
This Kiss	134
This Magic Moment	140
Up Where We Belong	146
Valentine	150
Weekend in New England	154
When a Man Loves a Woman	158
Where or When	162
A Whole New World	174
The Wind Beneath My Wings	166
You Light Up My Life	143
You Make Me Feel So Young	170
You Raise Me Up	177
You'll Never Know	186
(Your Love Has Lifted Me) Higher and Higher	182

AMAZED

Words and Music by Marv Green,
Aimee Mayo and Chris Lindsey
Arranged by Dan Coates

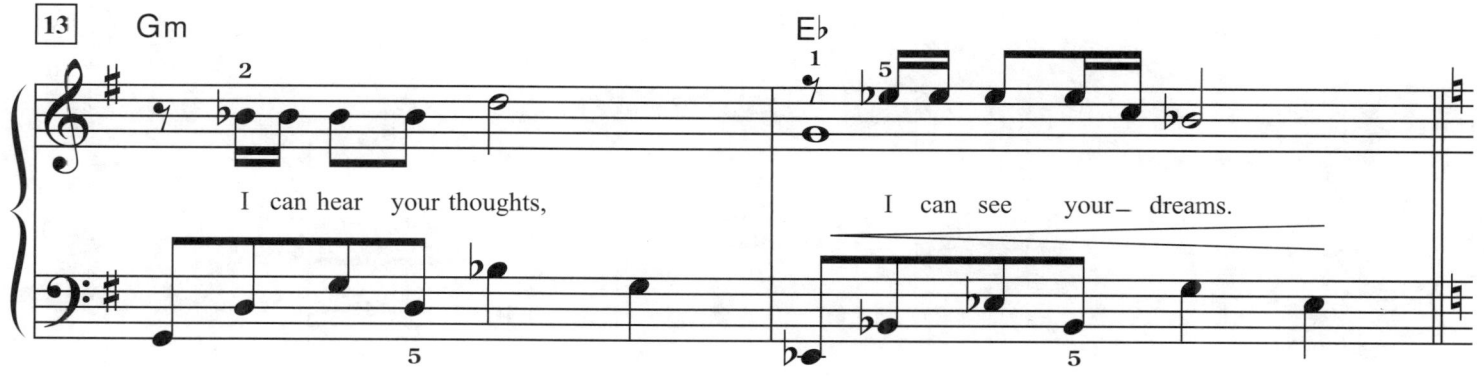

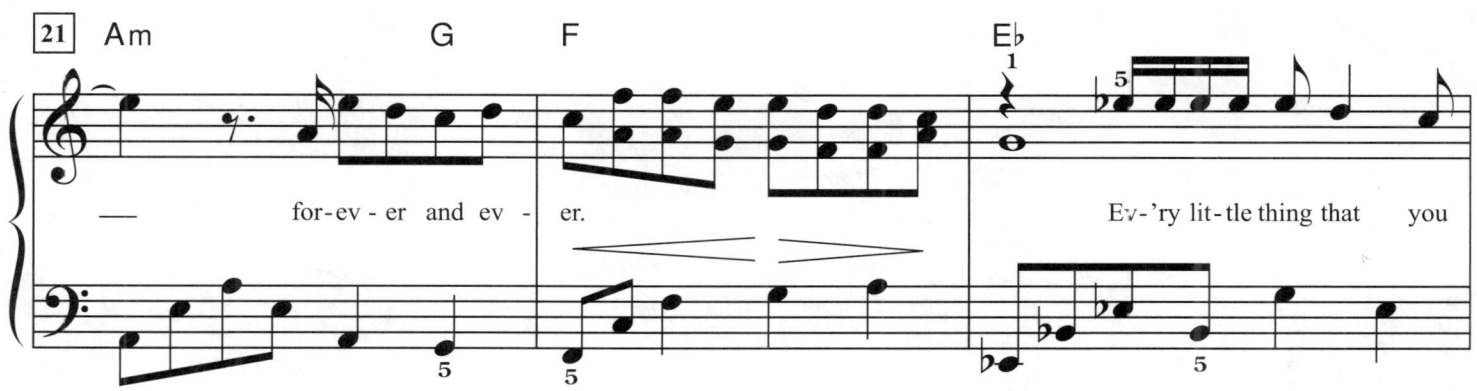

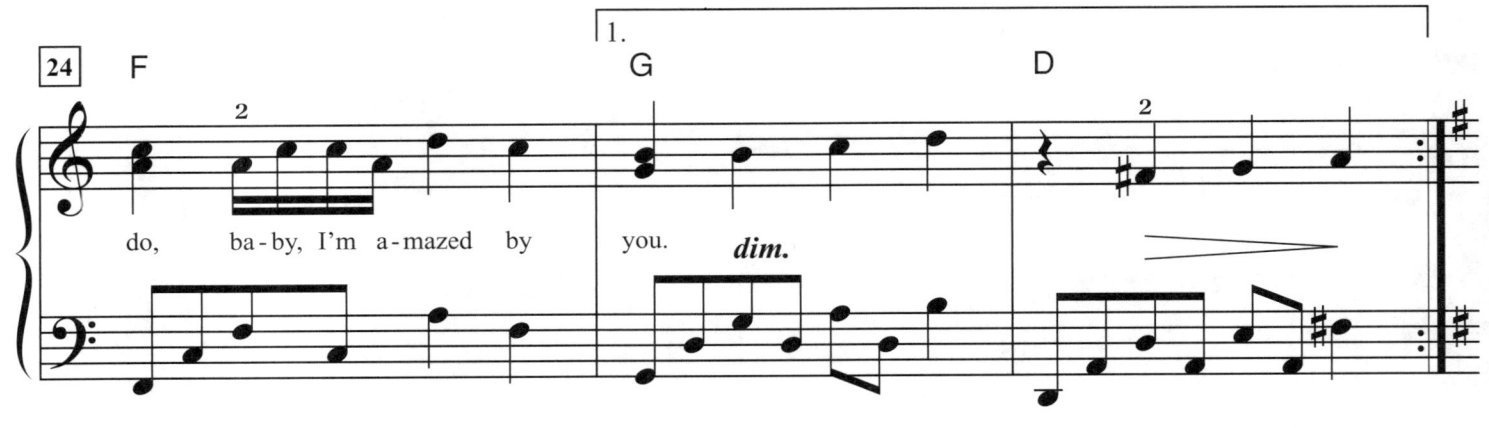
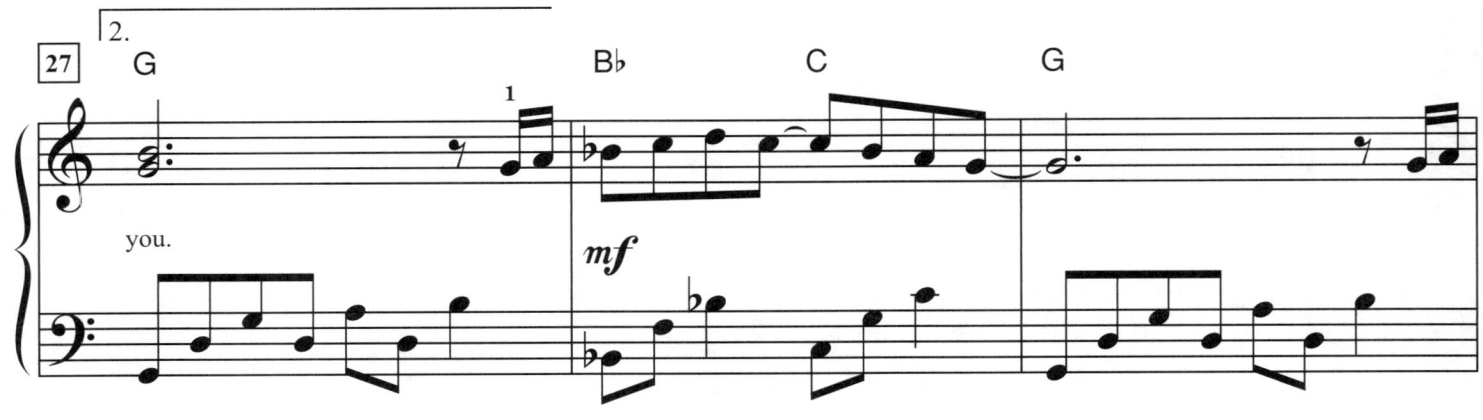
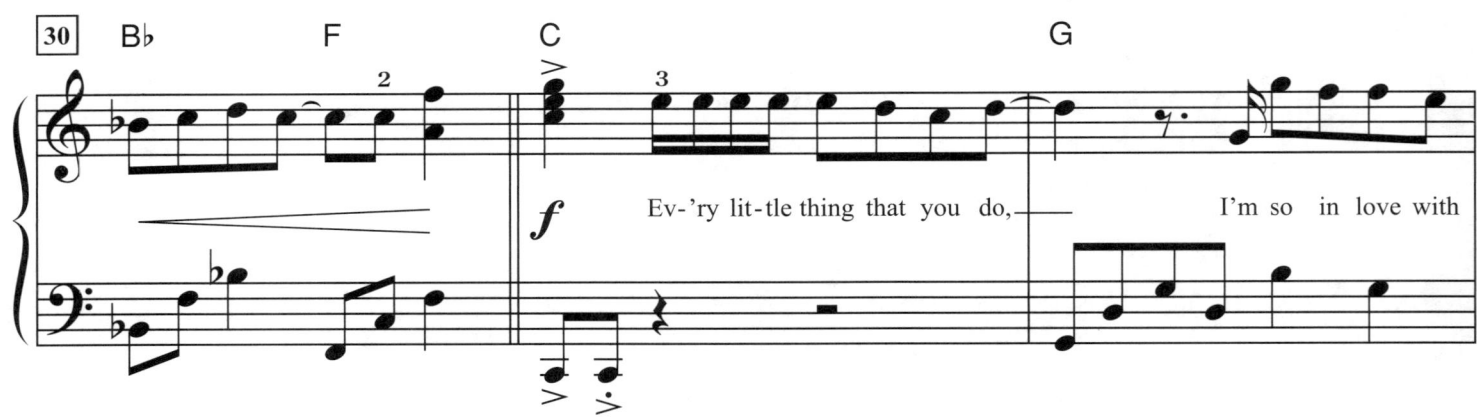
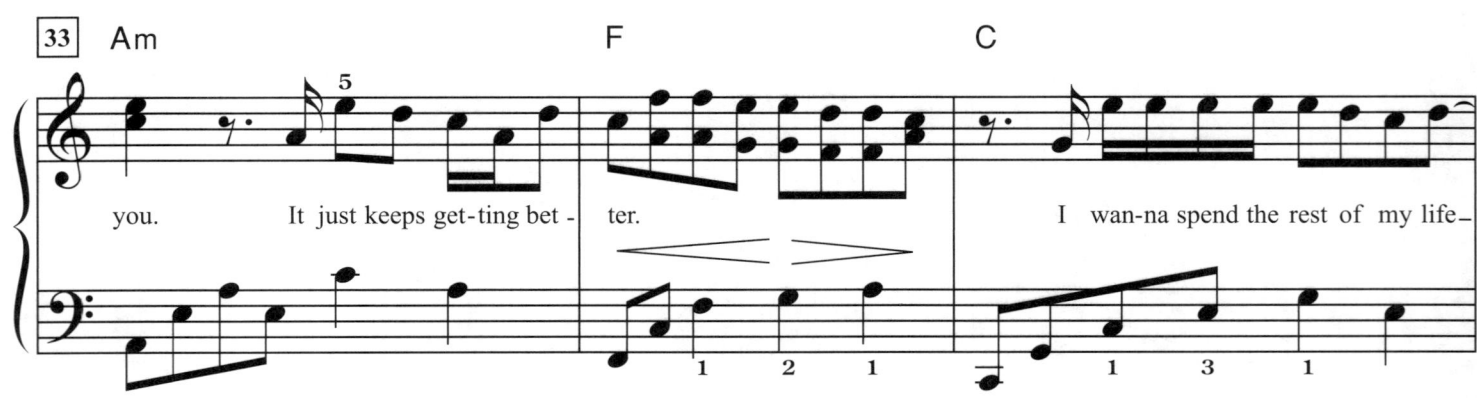

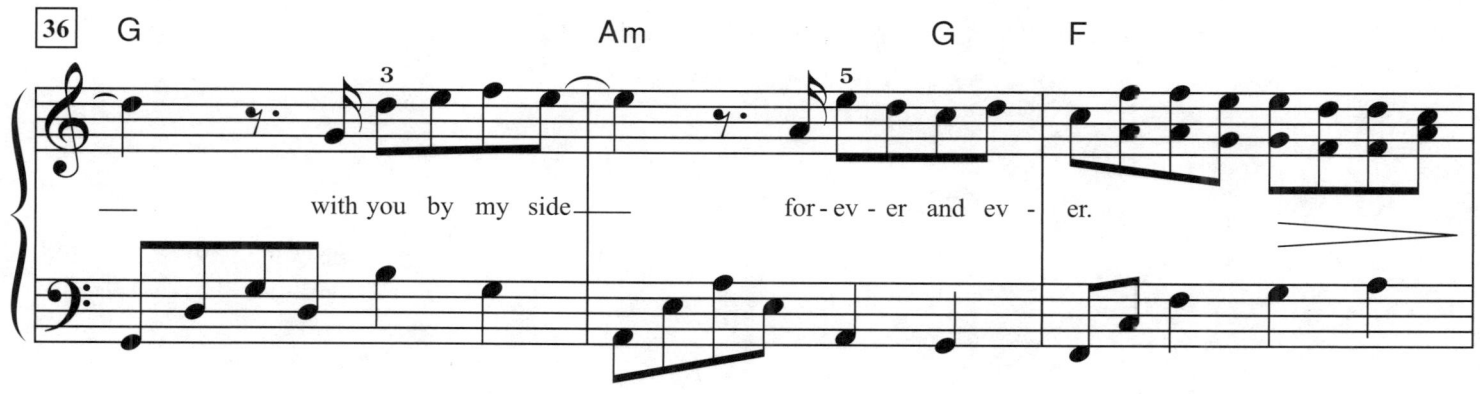
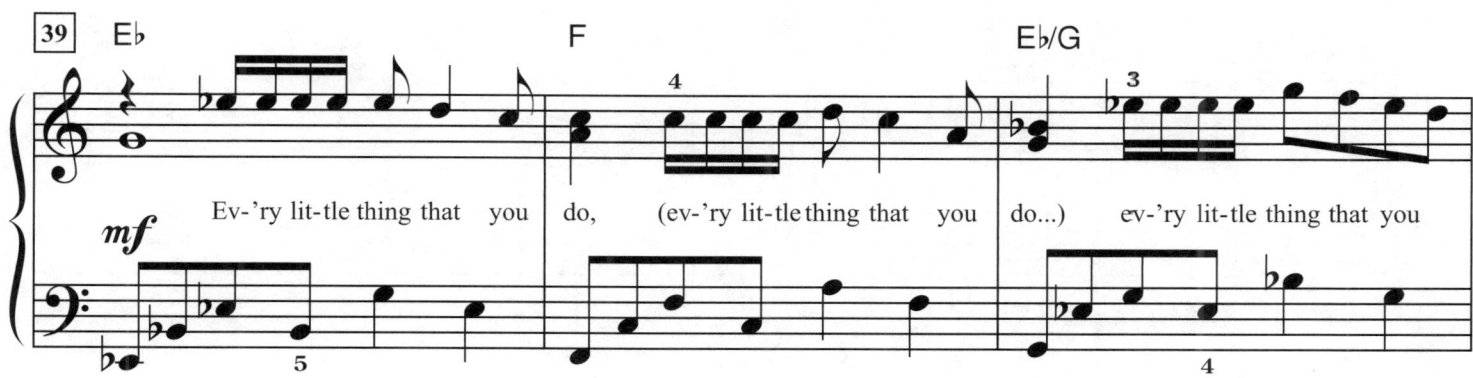
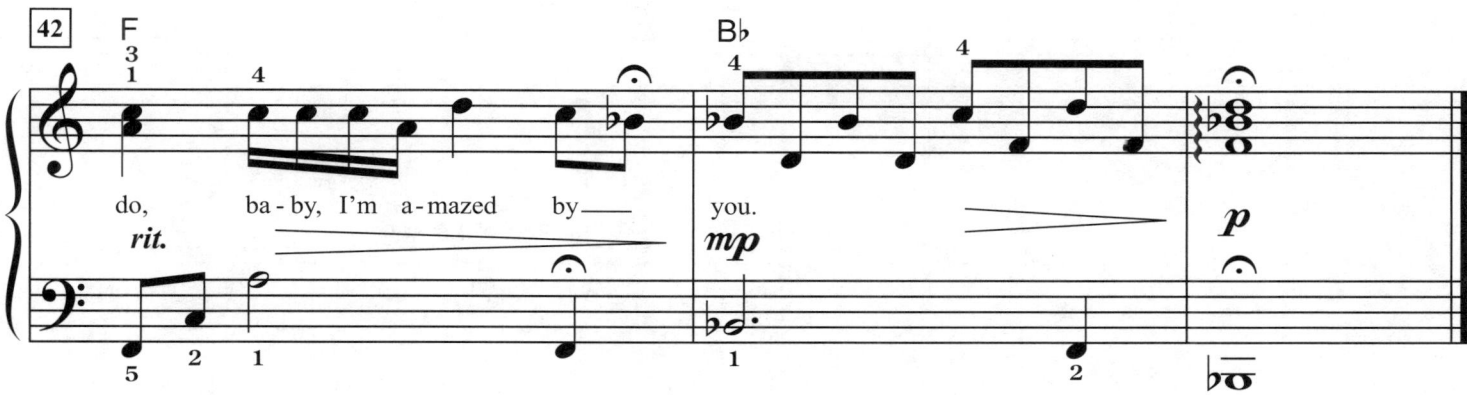

Verse 2:
The smell of your skin,
The taste of your kiss,
The way you whisper in the dark.
Your hair all around me,
Baby, you surround me.
You touch every place in my heart.
Oh, it feels like the first time every time.
I wanna spend the whole night in your eyes.
(To Chorus:)

A CERTAIN SMILE

Music by Sammy Fain and Paul Francis Webster
Arranged by Dan Coates

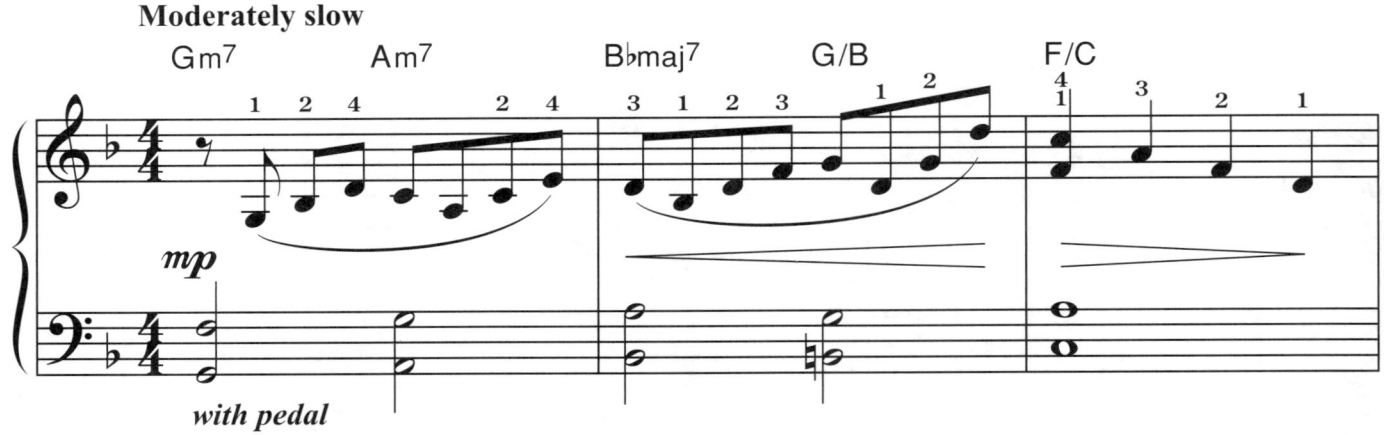

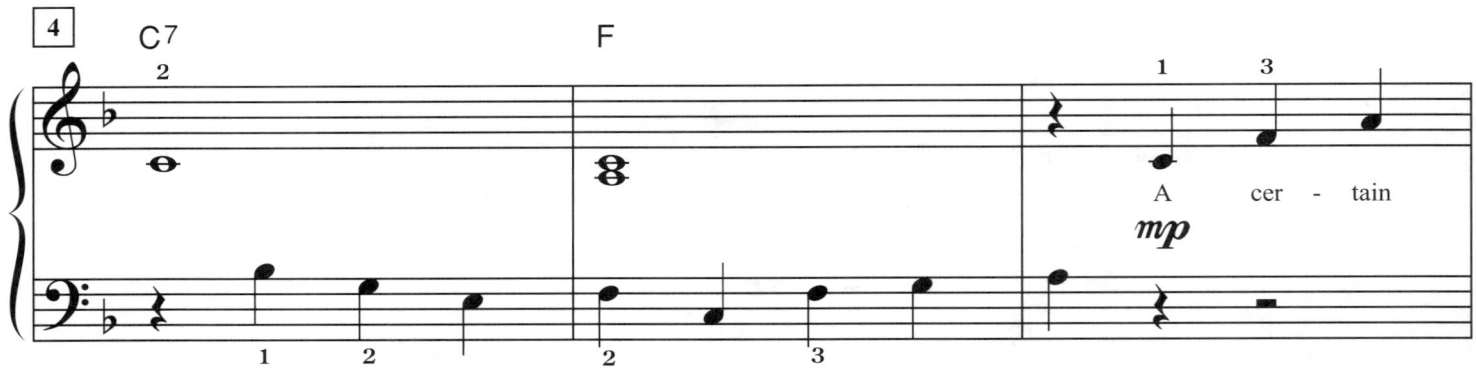

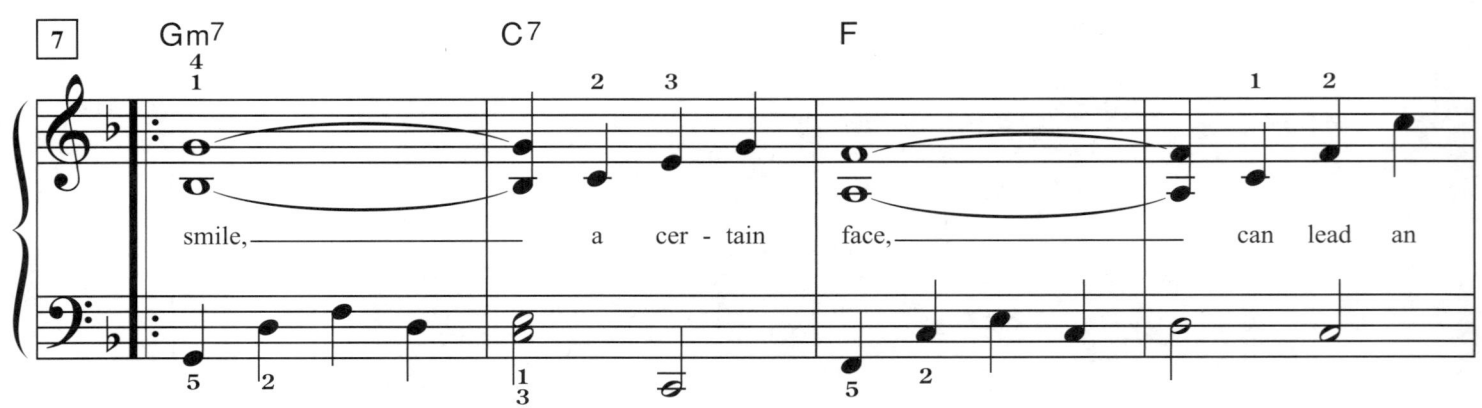

© 1958 (Renewed) TWENTIETH CENTURY MUSIC CORPORATION
All Rights Controlled by EMI MILLER CATALOG INC. (Publishing)
and ALFRED PUBLISHING CO., INC. (Print)
All Rights Reserved

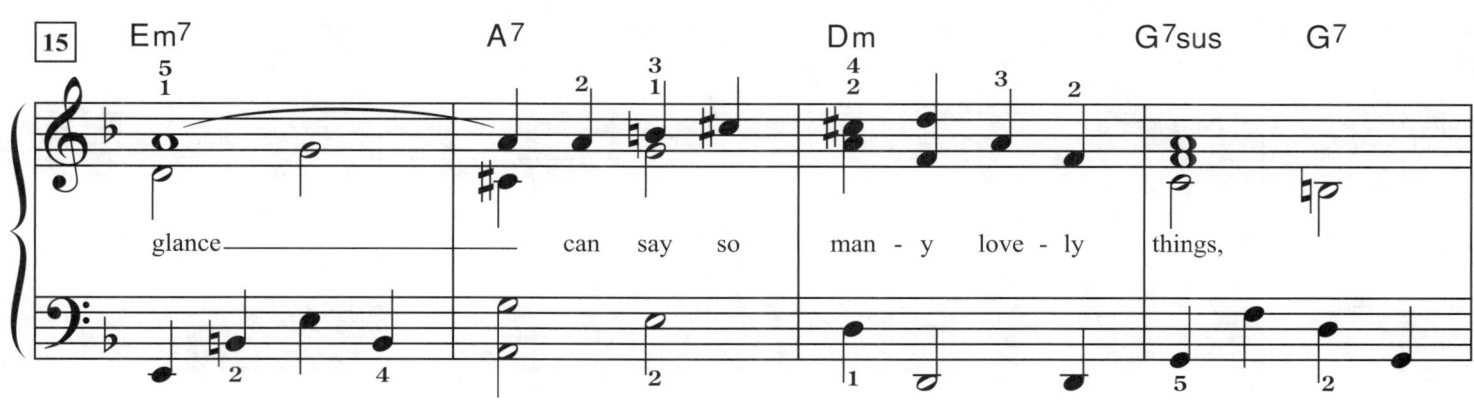
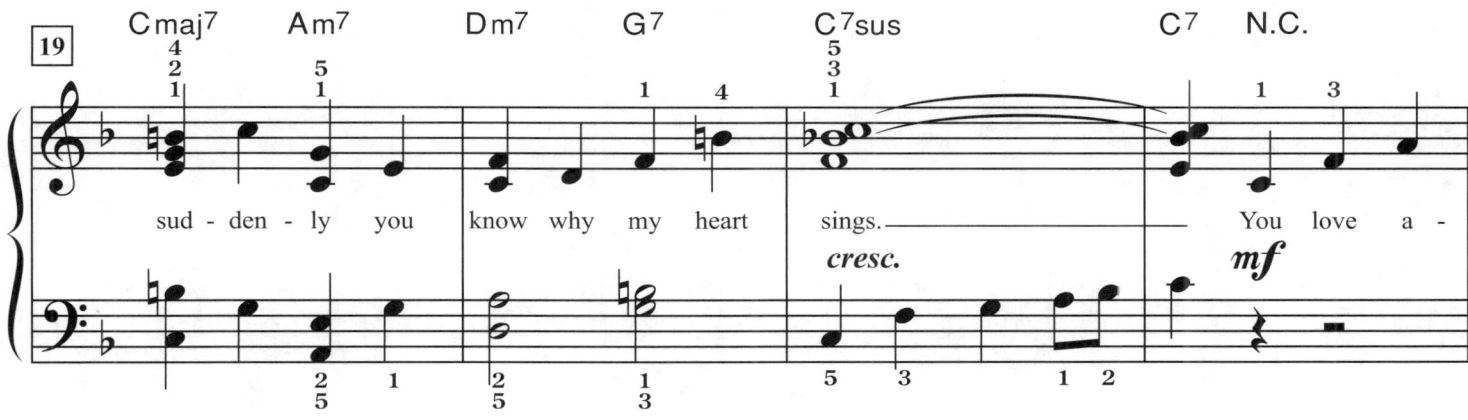
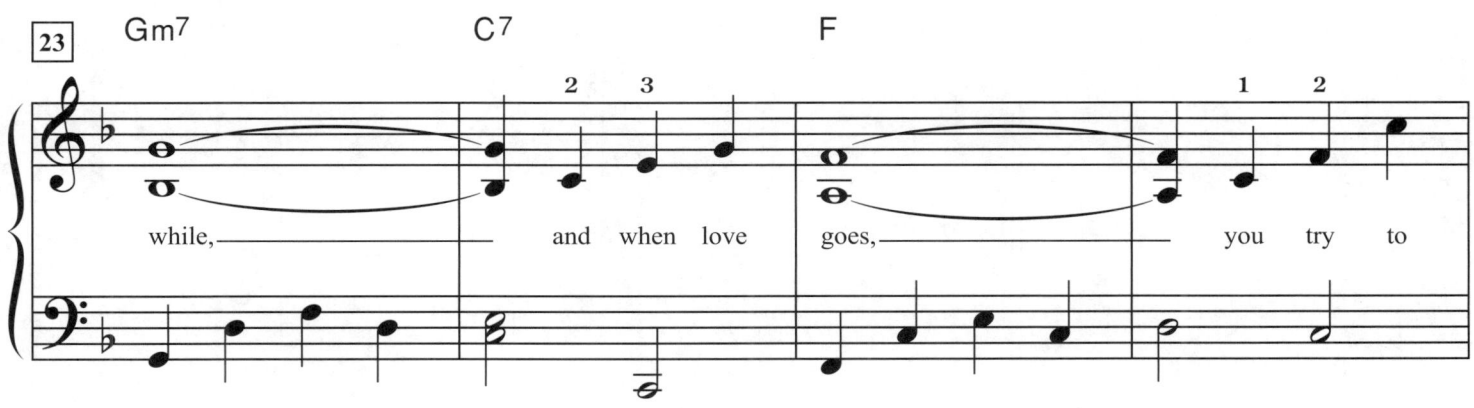

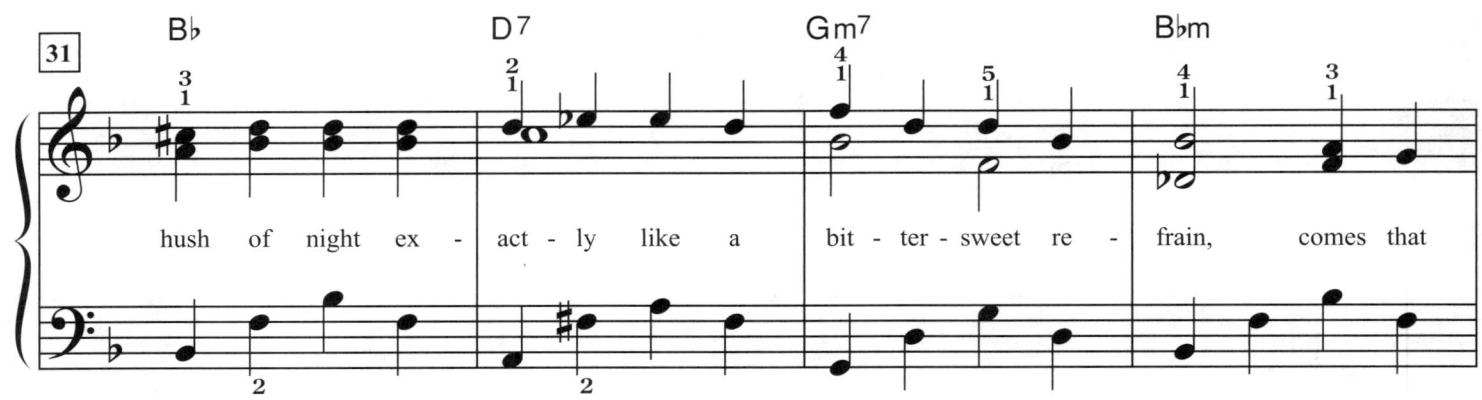
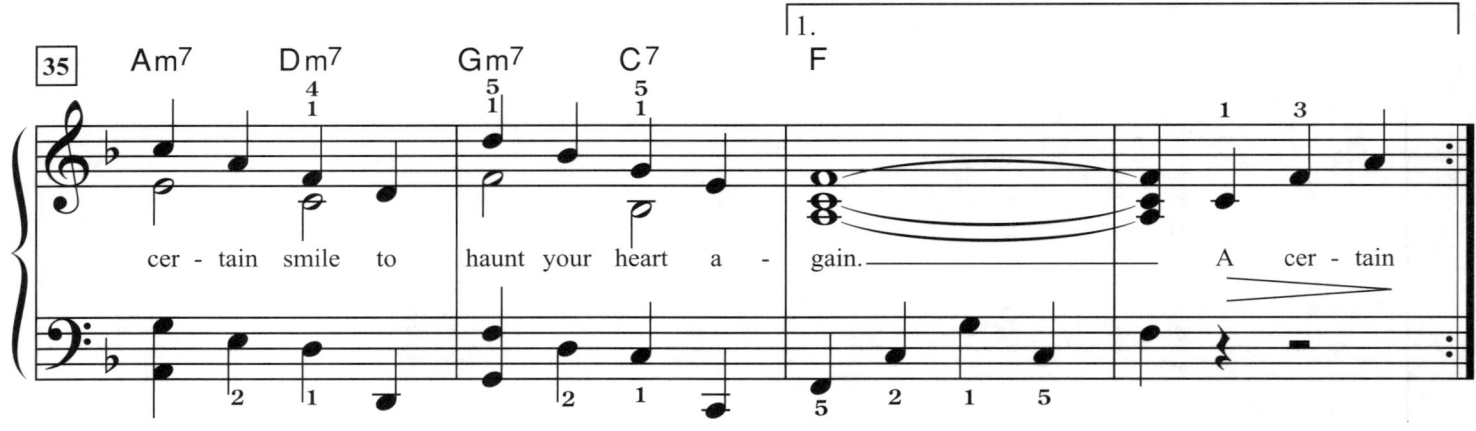

ANGEL EYES

Composed by Jim Brickman
Arranged by Dan Coates

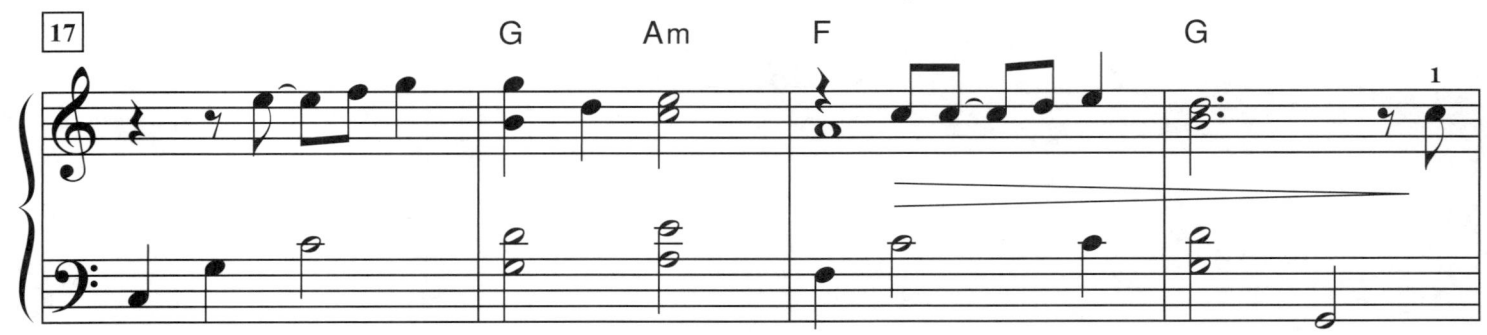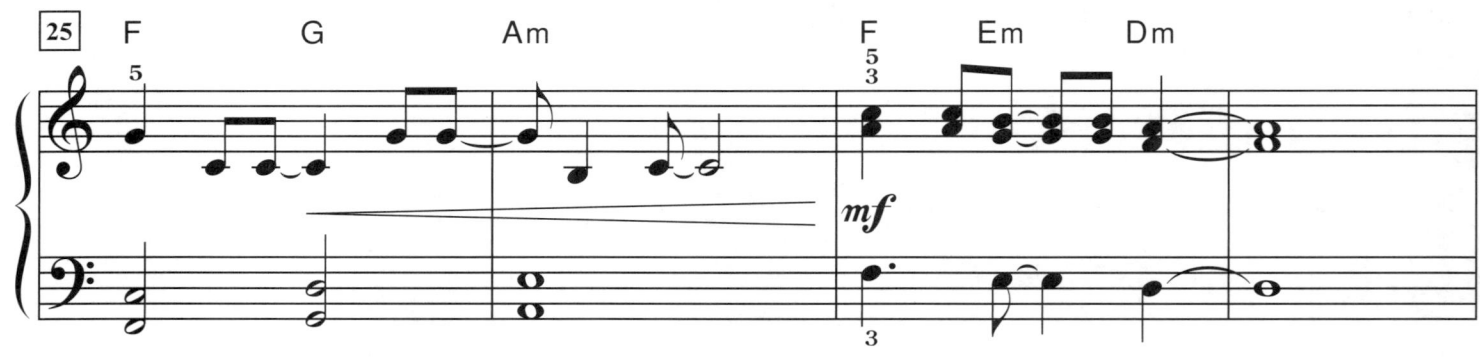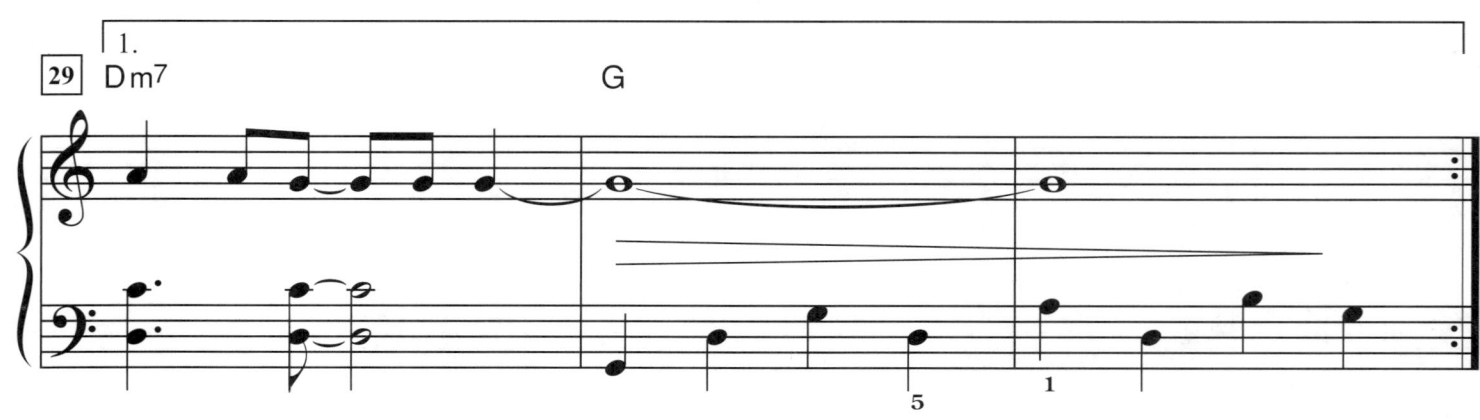

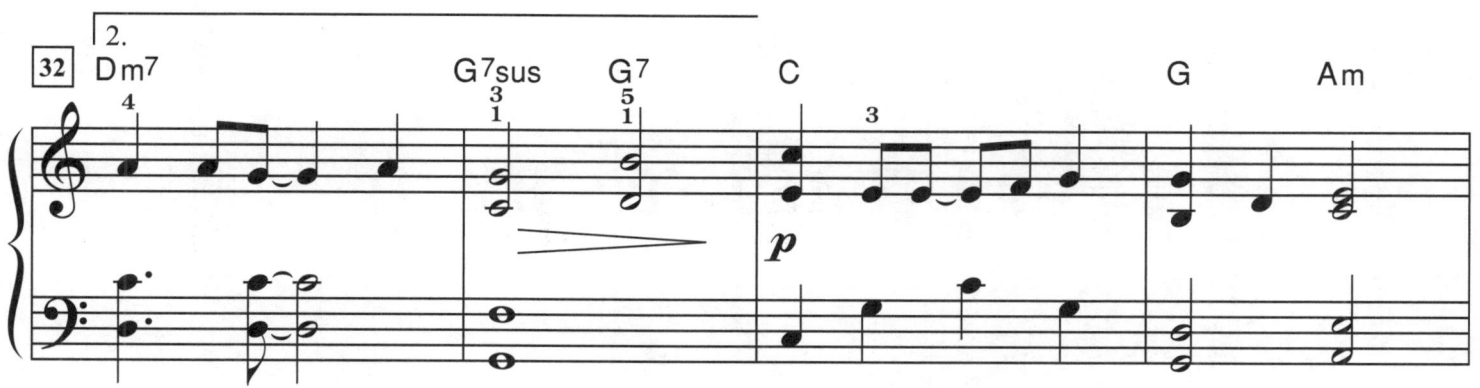
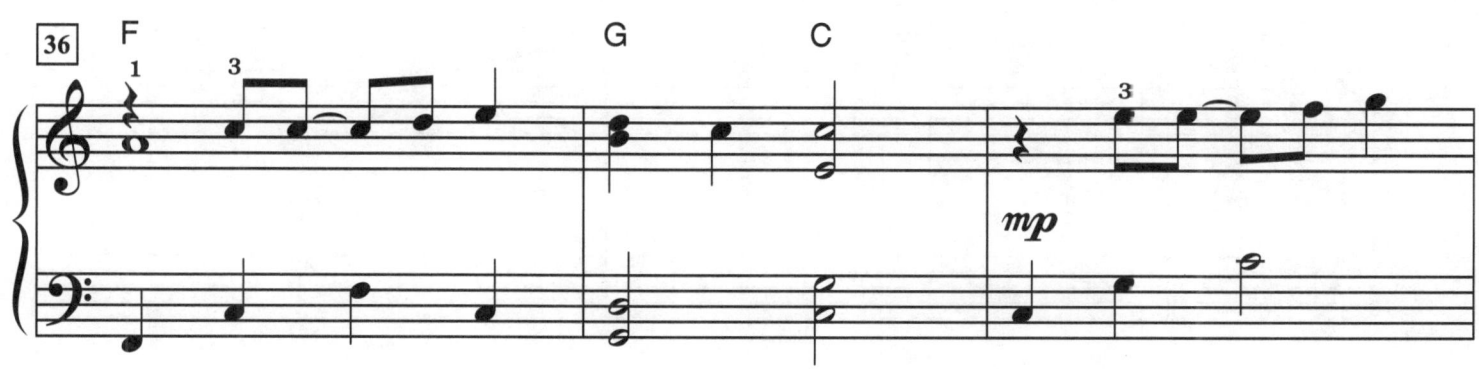
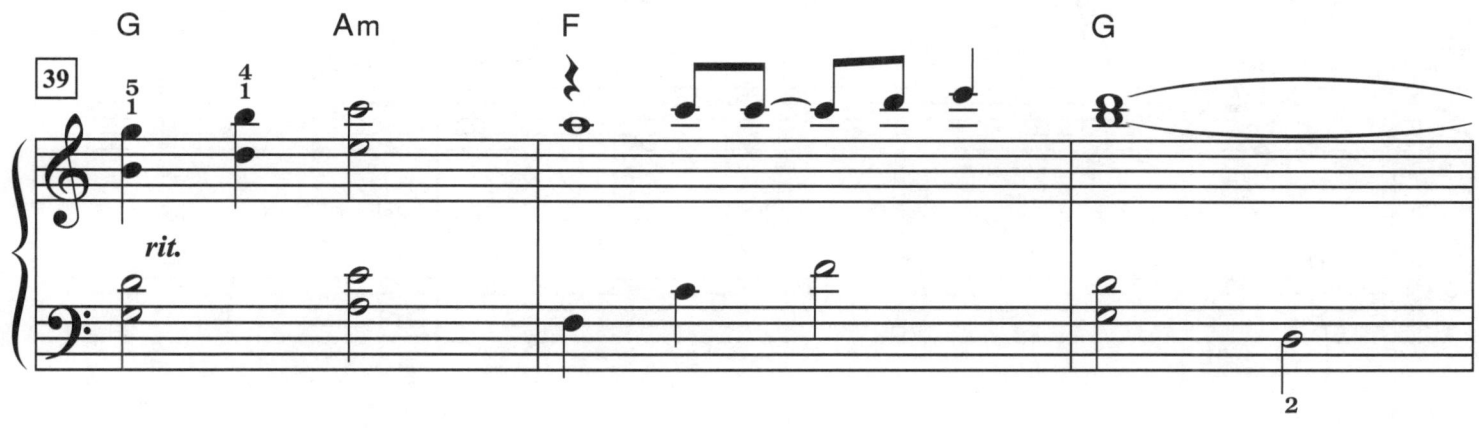
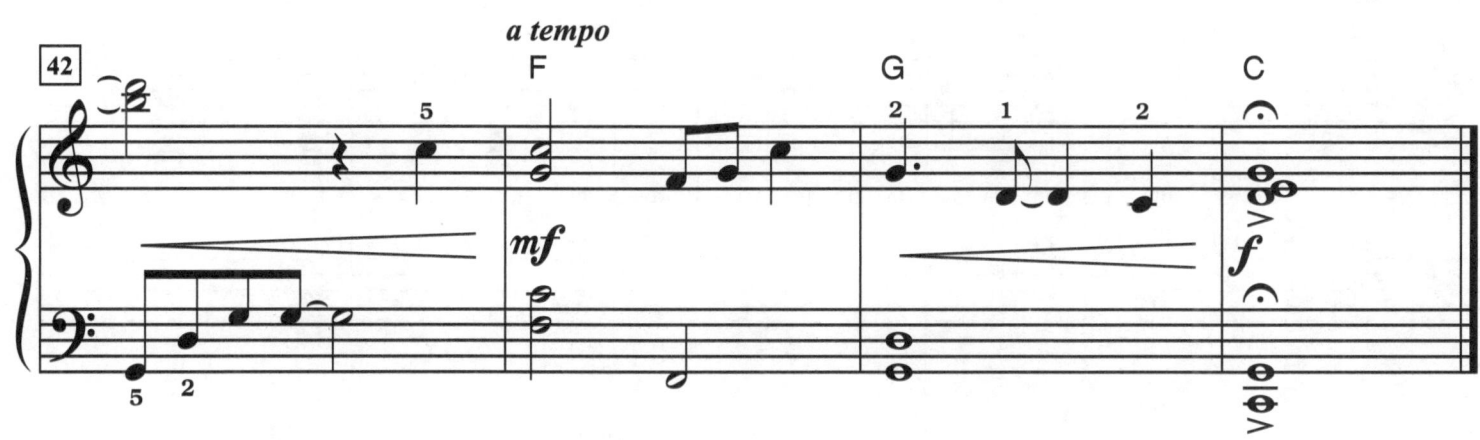

AS TIME GOES BY

Words and Music by Herman Hupfeld
Arranged by Dan Coates

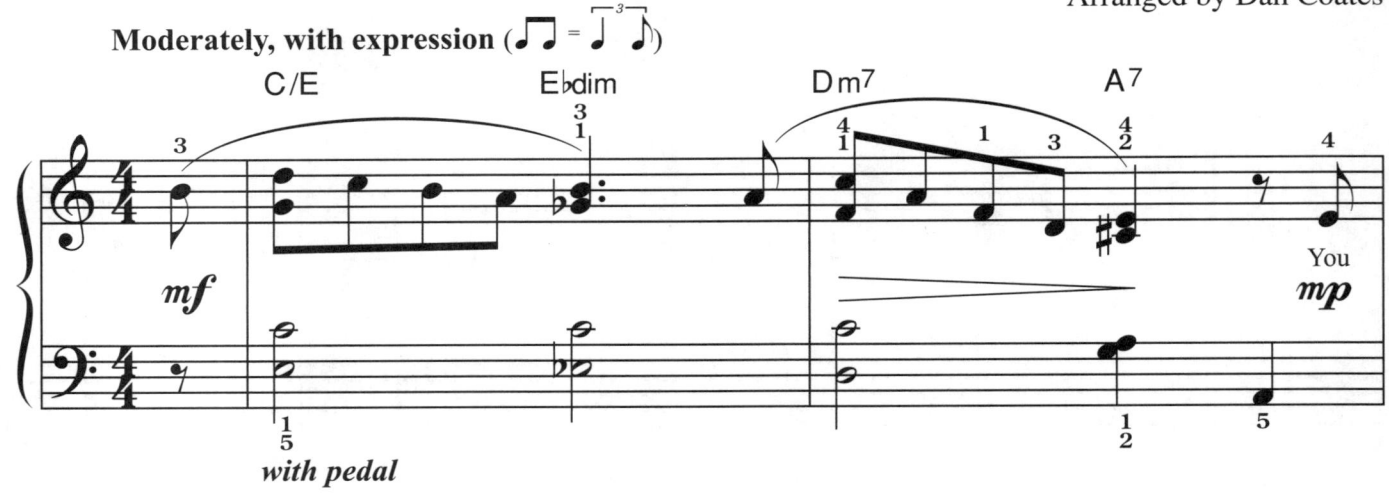

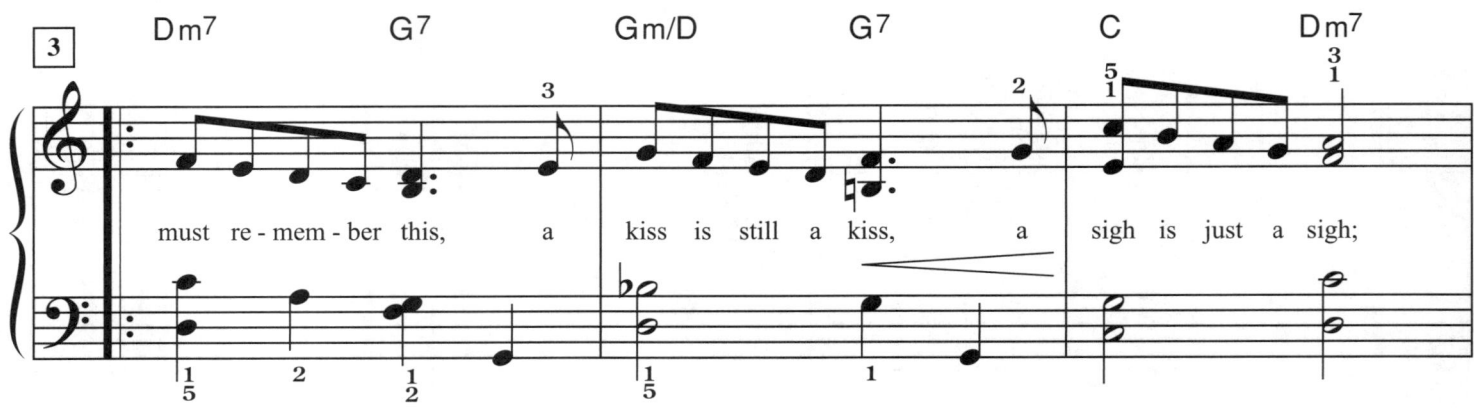

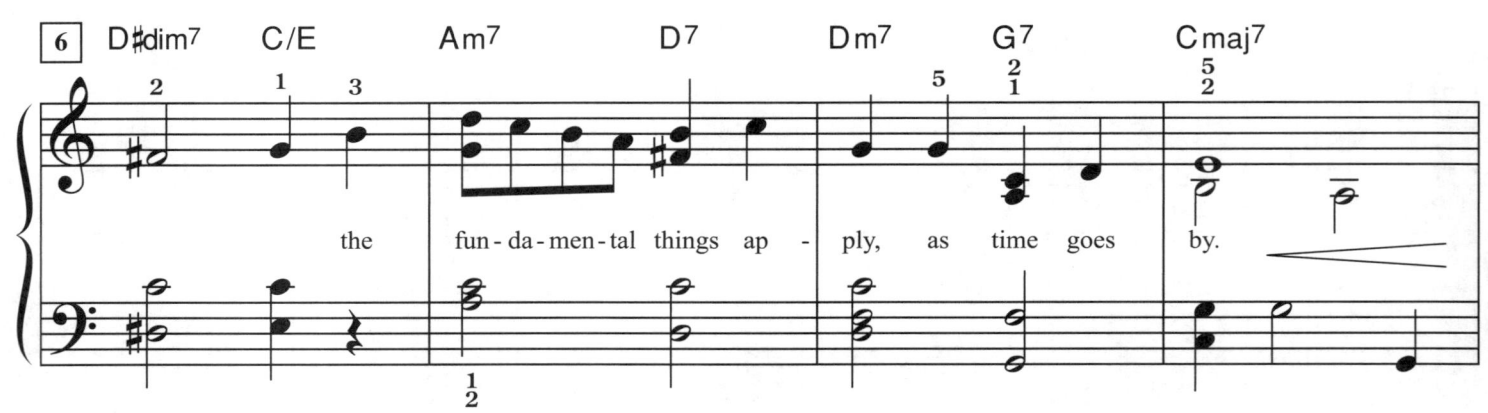

© 1931 (Renewed) WARNER BROS. INC.
All Rights Administered by WB MUSIC CORP.
All Rights Reserved

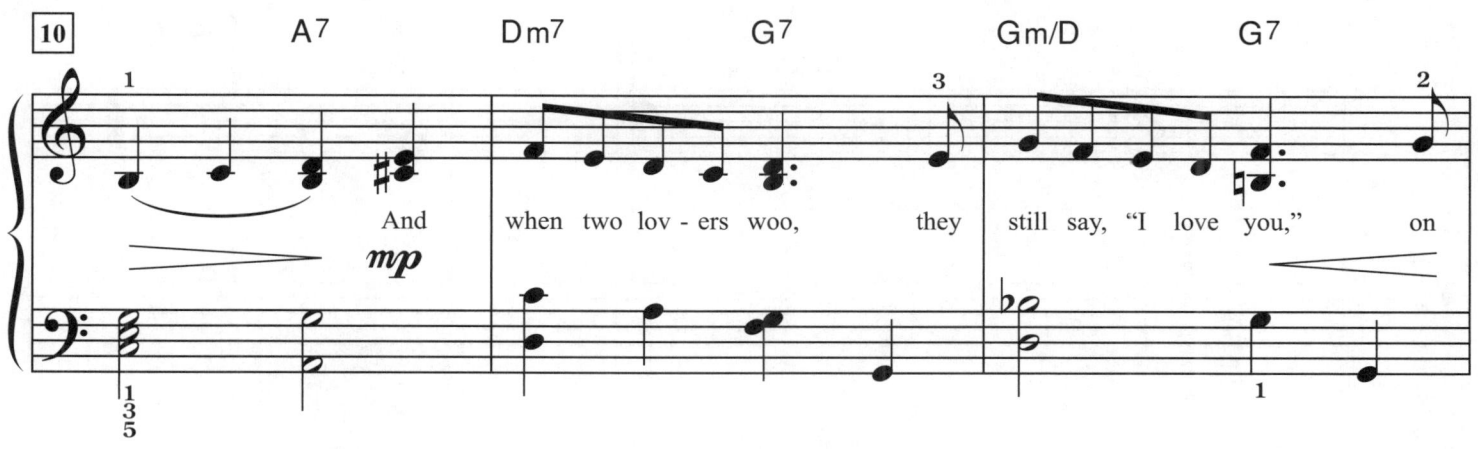
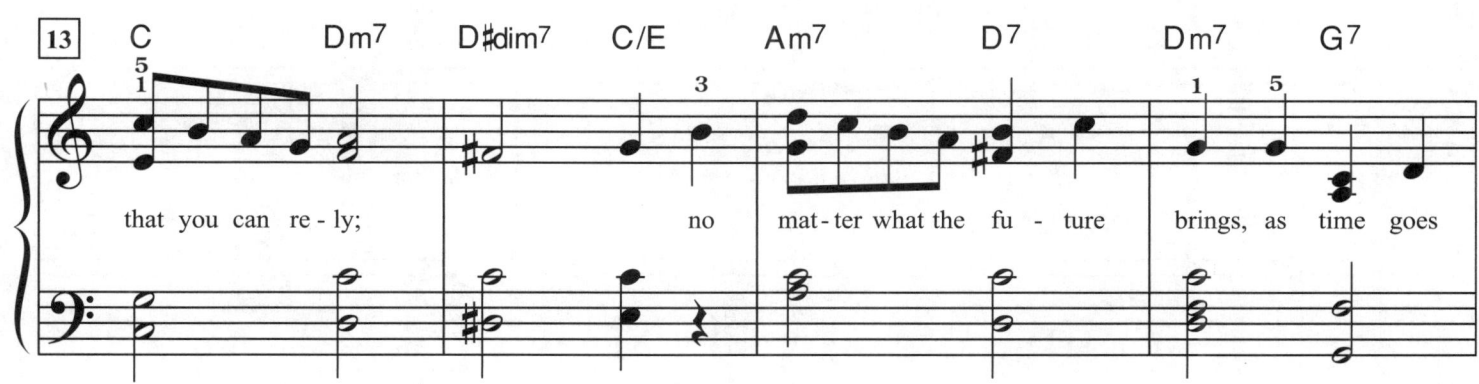
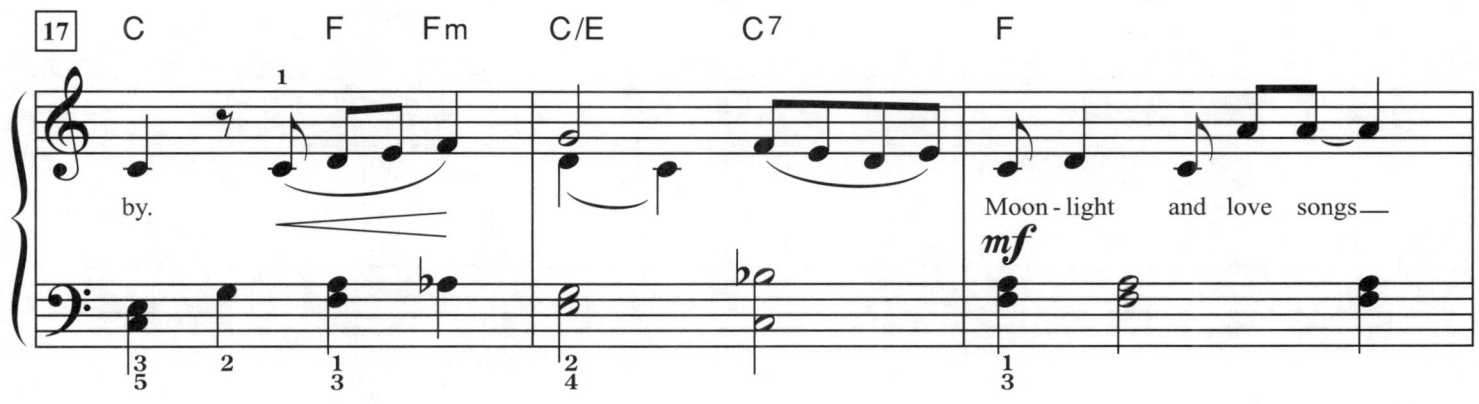
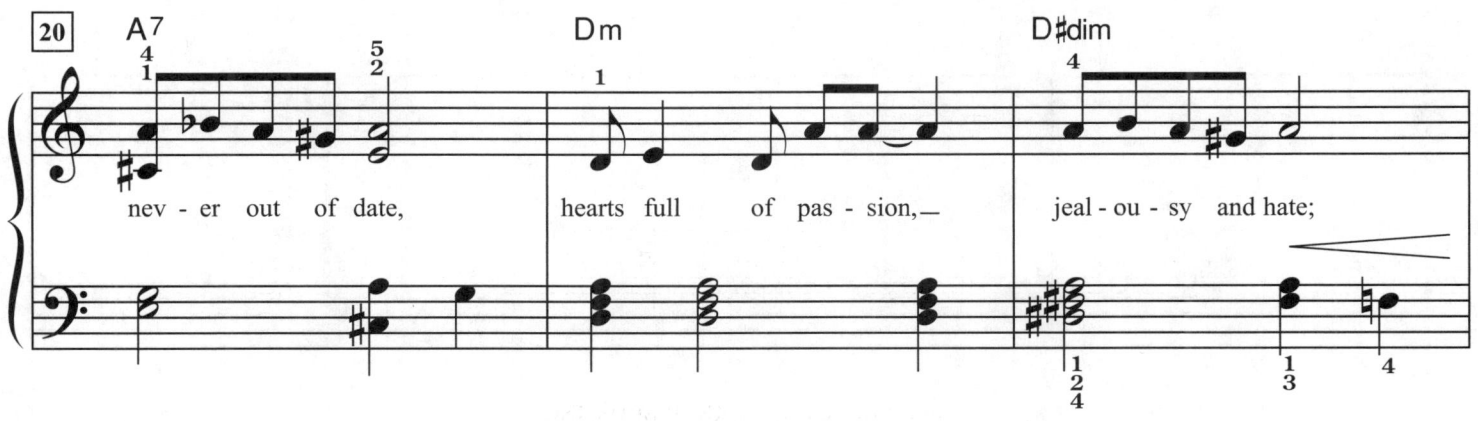

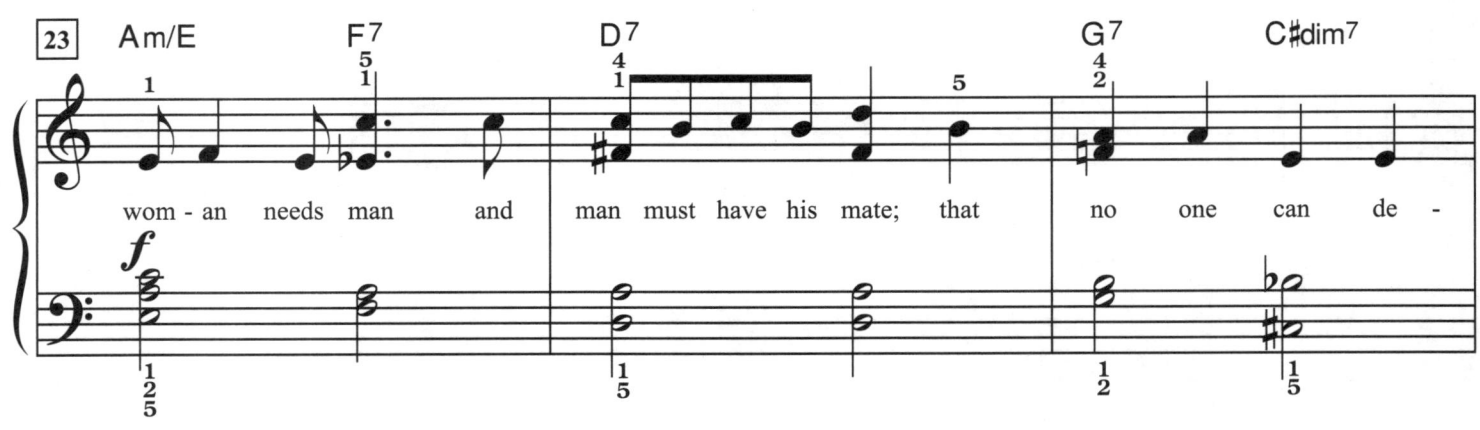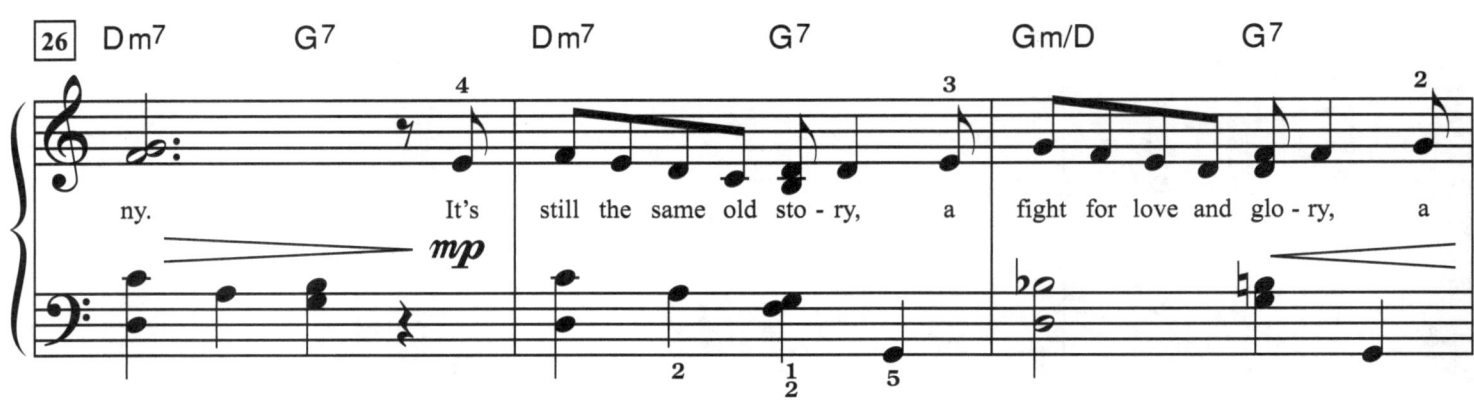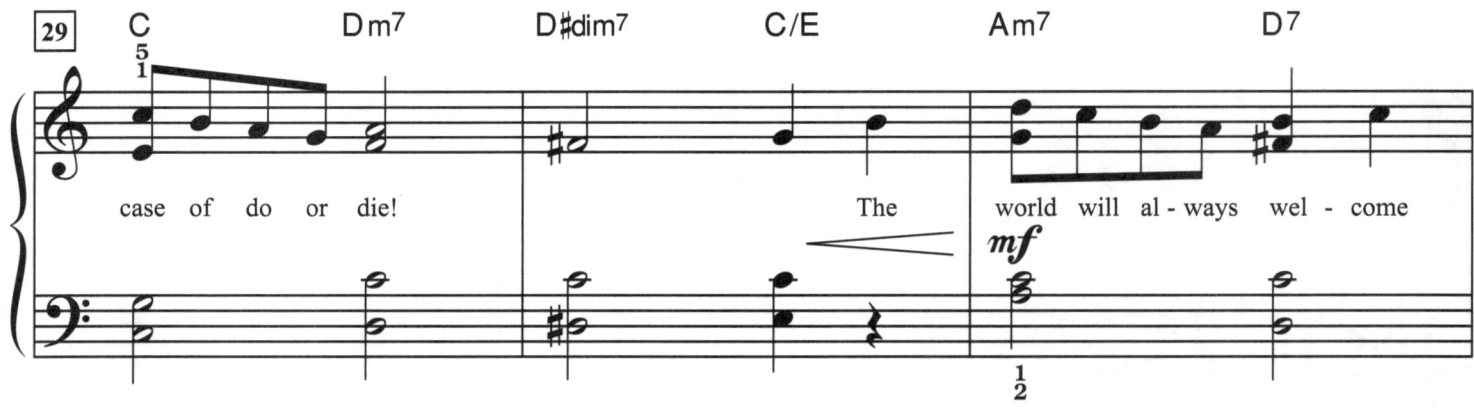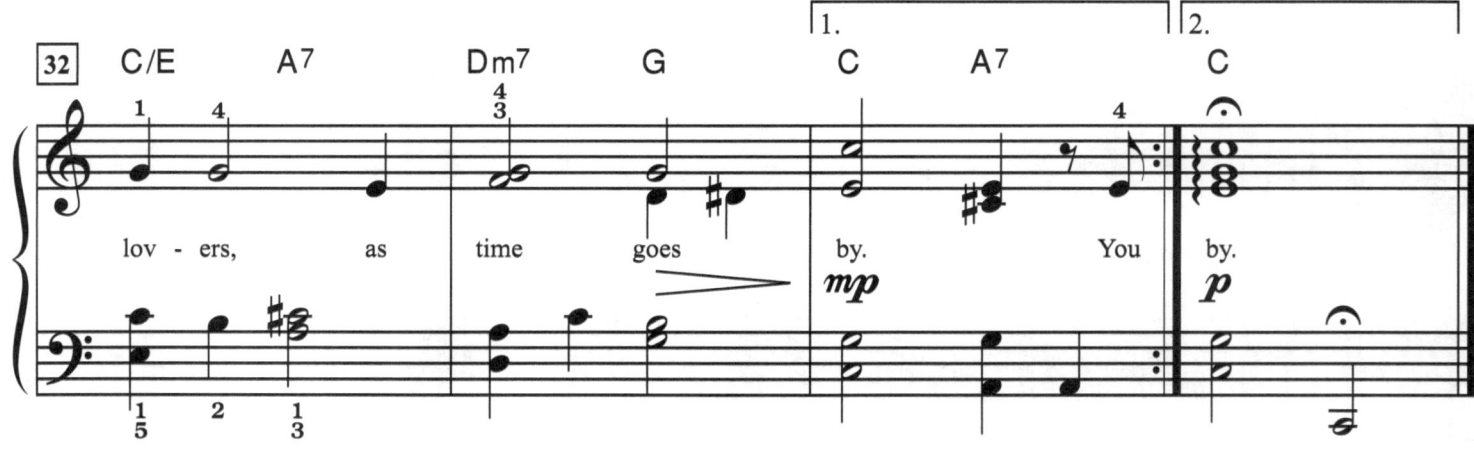

AT LAST

Music by Harry Warren
Lyrics by Mack Gordon
Arranged by Dan Coates

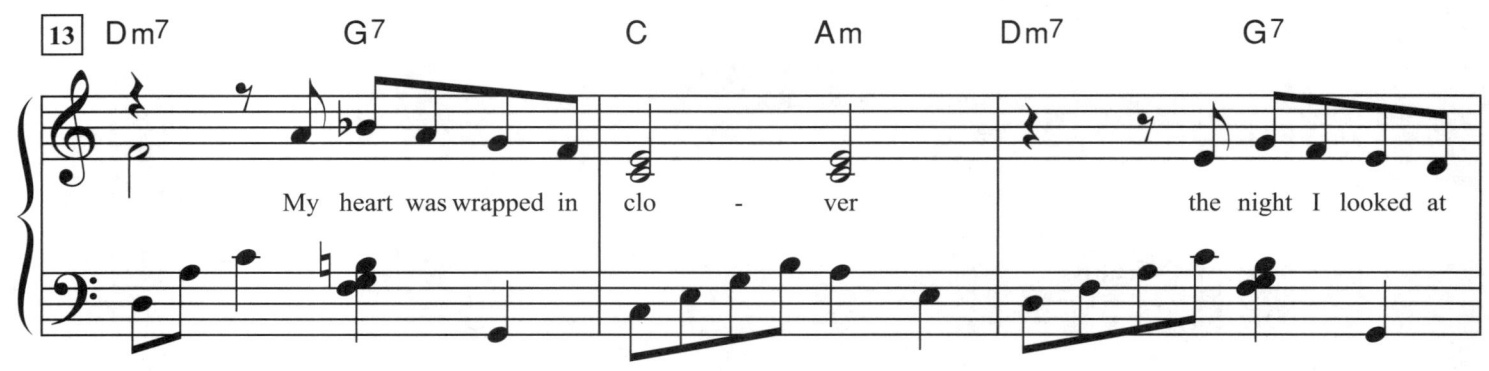
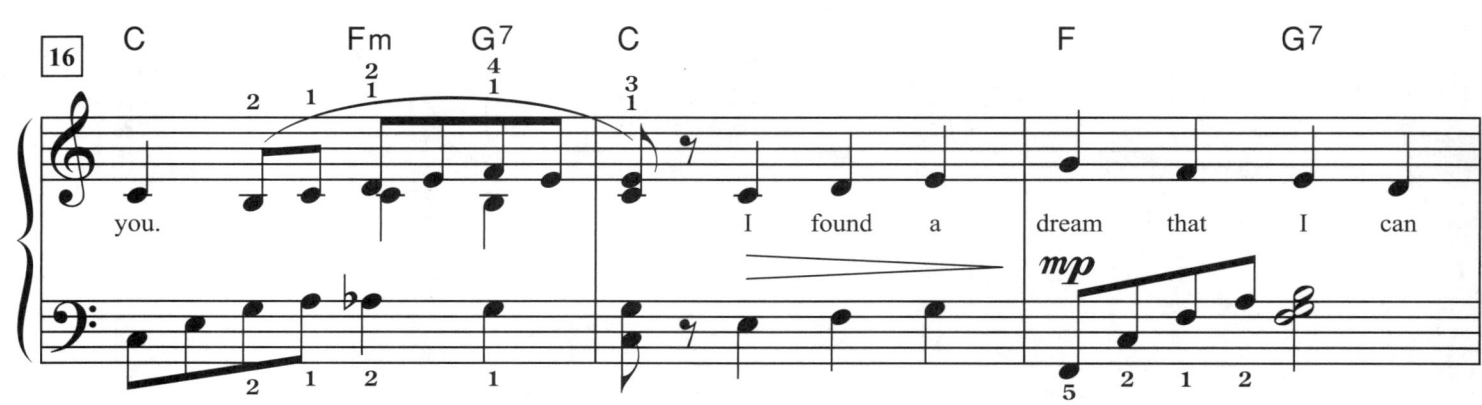
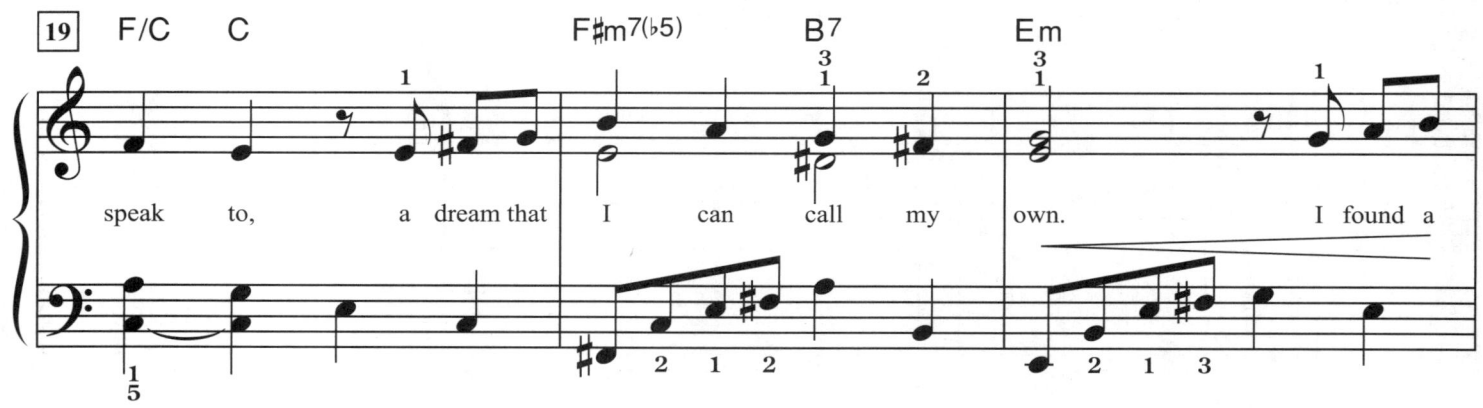

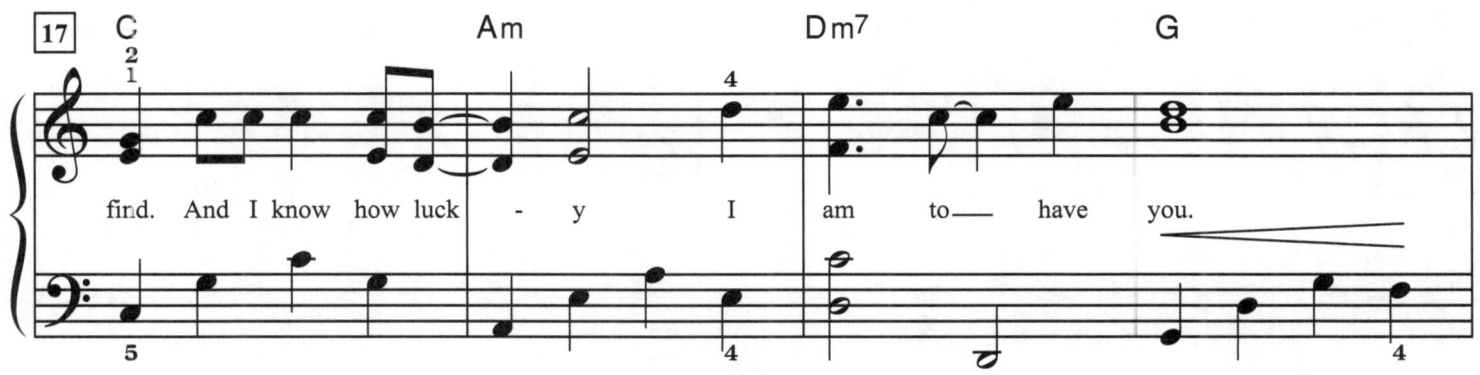

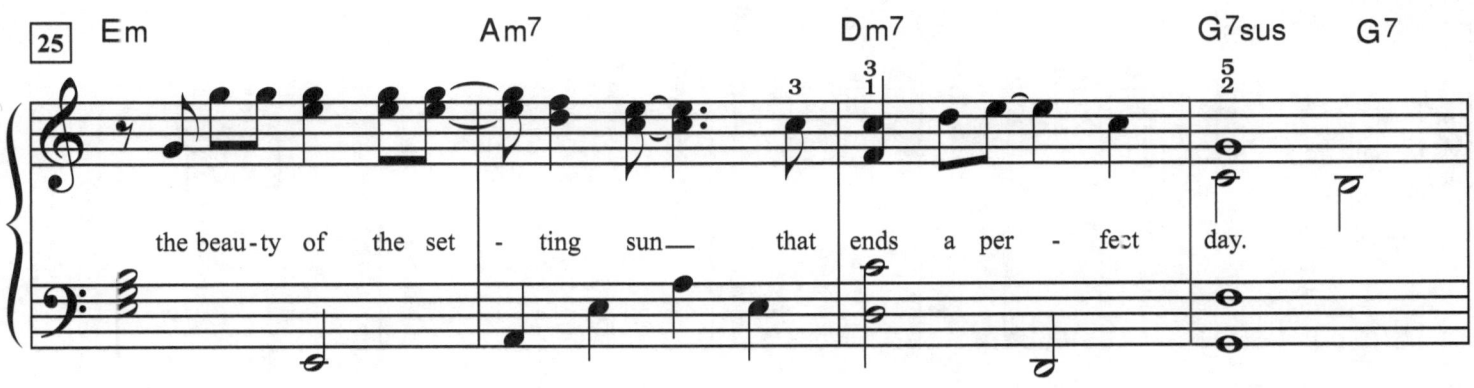
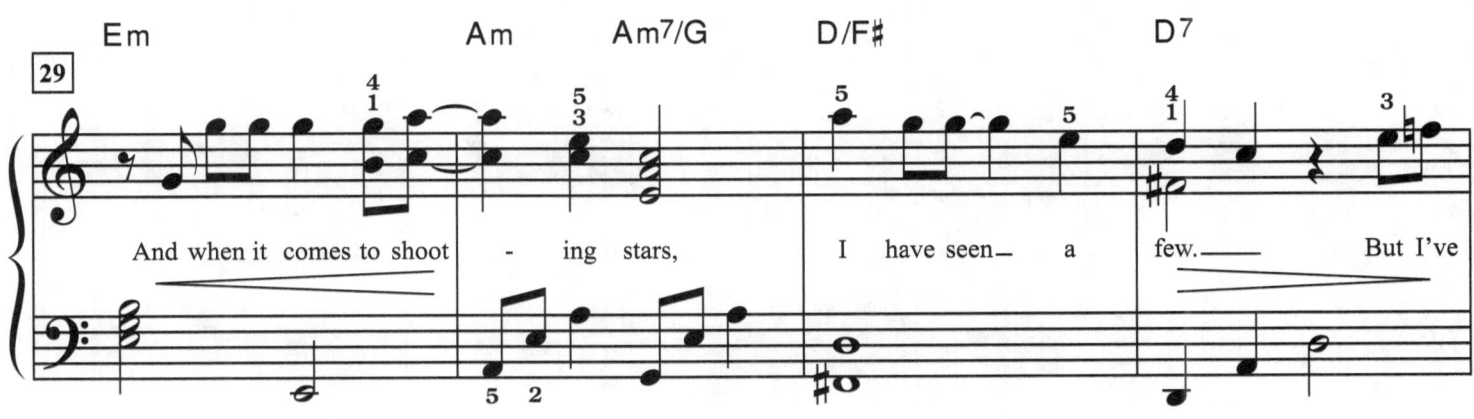

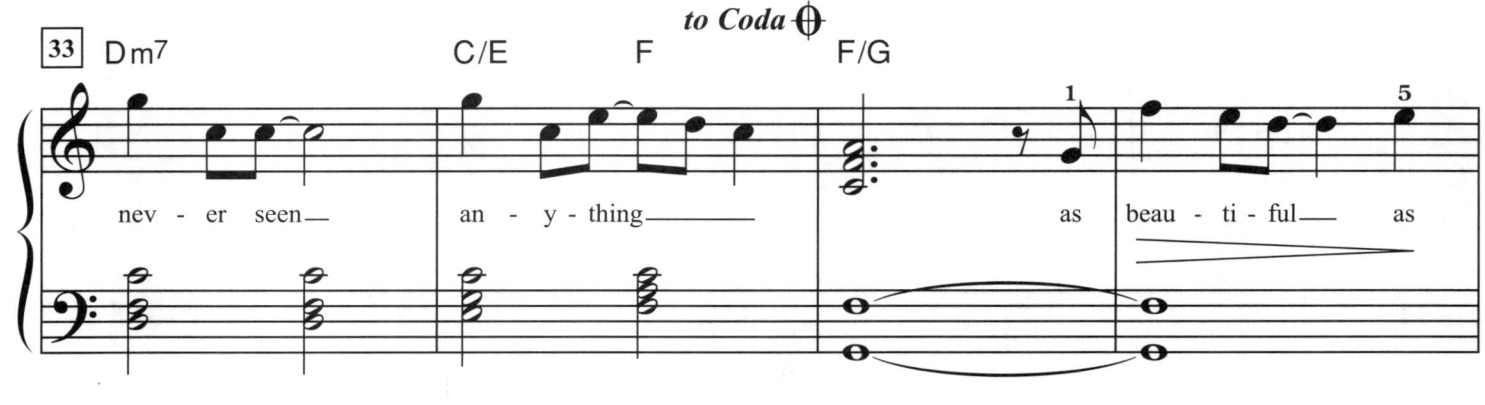
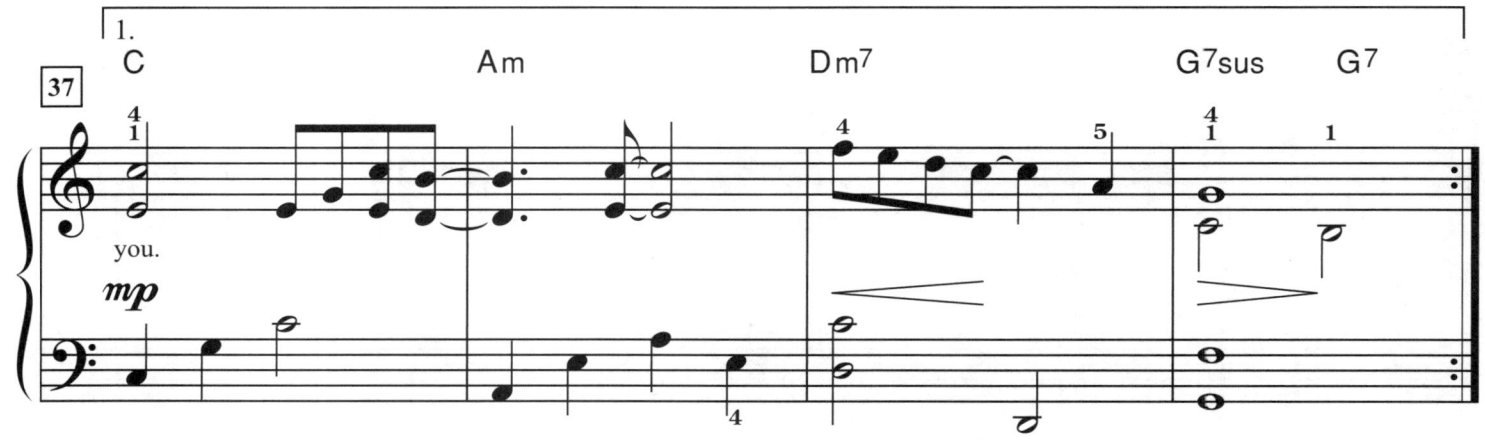
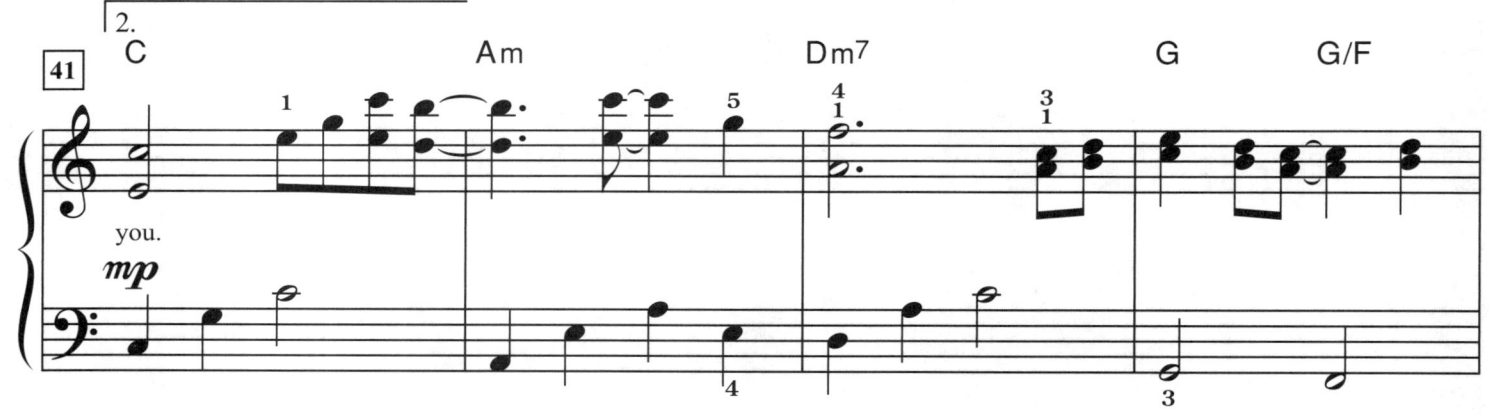
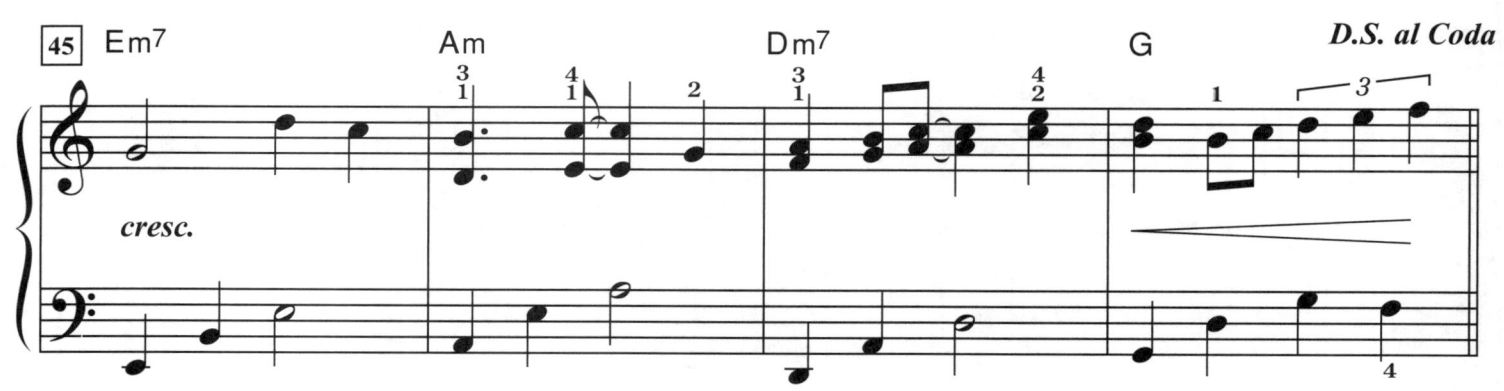

Verse 2:
Holding you in my arms,
No one else has fit so perfectly.
I could dance forever with you, with you.
And at the stroke of midnight,
Please forgive me if I can't let go,
'Cause I never dreamed I'd find
A Cinderella of my own.
(To Chorus:)

BEAUTY AND THE BEAST

(from Walt Disney's *Beauty and the Beast*)

Lyrics by Howard Ashman
Music by Alan Menken
Arranged by Dan Coates

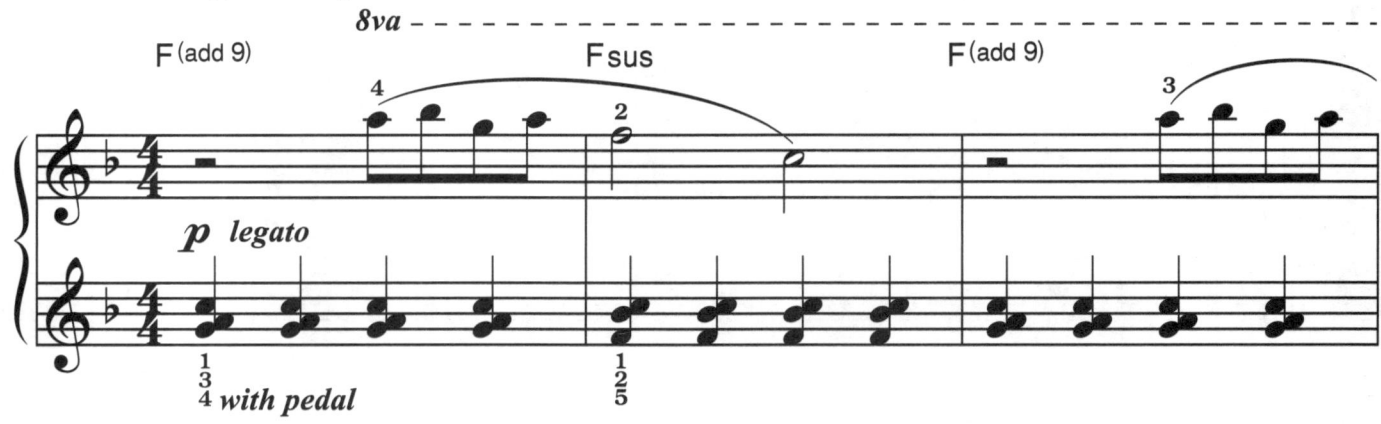

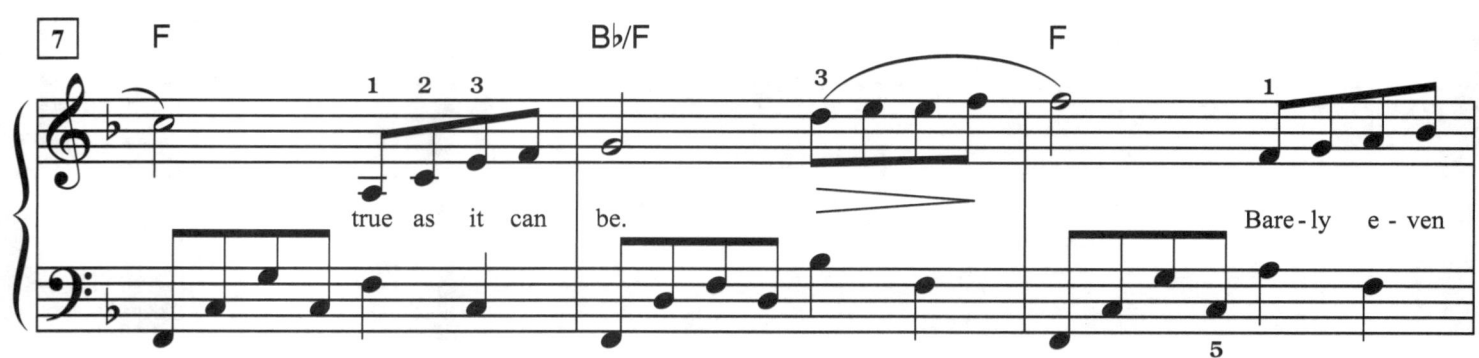

© 1991 WALT DISNEY MUSIC COMPANY and WONDERLAND MUSIC COMPANY, INC.
All Rights Reserved   Used by Permission

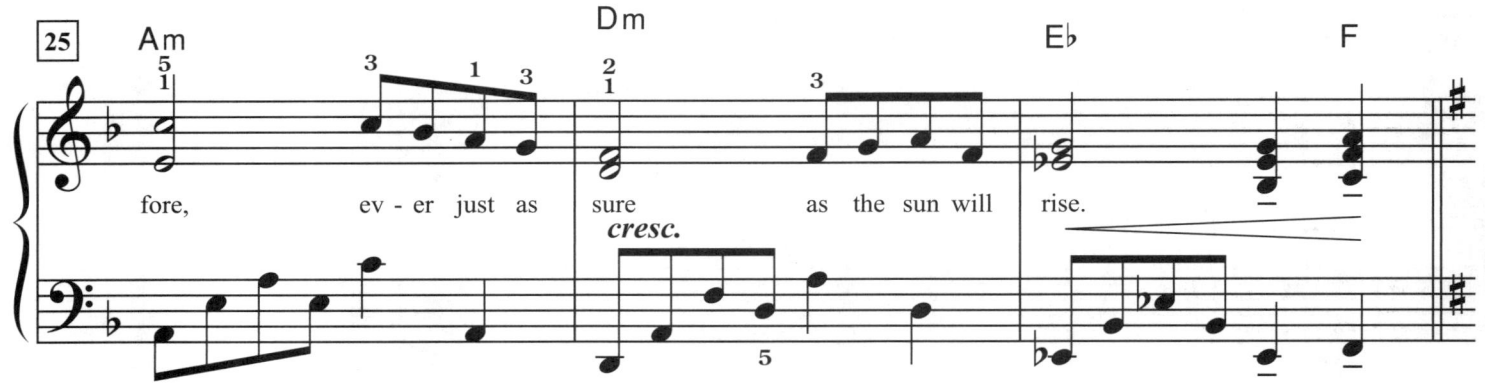
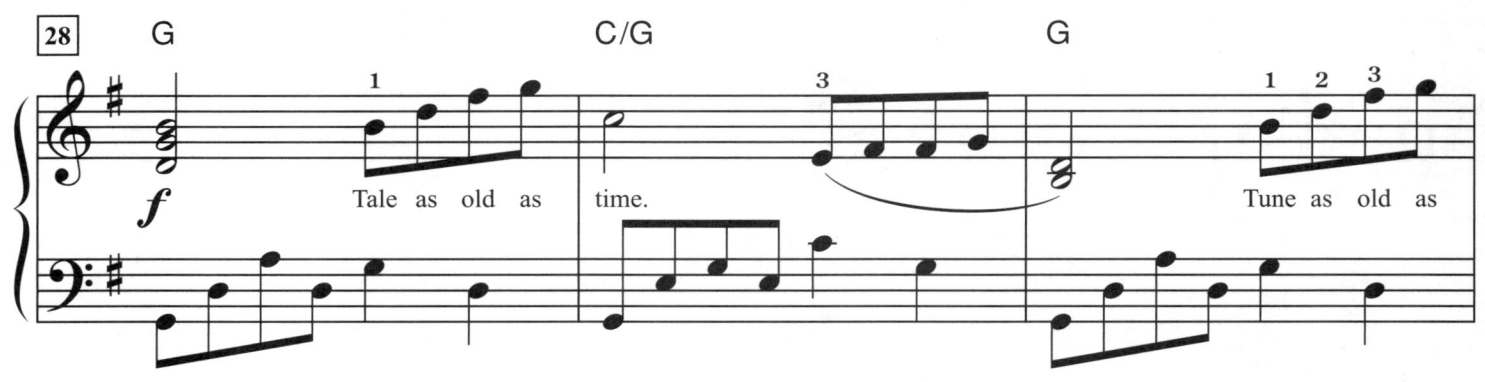
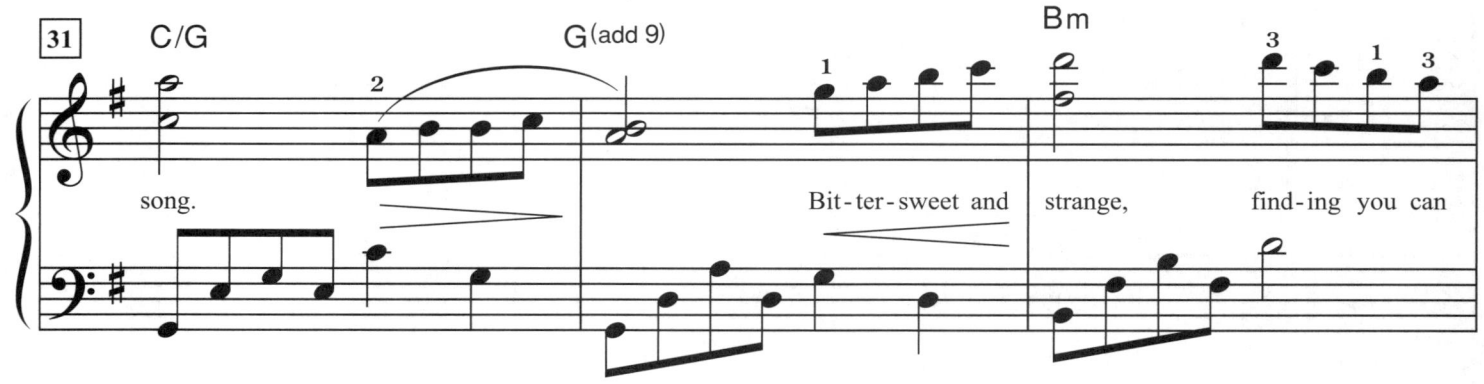
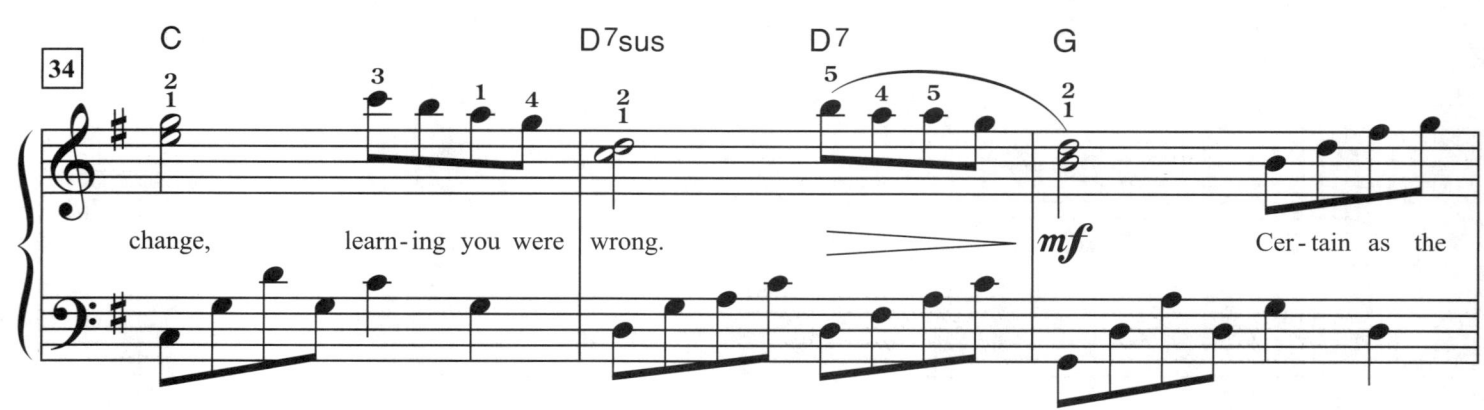

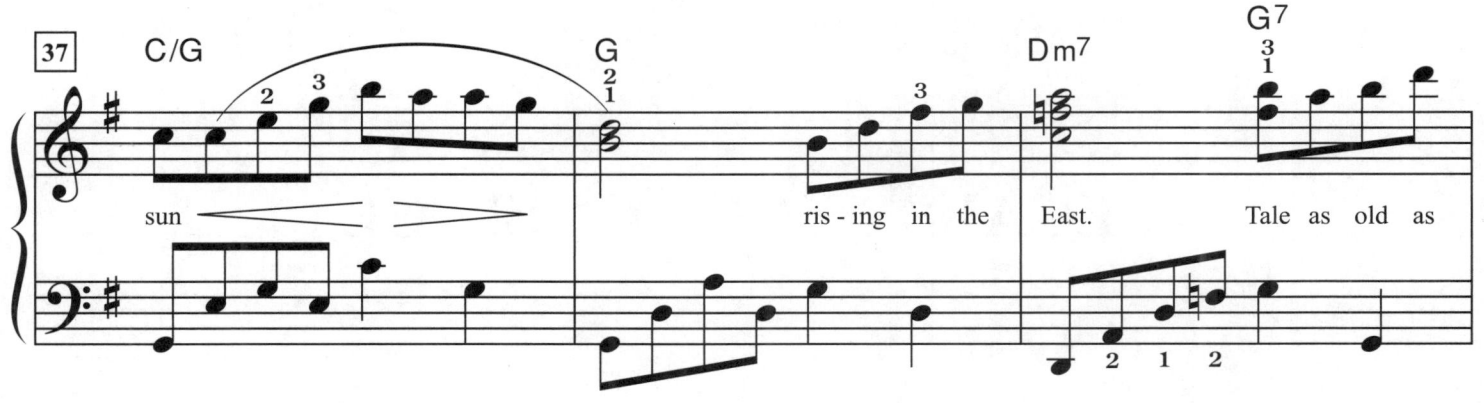
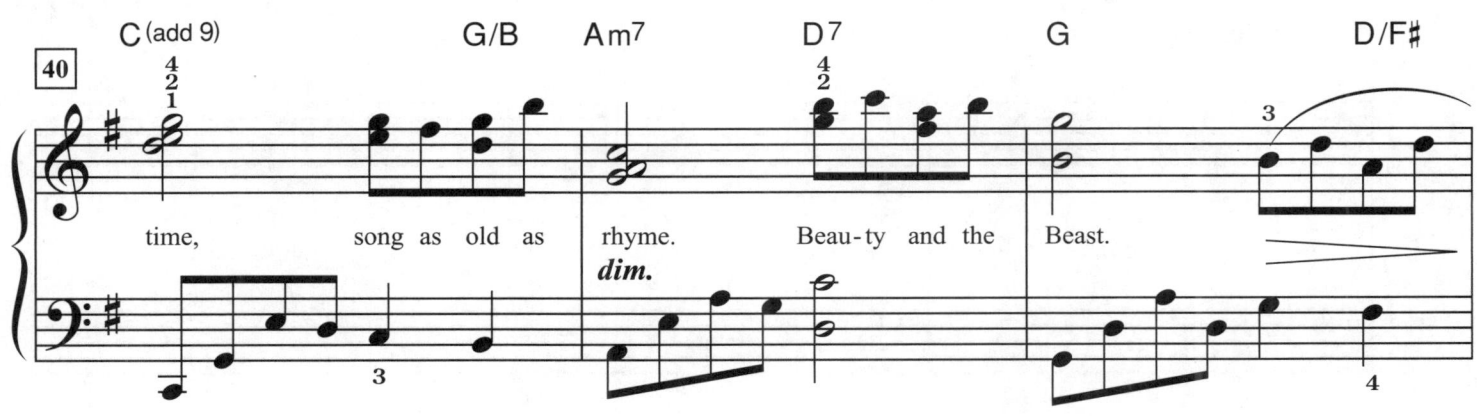
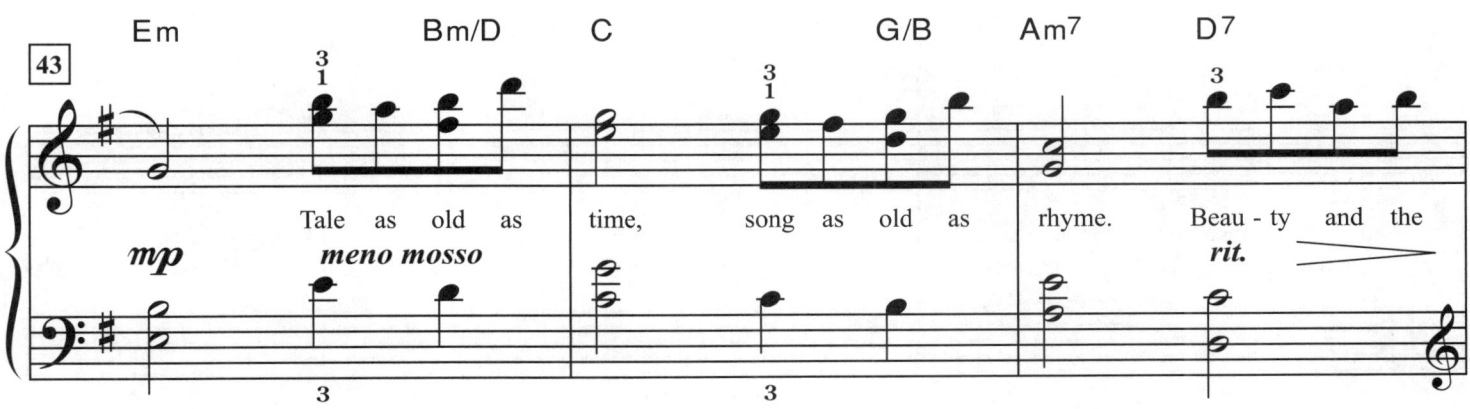
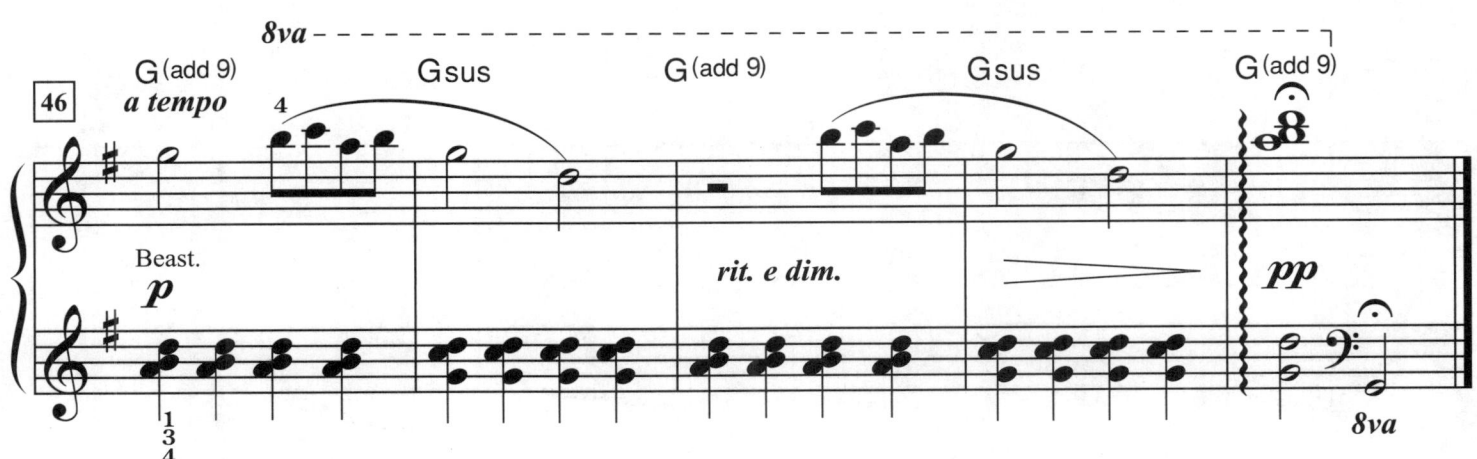

BECAUSE YOU LOVED ME

Words and Music by Diane Warren
Arranged by Dan Coates

© 1996 REALSONGS (ASCAP) and TOUCHSTONE PICTURES SONGS & MUSIC, INC. (ASCAP)
All Rights Reserved

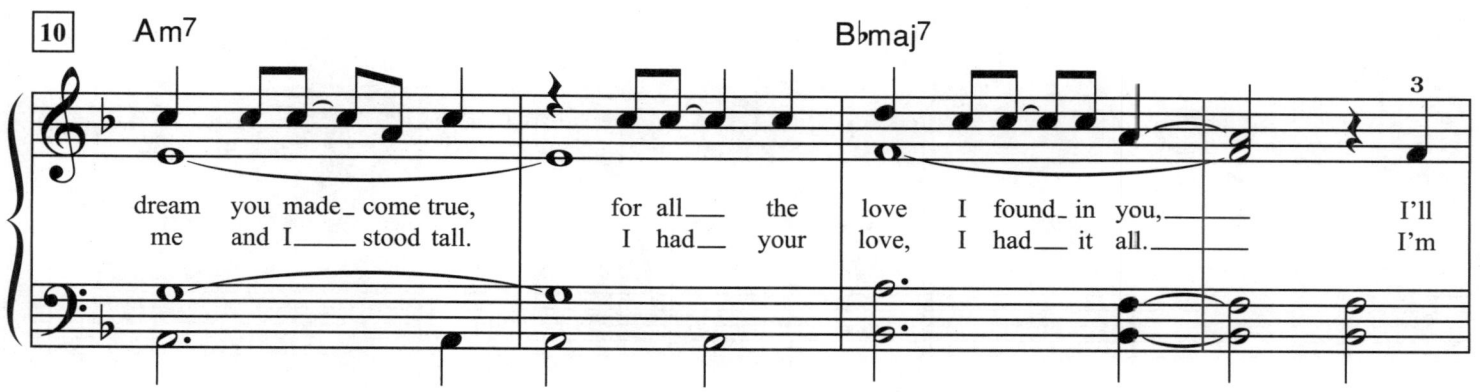

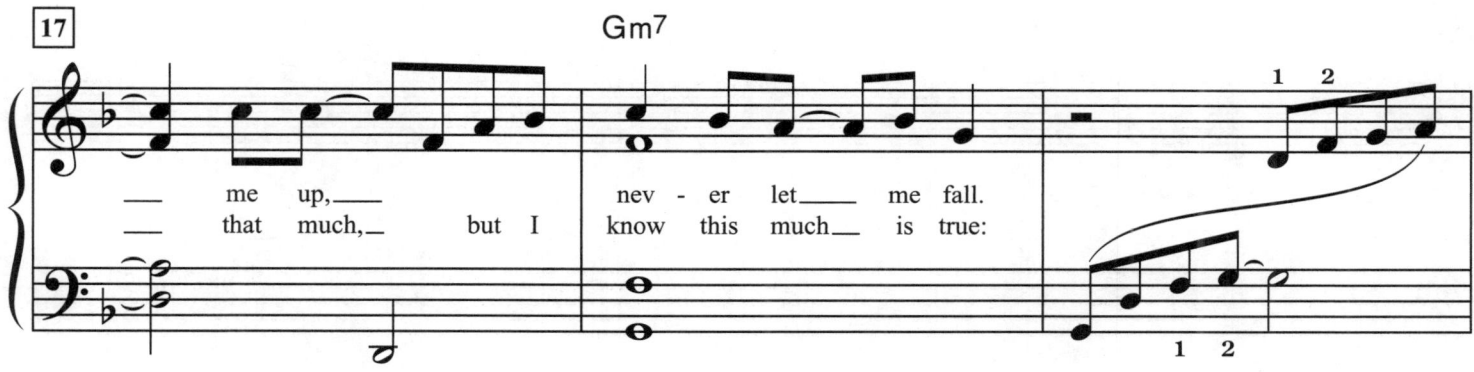

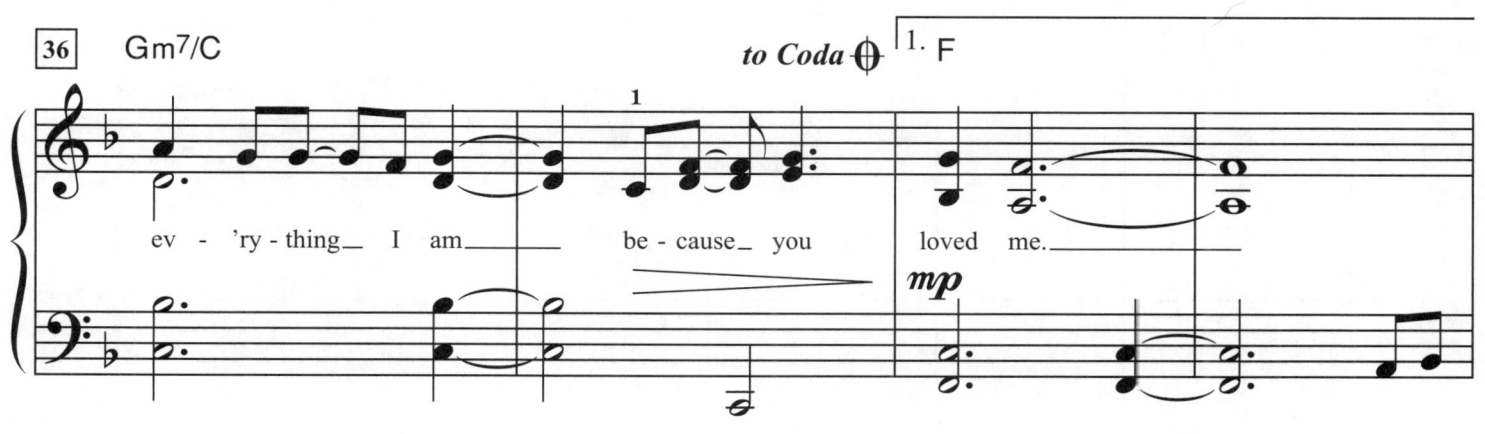
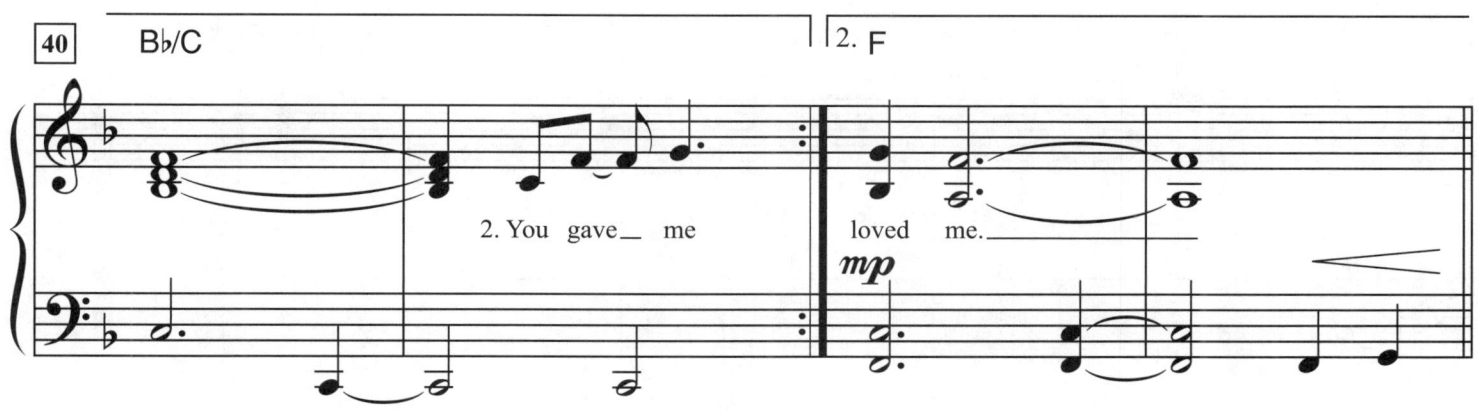

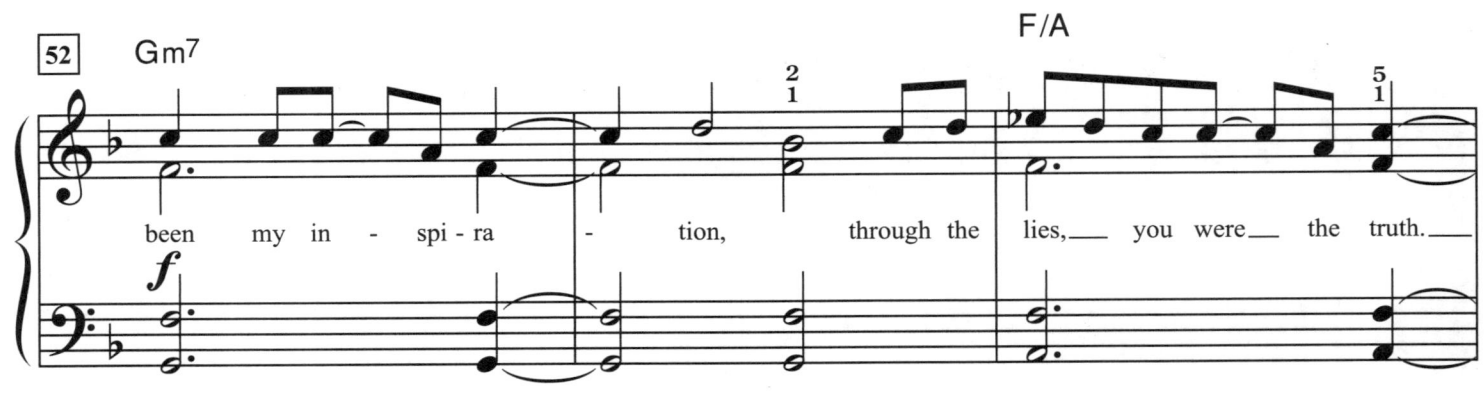
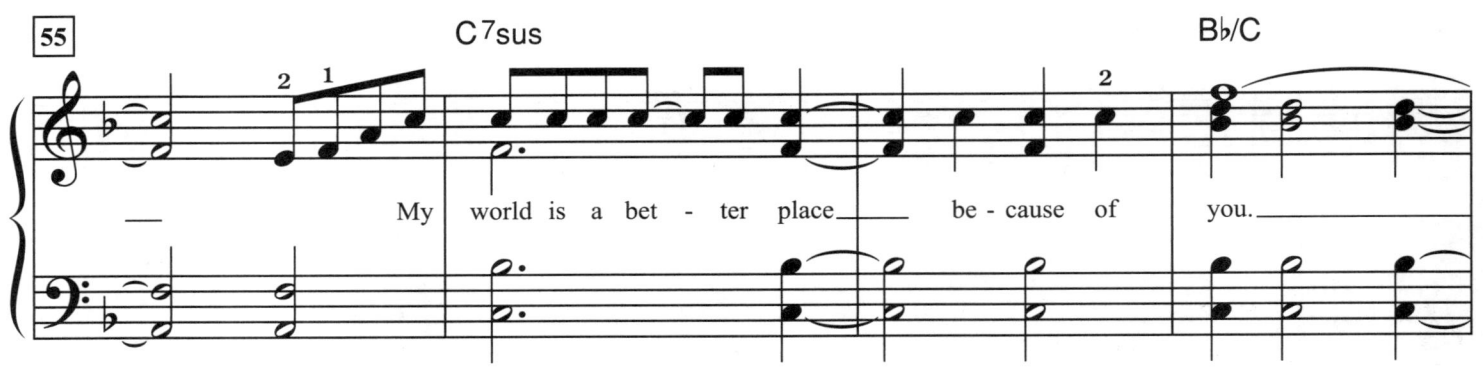
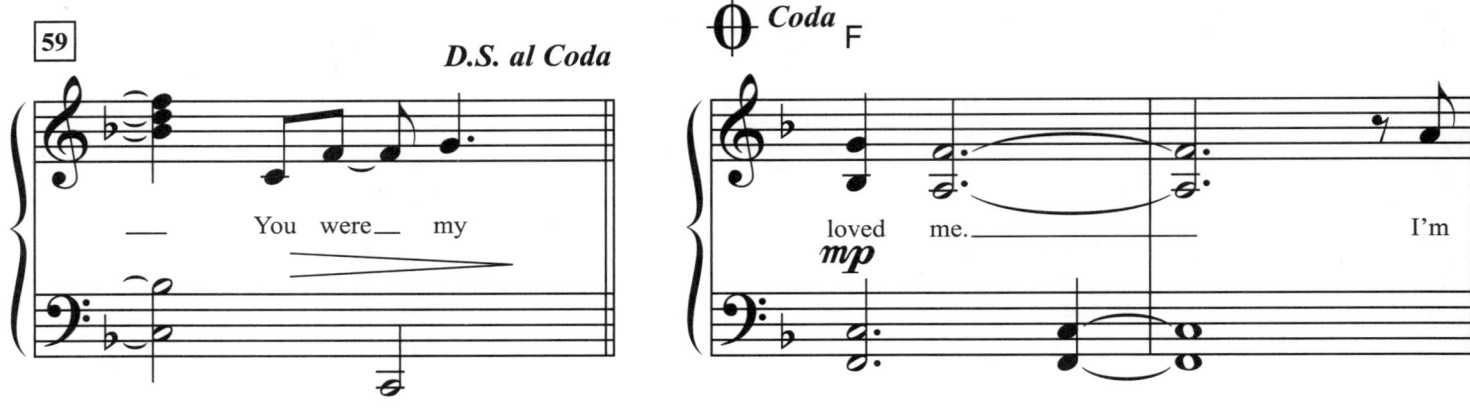

CAN YOU FEEL THE LOVE TONIGHT

(from Walt Disney's *The Lion King*)

Music by Elton John
Words by Tim Rice
Arranged by Dan Coates

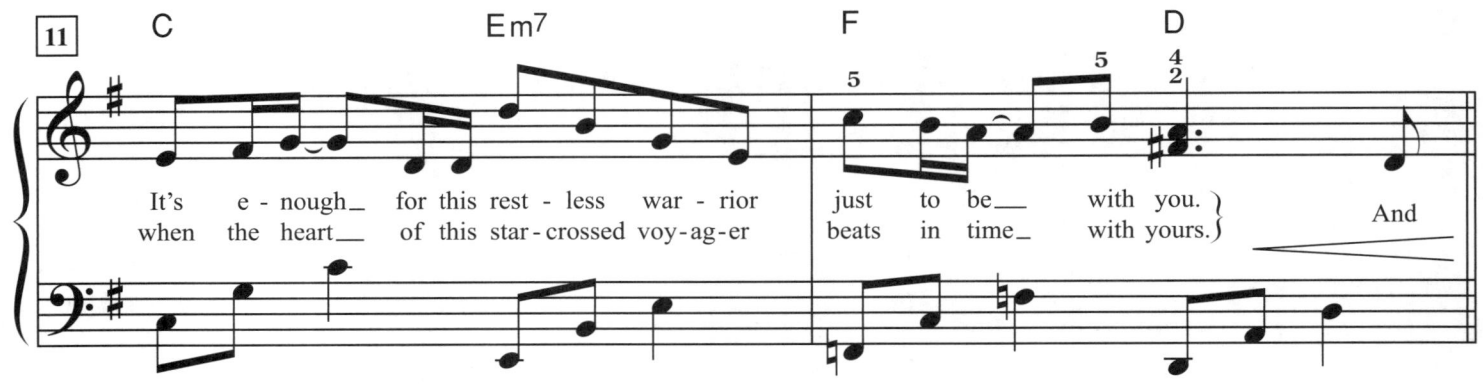

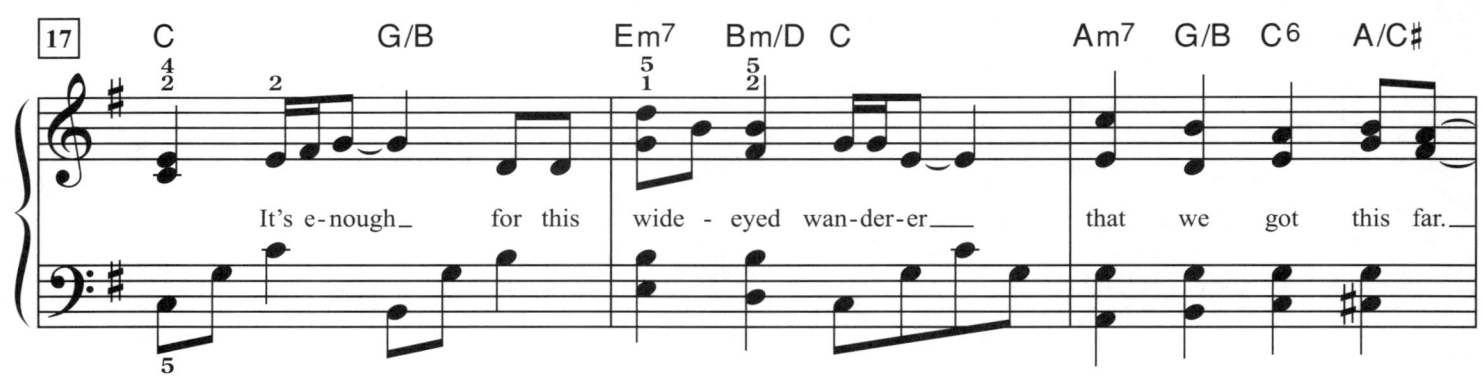
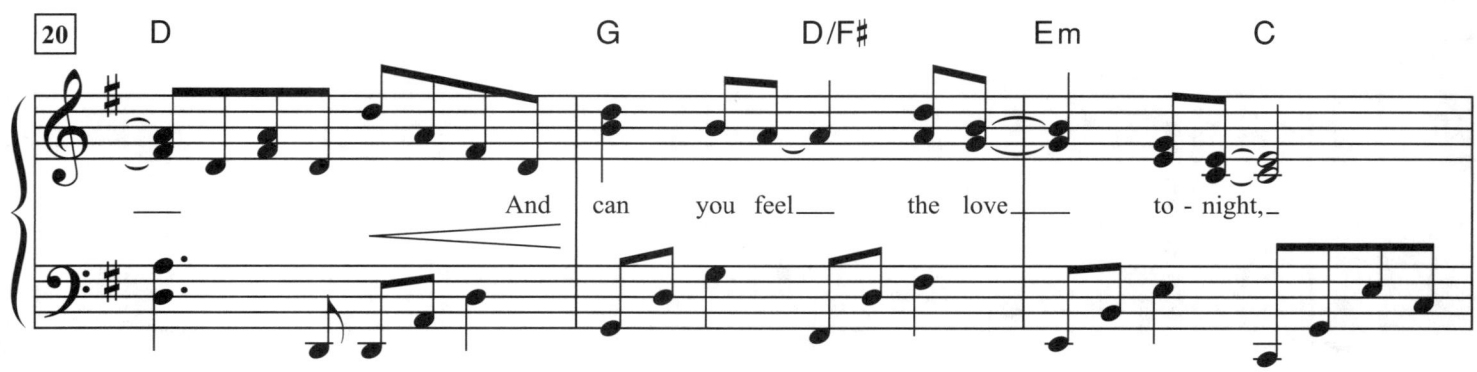

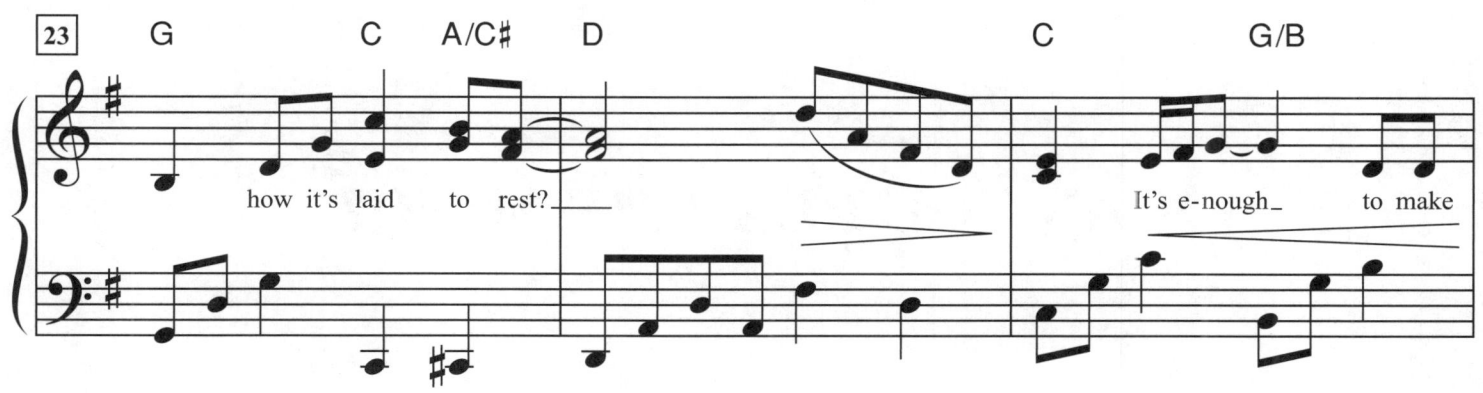
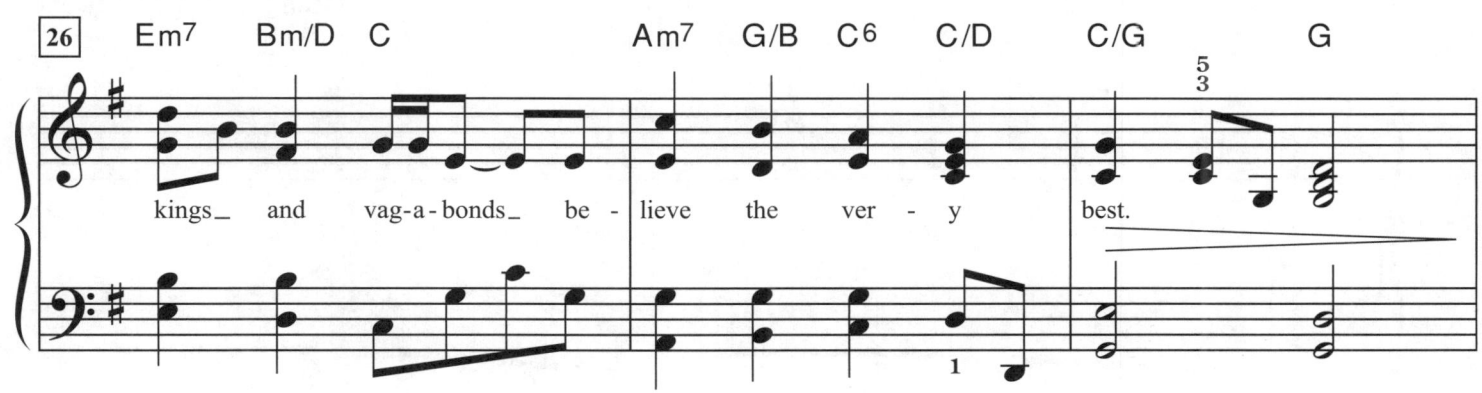
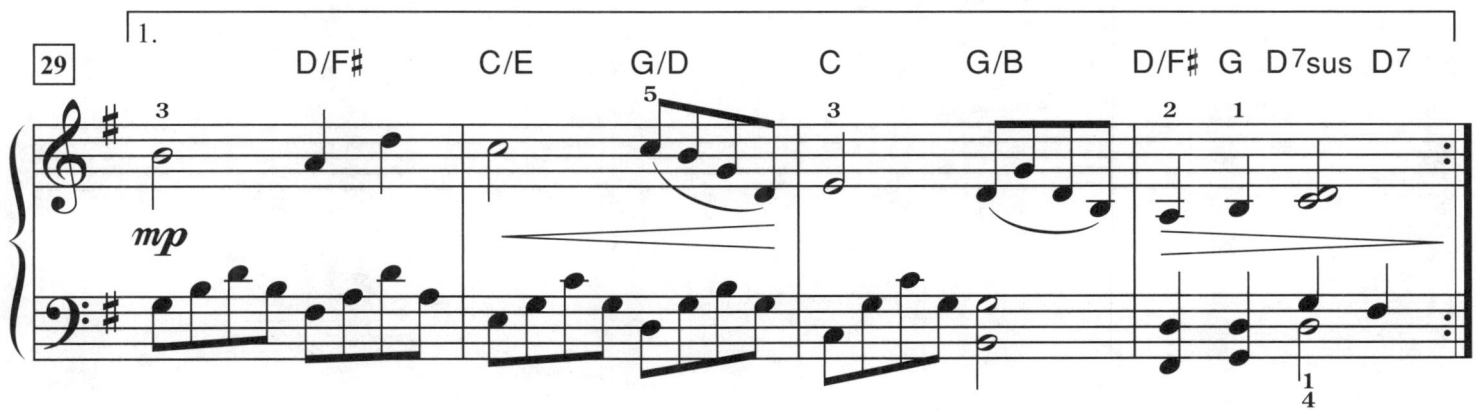
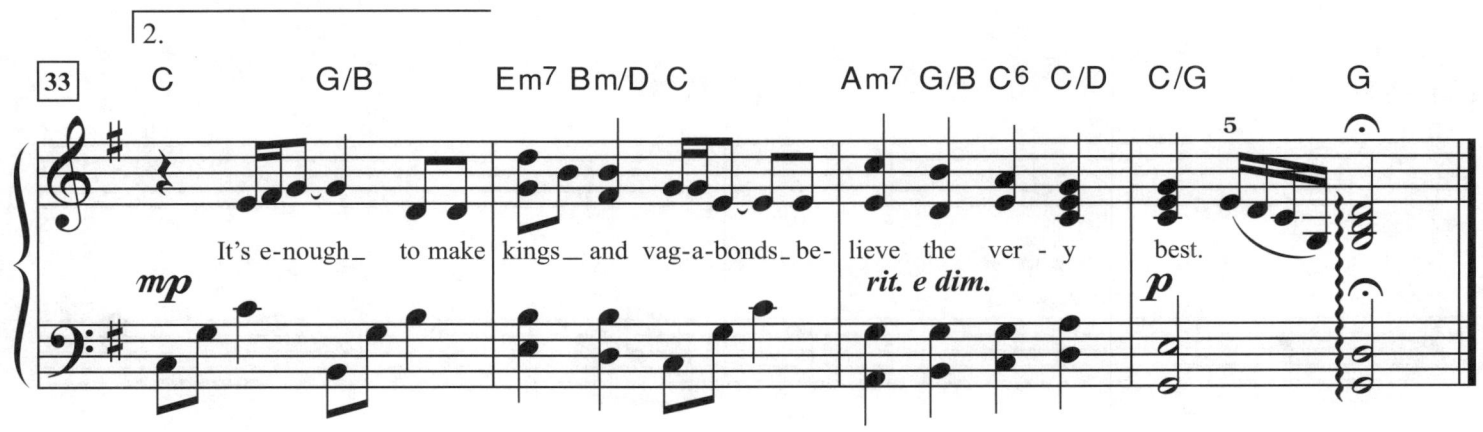

CAN YOU READ MY MIND?

Words by Leslie Bricusse
Music by **JOHN WILLIAMS**
Arranged by Dan Coates

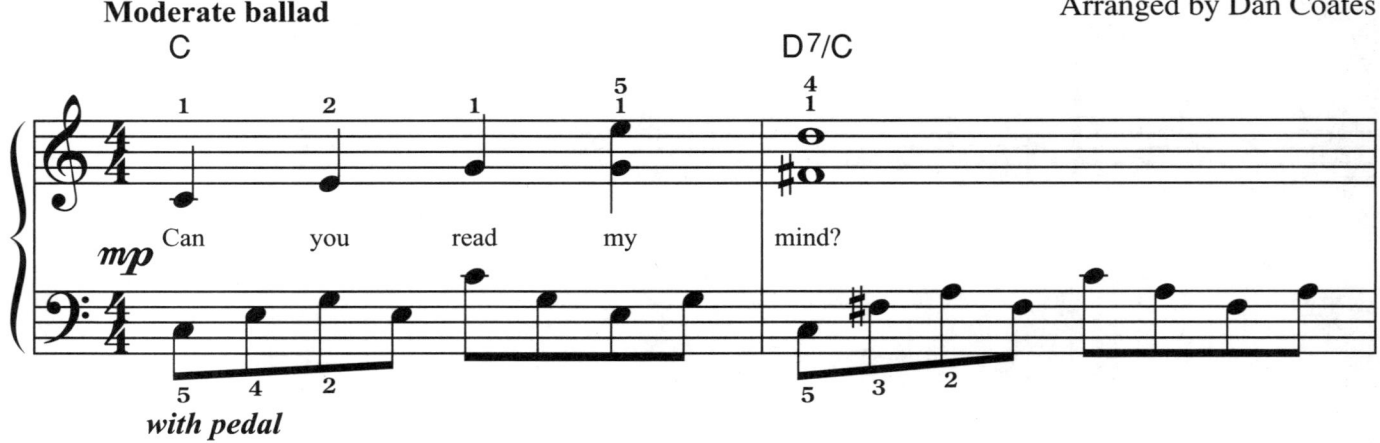

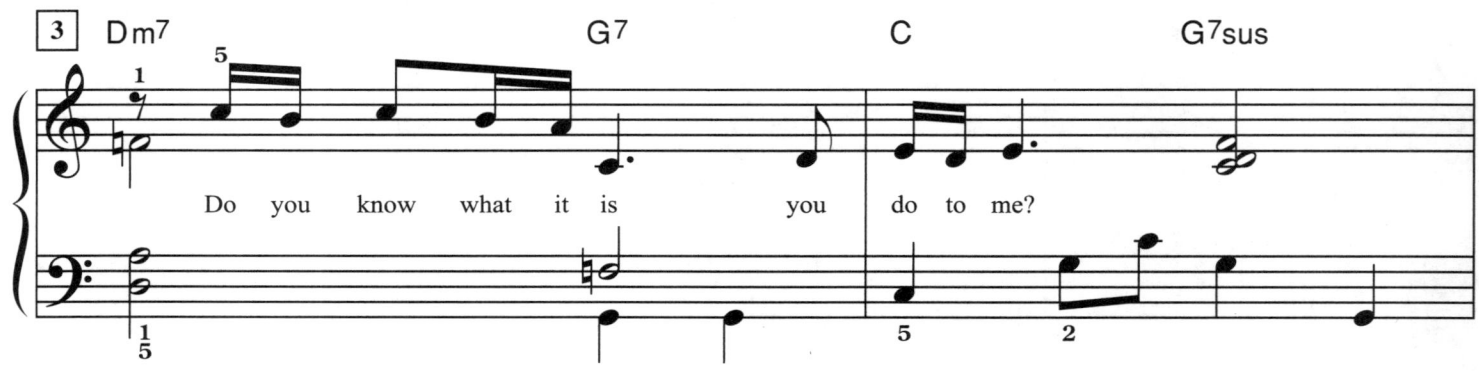

© 1978 (Renewed) WARNER-TAMERLANE PUBLISHING CORP.
Copyright Renewed
All Rights Reserved

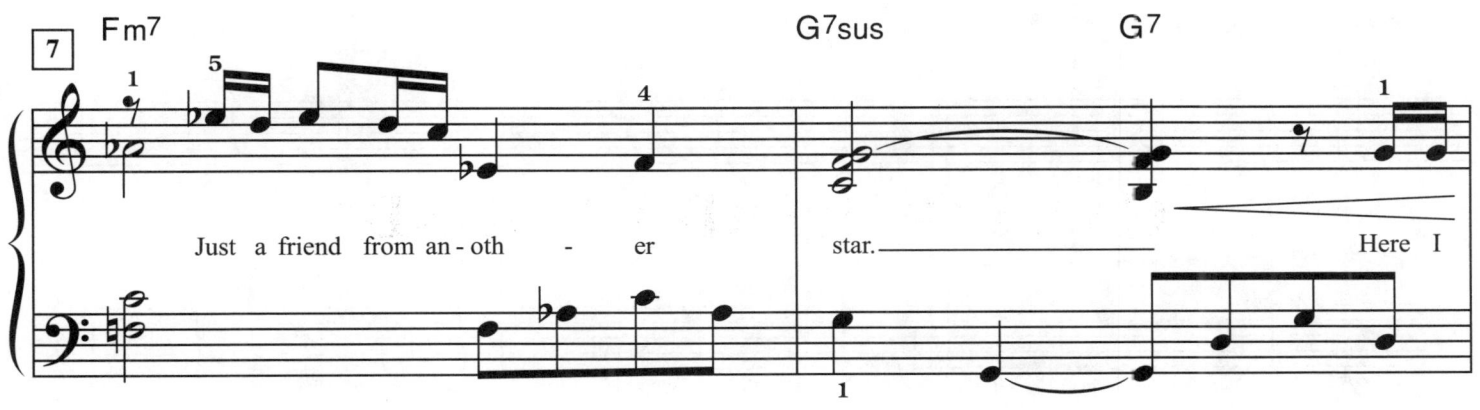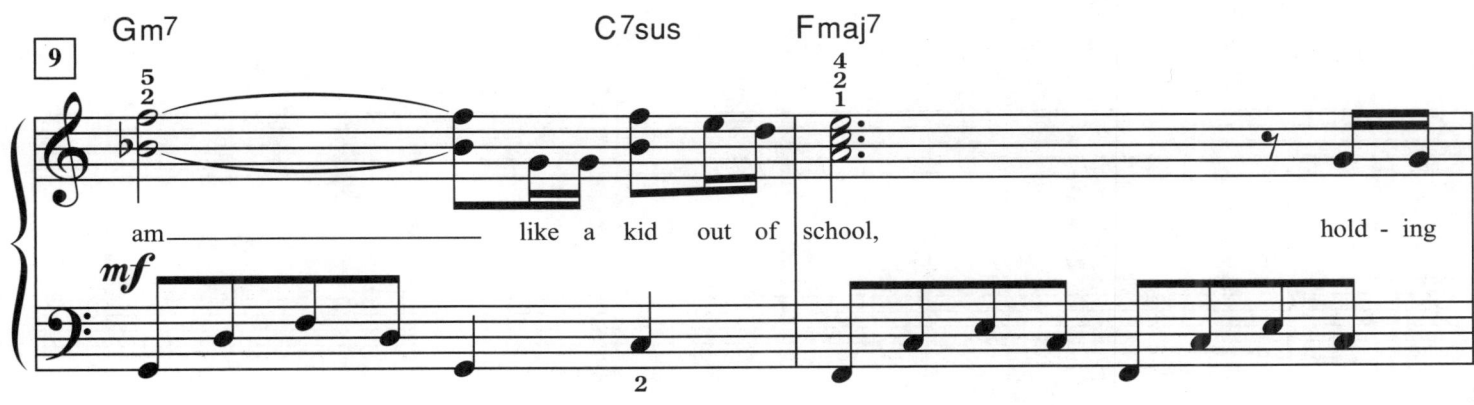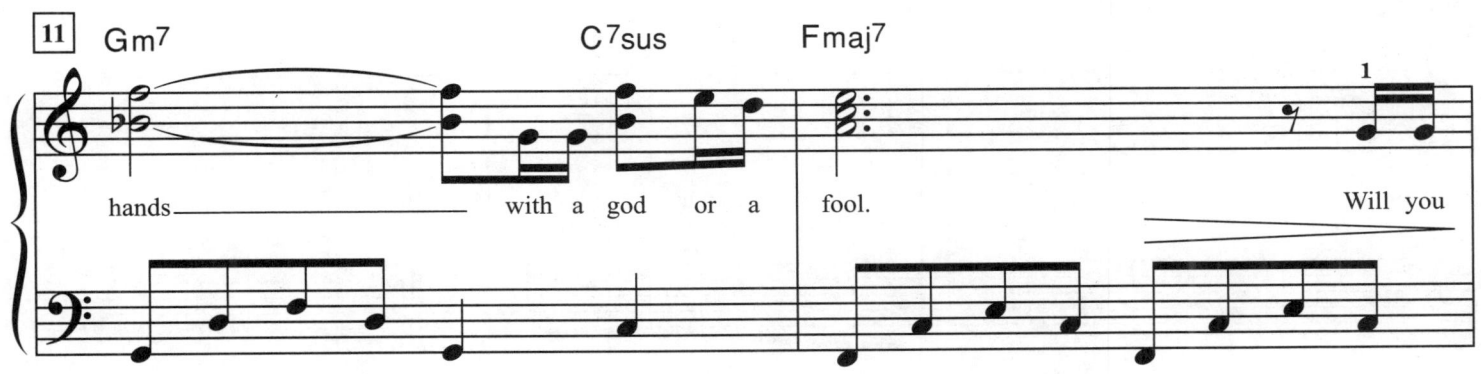

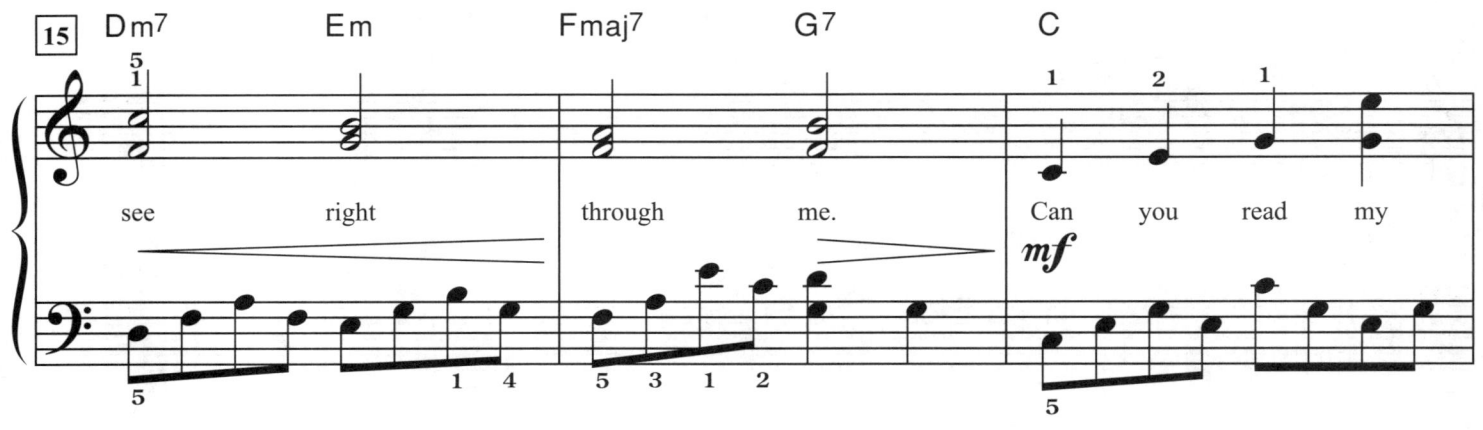
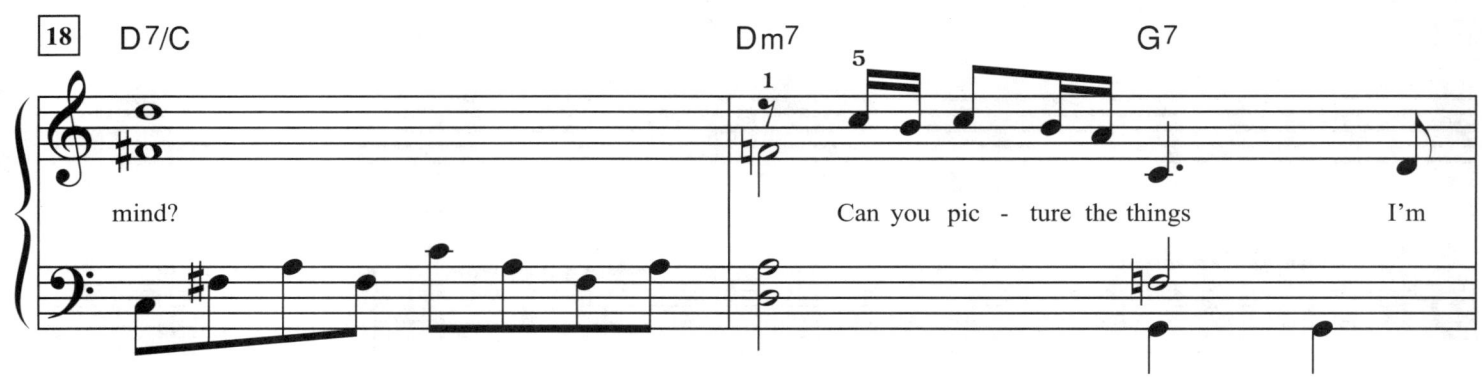
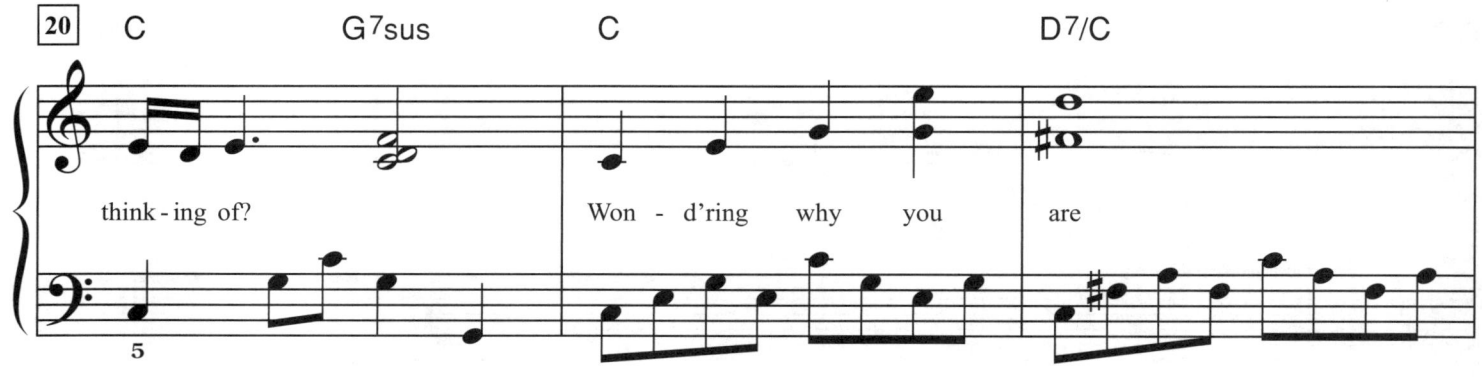
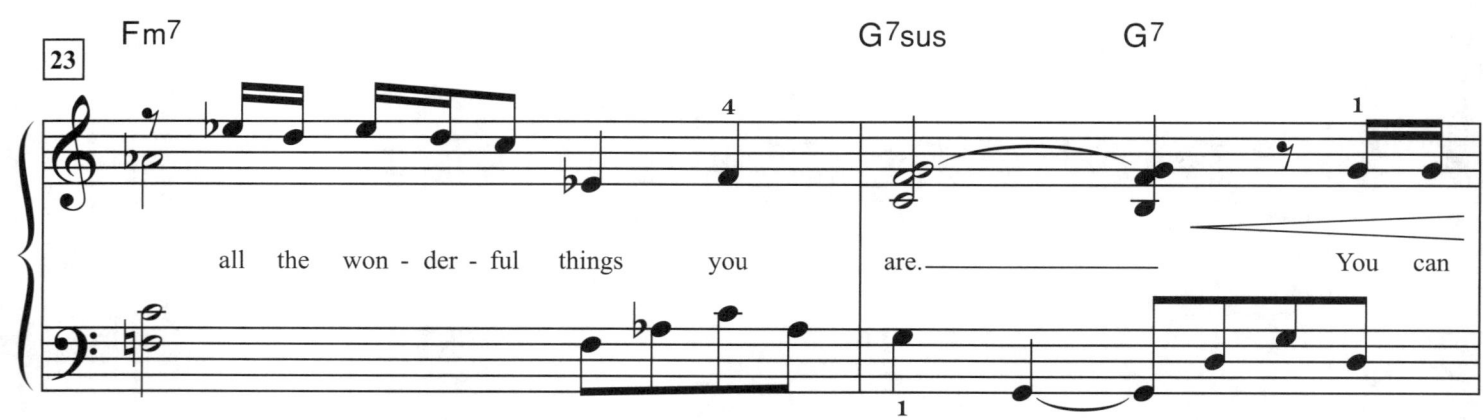

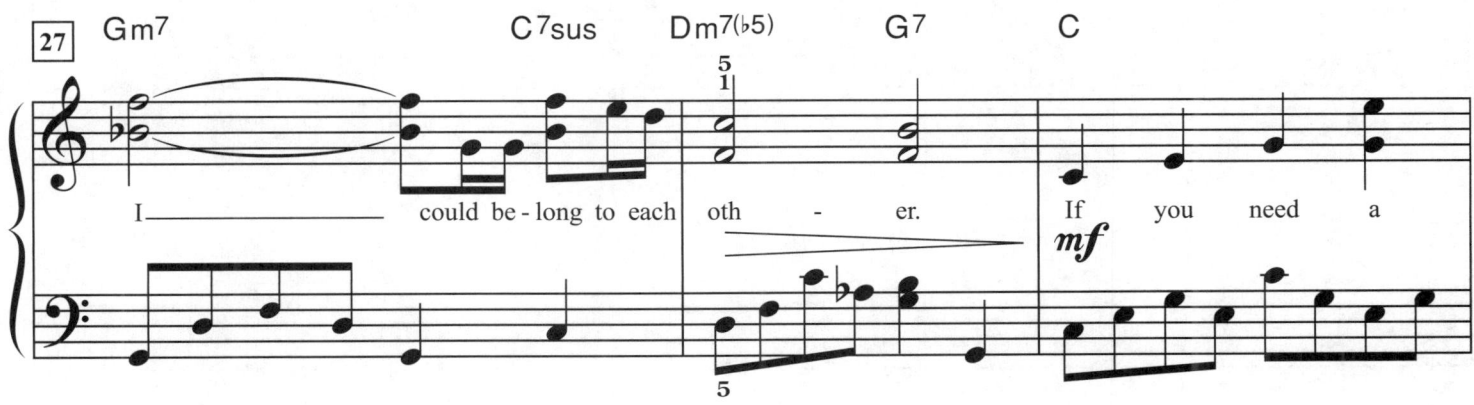
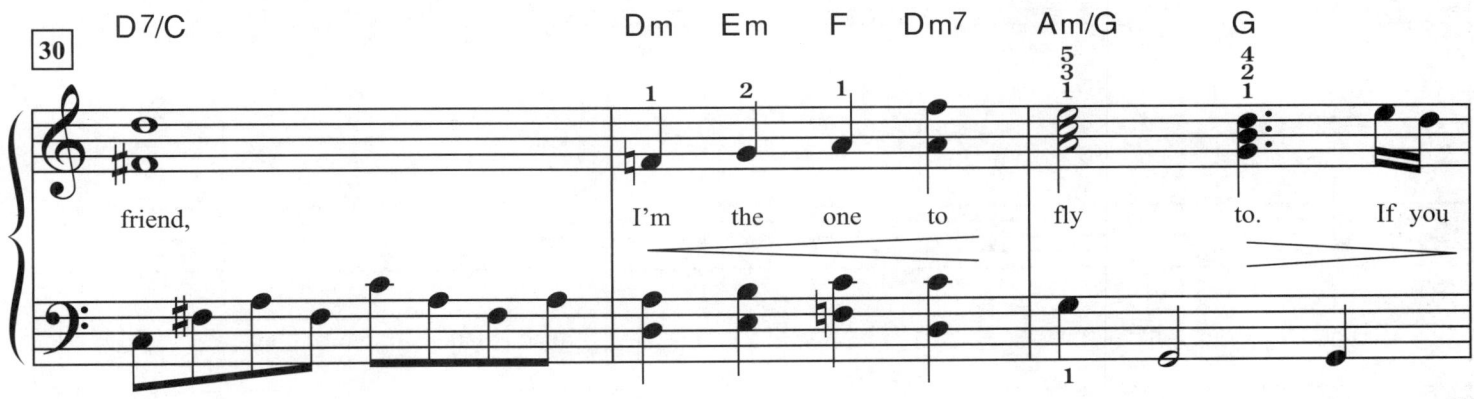
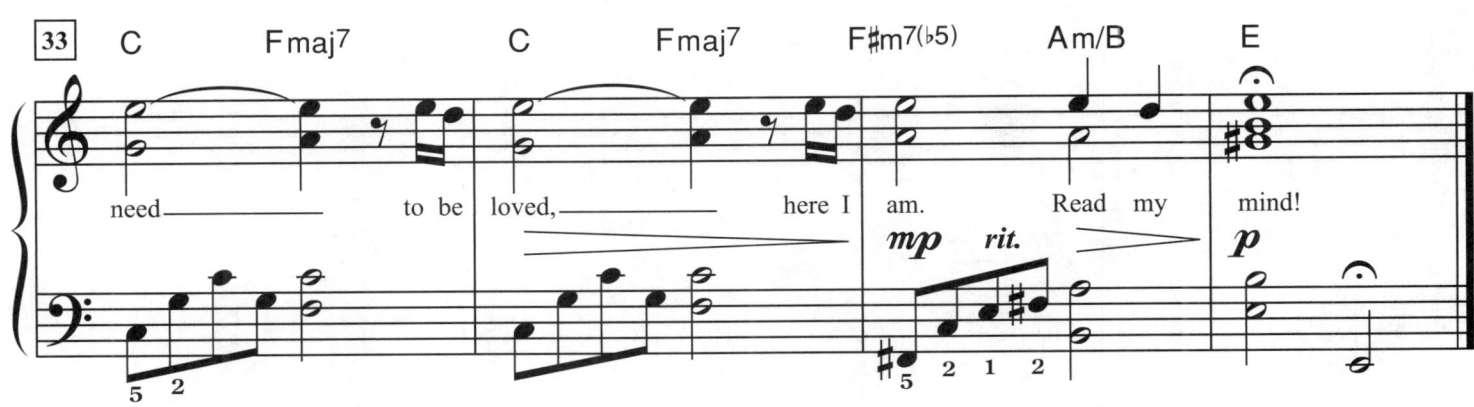

COME RAIN OR COME SHINE

Lyrics by Johnny Mercer
Music by Harold Arlen
Arranged by Dan Coates

© 1946 (Renewed) CHAPPELL & CO., INC.
All Rights for the Extended Renewal Term in the U.S. Assigned to THE JOHNNY MERCER FOUNDATION and SA MUSIC
All Rights for THE JOHNNY MERCER FOUNDATION Administered by WB MUSIC CORP.
All Rights Reserved

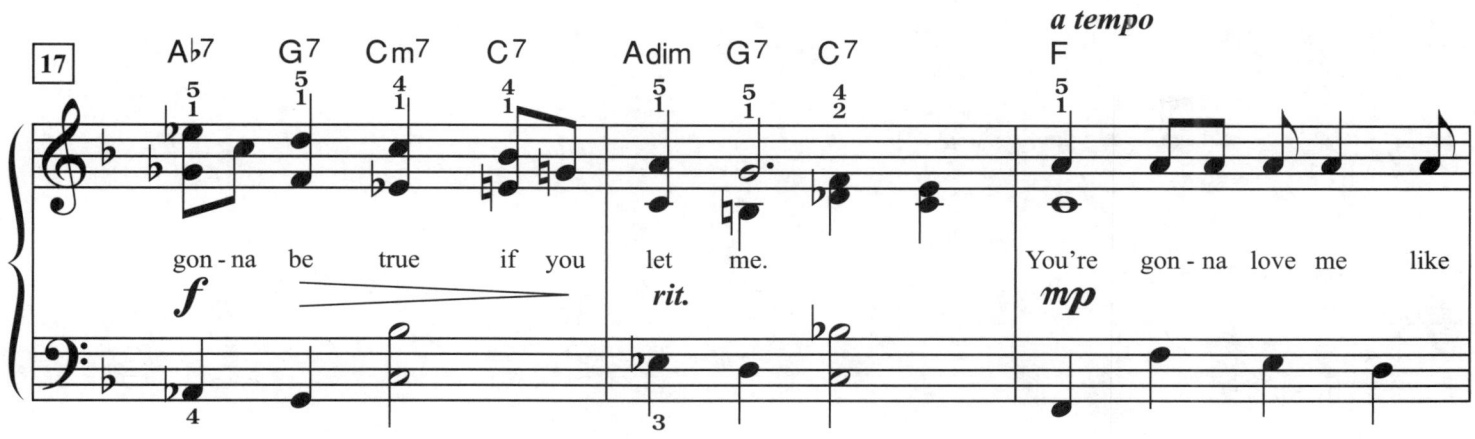

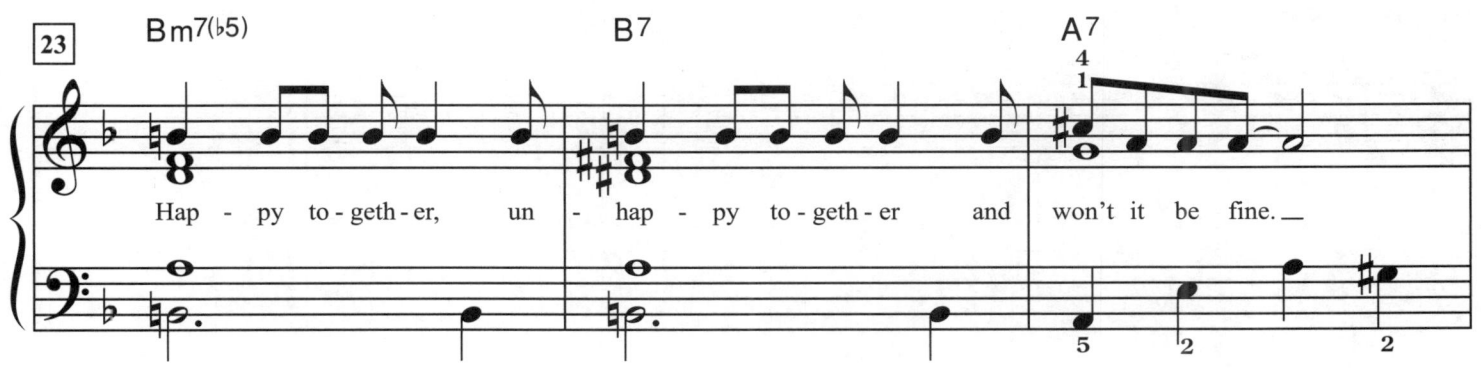

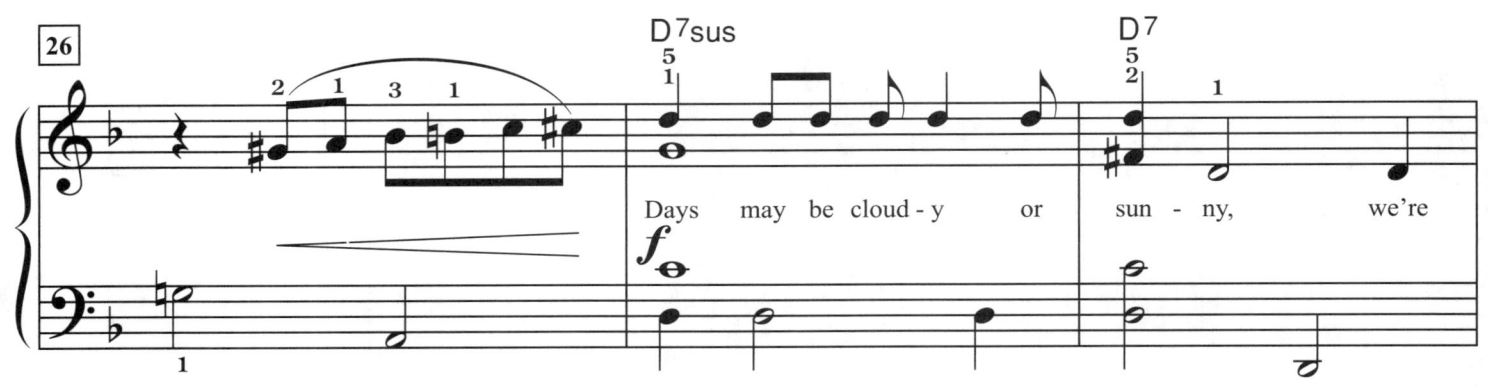
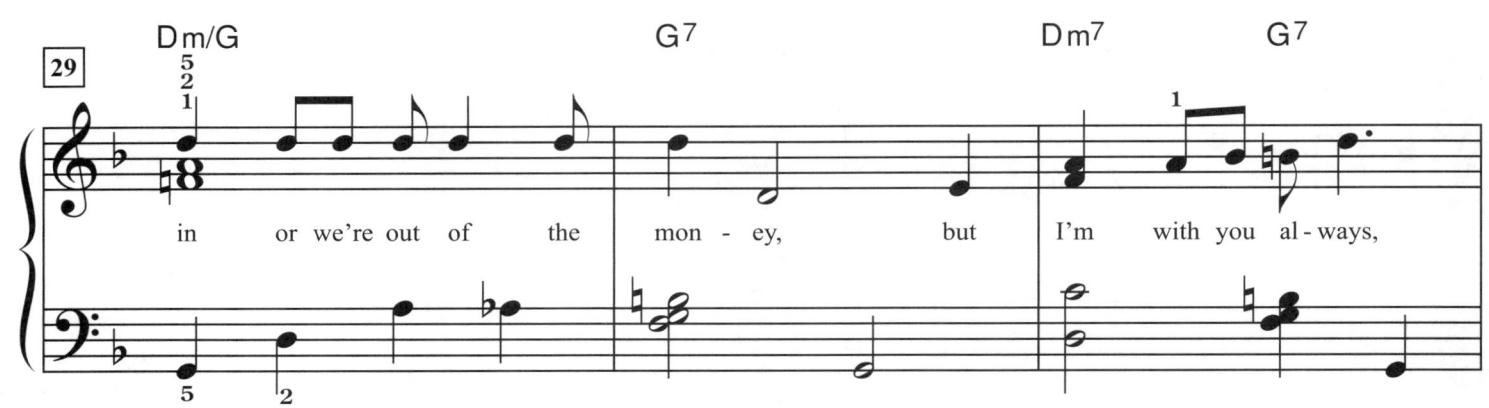
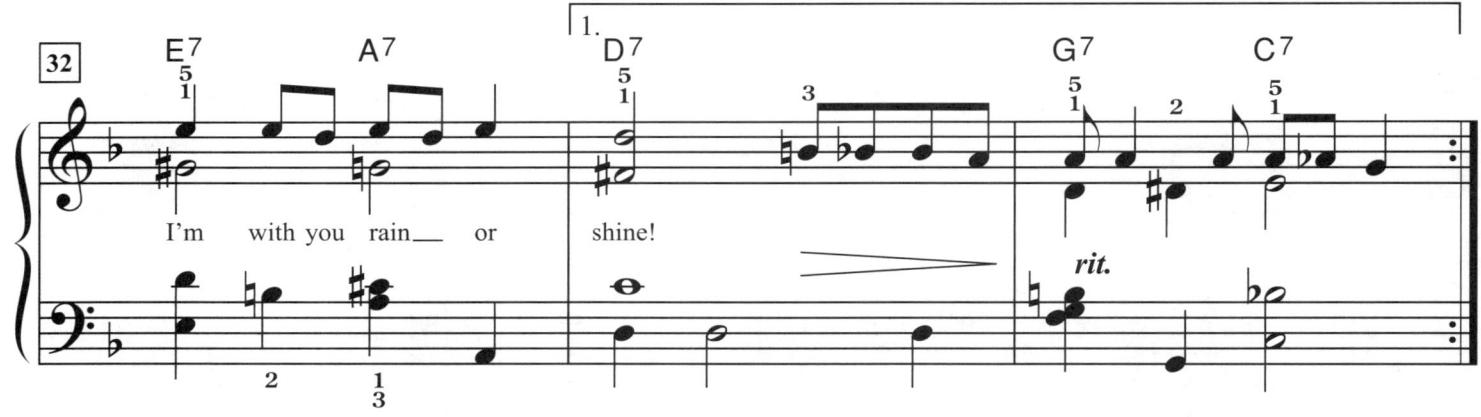
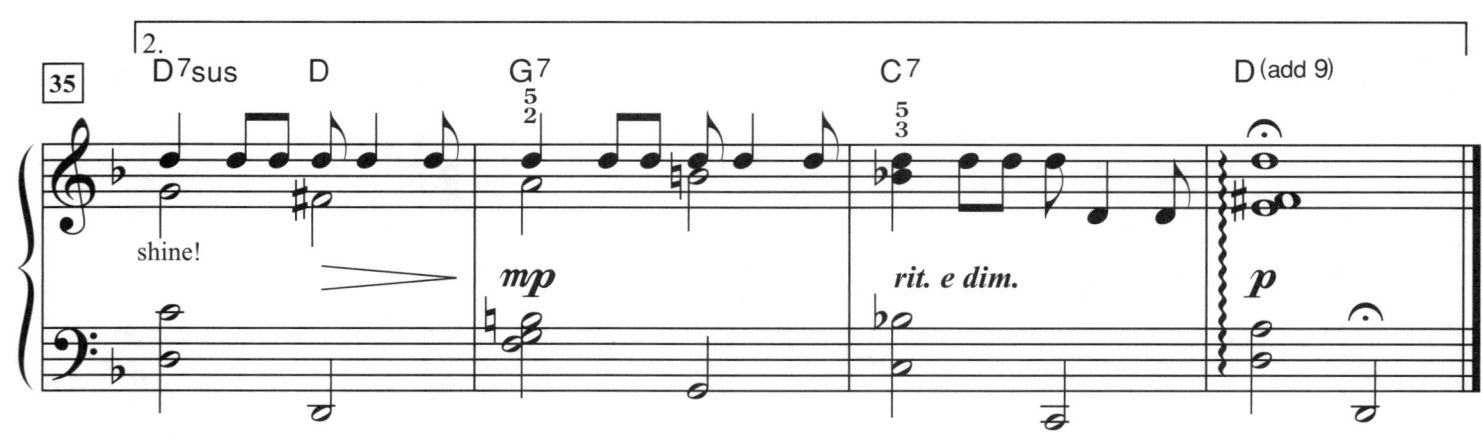

ENDLESS LOVE

Words and Music by Lionel Richie
Arranged by Dan Coates

© 1981 PGP MUSIC and BROCKMAN MUSIC
All Rights in the U.S. Administered by WB MUSIC CORP. and Elsewhere Throughout the World by INTERSONG-USA, INC.
All Rights Reserved

34
G
C
G/B
Am
Em/G
I'll be that fool for you, I'm
37
F
G
C
sure; you know I don't mind.
40
B♭/C
C
F
G
And yes, you'll be the
43
C
Am
Em/G
Fmaj7
on - ly one. No one can de -
f

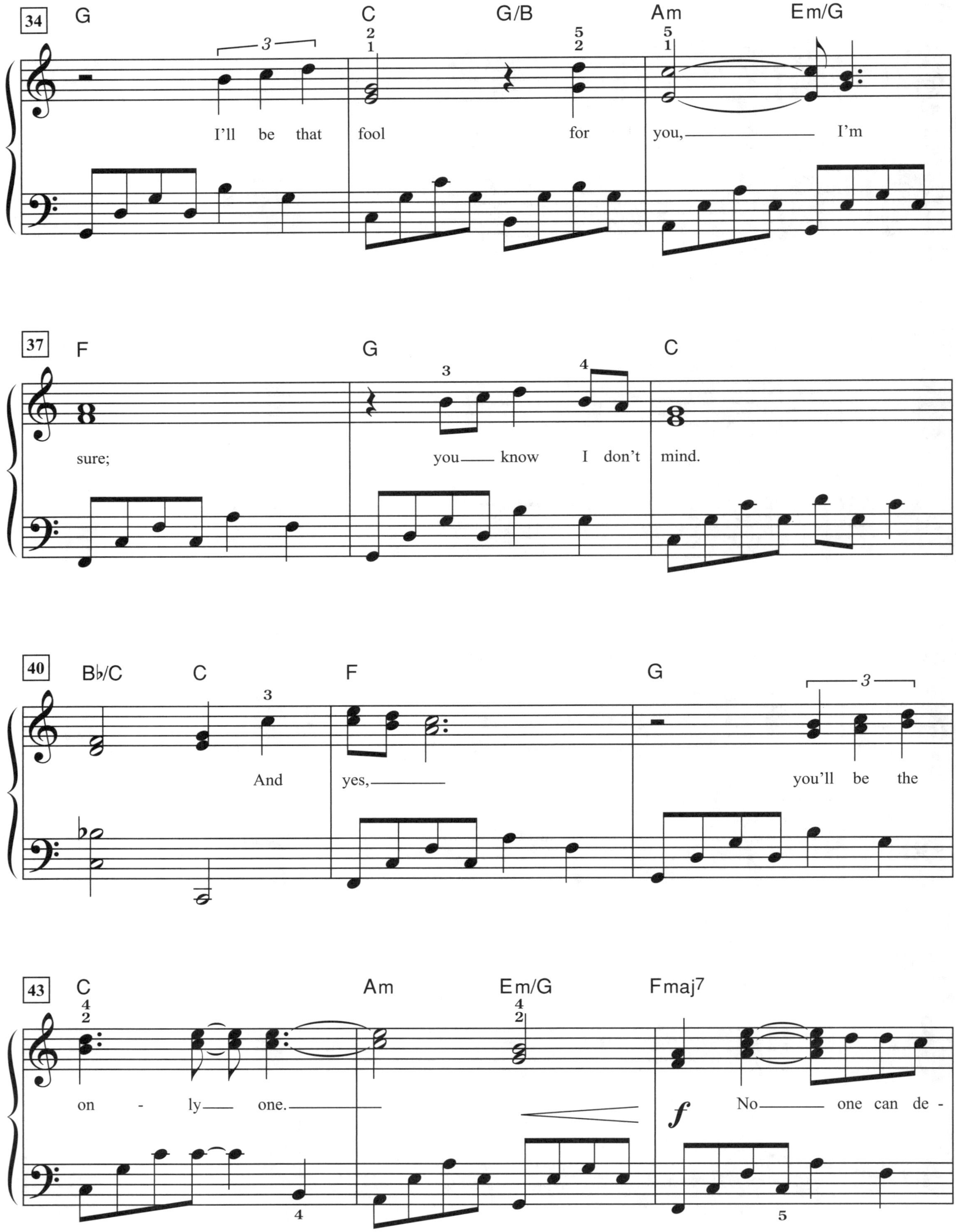

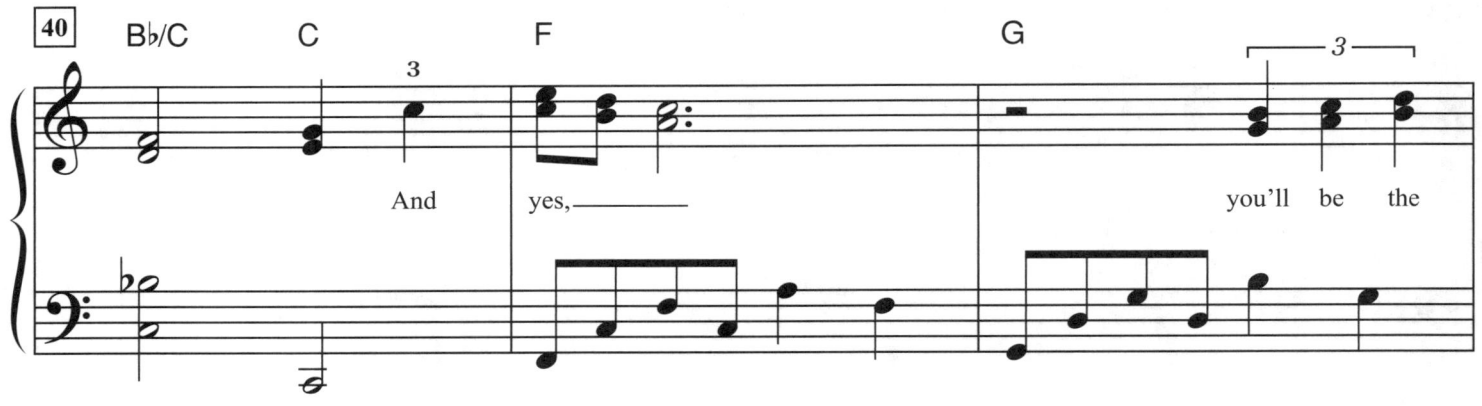

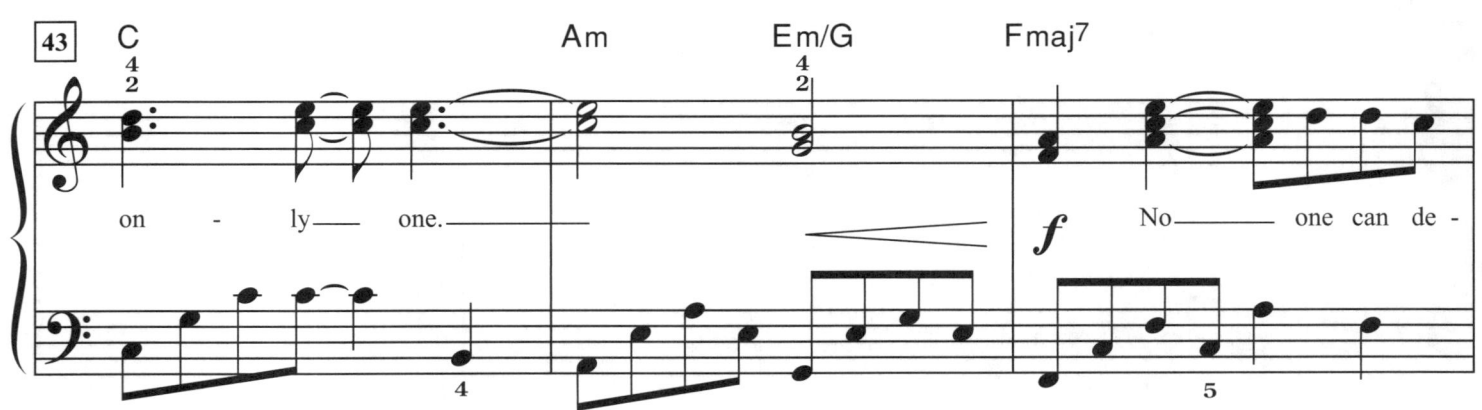

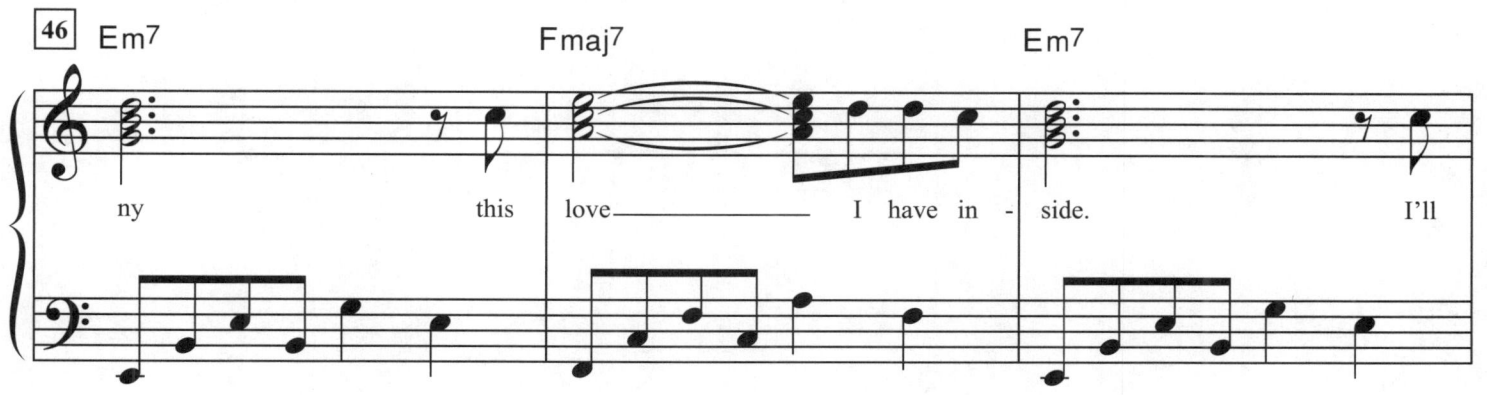
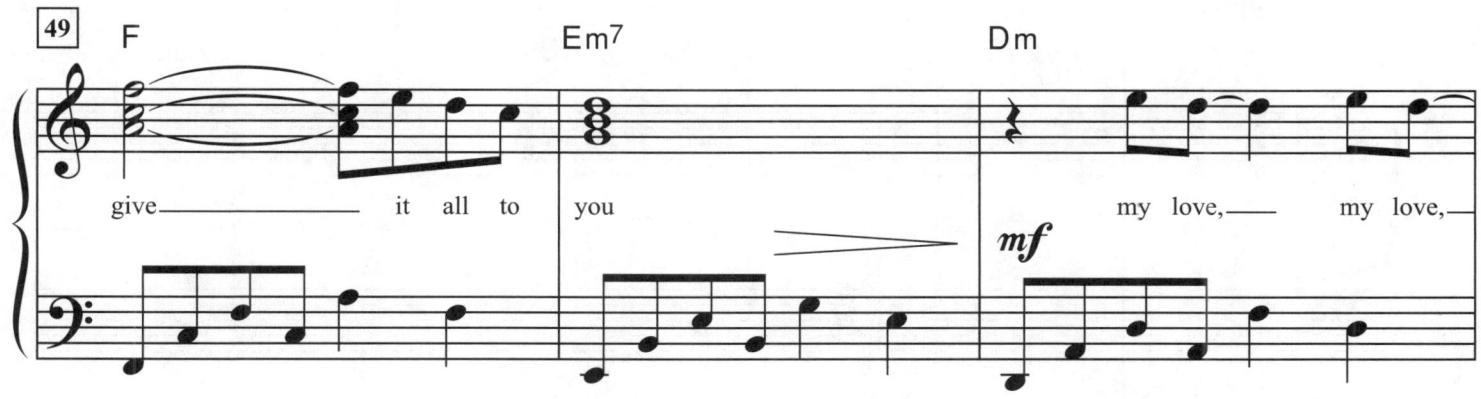
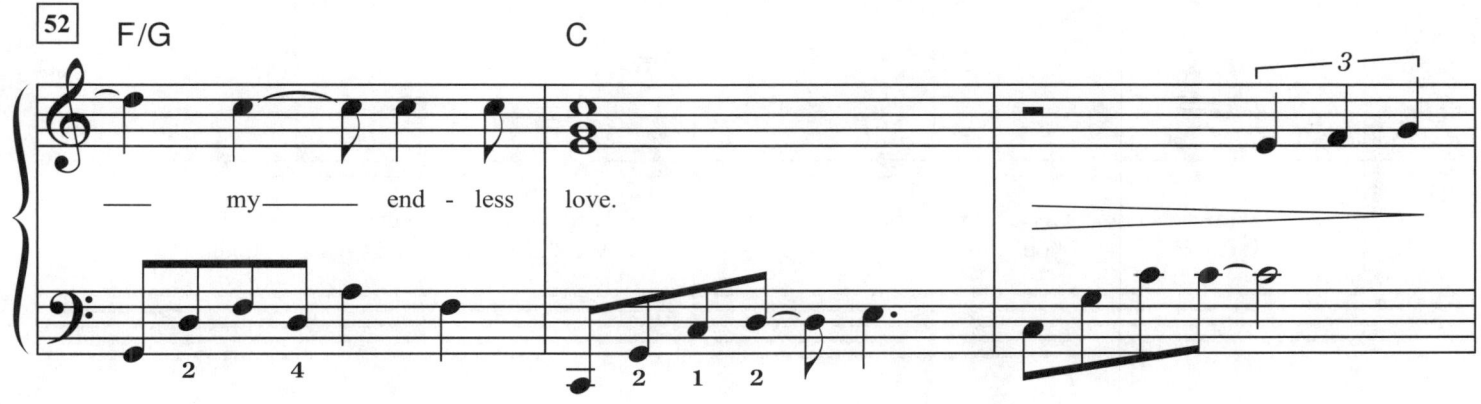

THE GIFT

Words and Music by
Jim Brickman and Tom Douglas
Arranged by Dan Coates

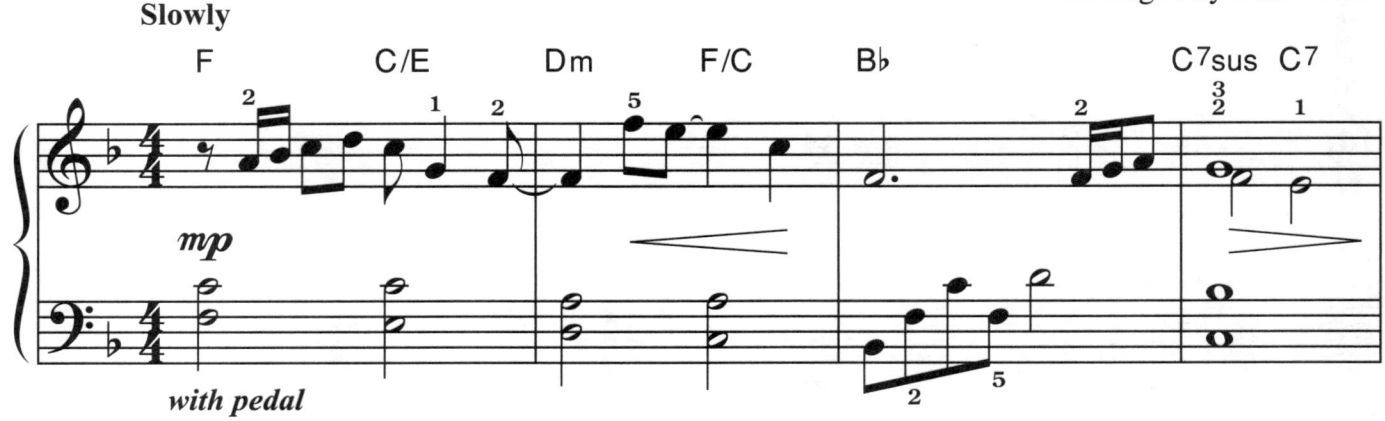

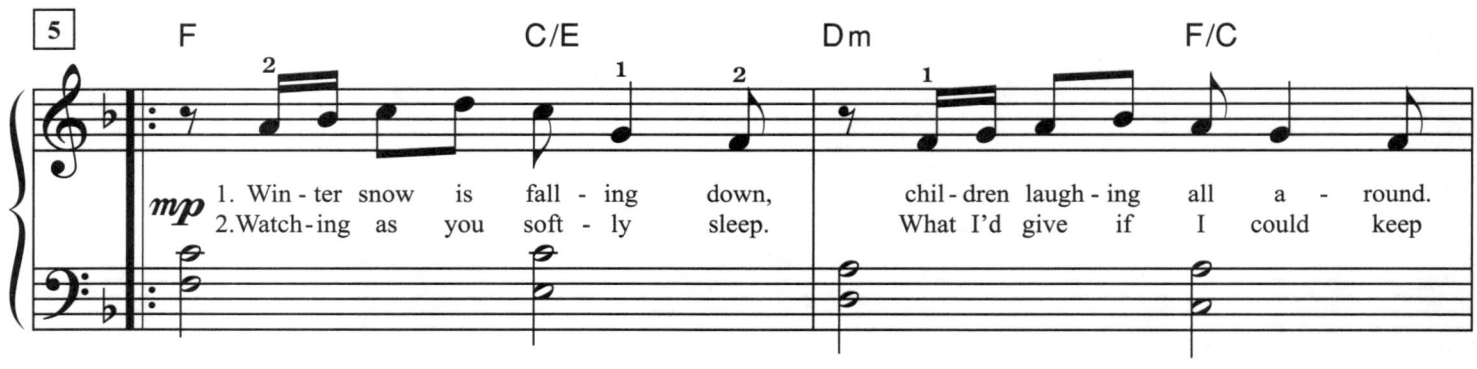

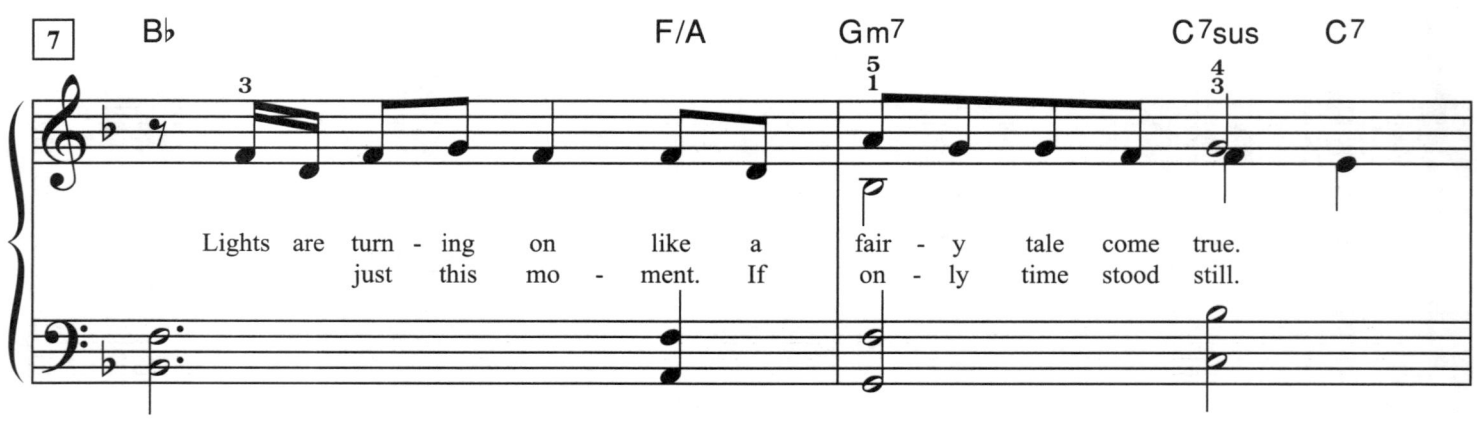

© 1997 BRICKMAN ARRANGEMENT / MULTISONGS, INC. (A Division of Careers BMG Music Publishing)
and SONY/ATV SONGS LLC d/b/a TREE PUBLISHING CO.
Print Rights for BRICKMAN ARRANGEMENT Administered Worldwide by ALFRED PUBLISHING CO., INC.
All Rights Reserved

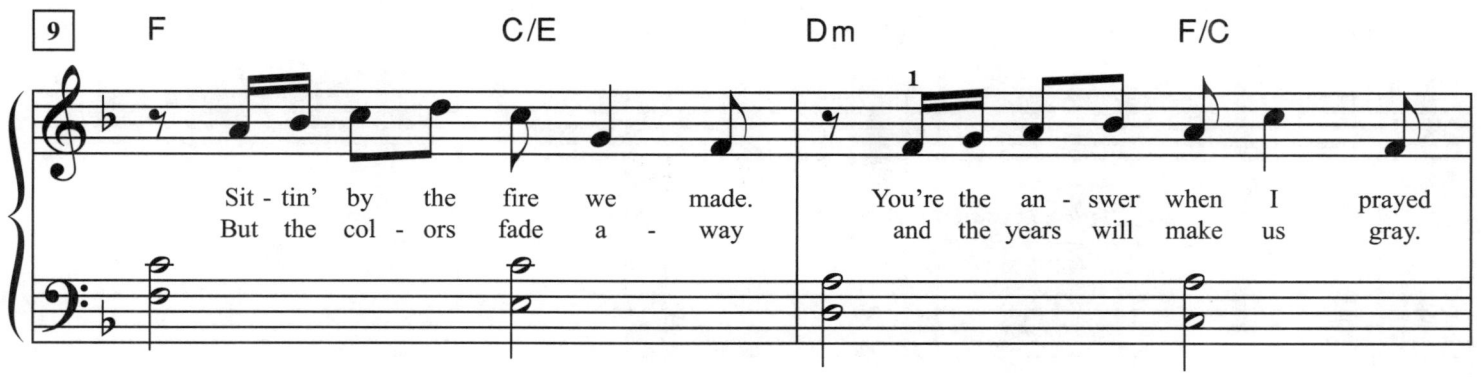
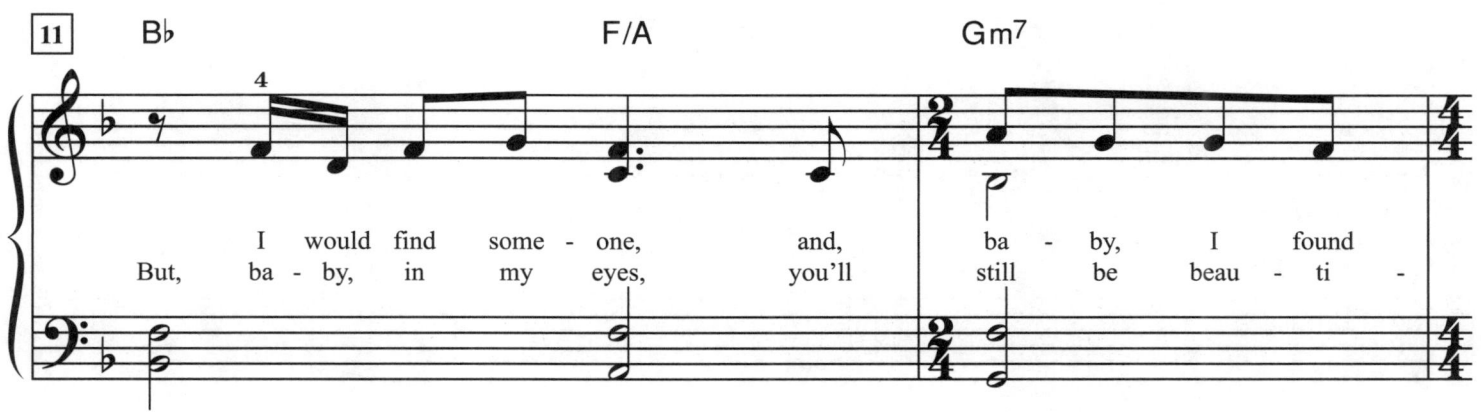
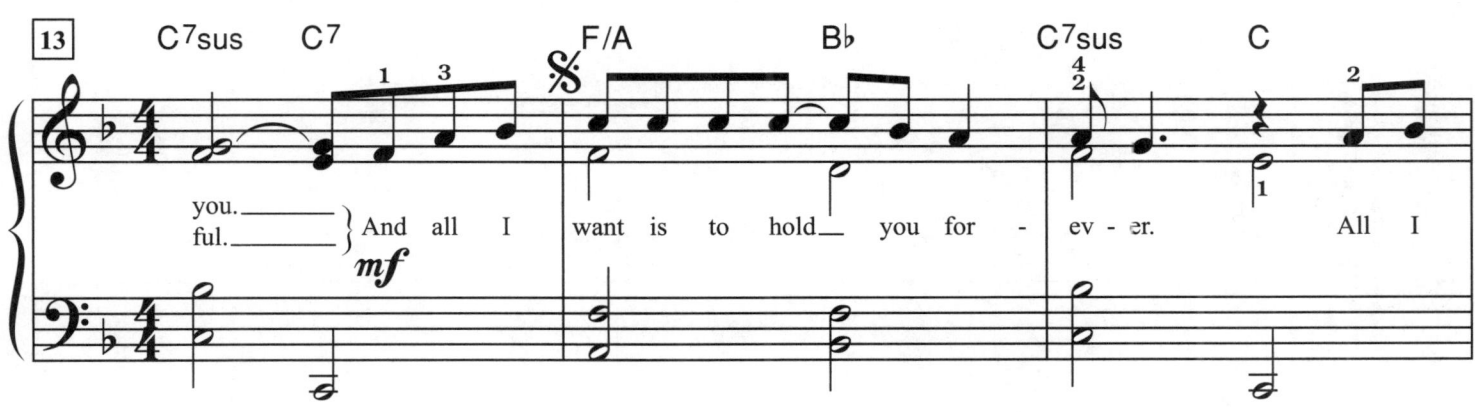
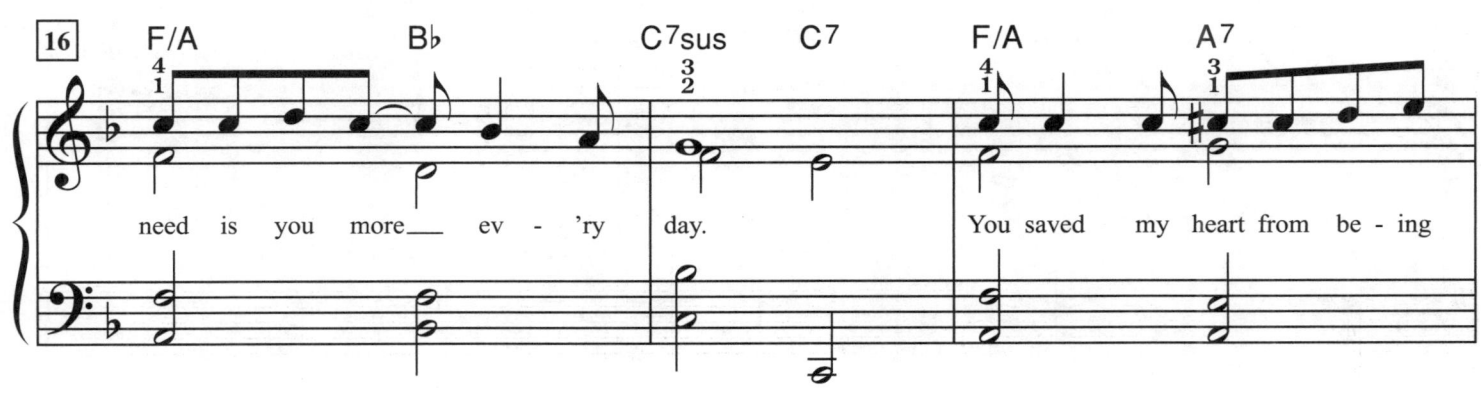

50

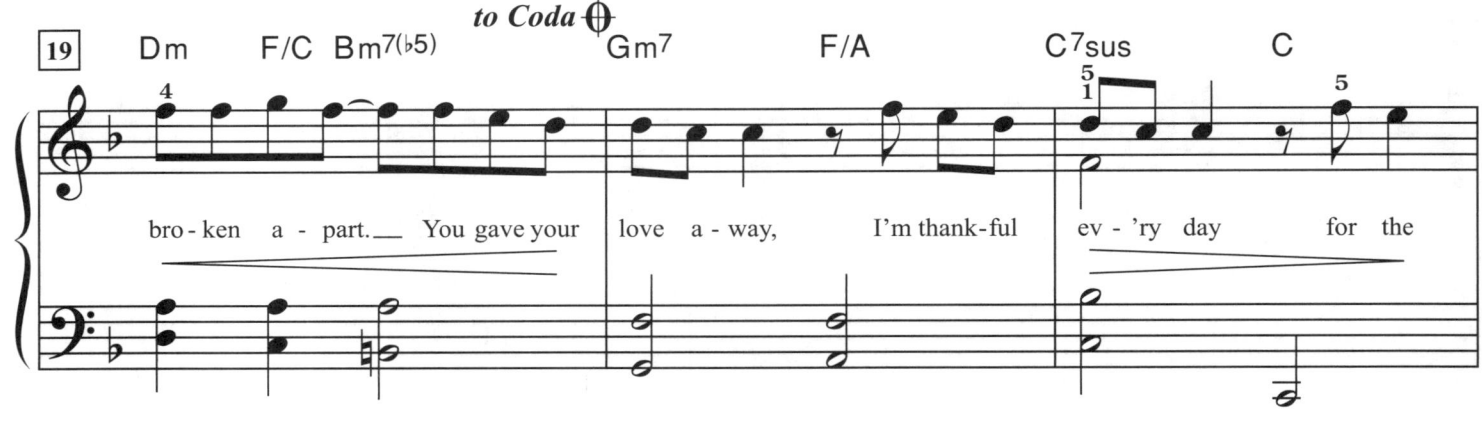

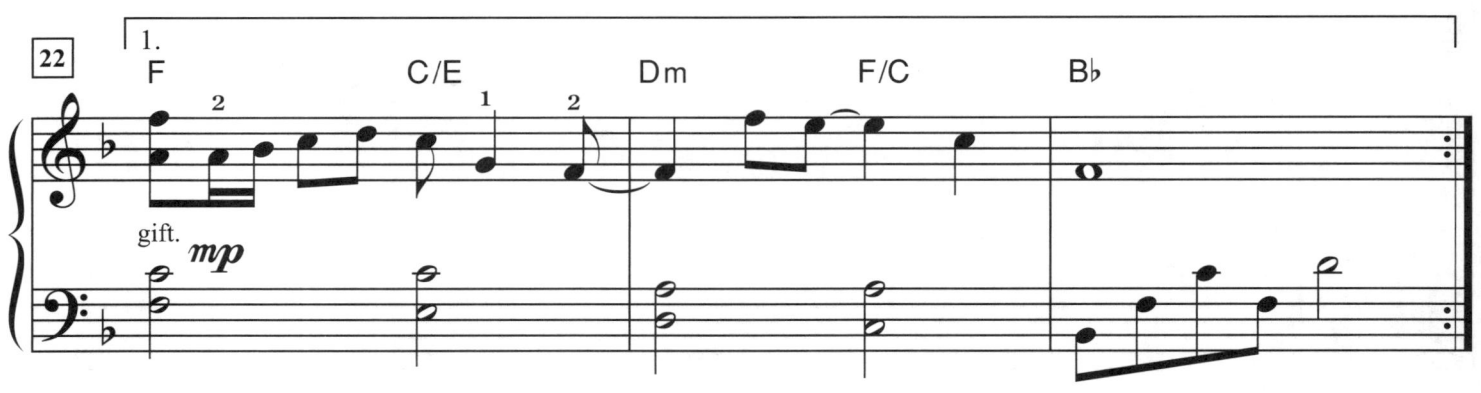

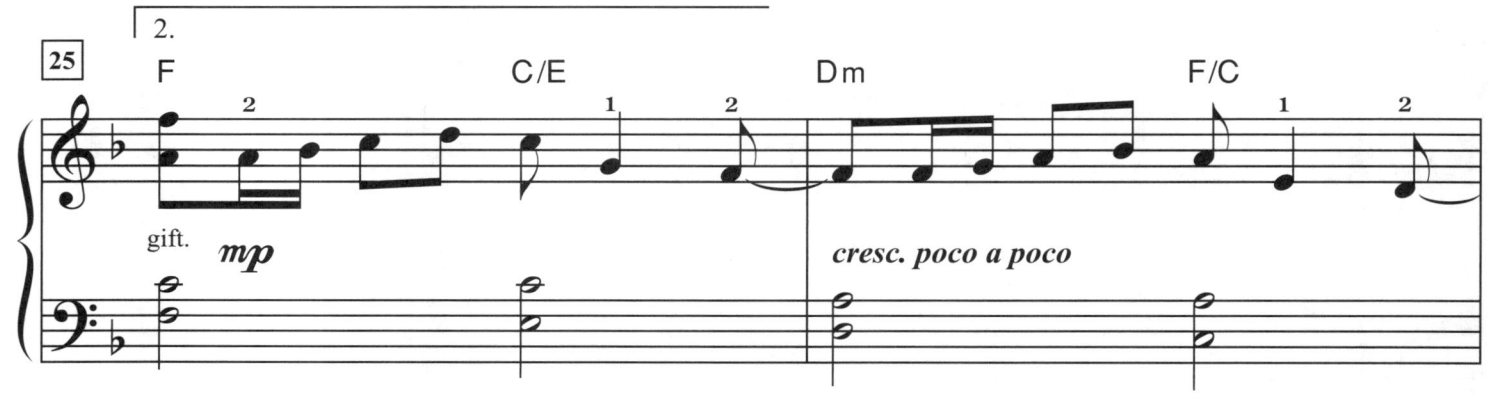

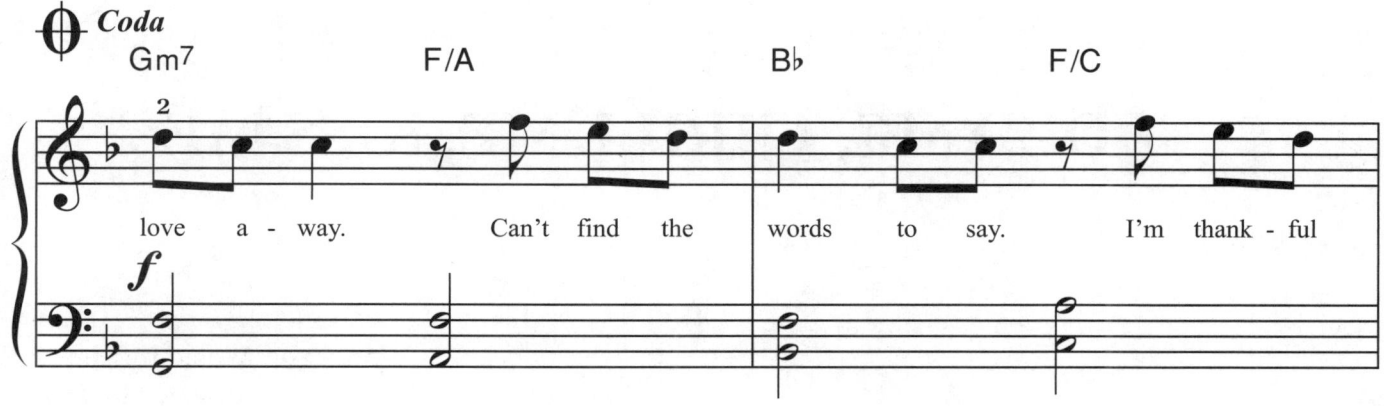
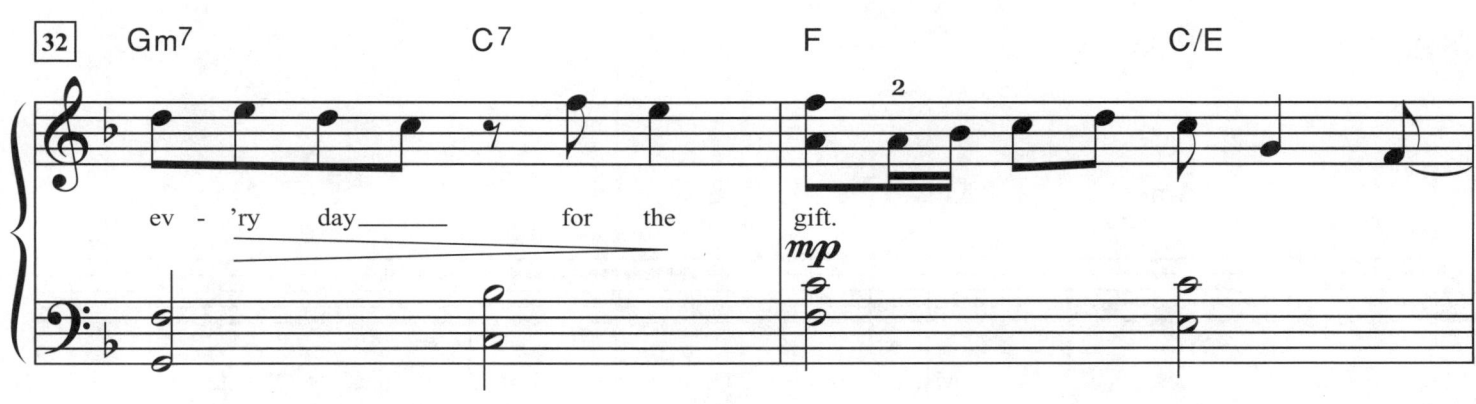

HOLD ME, THRILL ME, KISS ME

Words and Music by Harry Noble
Arranged by Dan Coates

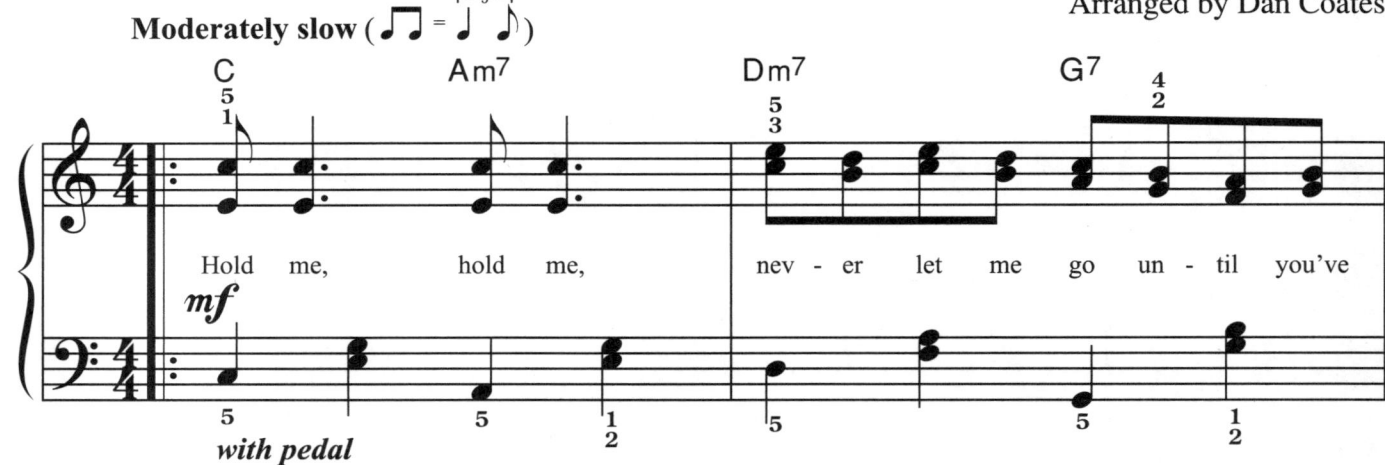

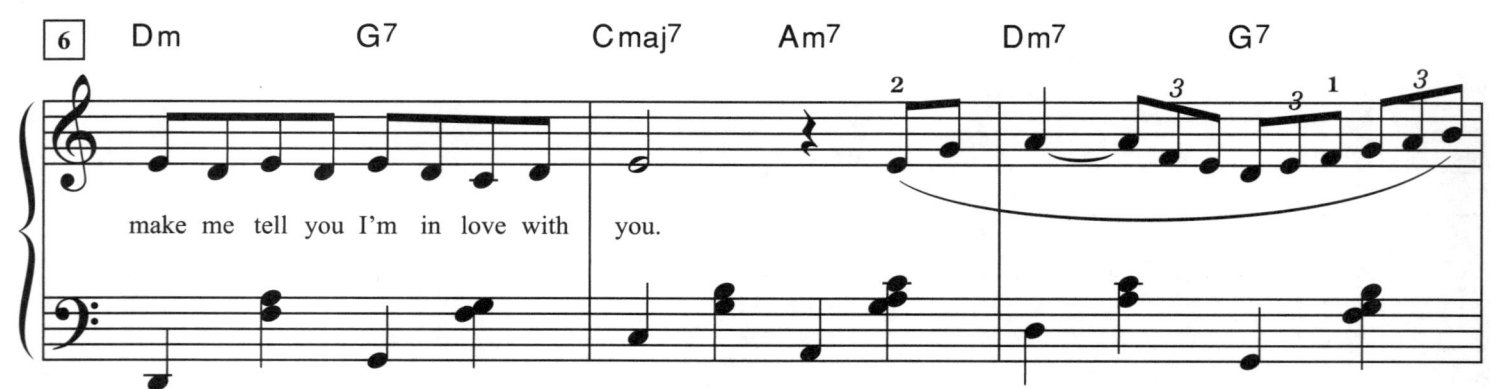

© 1952 (Renewed) EMI MILLS MUSIC, INC.
All Rights Controlled by EMI MILLS MUSIC, INC. (Publishing)
and ALFRED PUBLISHING CO., INC. (Print)
All Rights Reserved

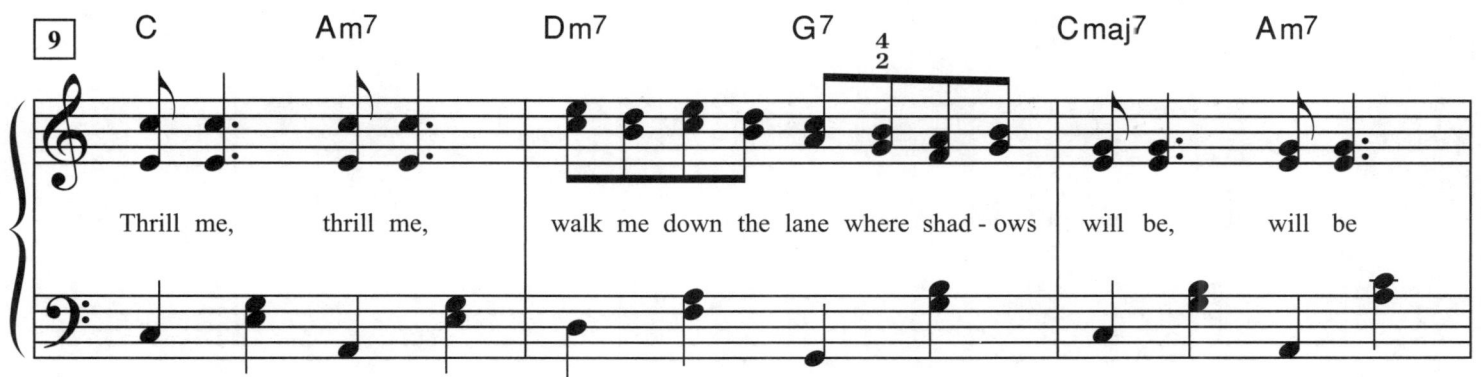
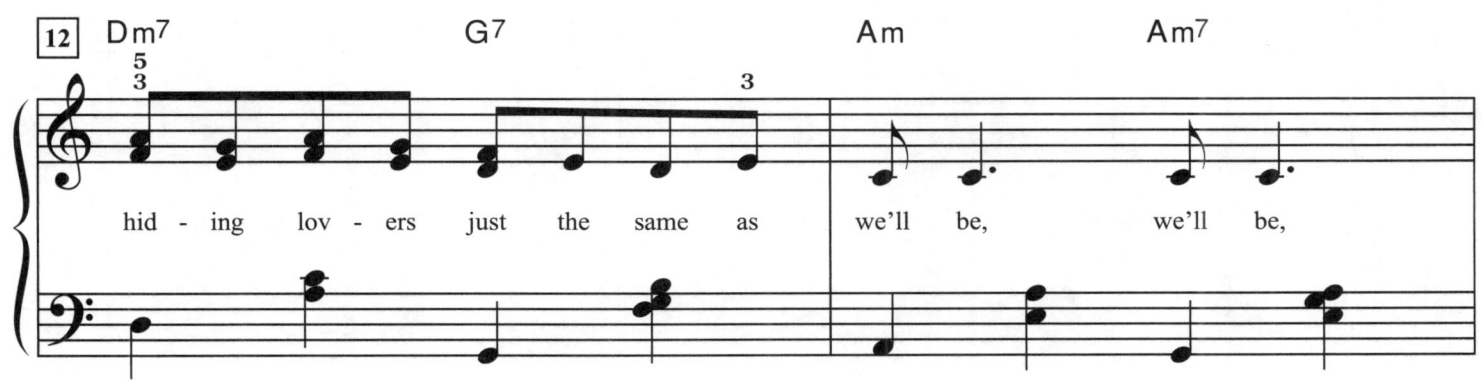

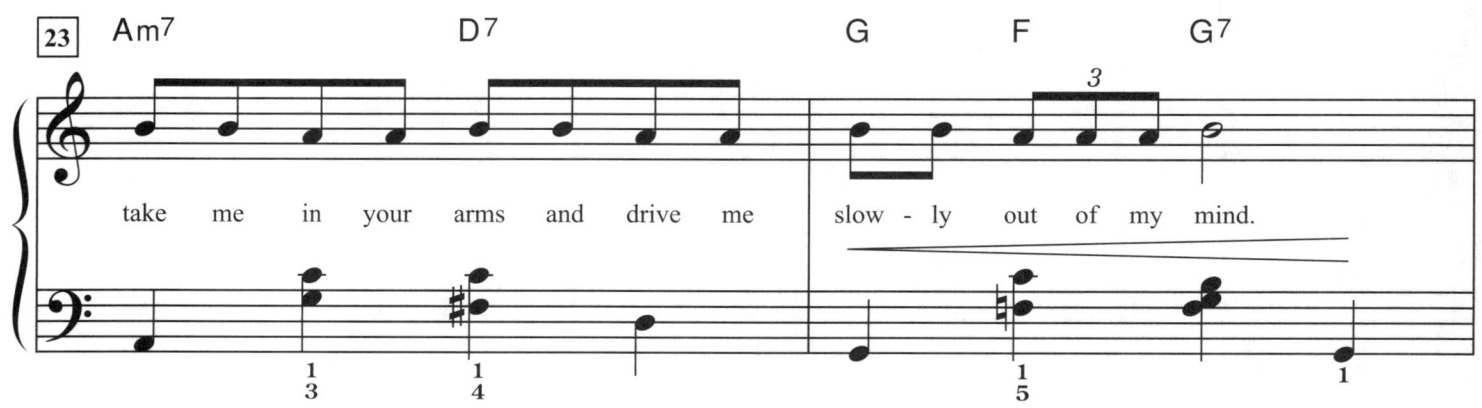

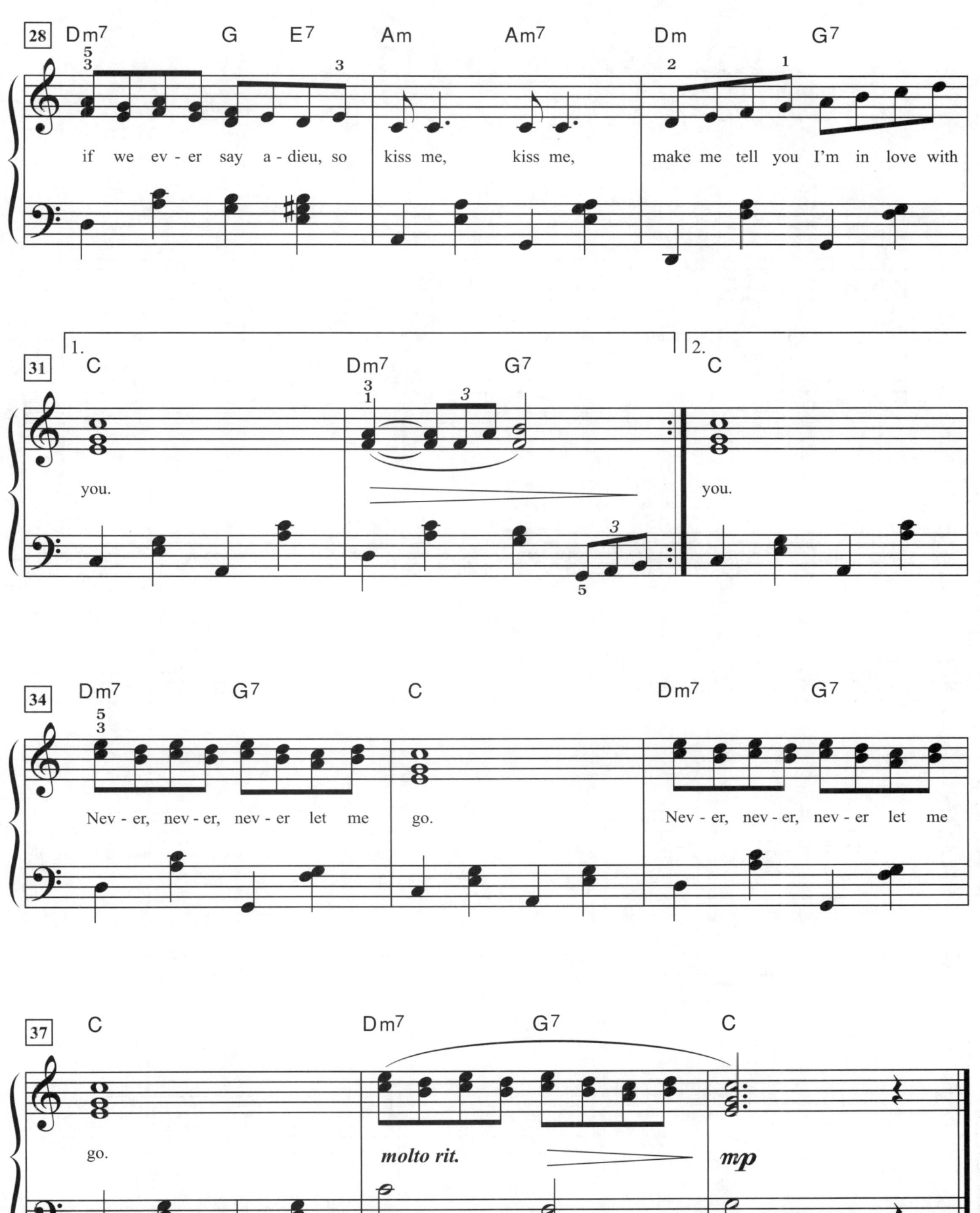

HOW COULD I EVER KNOW

Lyrics by Marsha Norman
Music by Lucy Simon
Arranged by Dan Coates

© 1991, 1992 ABCDE PUBLISHING LTD. and CALOUGIE MUSIC
All Rights Administered by WB MUSIC CORP.
All Rights Reserved

HOW DEEP IS YOUR LOVE

Words and Music by Barry Gibb,
Maurice Gibb and Robin Gibb
Arranged by Dan Coates

HOW DO I LIVE

Words and Music by Diane Warren
Arranged by Dan Coates

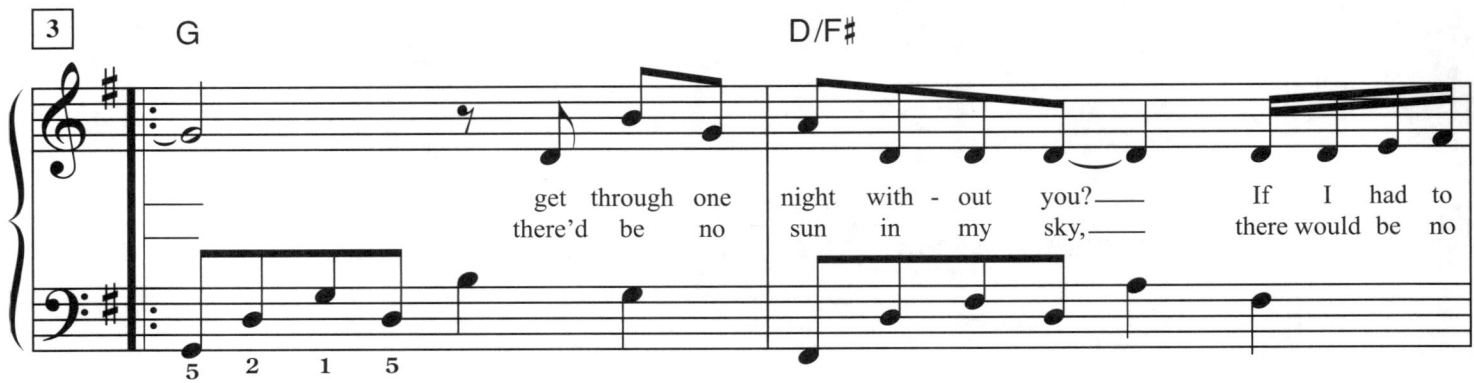

© 1997 REALSONGS (ASCAP)
All Rights Reserved

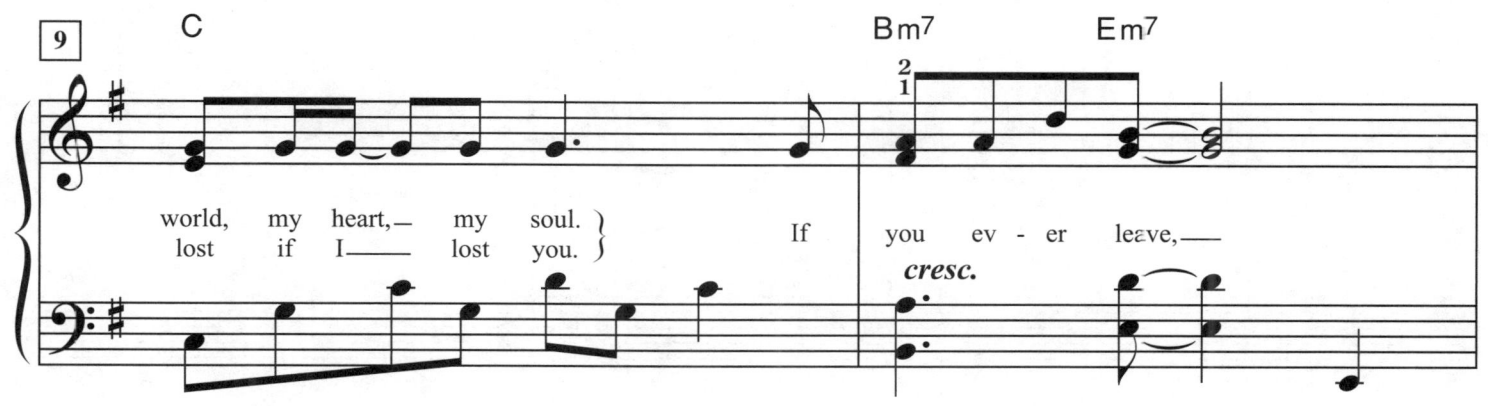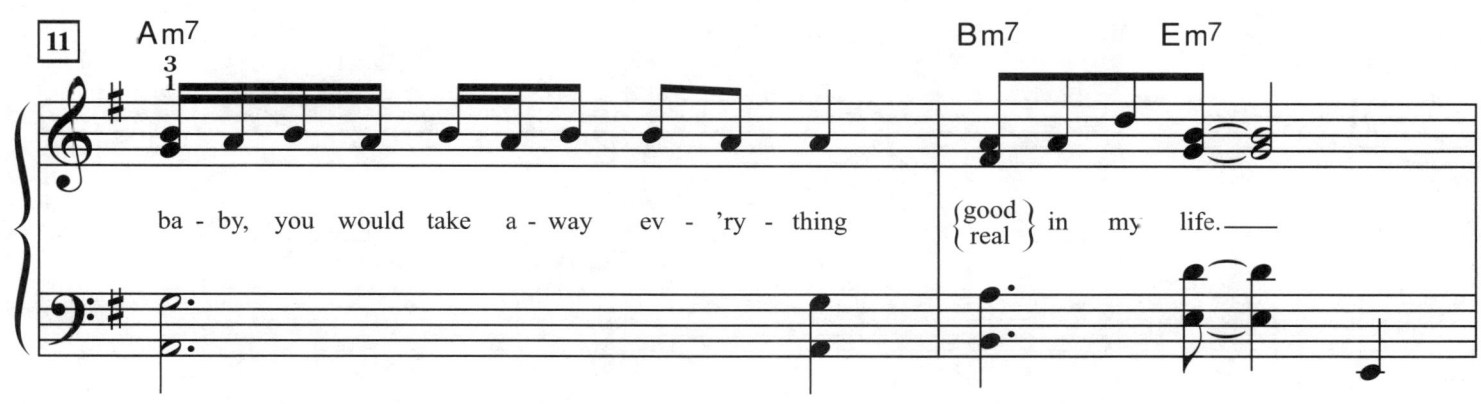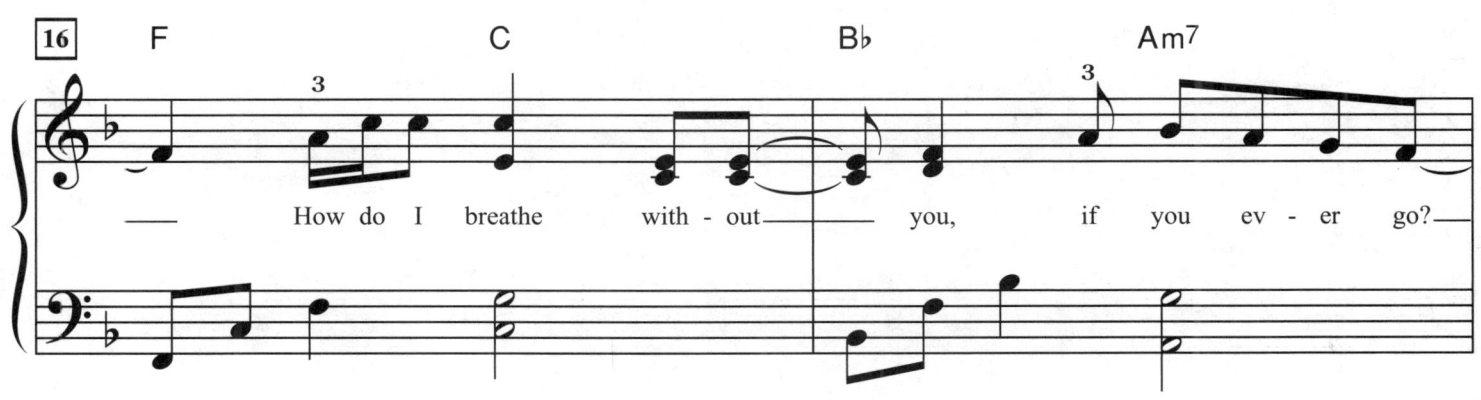

64

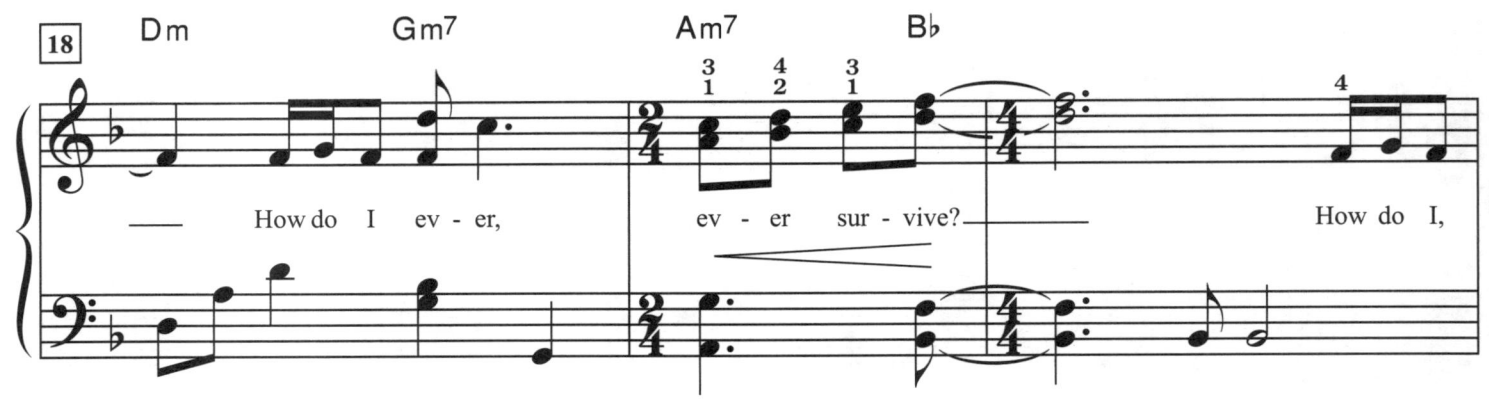
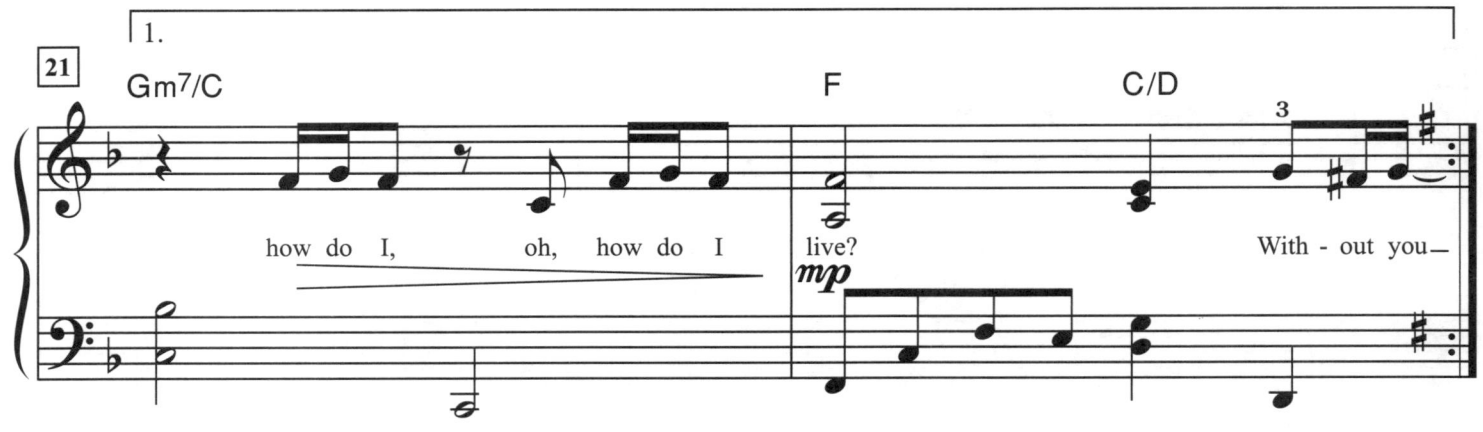

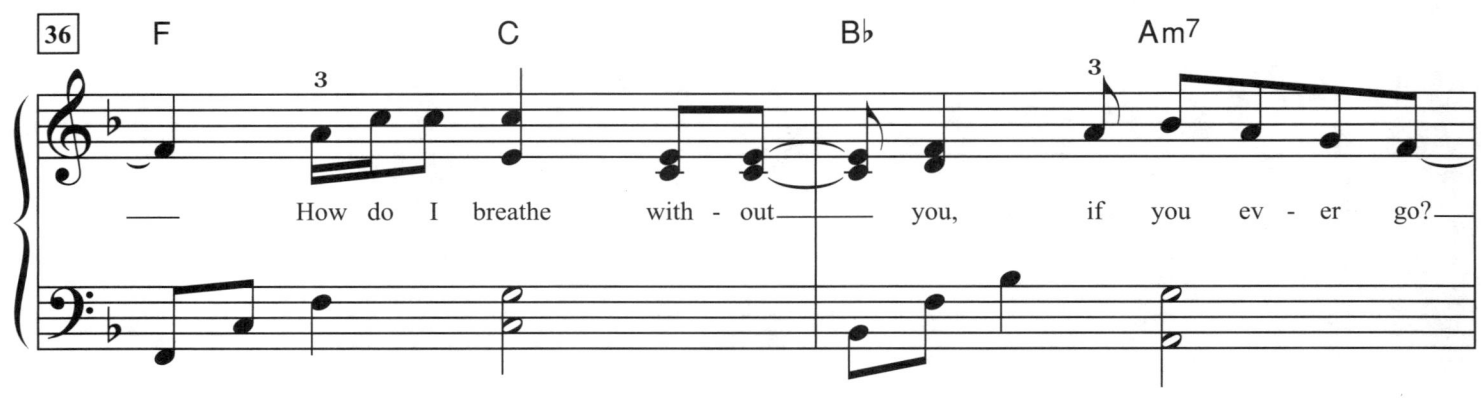
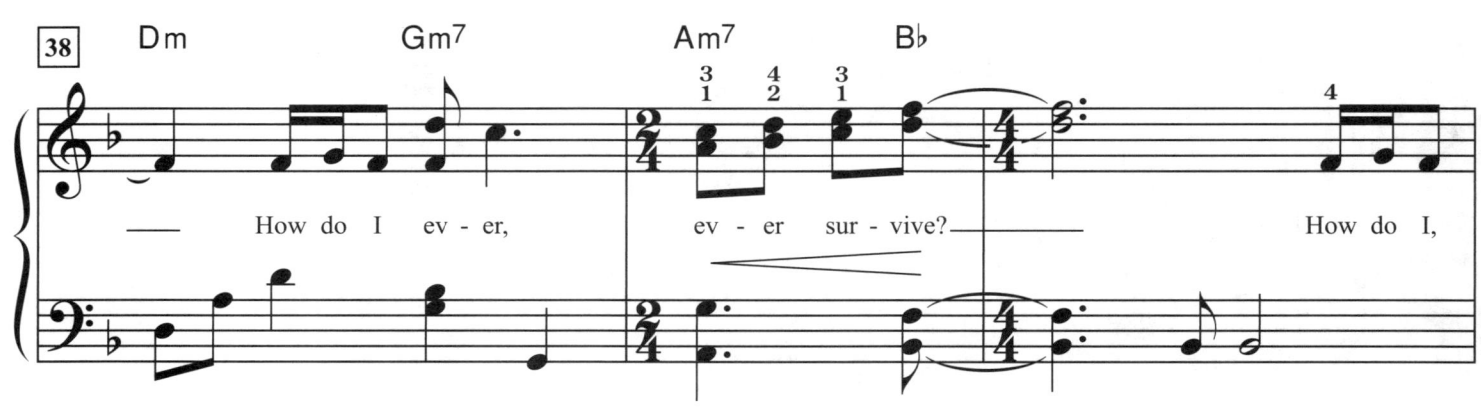
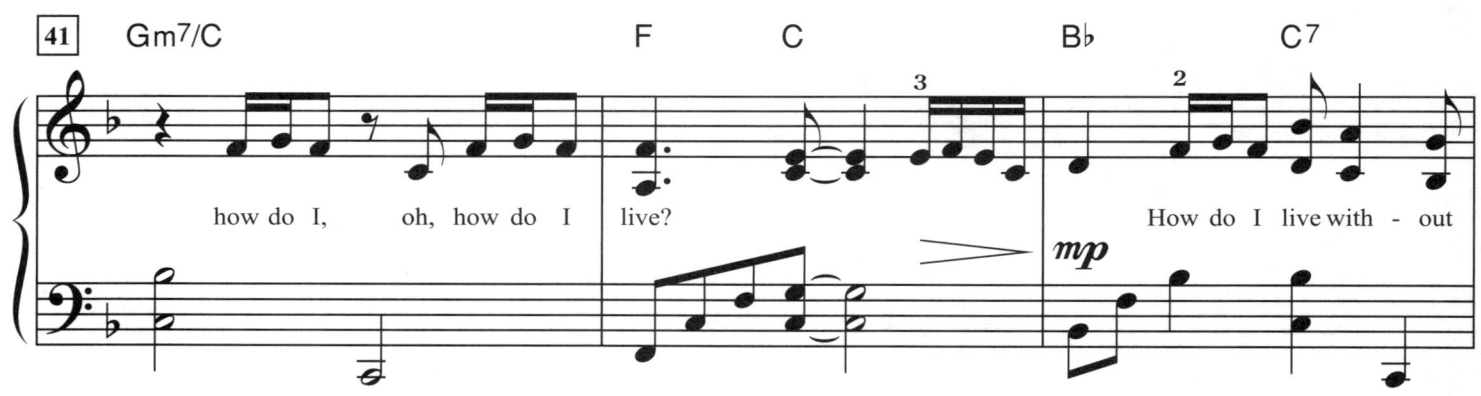
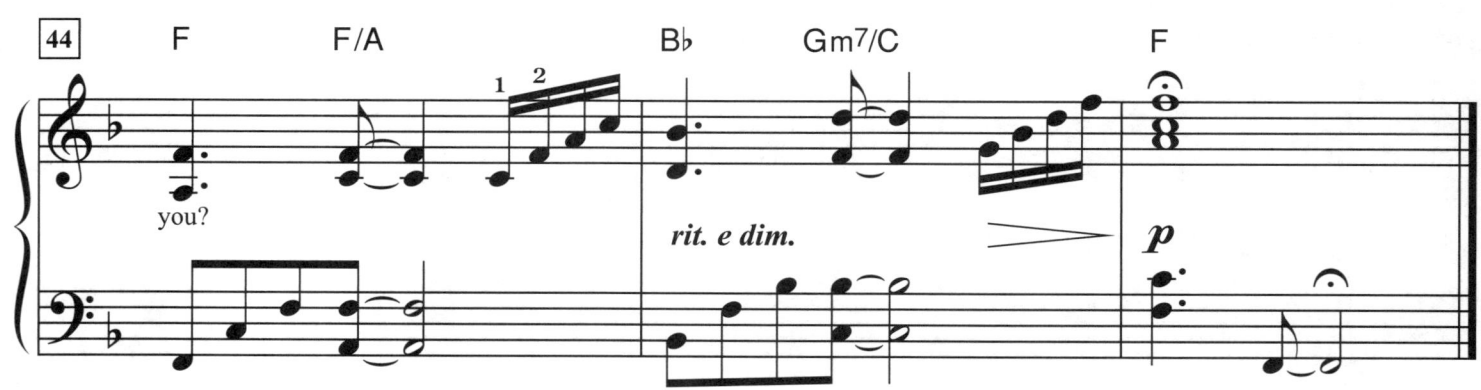

I GET A KICK OUT OF YOU

Words and Music by Cole Porter
Arranged by Dan Coates

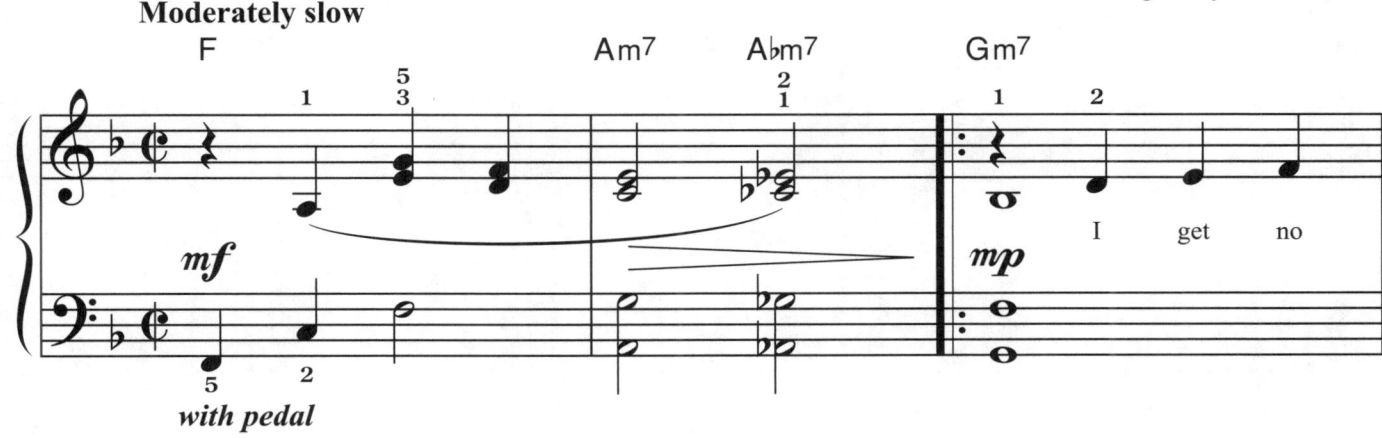

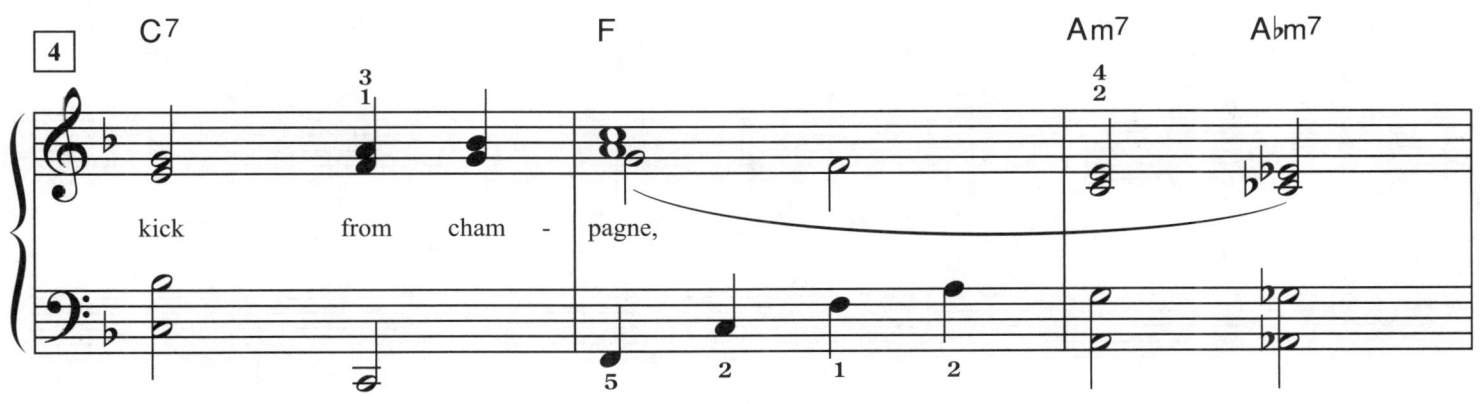

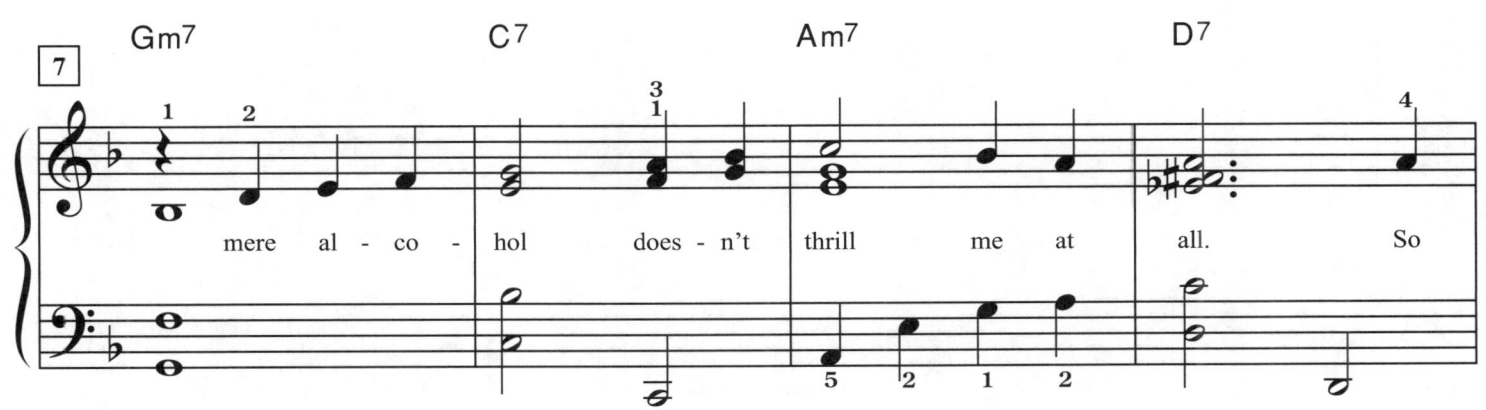

© 1934 (Renewed) WB MUSIC CORP.
All Rights Reserved

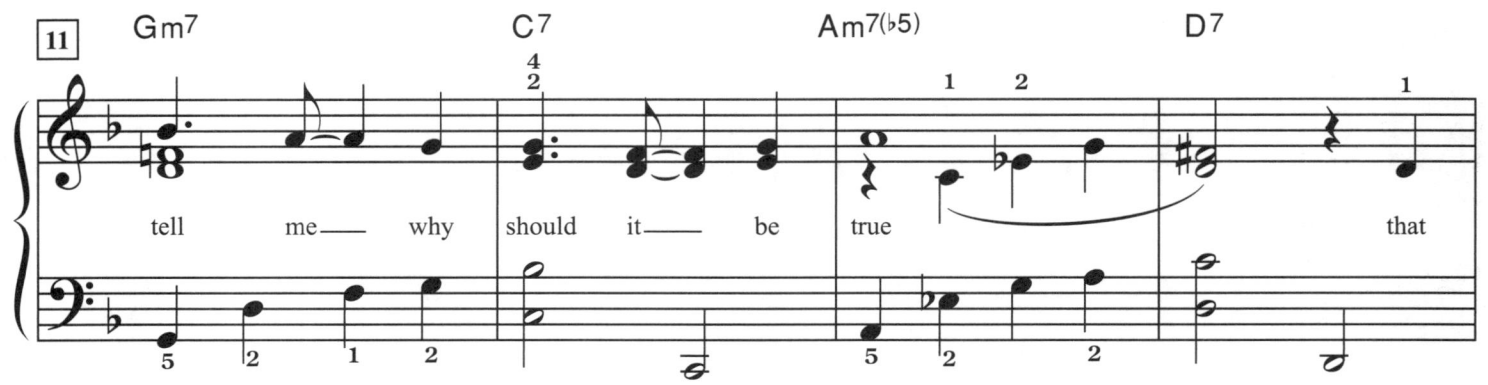
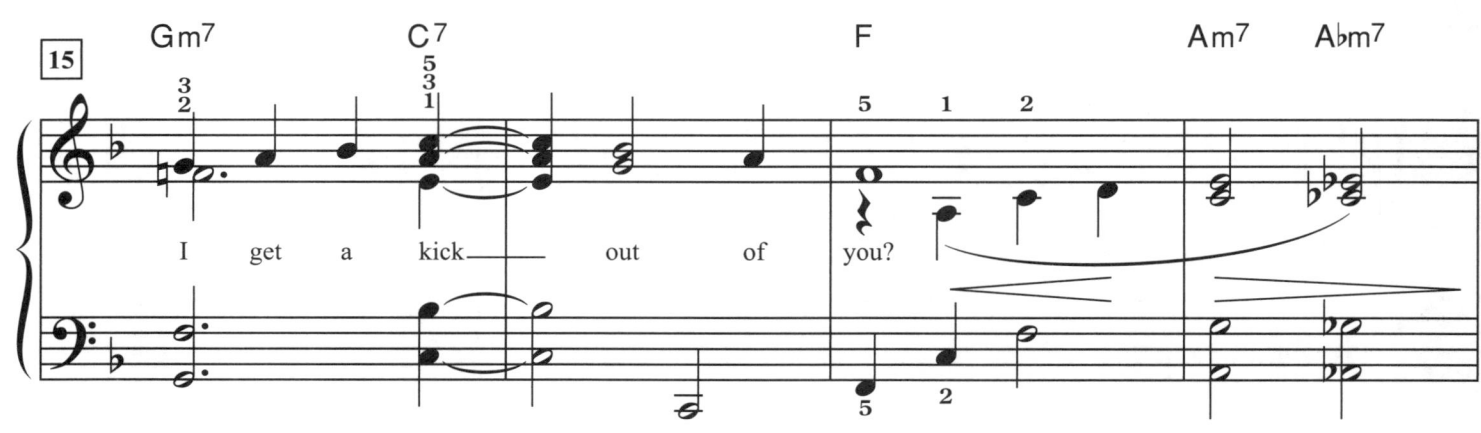
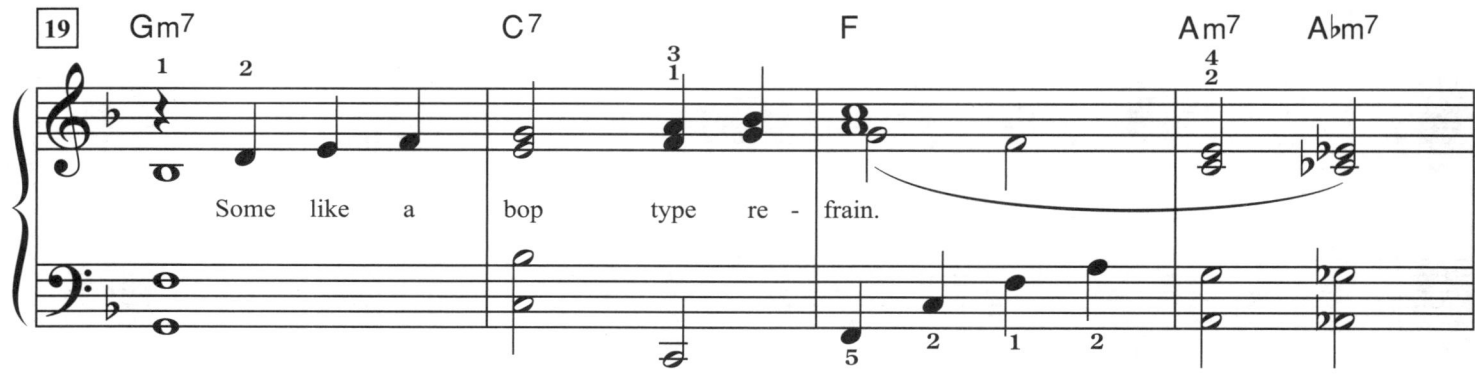
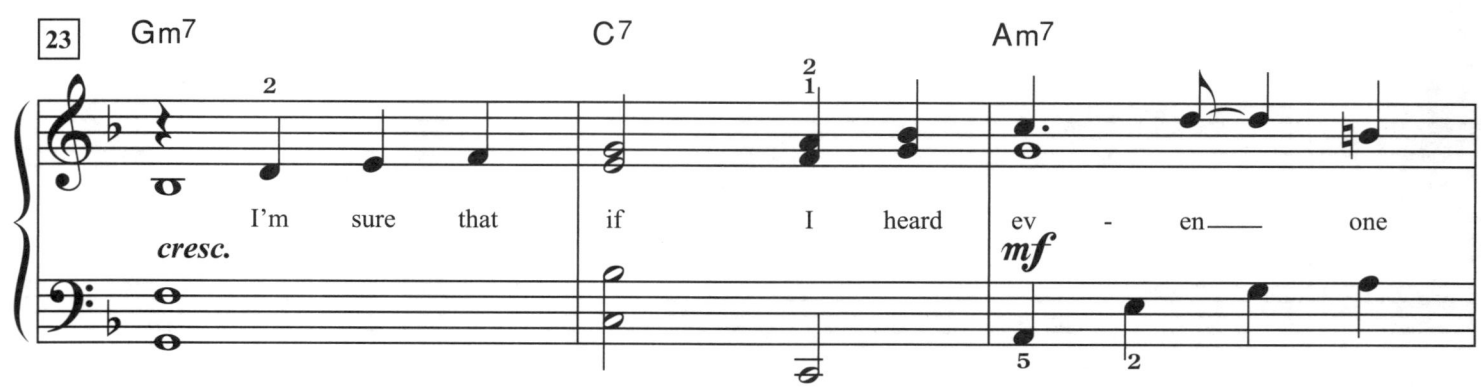

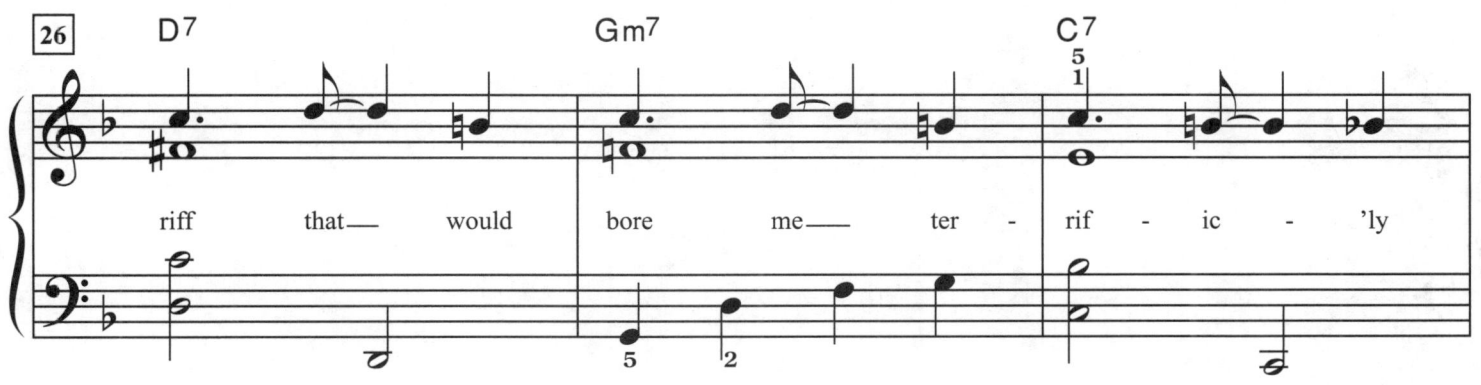
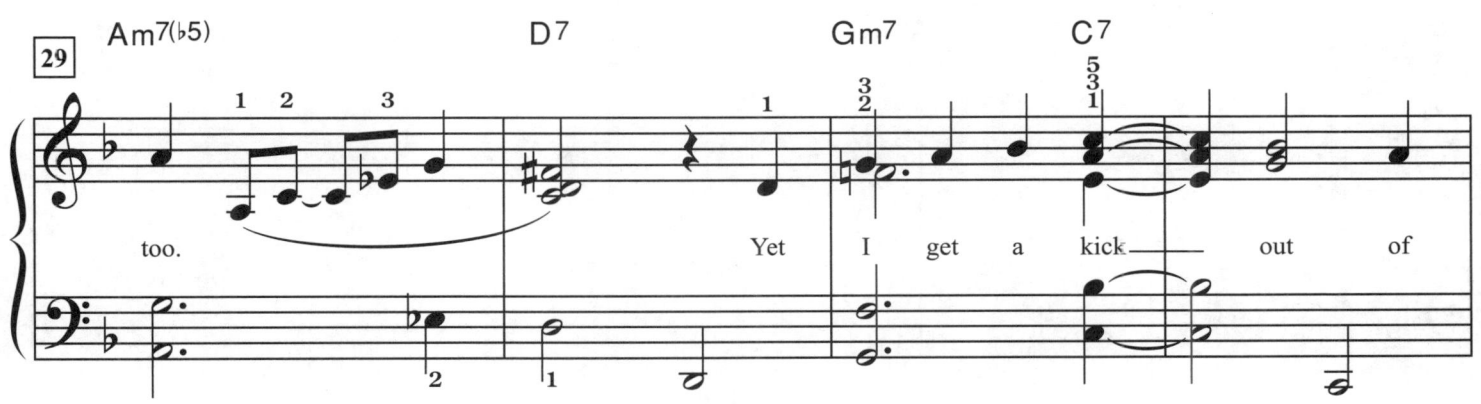
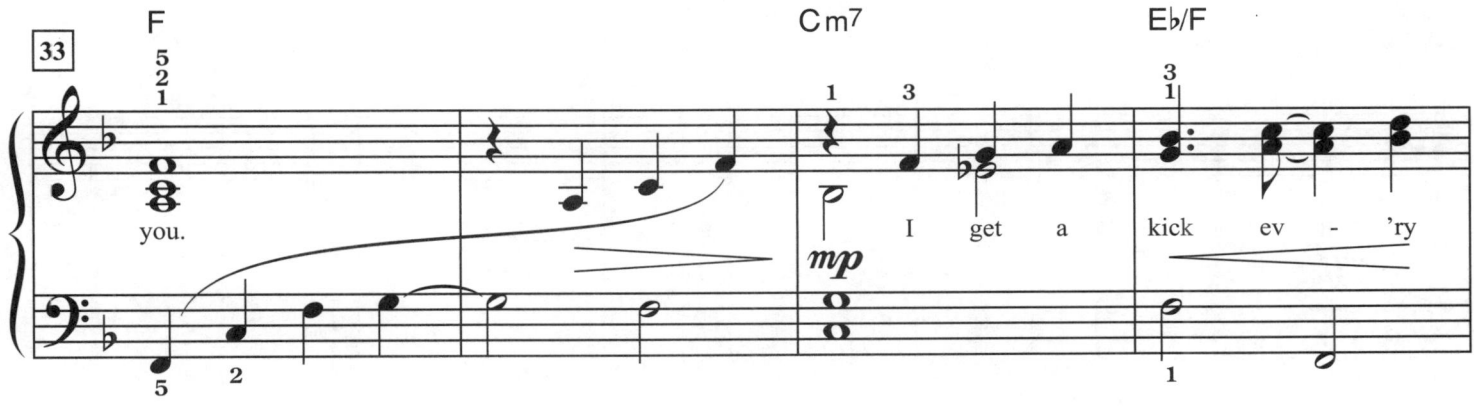
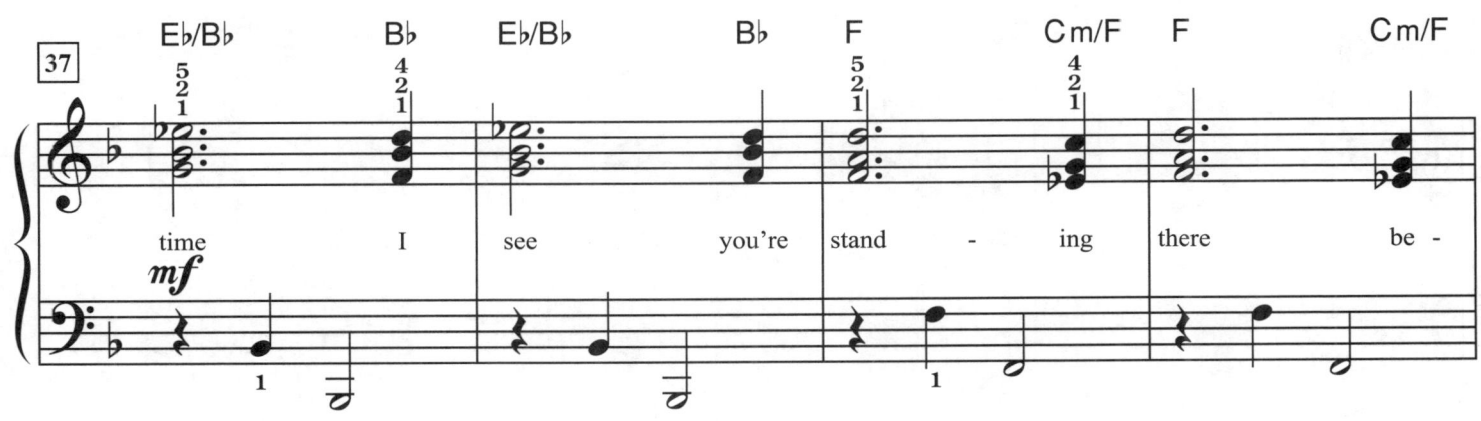

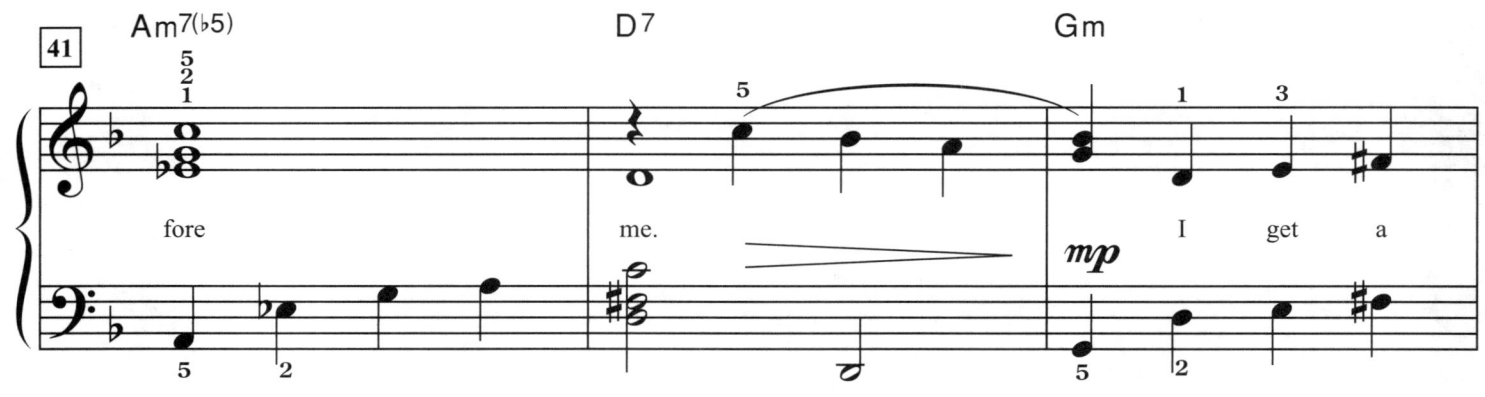
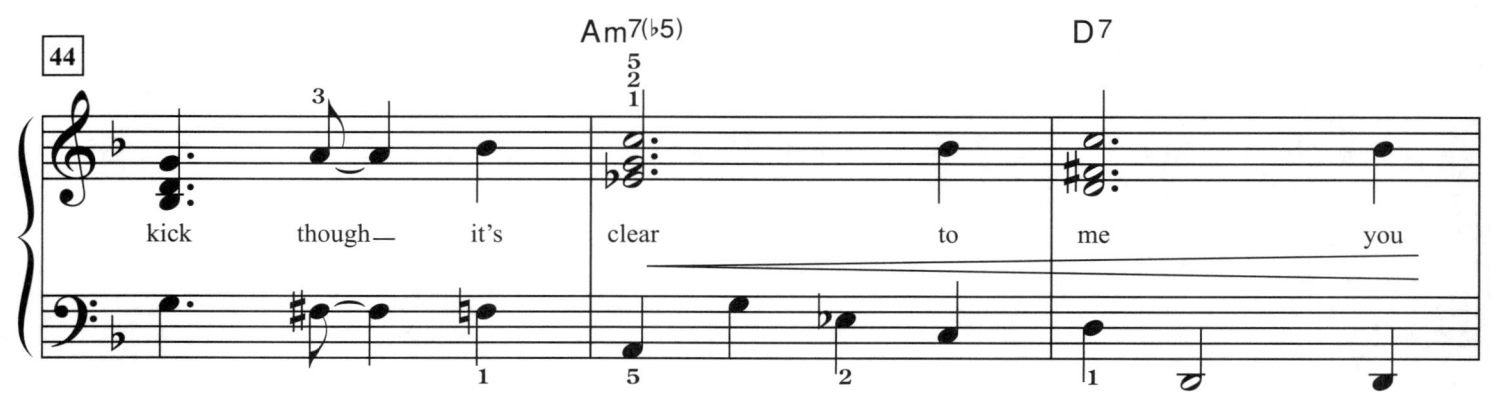
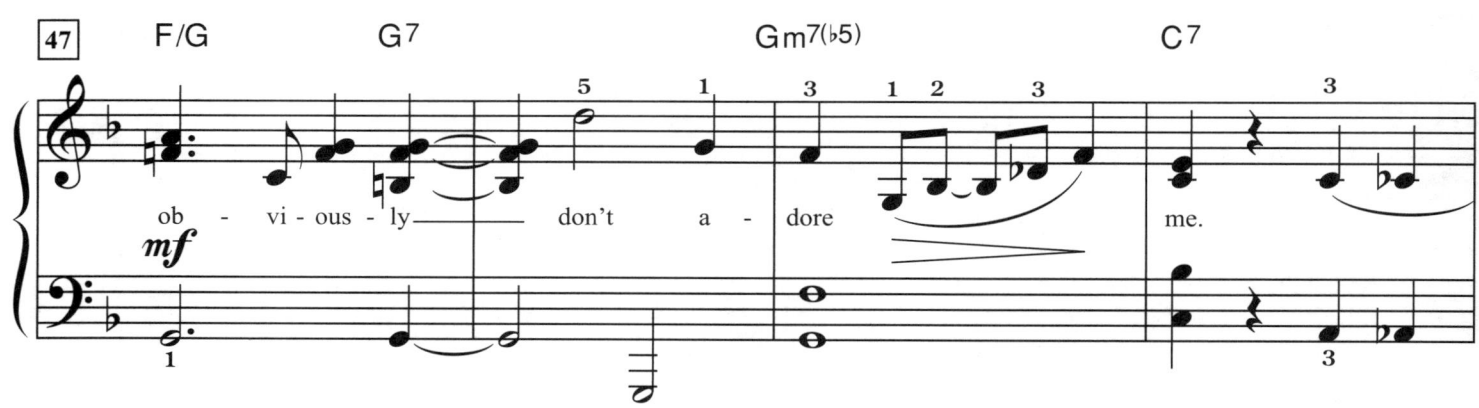
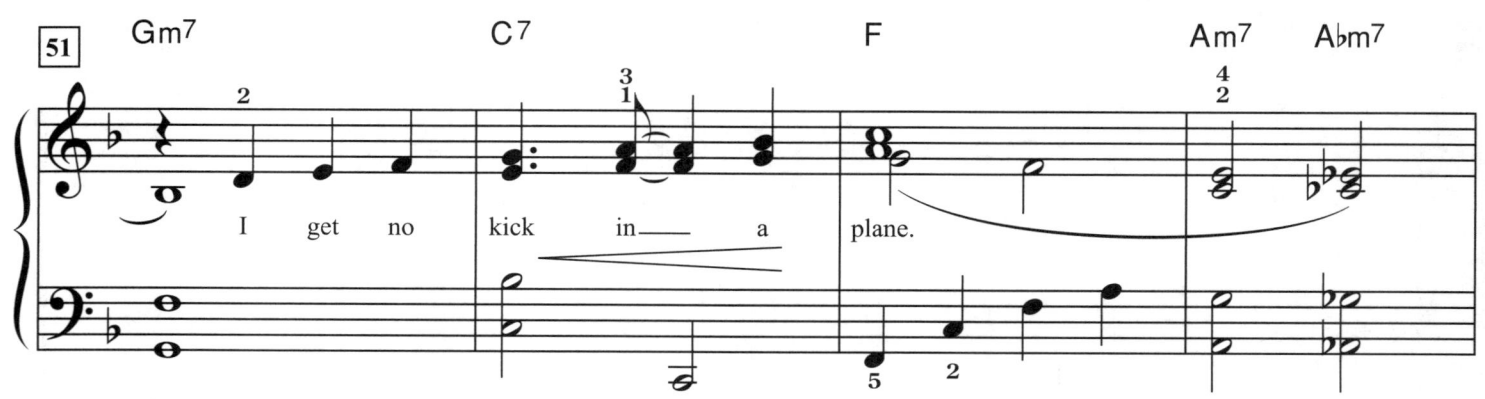

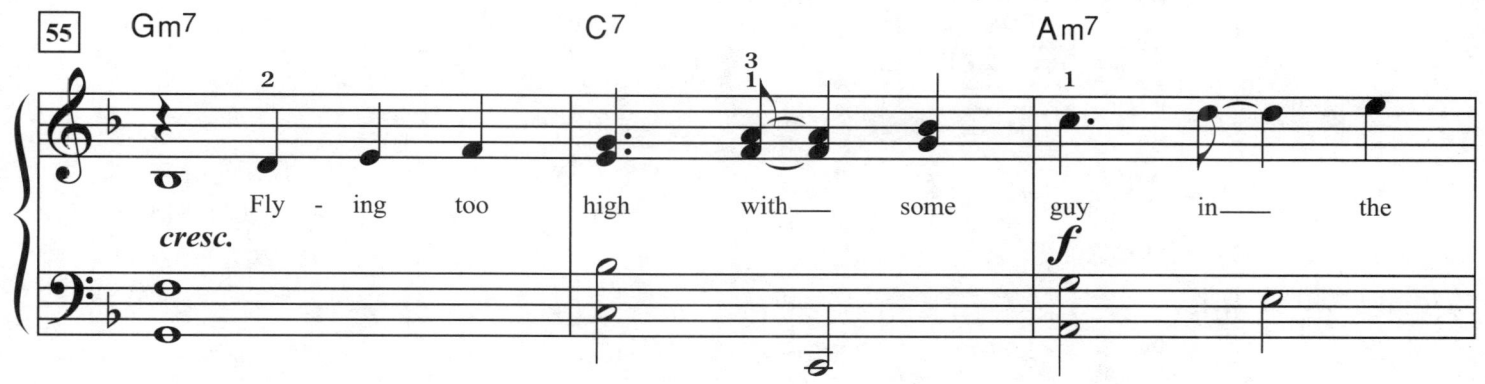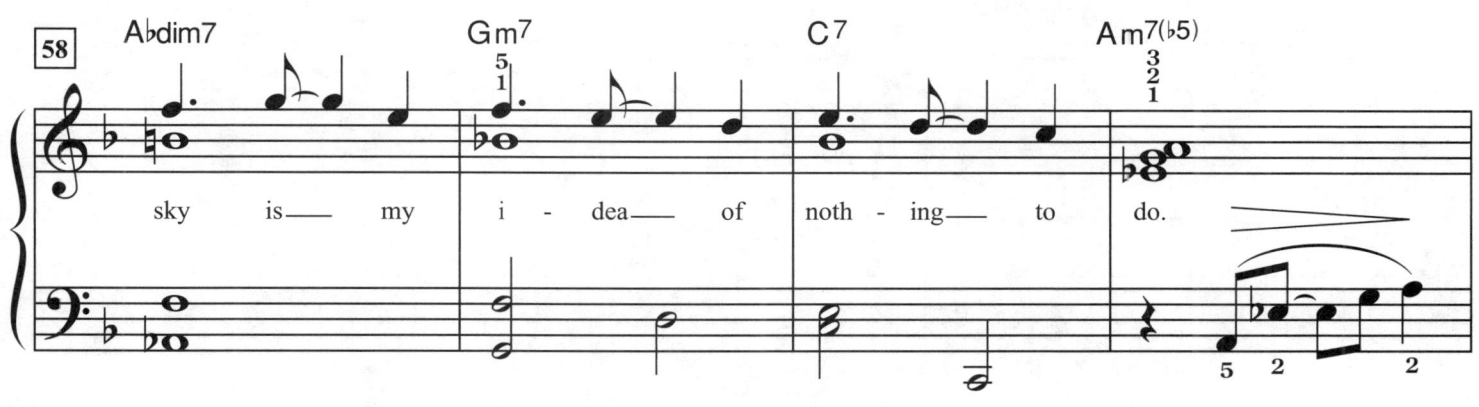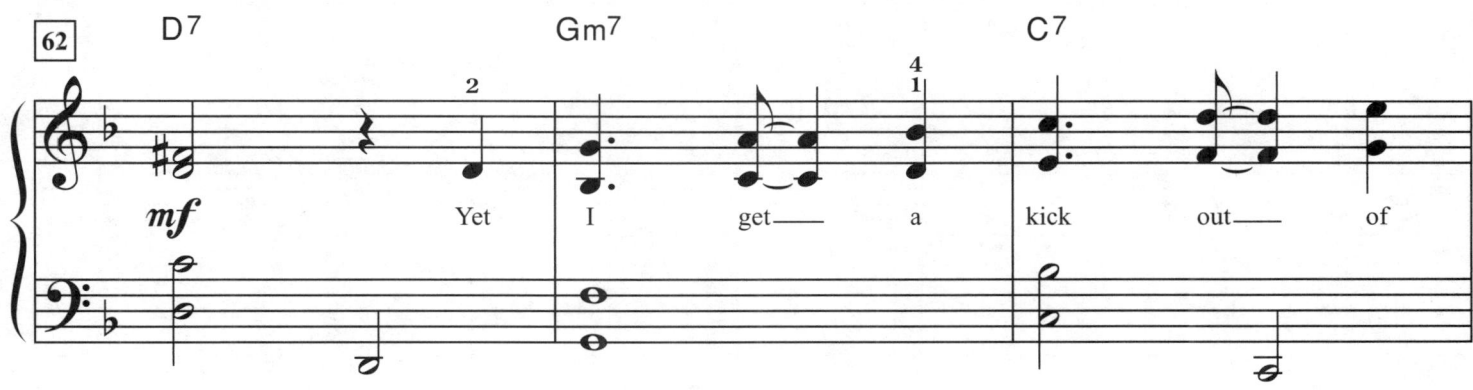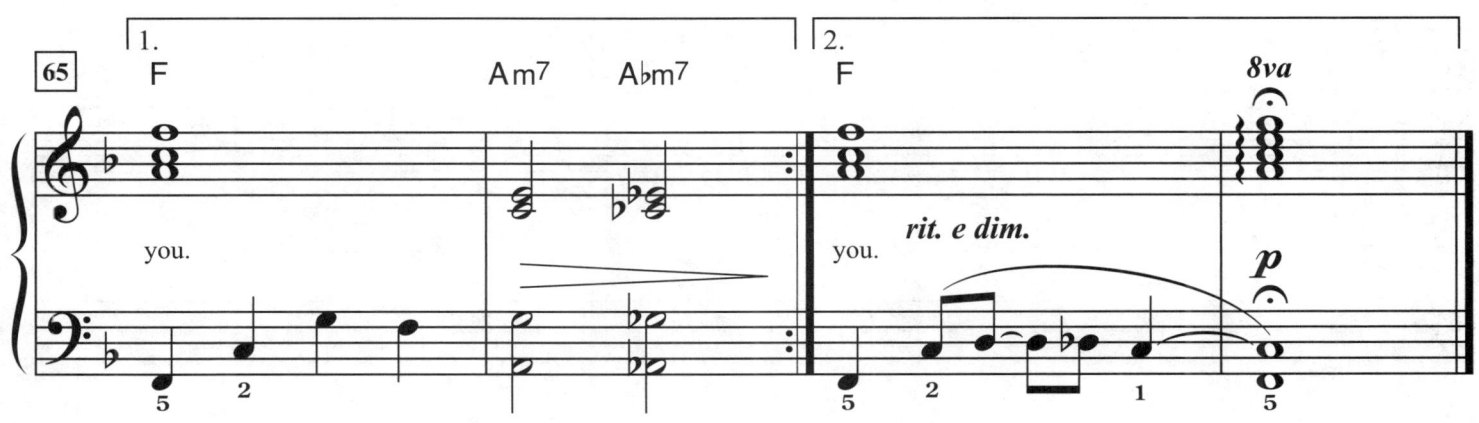

I BELIEVE IN YOU AND ME

Words and Music by
Sandy Linzer and David Wolfert
Arranged by Dan Coates

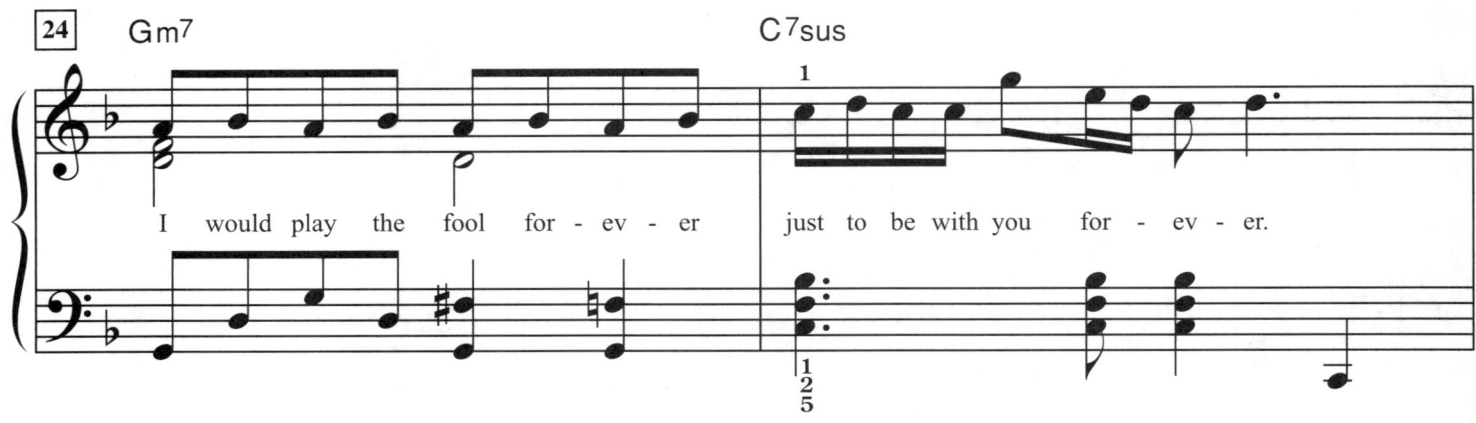

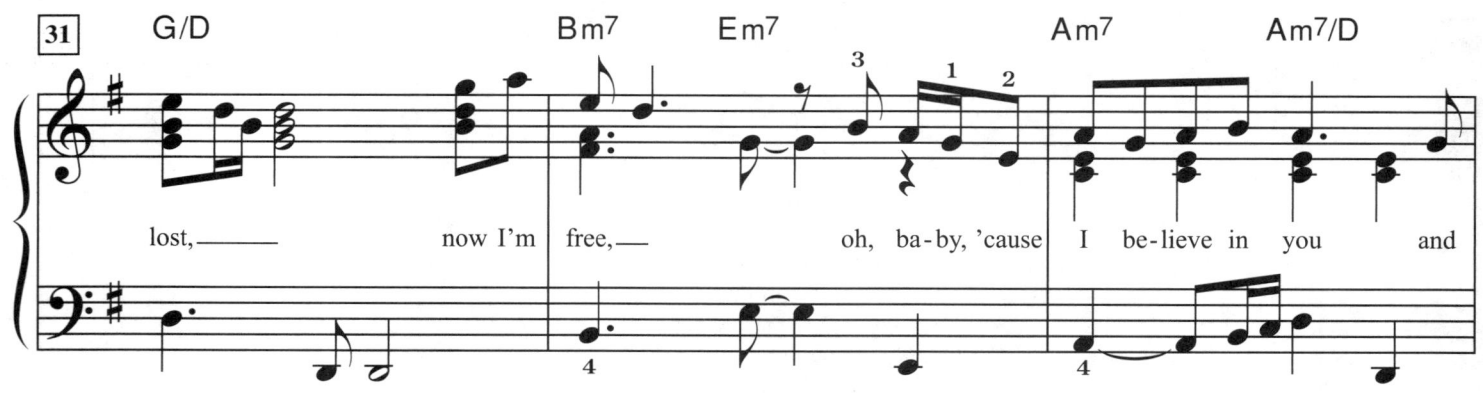

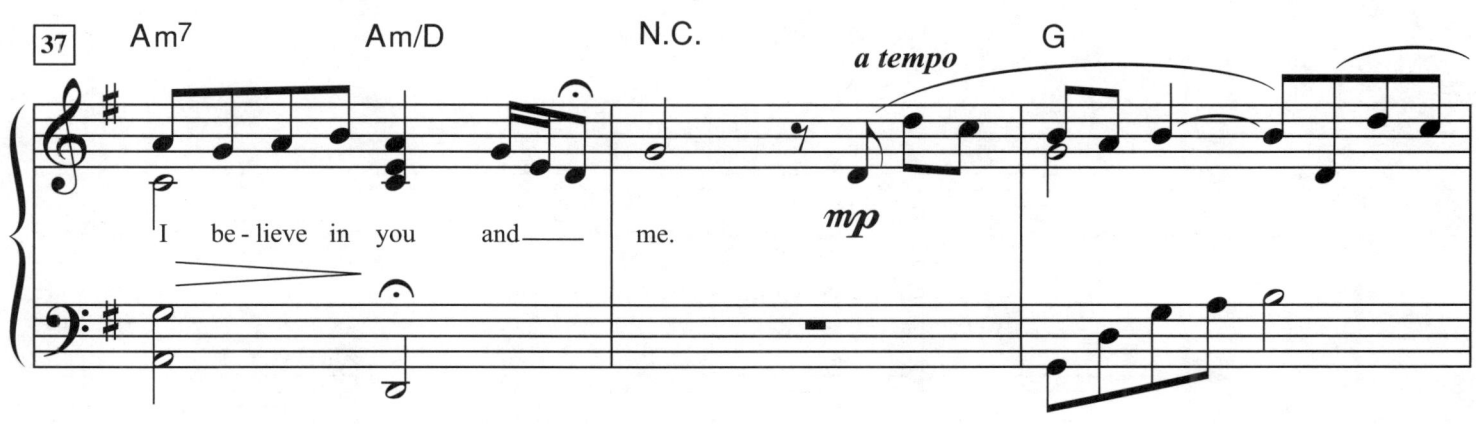
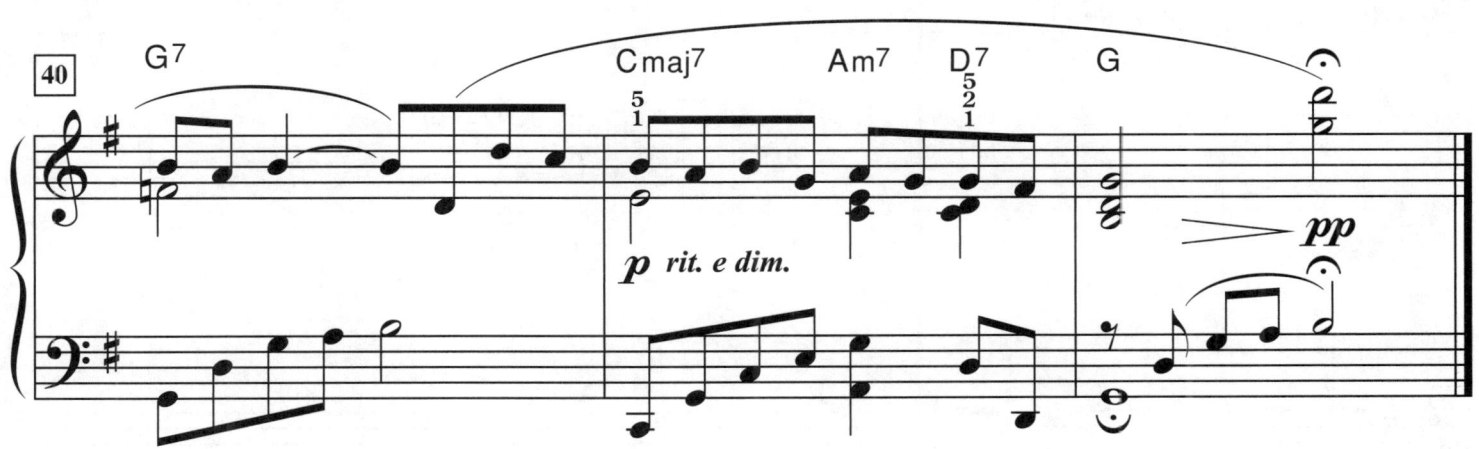

Verse 2:
I will never leave your side,
I will never hurt your pride.
When all the chips are down,
I will always be around
Just to be right where you are, my love.
Oh, I love you, boy.
I will never leave you out,
I will always let you in
To places no one has ever been.
Deep inside, can't you see?
I believe in you and me.

I DON'T WANT TO MISS A THING

Words and Music by Diane Warren
Arranged by Dan Coates

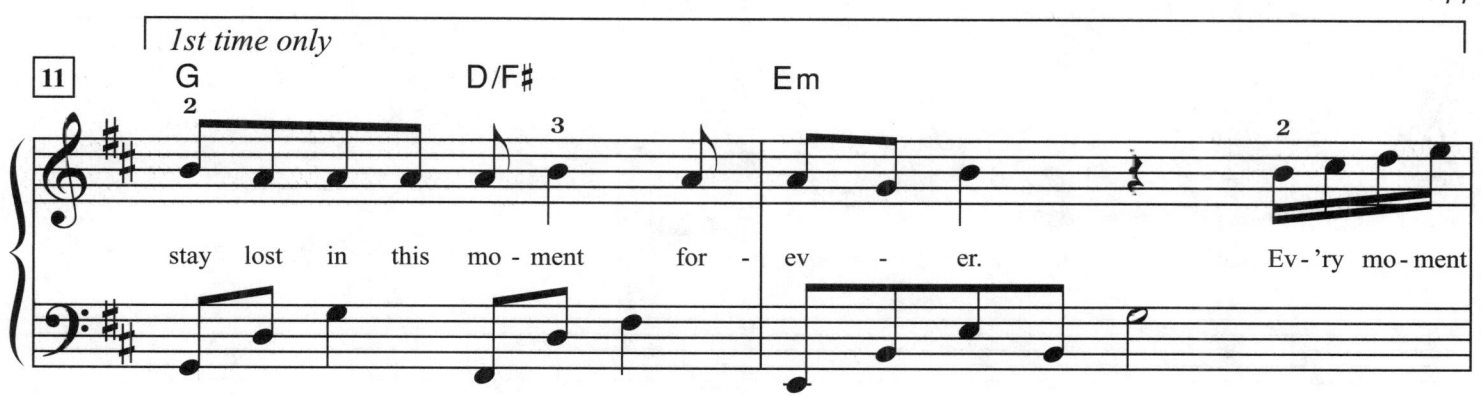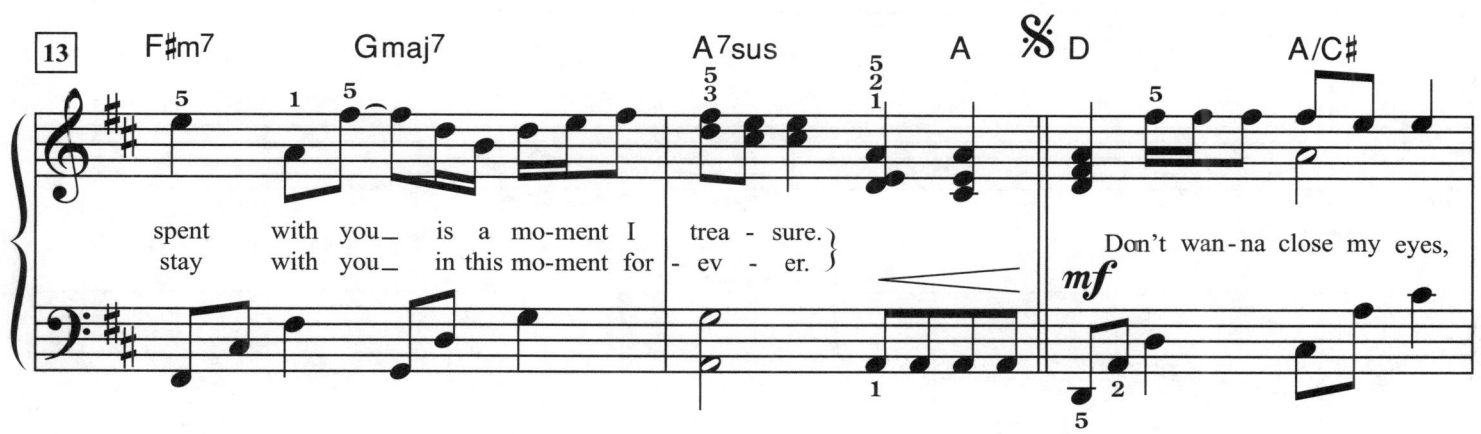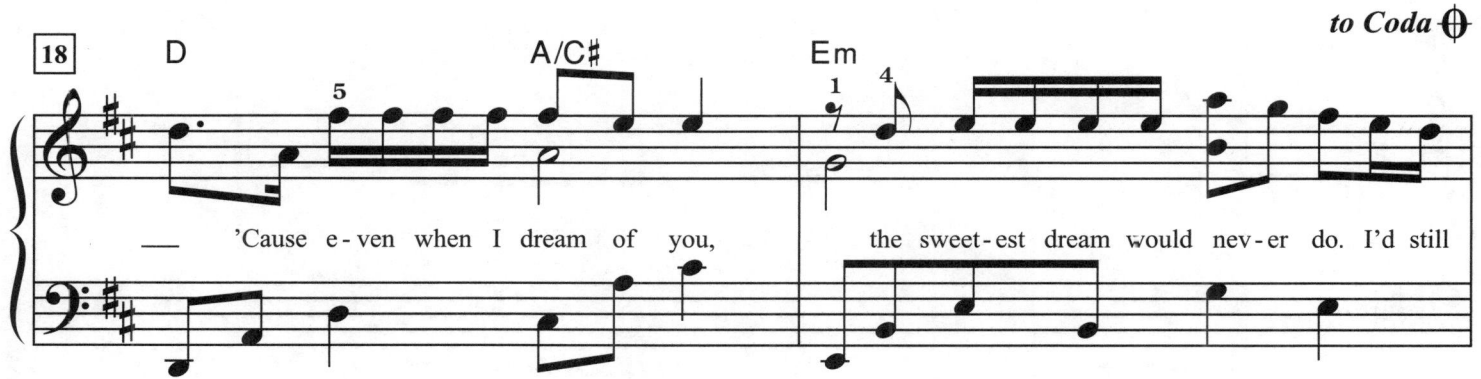

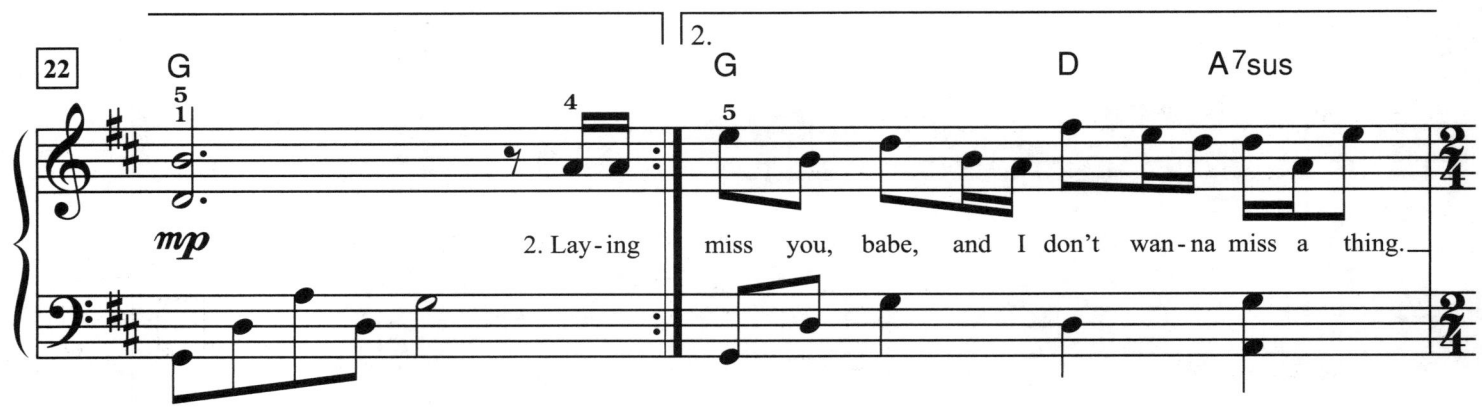
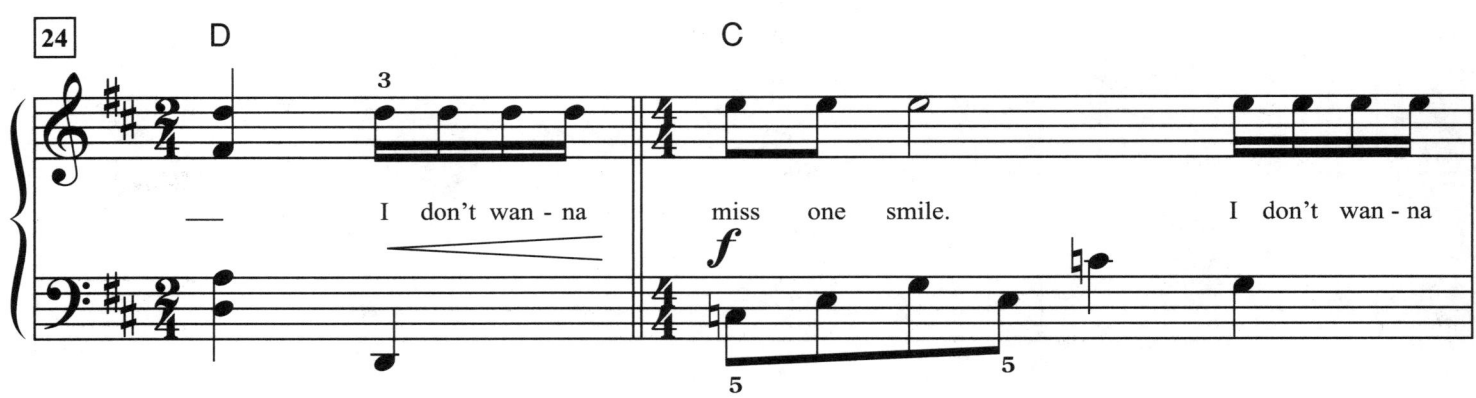
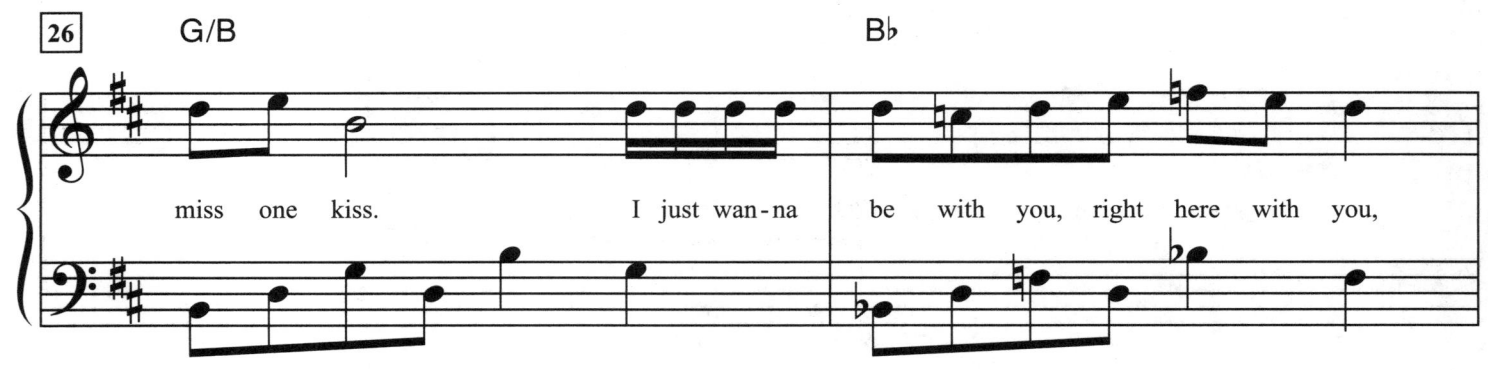

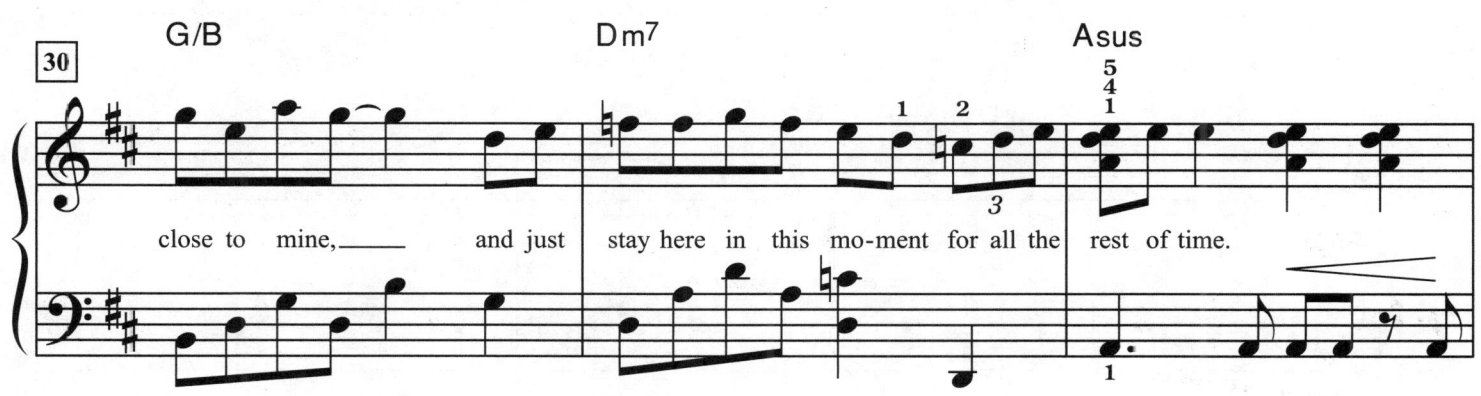

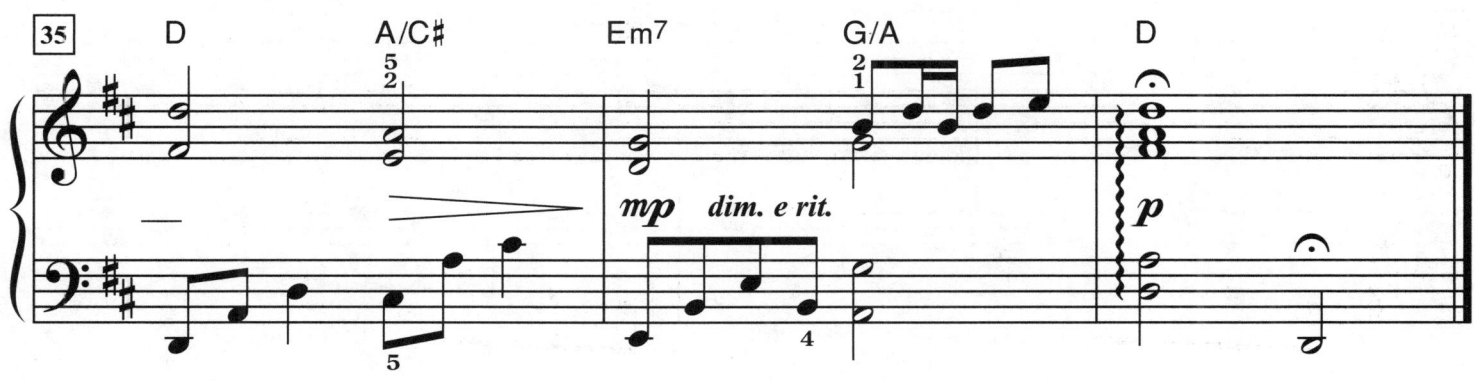

I ONLY HAVE EYES FOR YOU

Words by Al Dubin
Music by Harry Warren
Arranged by Dan Coates

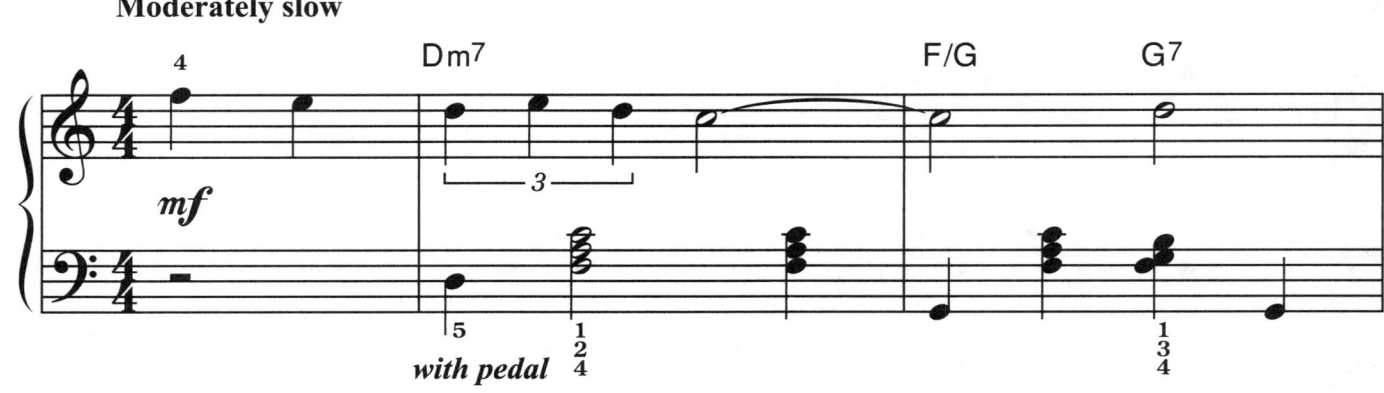

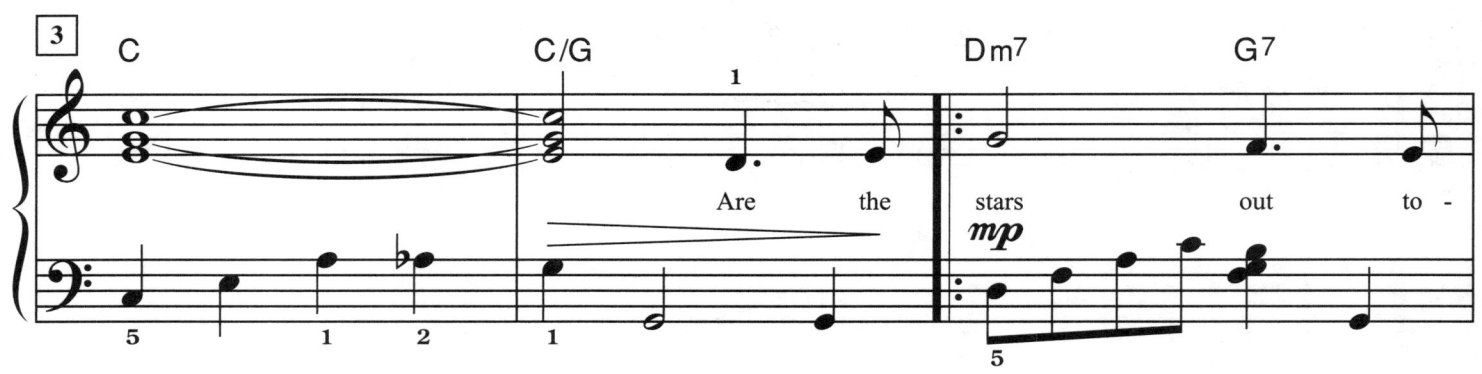

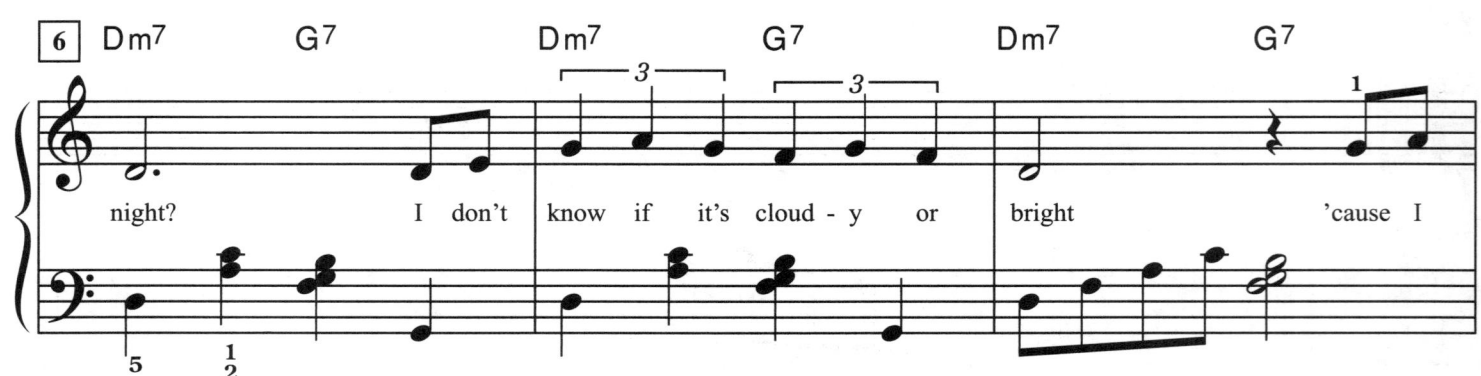

© 1934 (Renewed) WB MUSIC CORP.
All Rights Reserved

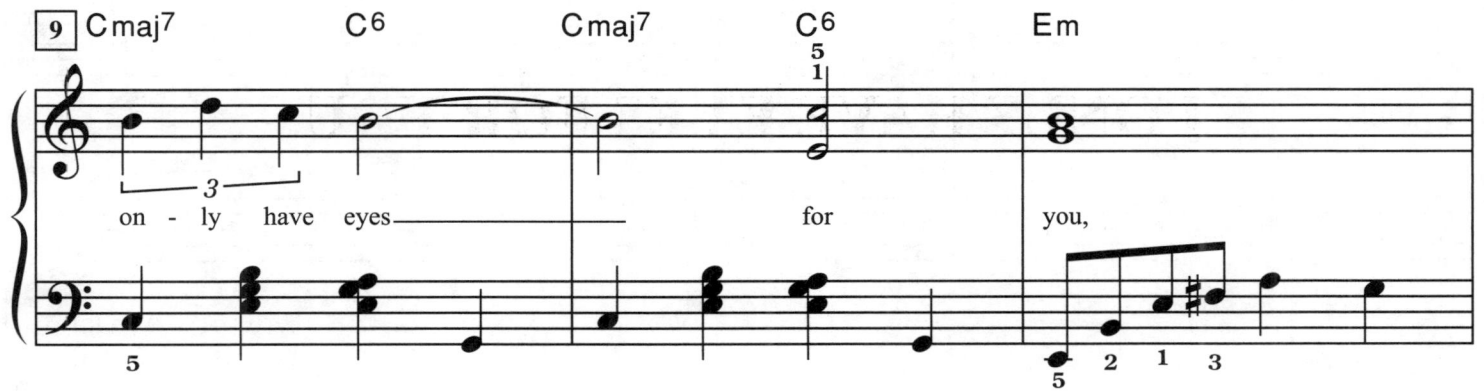
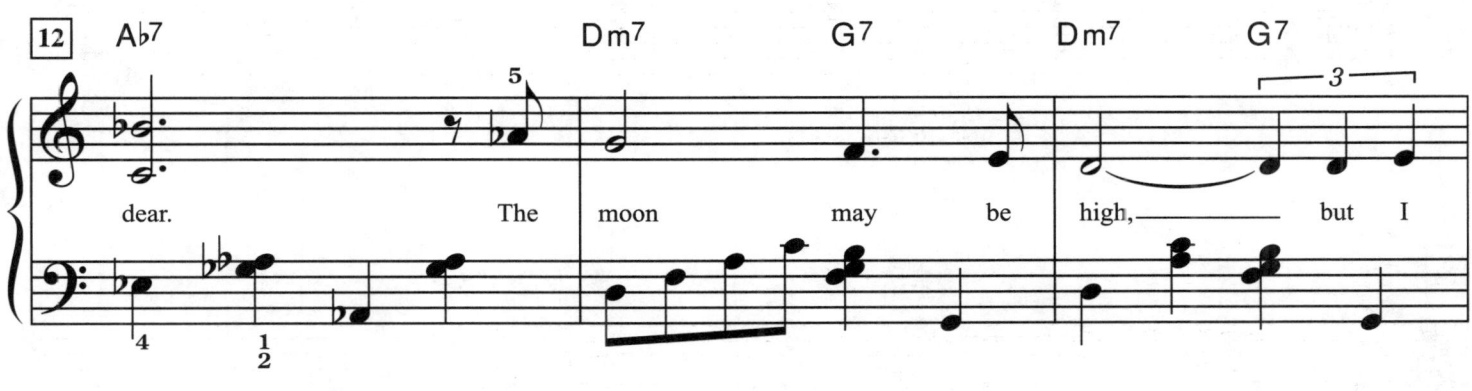
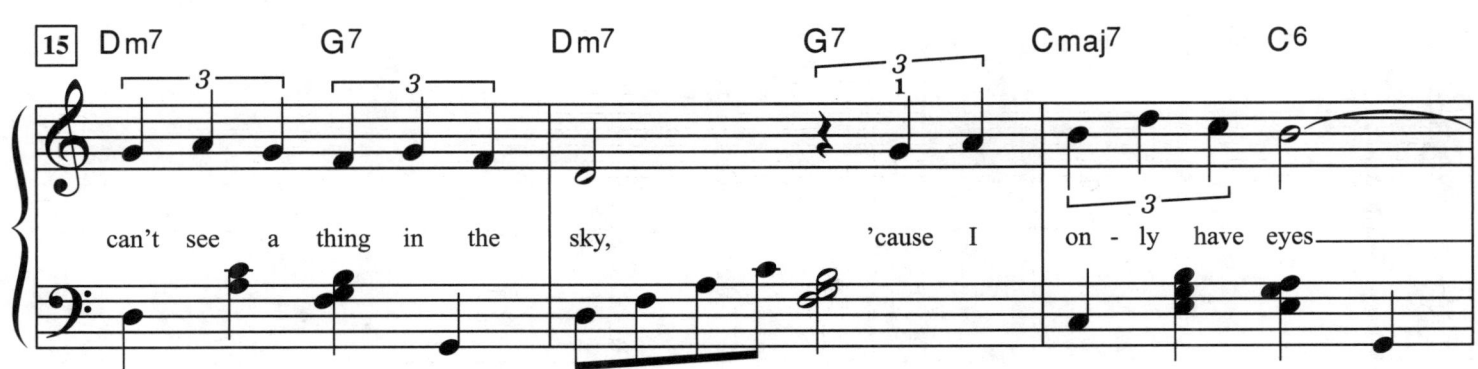

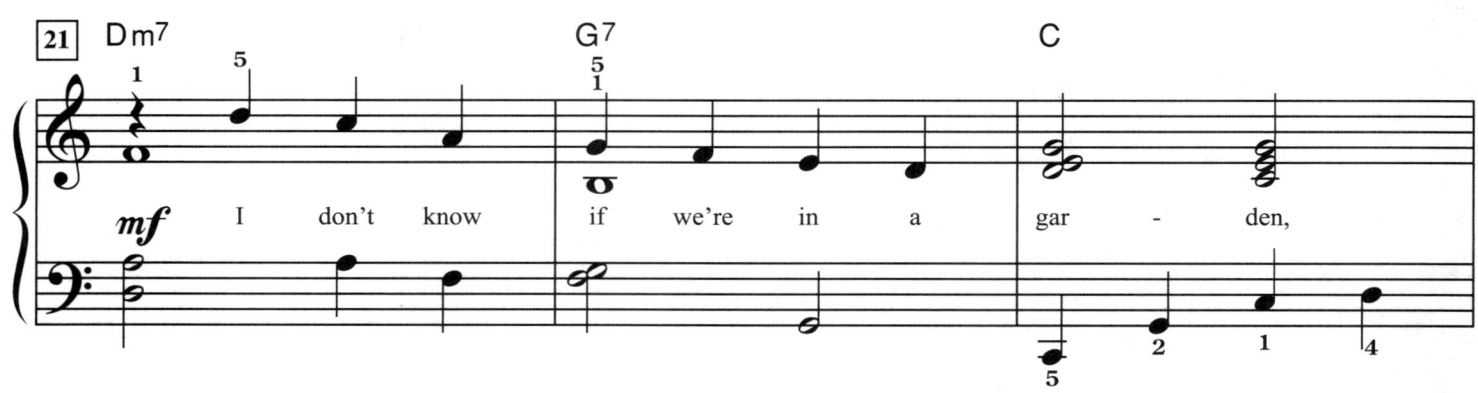
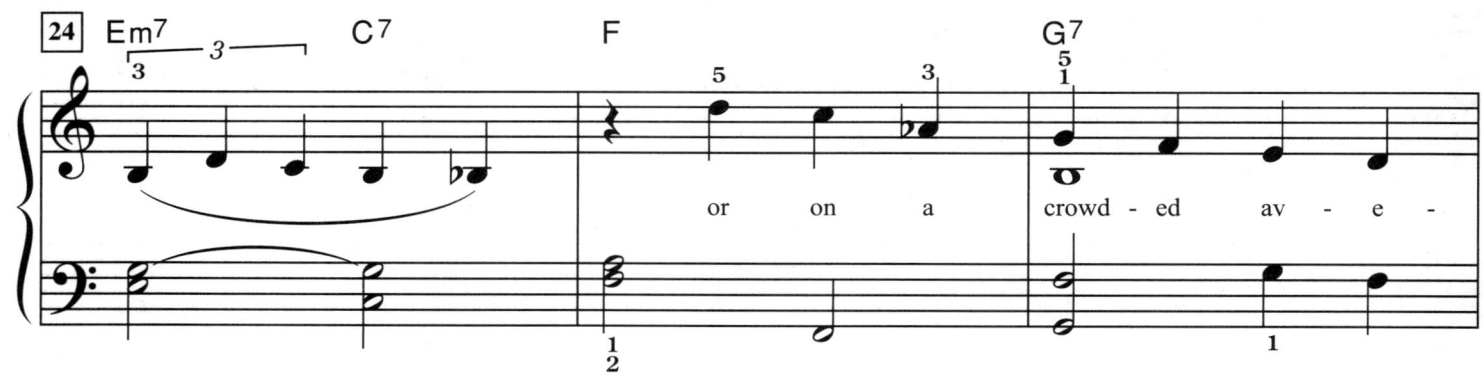
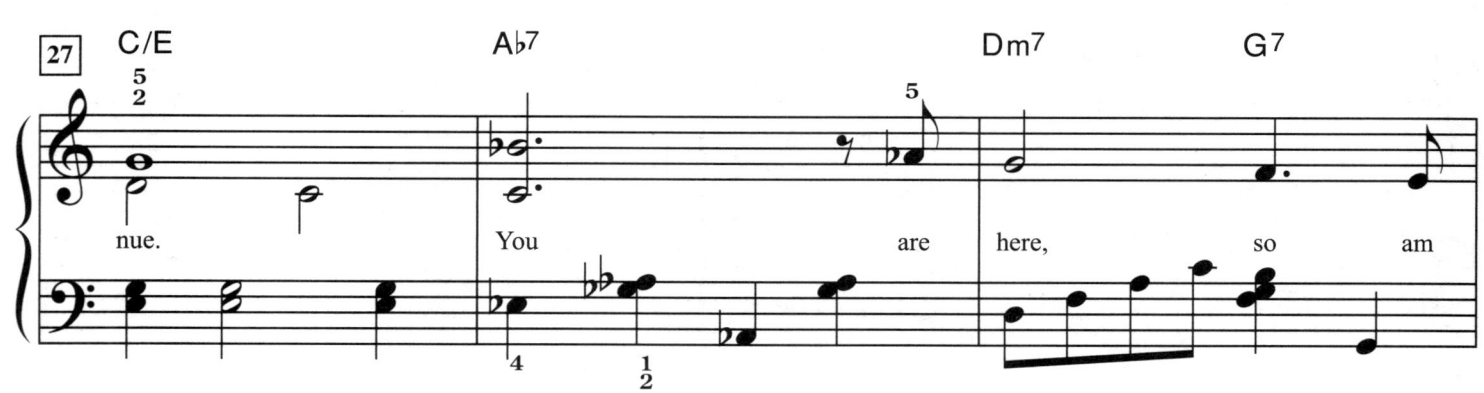

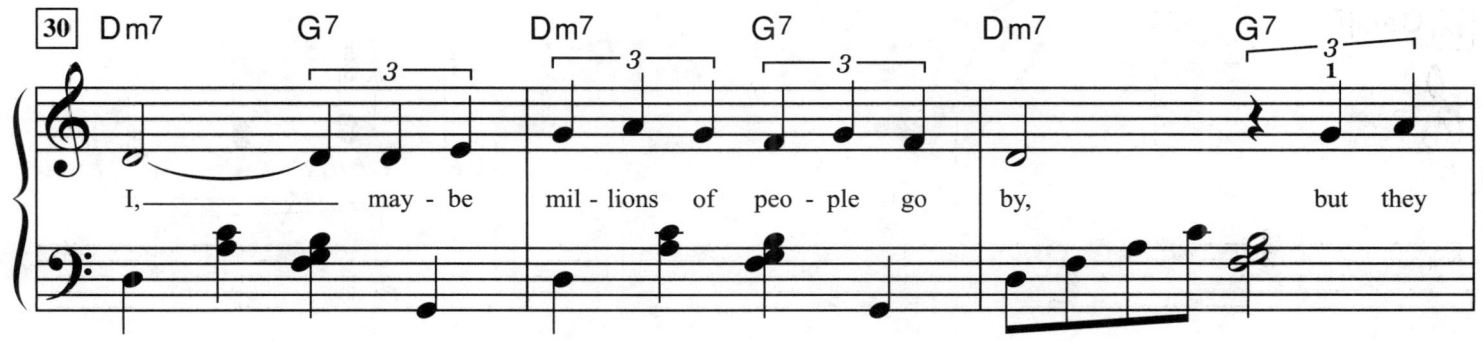
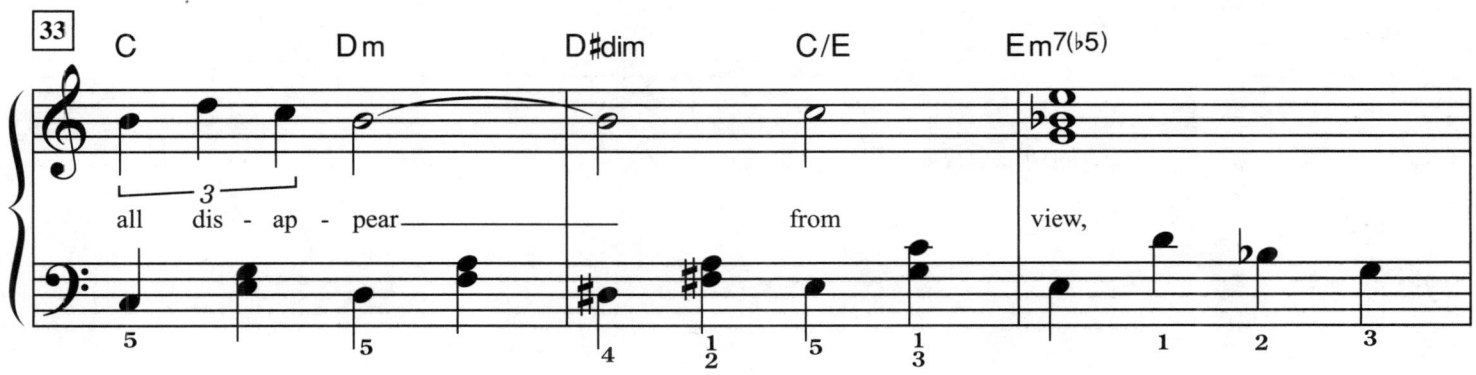
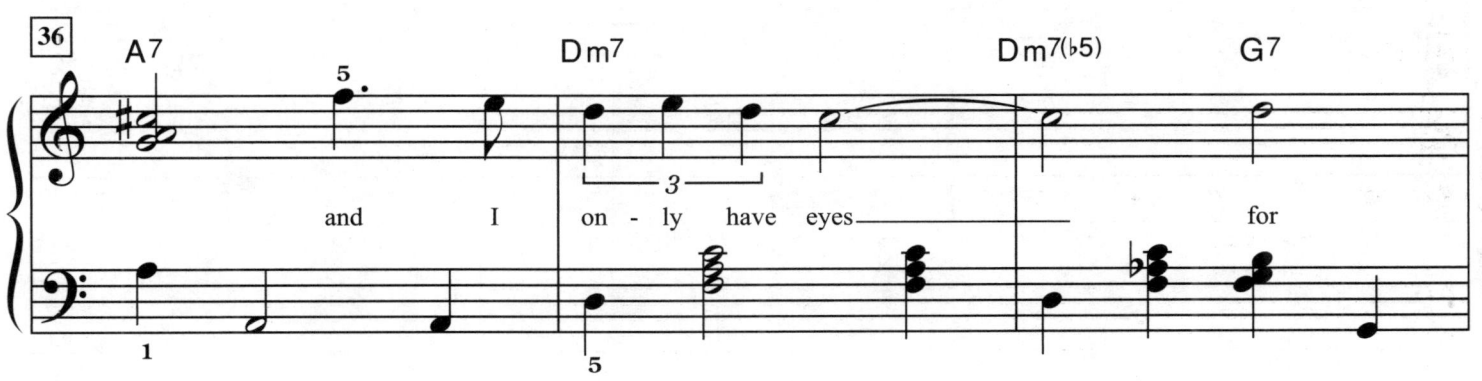
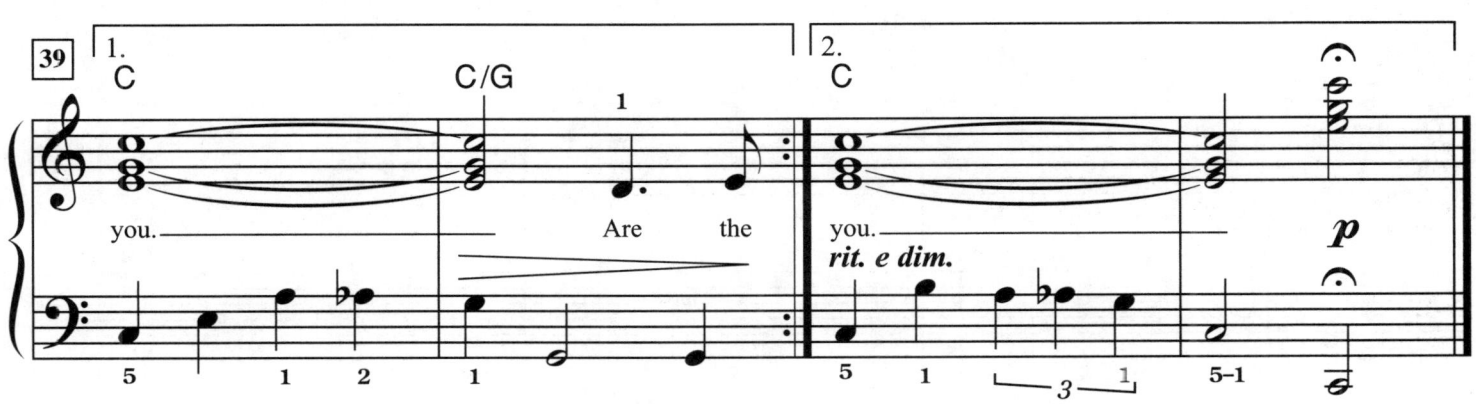

I'VE GROWN ACCUSTOMED TO HER FACE

Words by Alan Jay Lerner
Music by Frederick Loewe
Arranged by Dan Coates

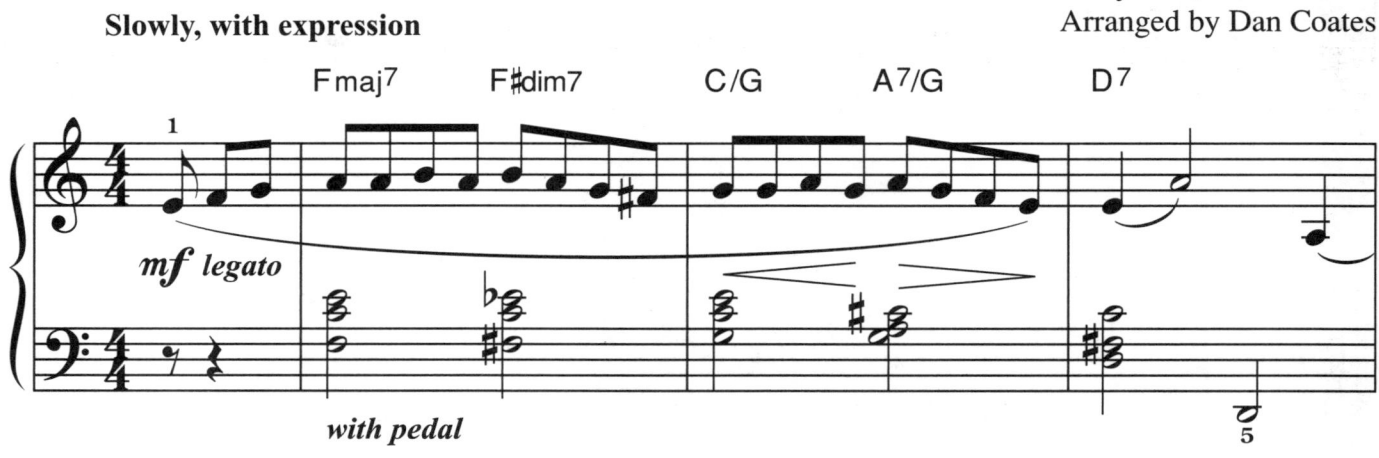

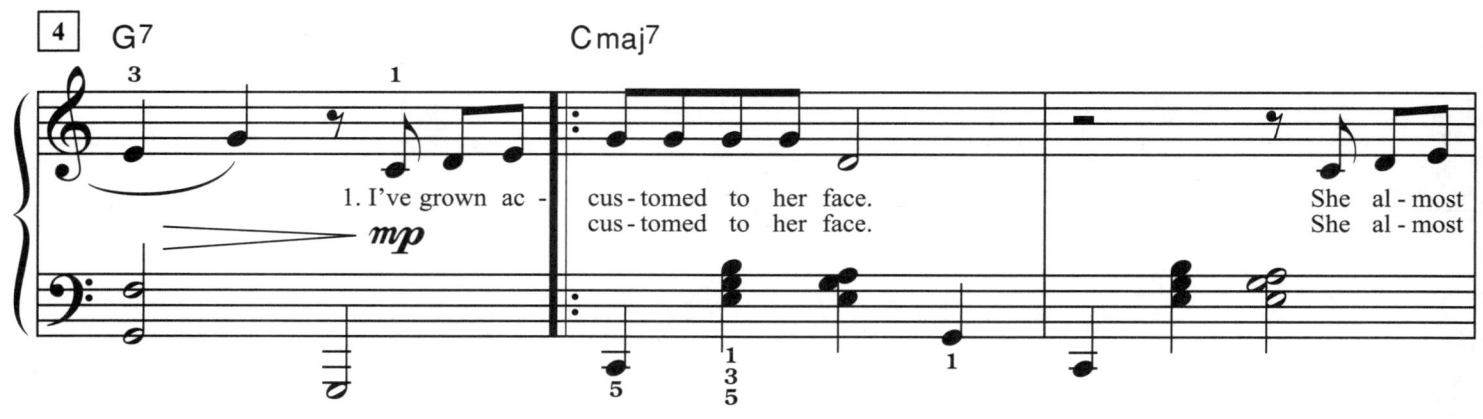

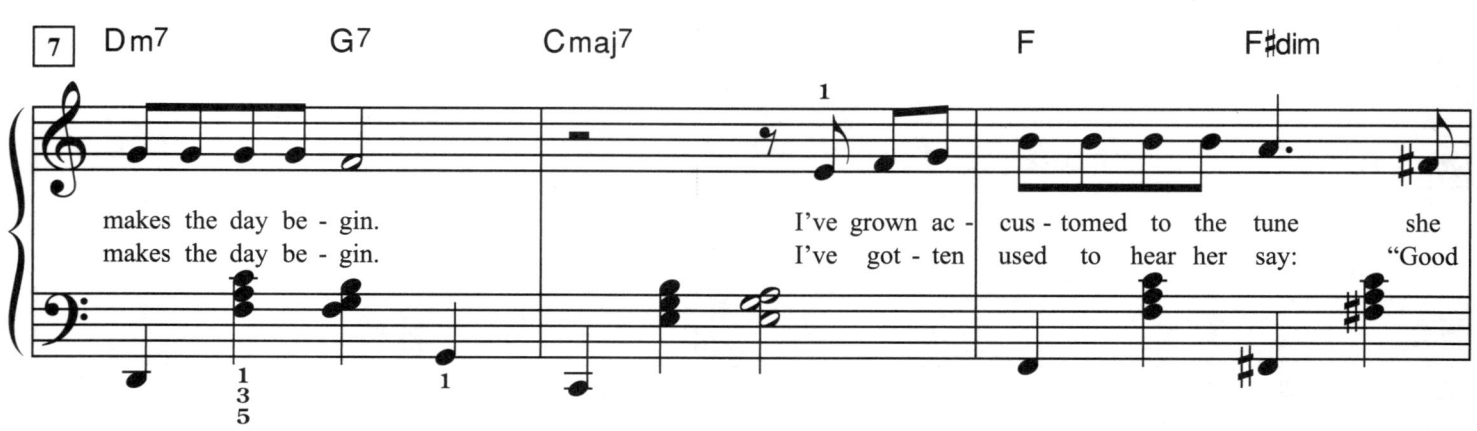

© 1956 (Renewed) ALAN JAY LERNER and FREDERICK LOEWE
Publication and Allied Rights Assigned to CHAPPELL & CO., INC.
All Rights Reserved

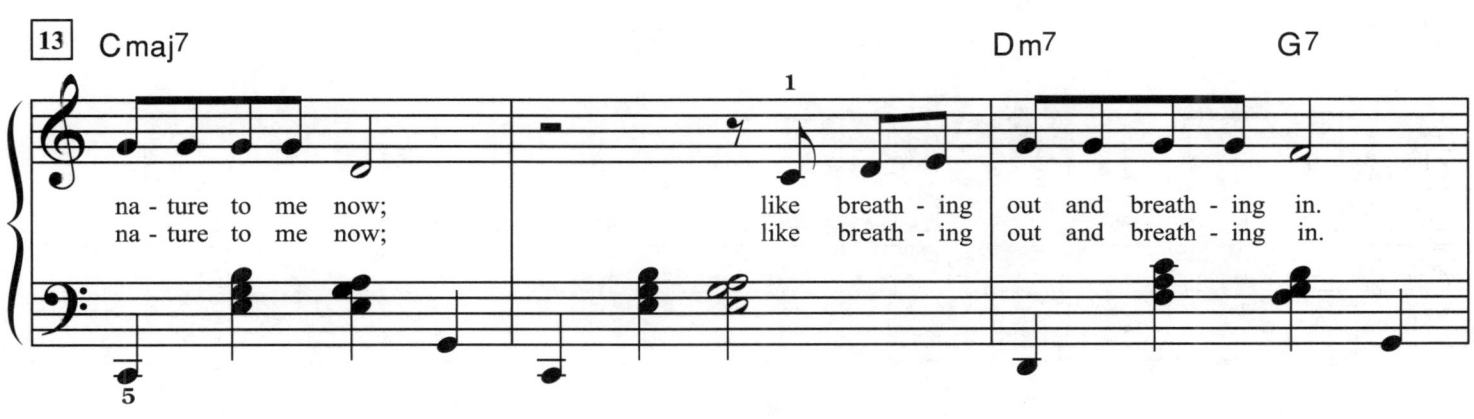
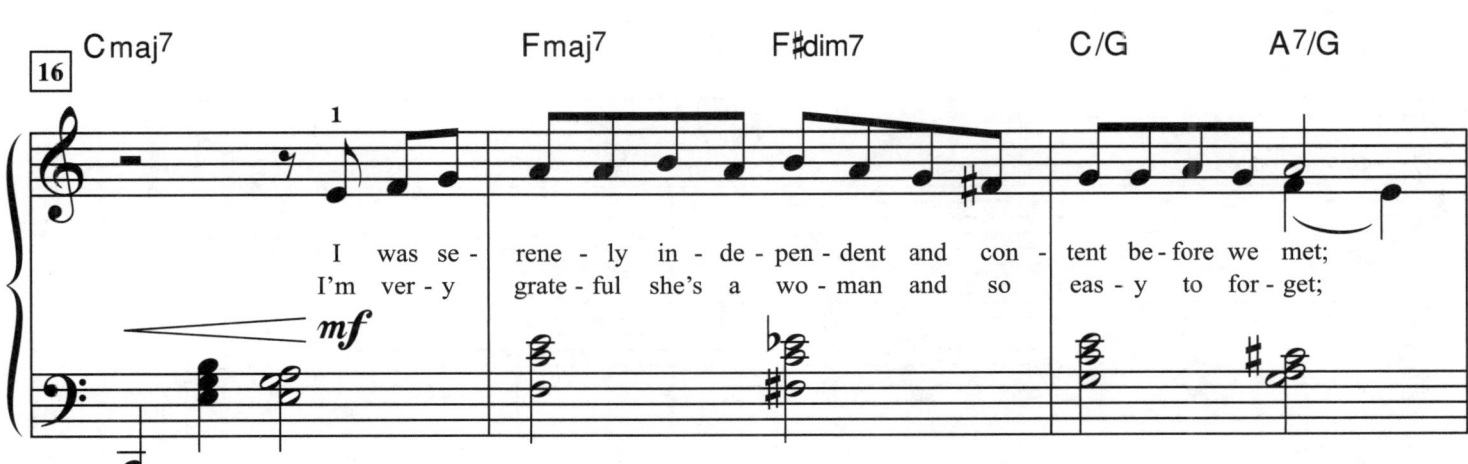

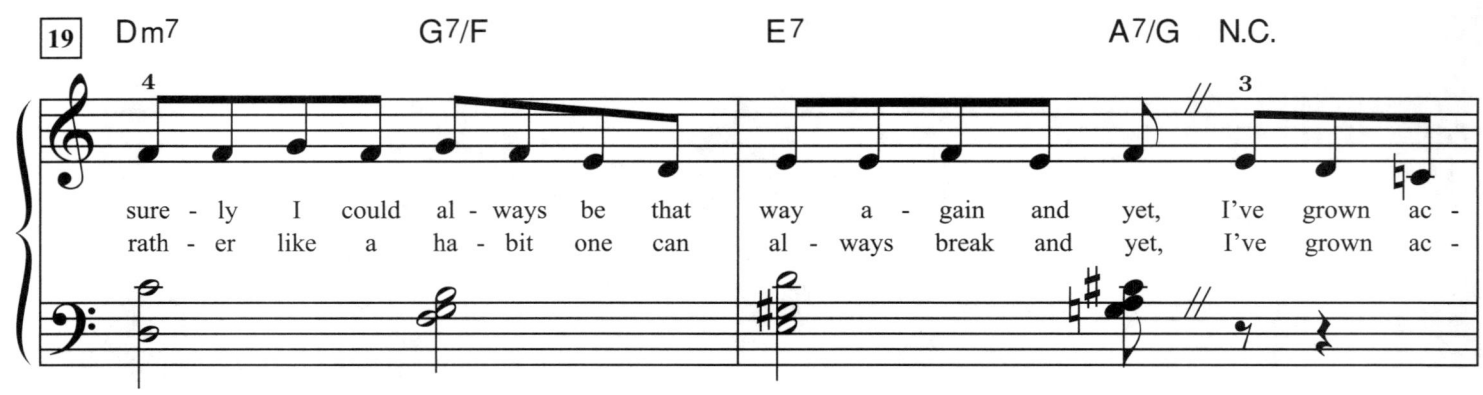
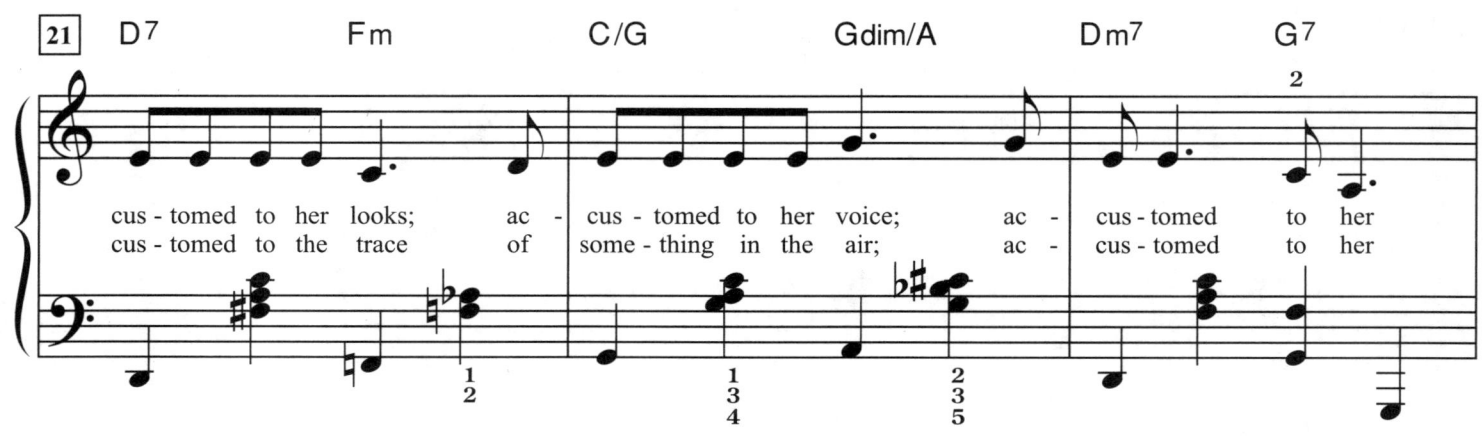
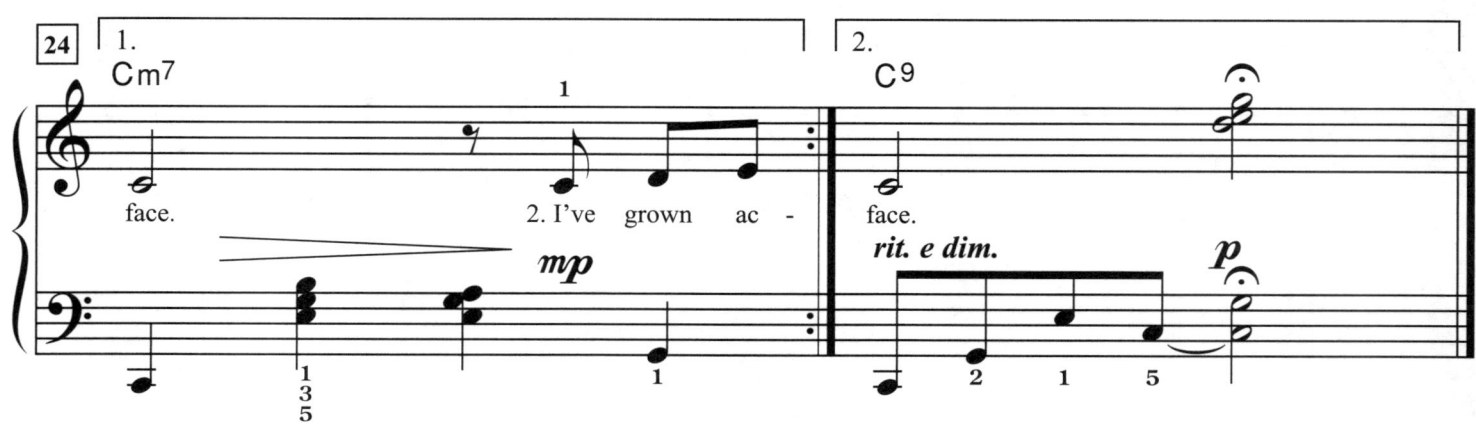

LA VIE EN ROSE

Original French Lyrics by Edith Piaf
English Lyrics by Mack David
Music by Luis Guglielmi
Arranged by Dan Coates

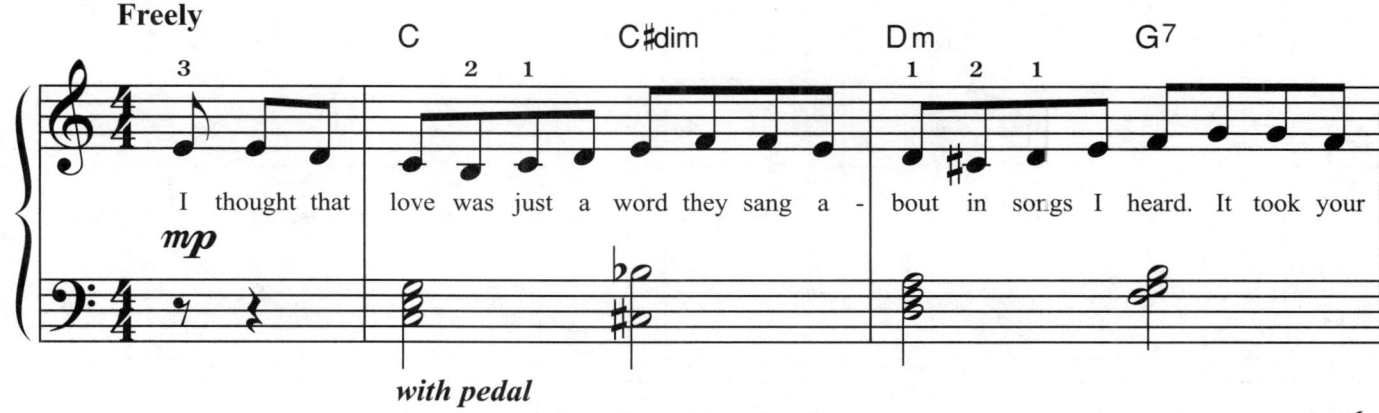

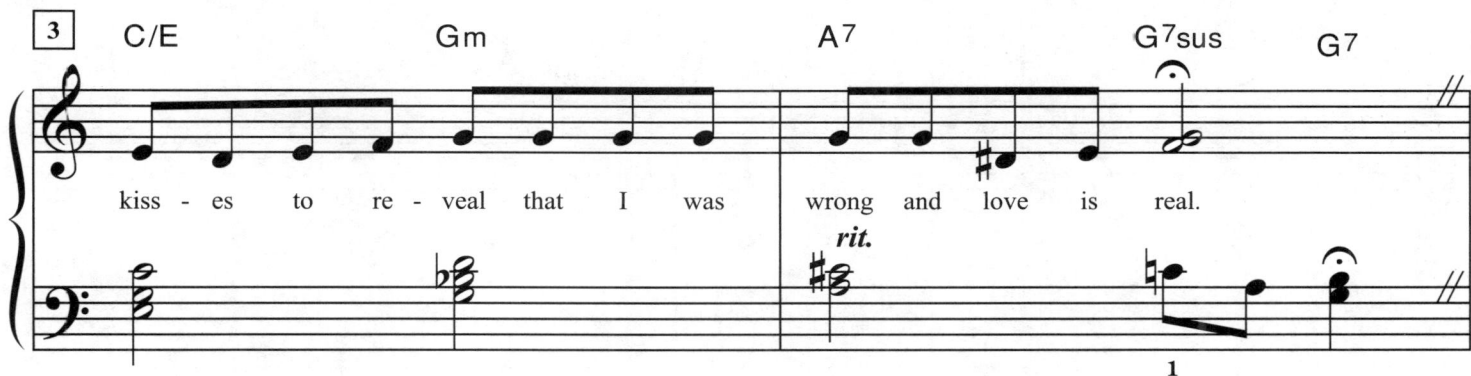

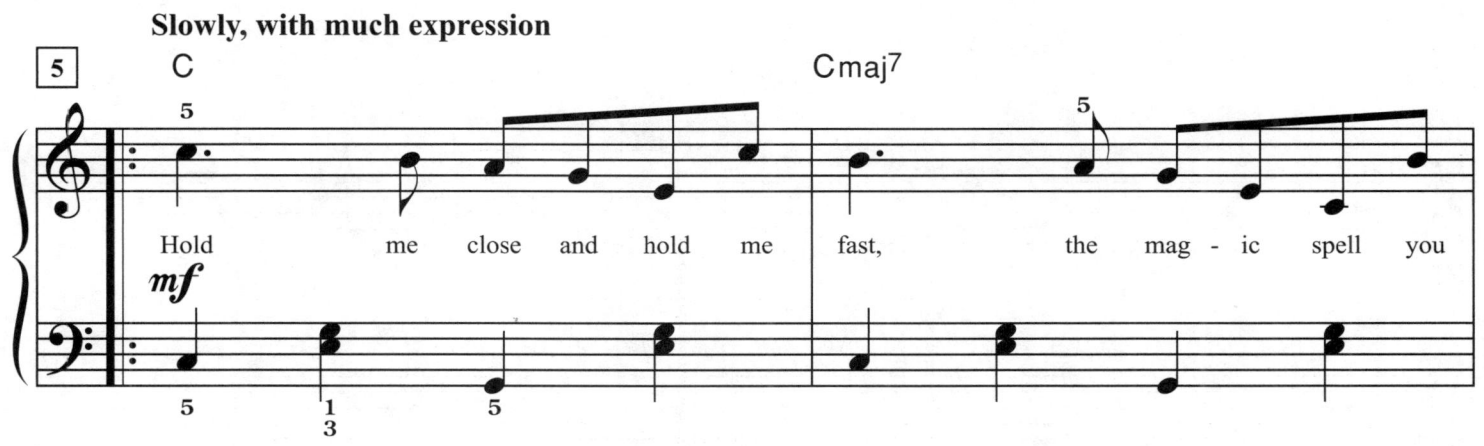

© 1947 EDITIONS ARPEGE, PARIS
© 1950 WARNER BROS. INC.
Copyrights Renewed and Assigned to EDITIONS PAUL BEUSCHER, WB MUSIC CORP. and UNIVERSAL POLYGRAM INTERNATIONAL
All Rights in the U.S. Administered by WB MUSIC CORP.
All Rights Reserved

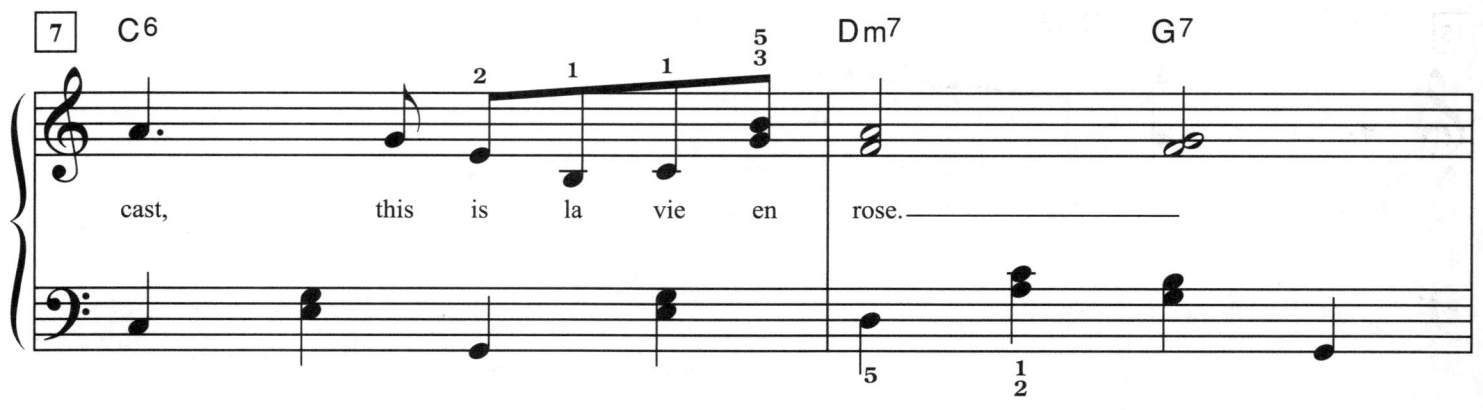
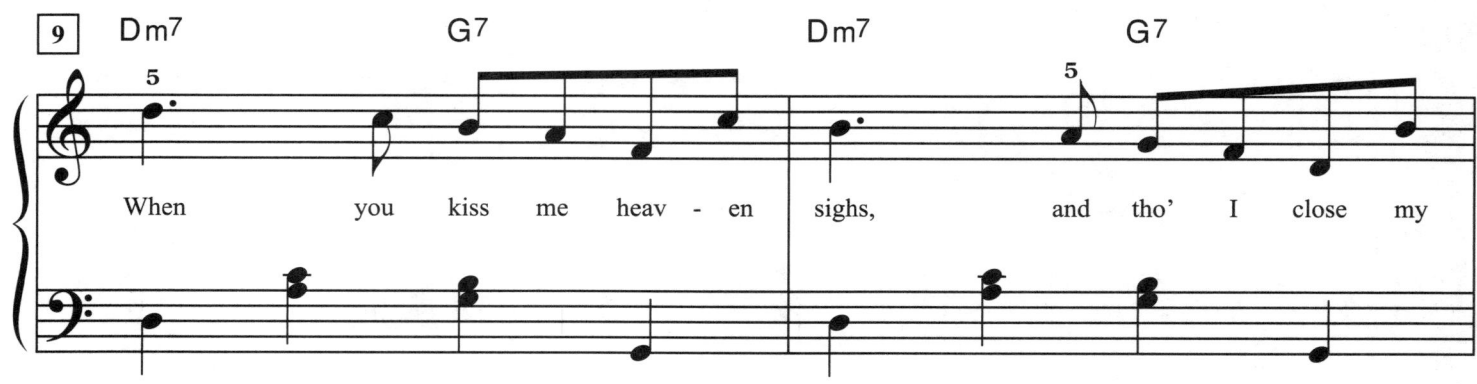
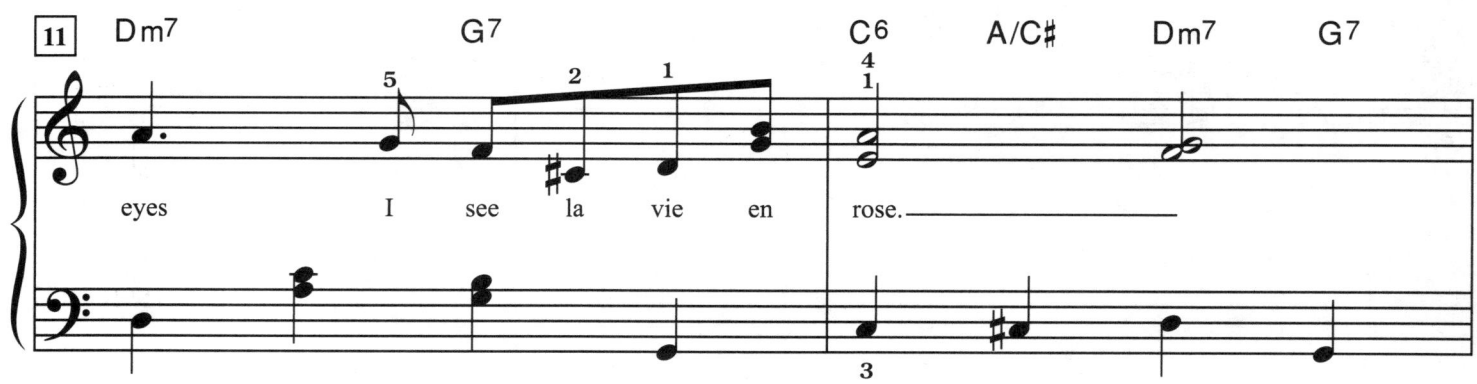

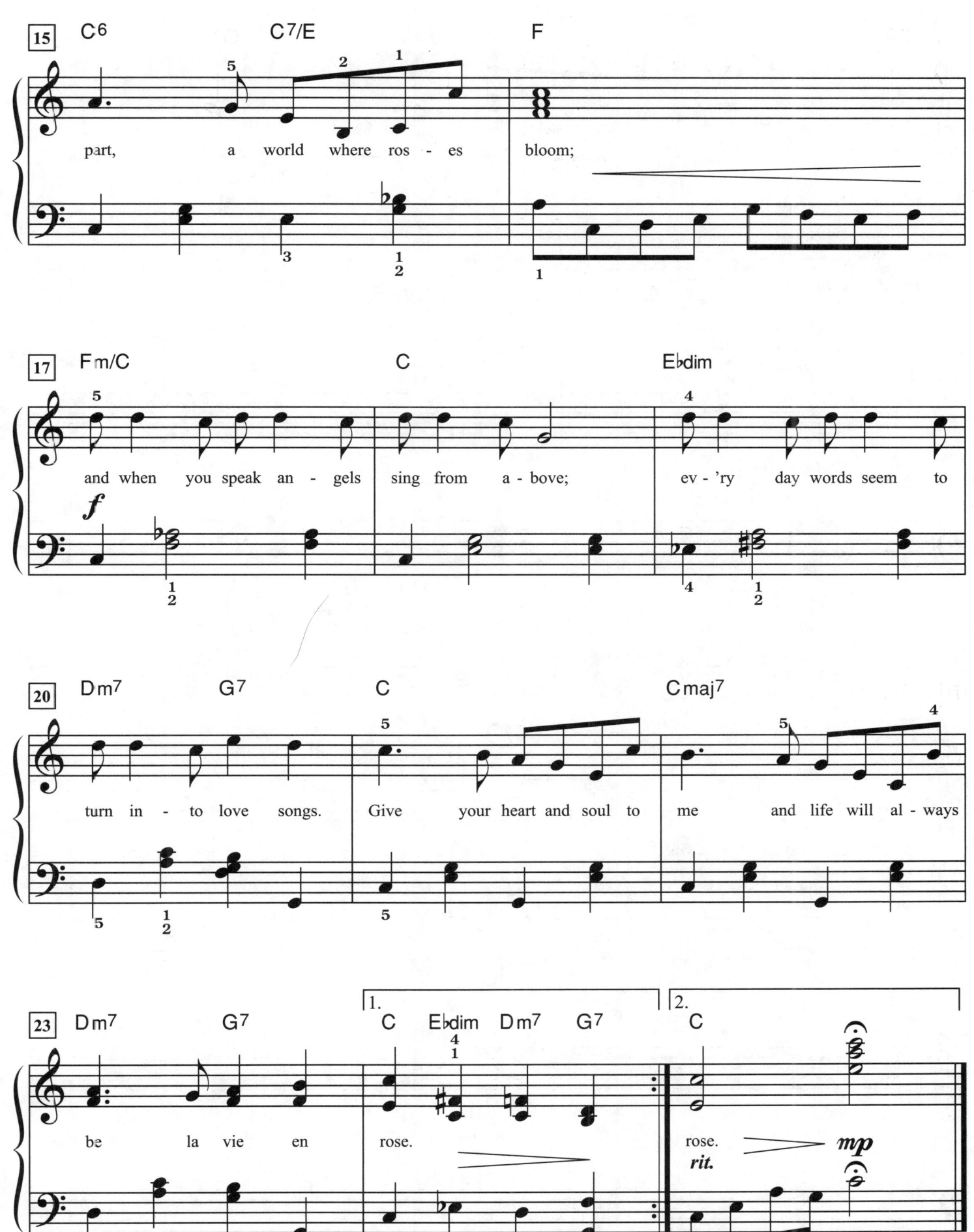

KILLING ME SOFTLY WITH HIS SONG

Words and Music by
Charles Fox and Norman Gimbel
Arranged by Dan Coates

LAURA

Lyrics by Johnny Mercer
Music by David Raksin
Arranged by Dan Coates

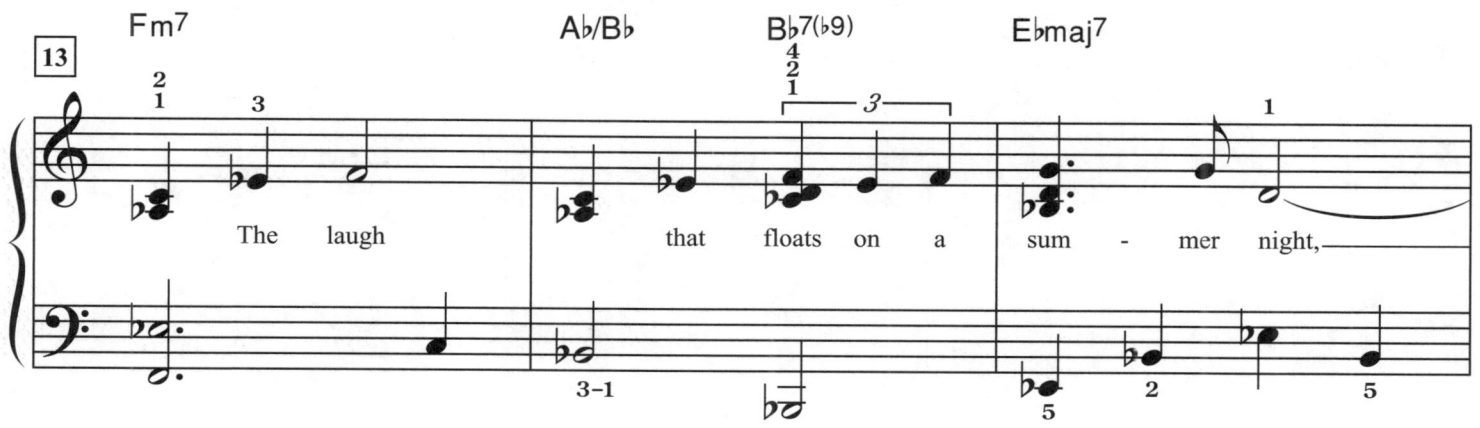

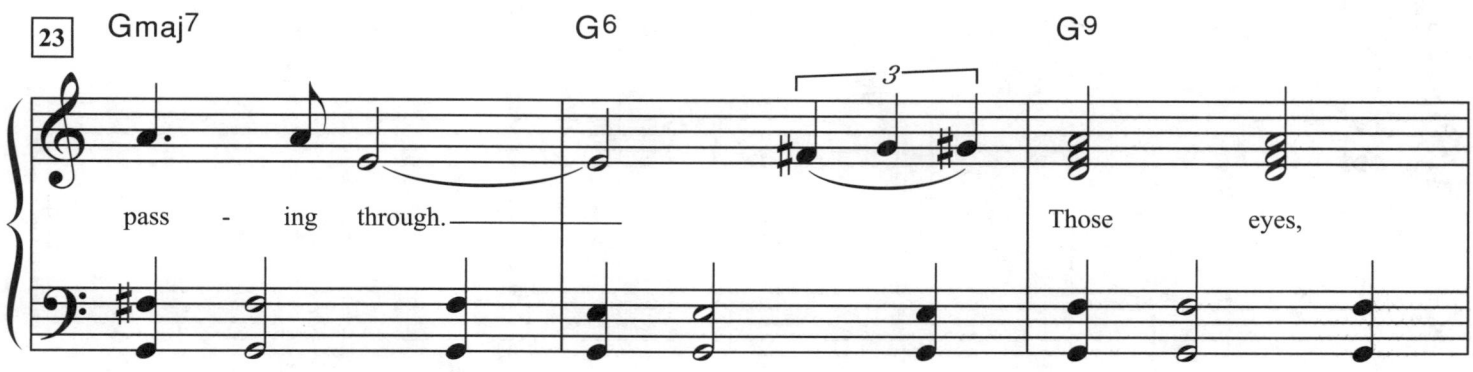

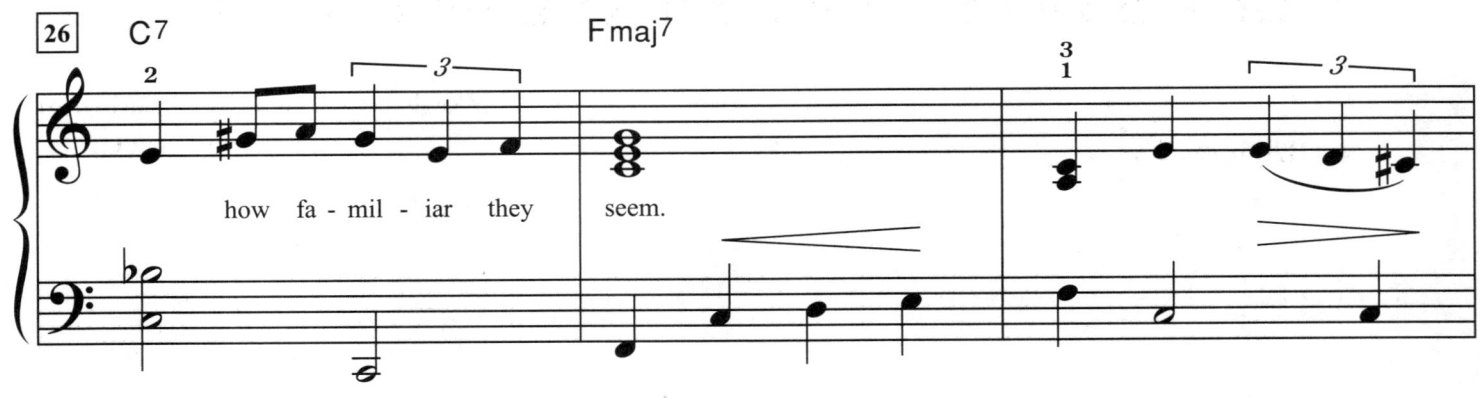
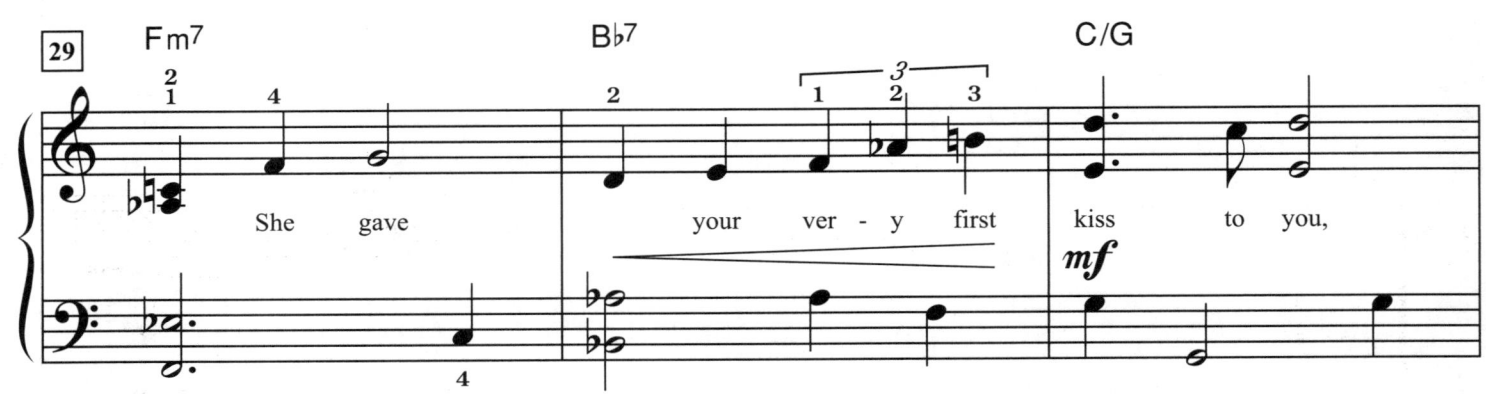
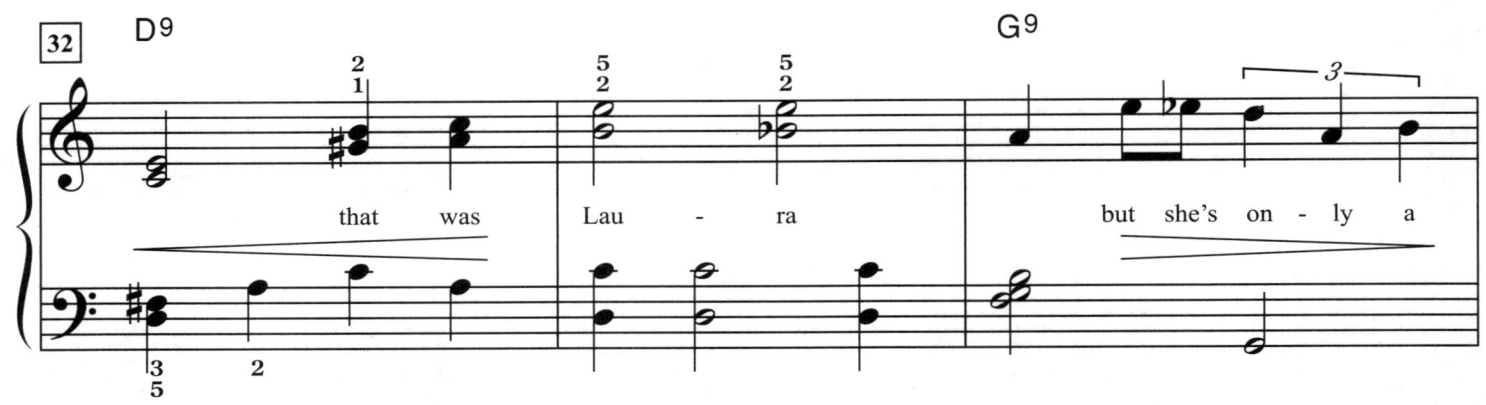

LET'S DO IT (LET'S FALL IN LOVE)

Words and Music by Cole Porter
Arranged by Dan Coates

© 1928 (Renewed) WB MUSIC CORP.
All Rights Reserved

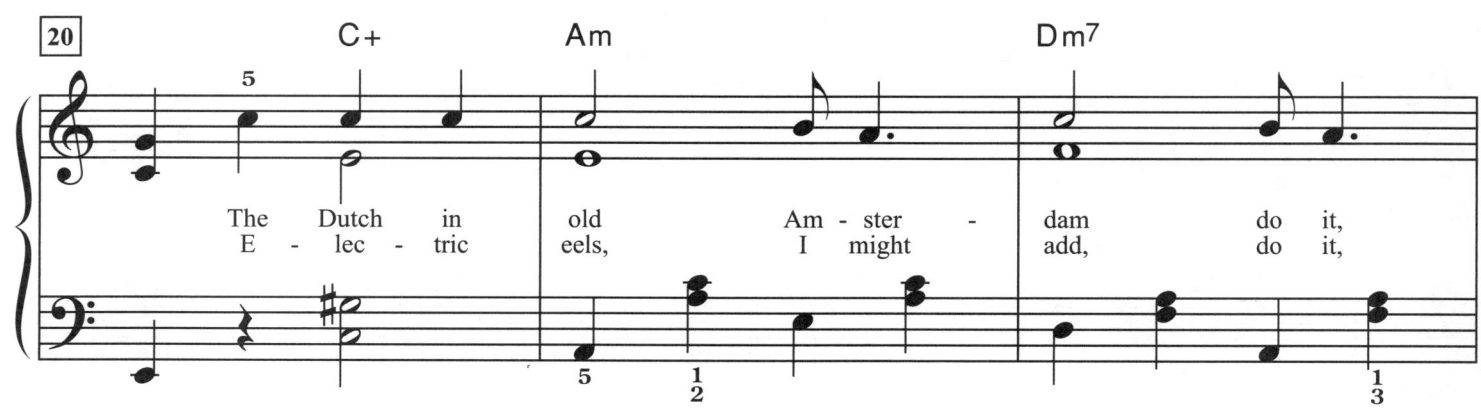
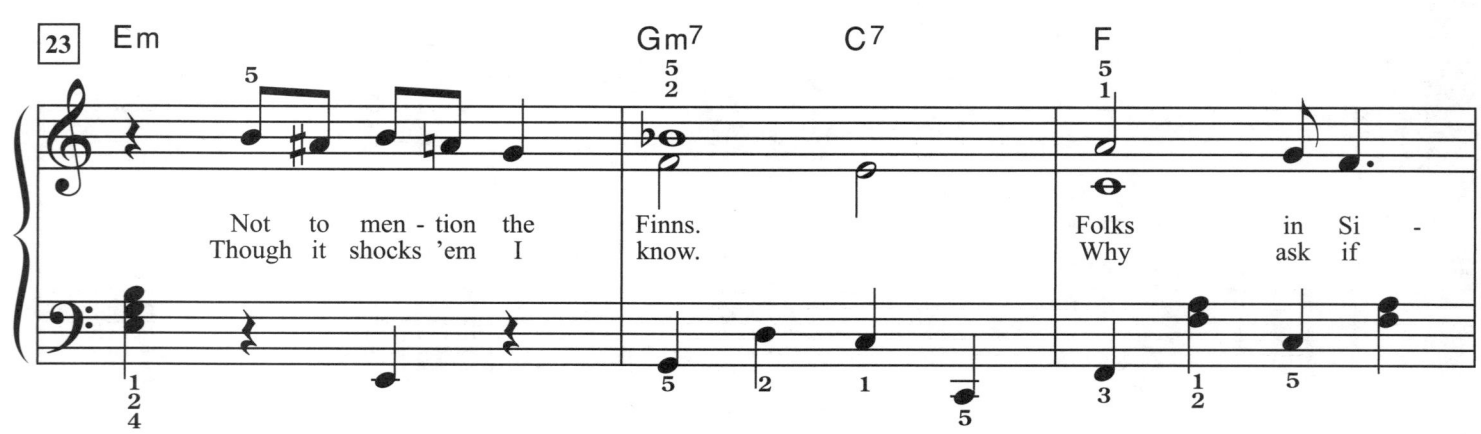

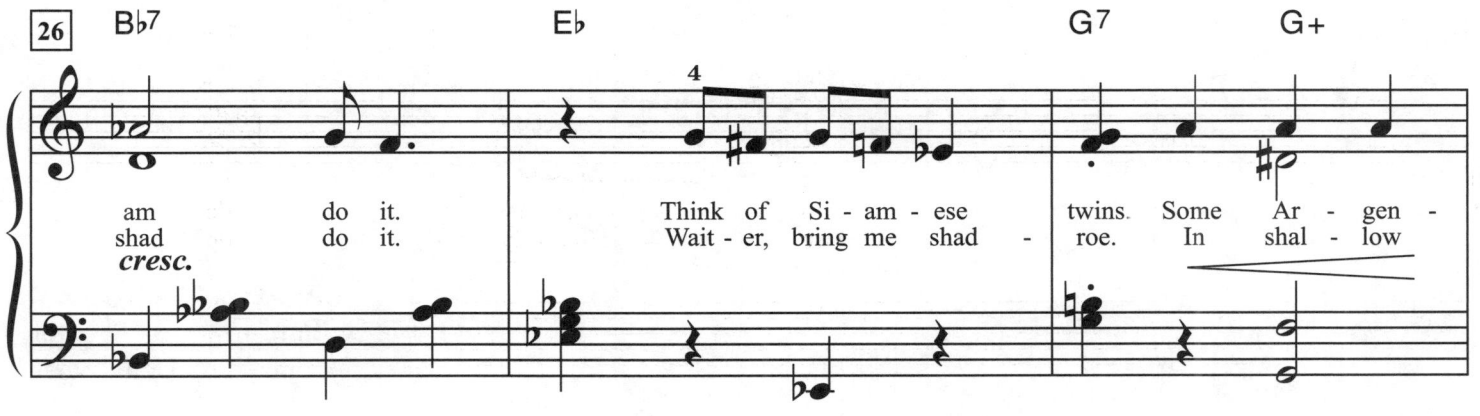

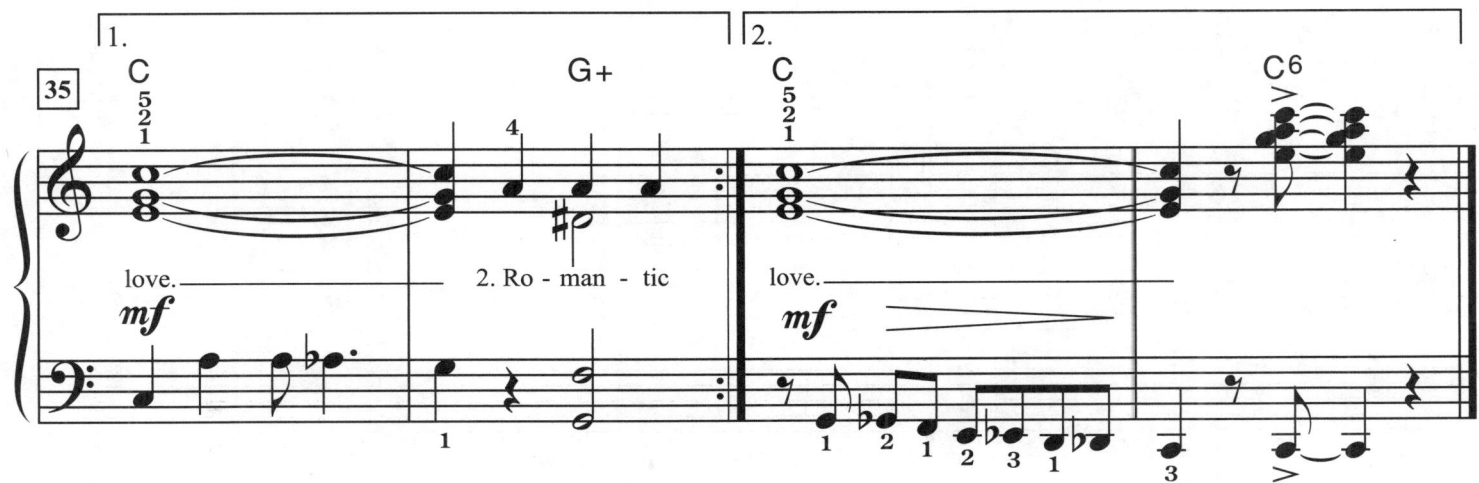

LOVE IS A MANY SPLENDORED THING

Music by Sammy Fain
Lyric by Paul Francis Webster
Arranged by Dan Coates

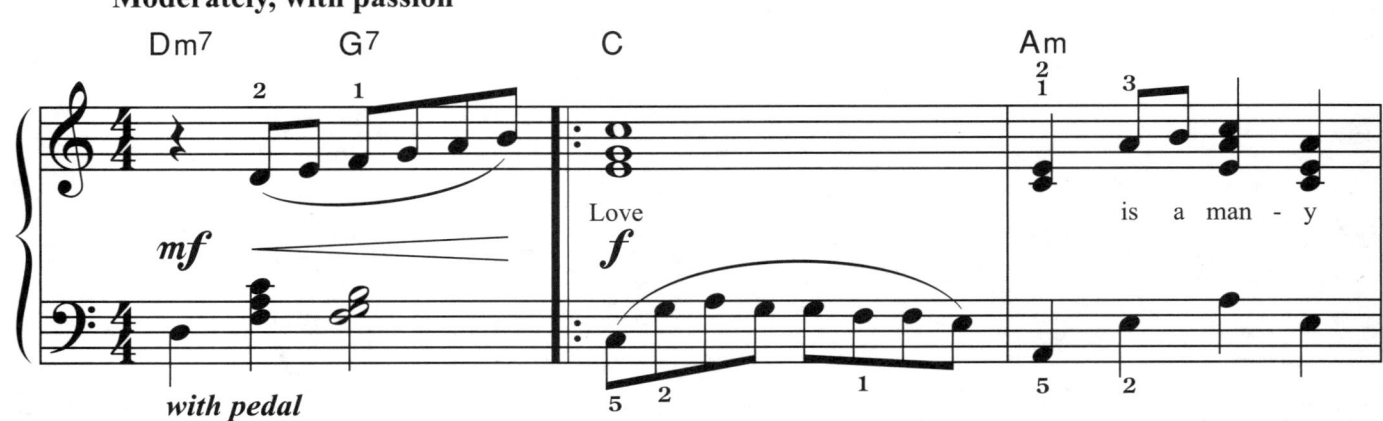
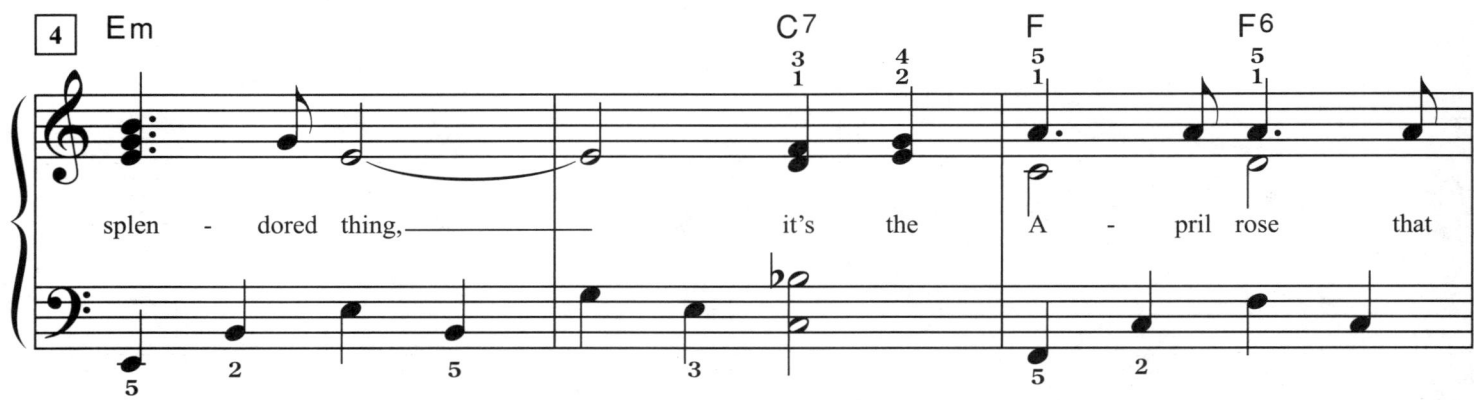
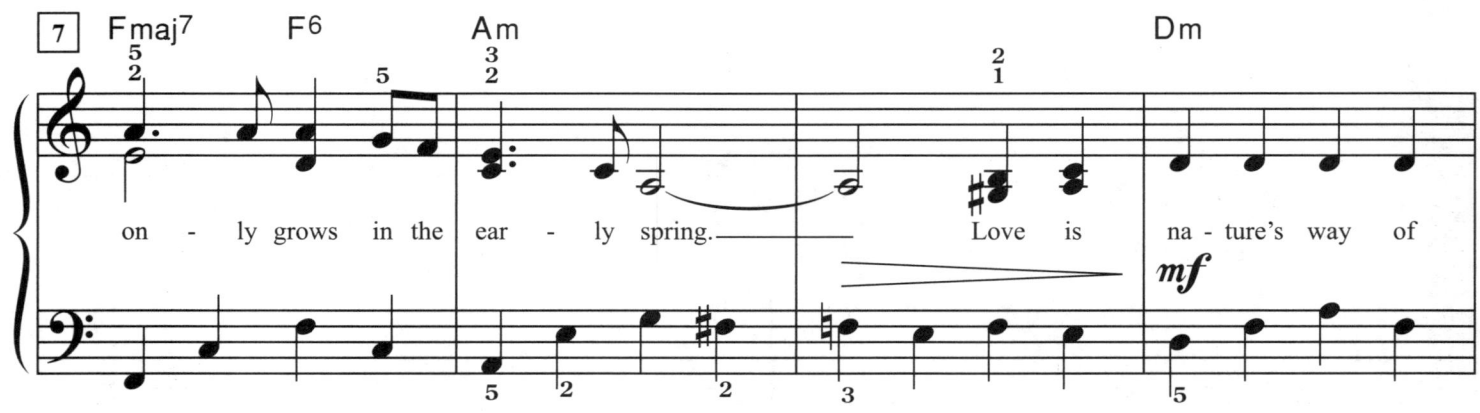

© 1955 (Renewed) TWENTIETH CENTURY MUSIC CORPORATION
All Rights Controlled by EMI Miller Catalog INC. (Publishing)
and ALFRED PUBLISHING CO., INC. (Print)
All Rights Reserved

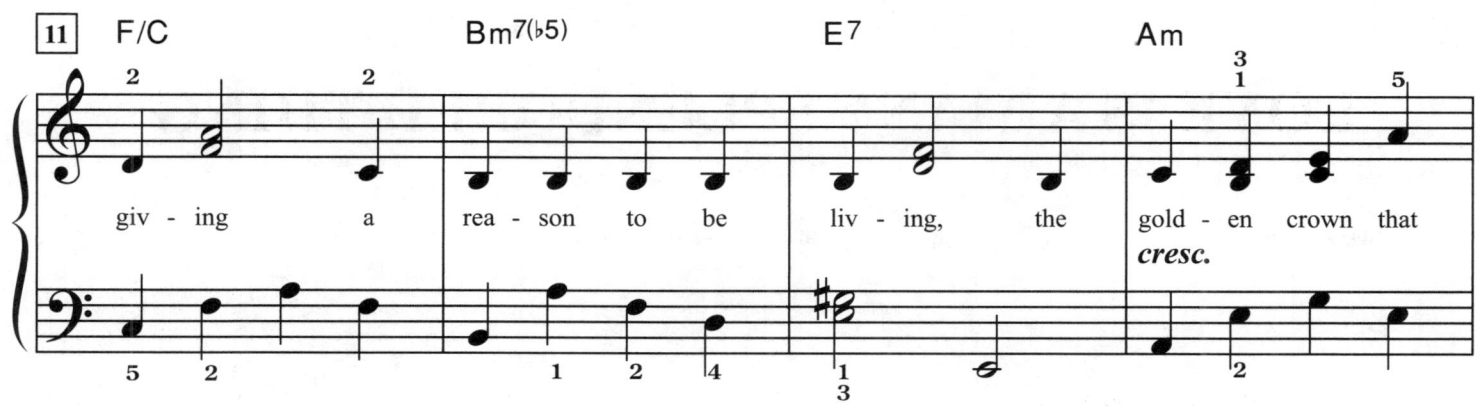
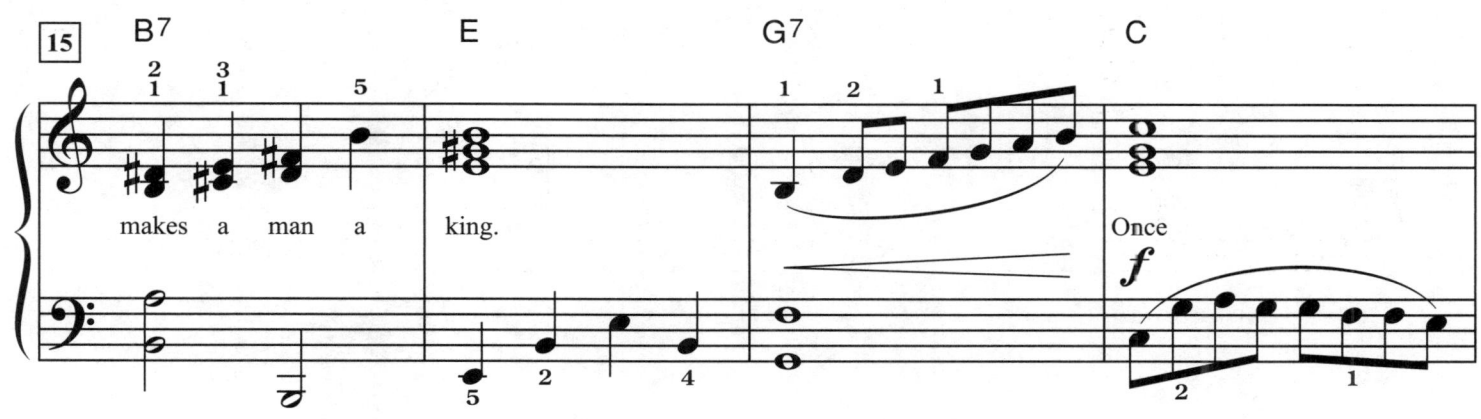
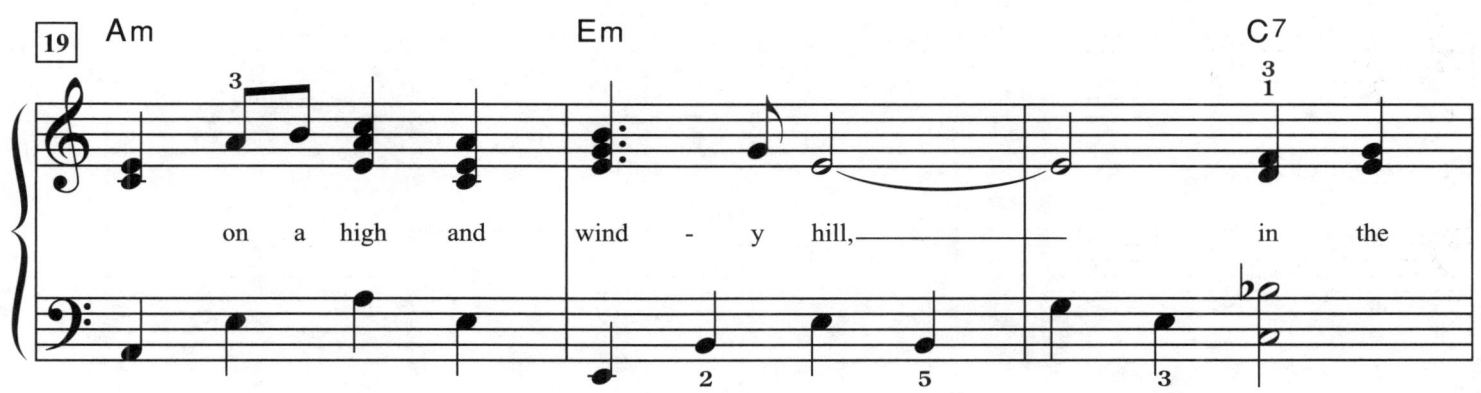
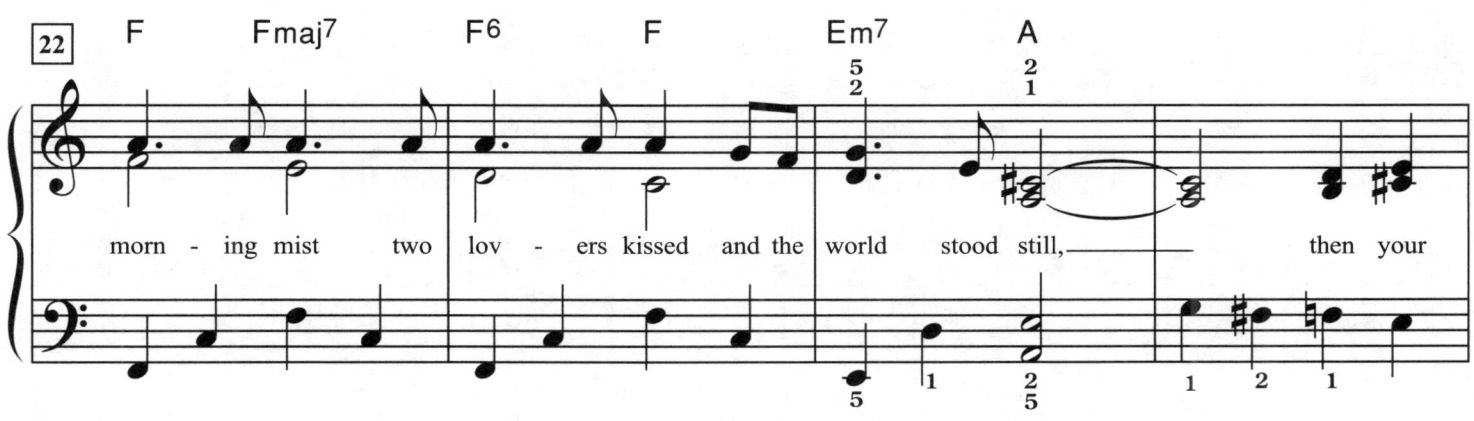

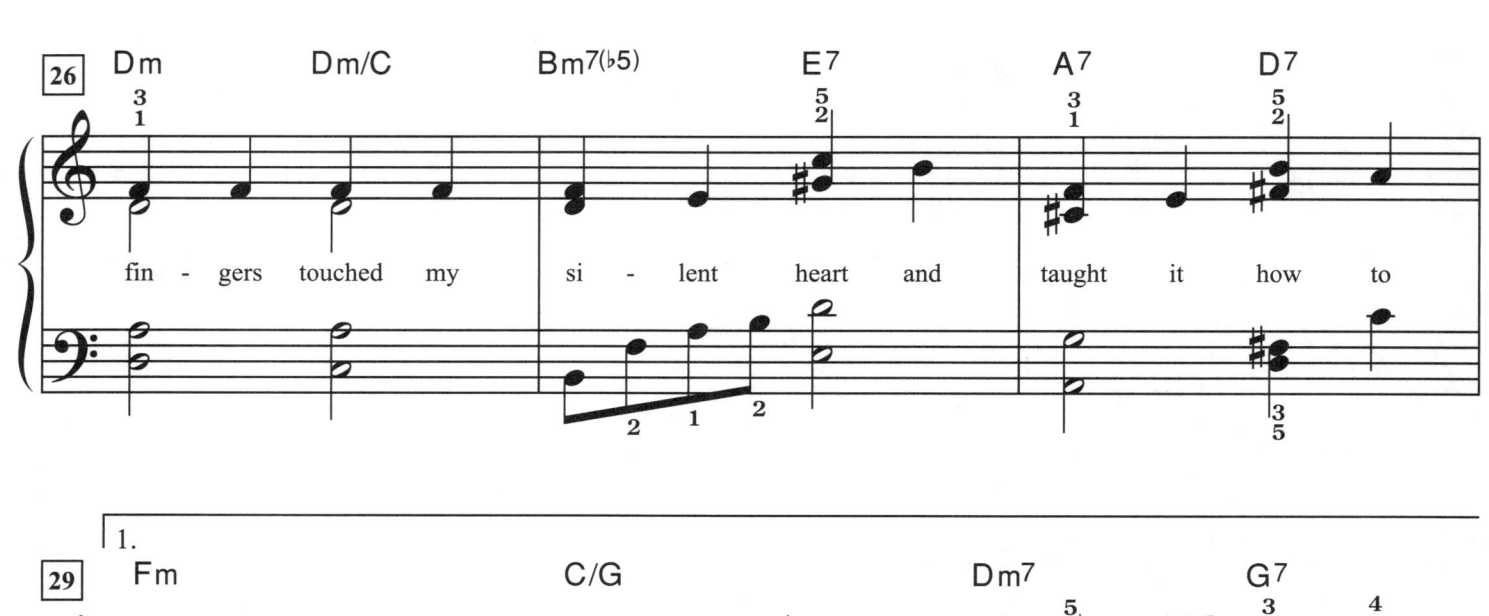

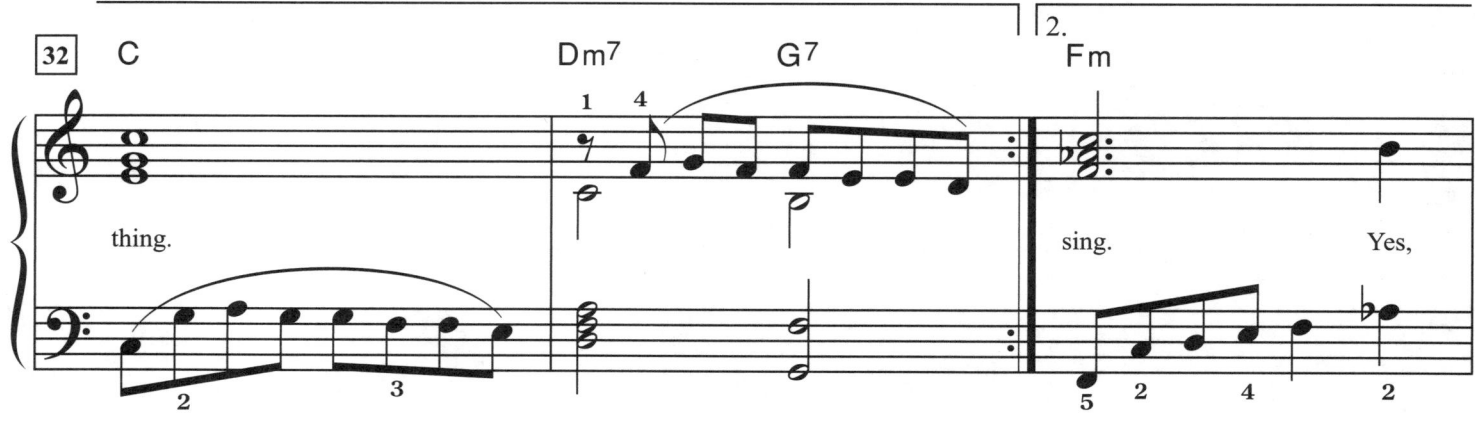
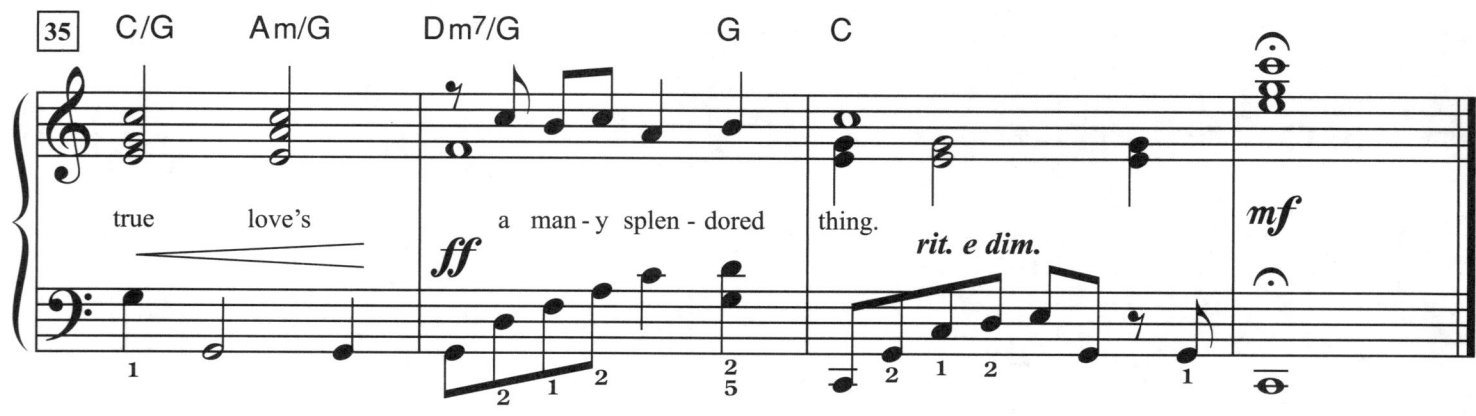

MISTY

Words by Johnny Burke
Music by Erroll Garner
Arranged by Dan Coates

Slowly, with expression

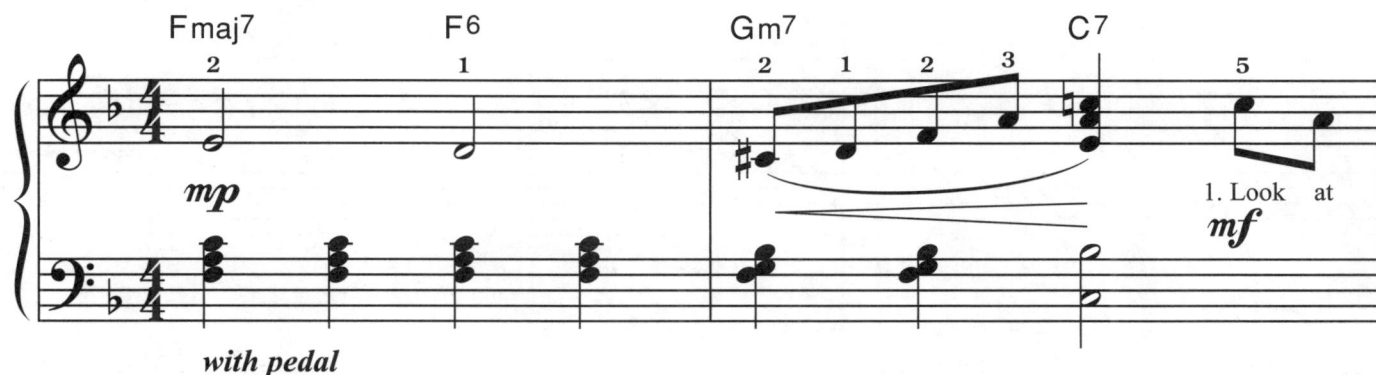

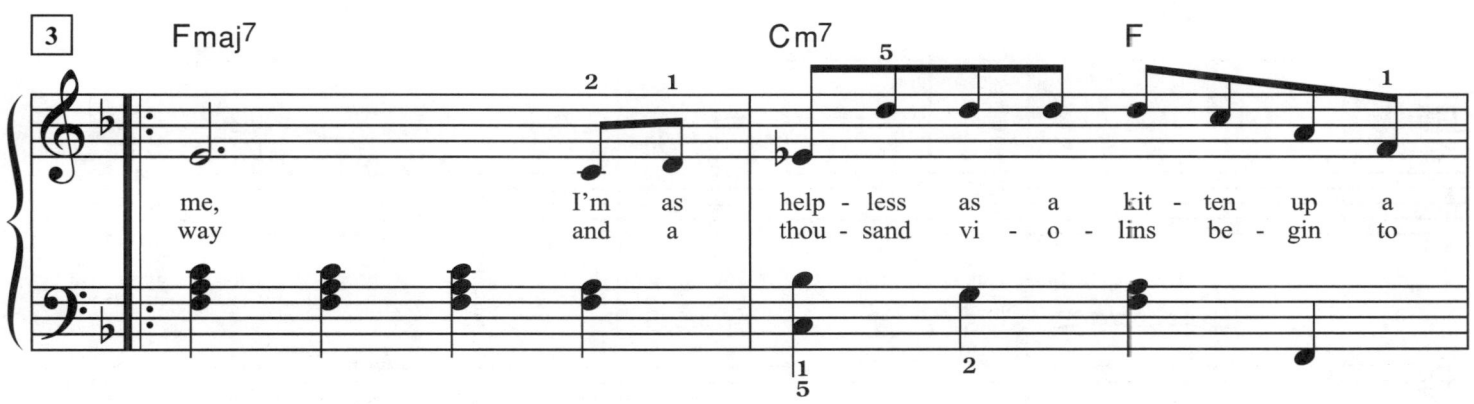

© 1954, 1955 (Copyrights Renewed) MARKE-MUSIC PUBLISHING CO., INC., MY DAD'S SONGS, INC., REGANESQUE MUSIC and
OCTAVE MUSIC PUBLISHING CORP.
All Rights For MARKE-MUSIC PUBLISHING CO., INC. Administered by WB MUSIC CORP.
All Rights Reserved

102

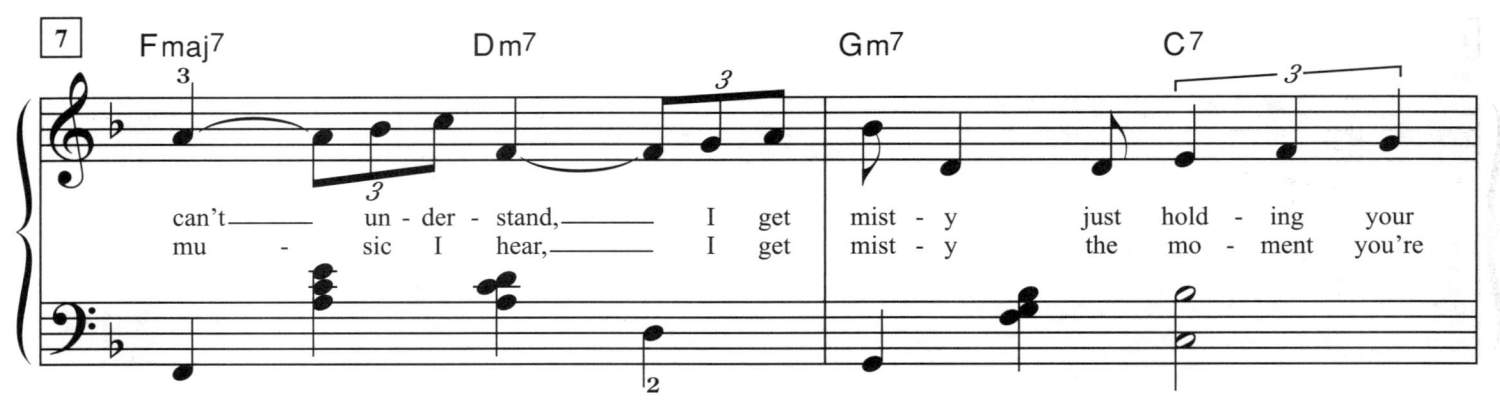
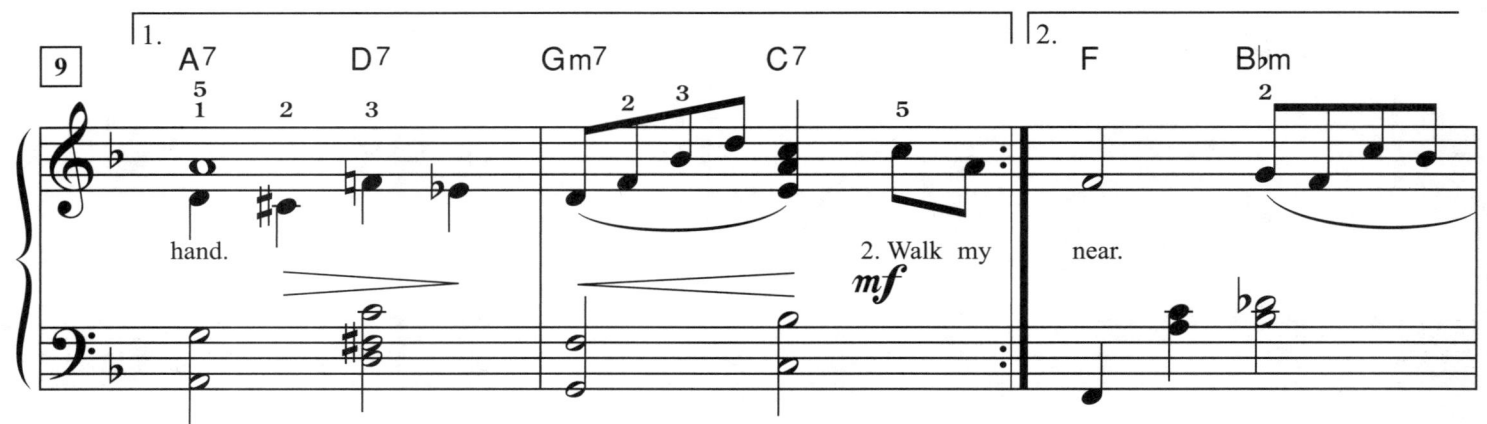
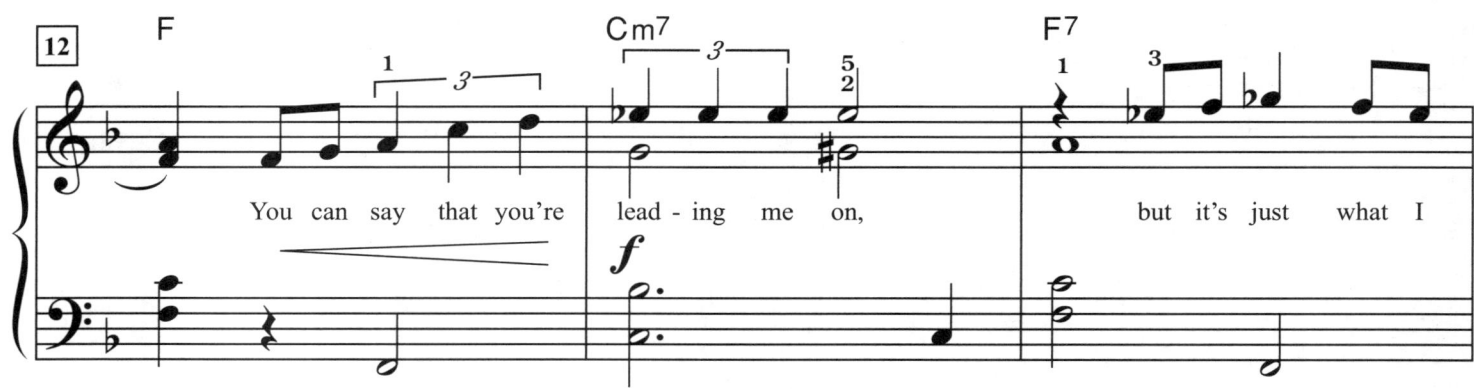
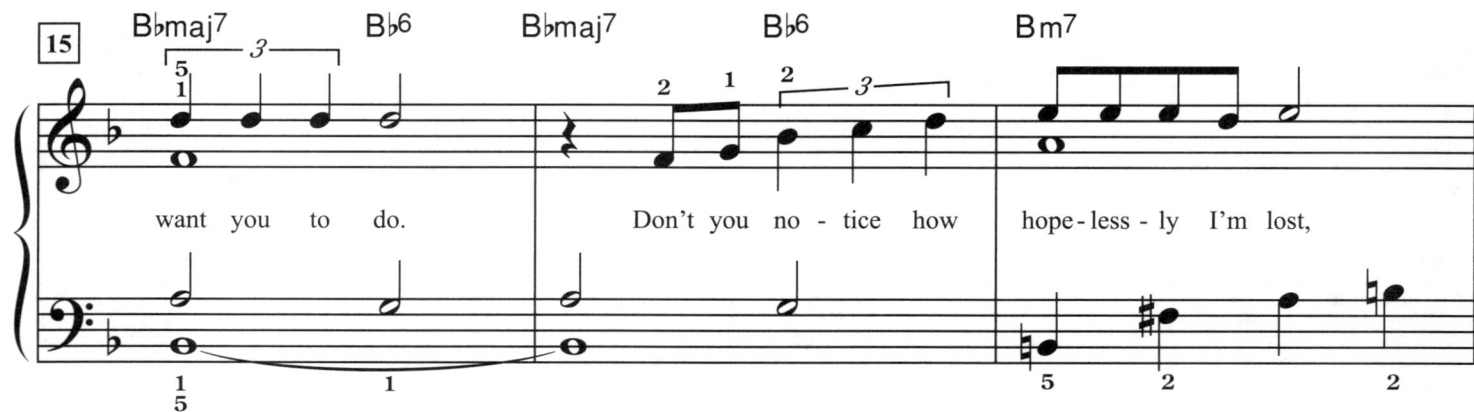

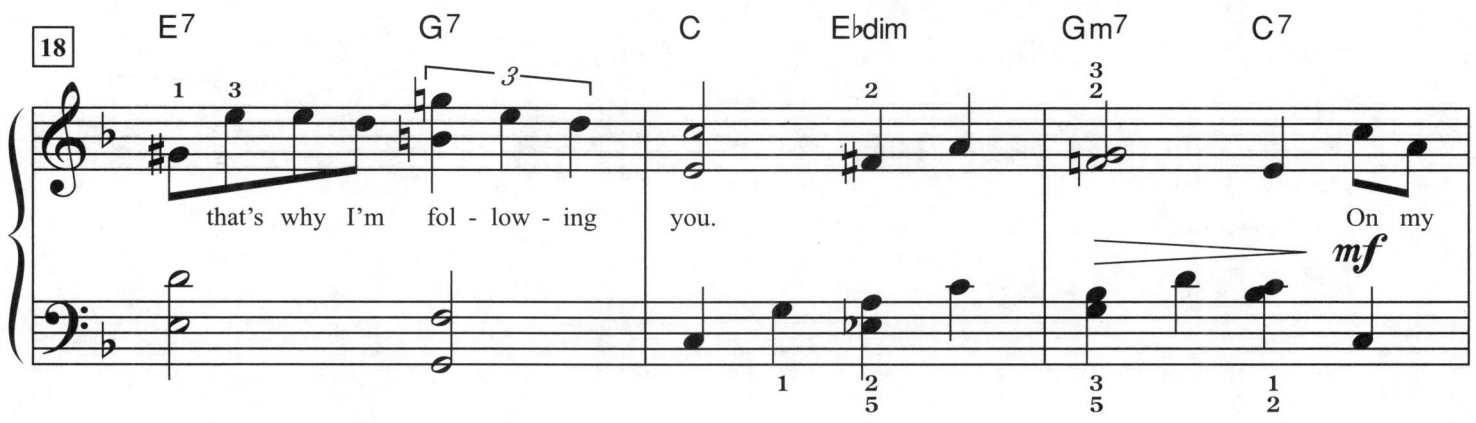
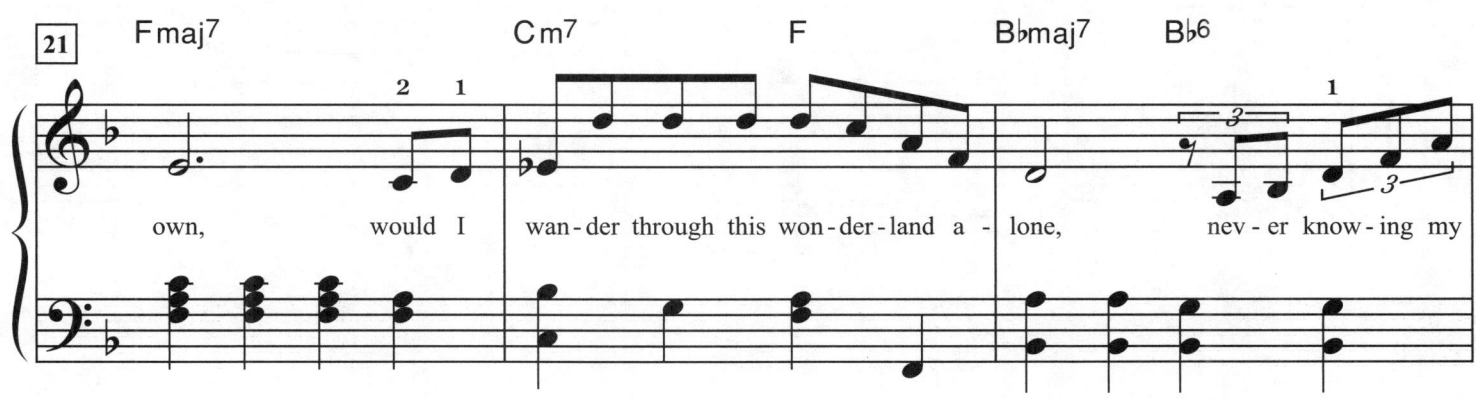

MOONLIGHT SERENADE

Music by Glenn Miller
Lyrics by Mitchell Parish
Arranged by Dan Coates

Moderately slow

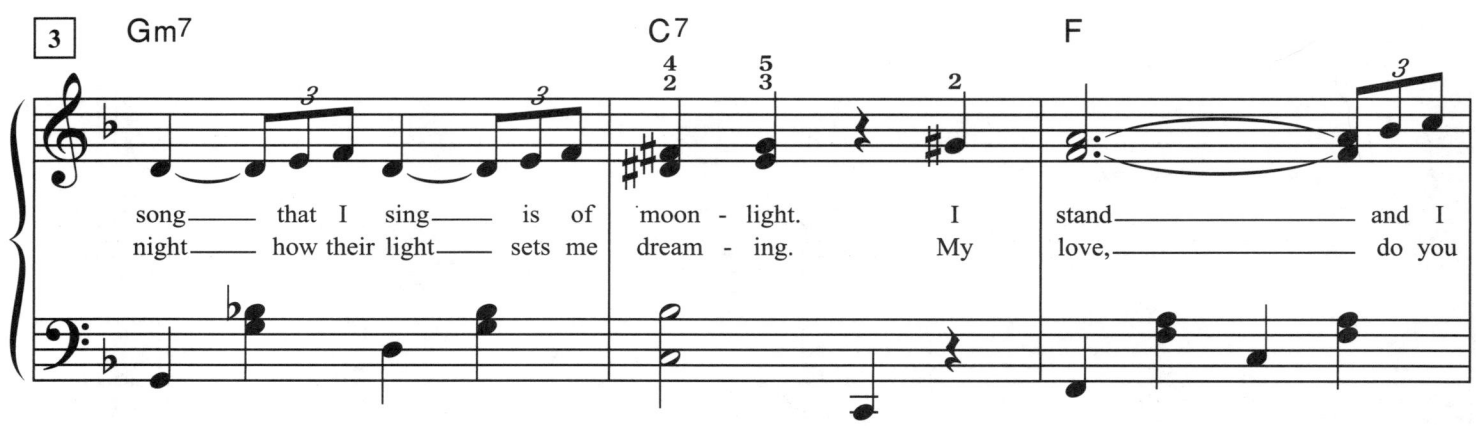

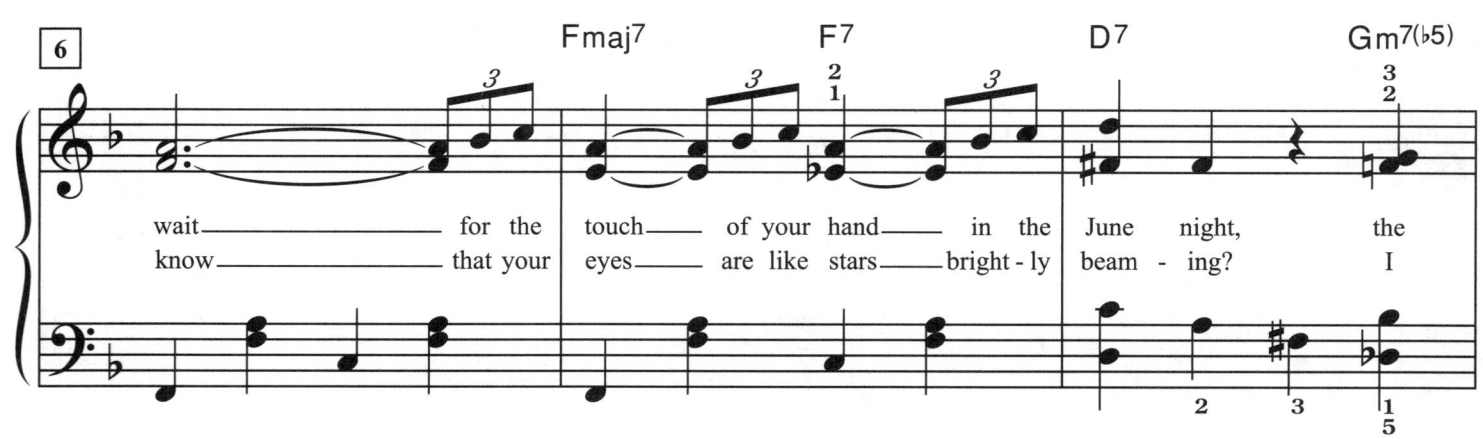

© 1939 (Renewed) EMI Robbins Catalog INC.
All Rights Controlled by EMI Robbins Catalog INC. (Publishing) and Alfred Publishing Co., Inc. (Print)
All Rights Reserved

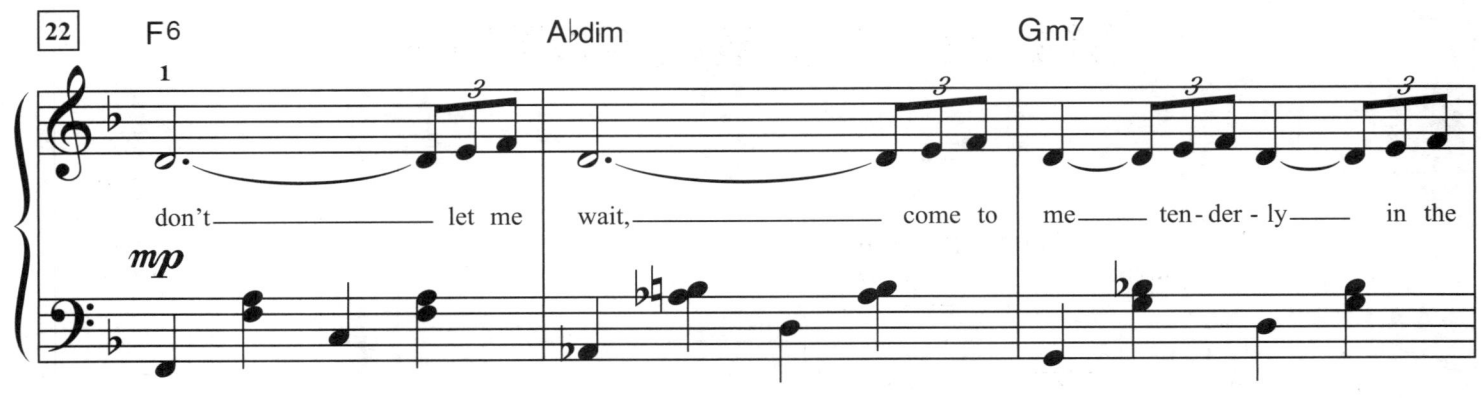
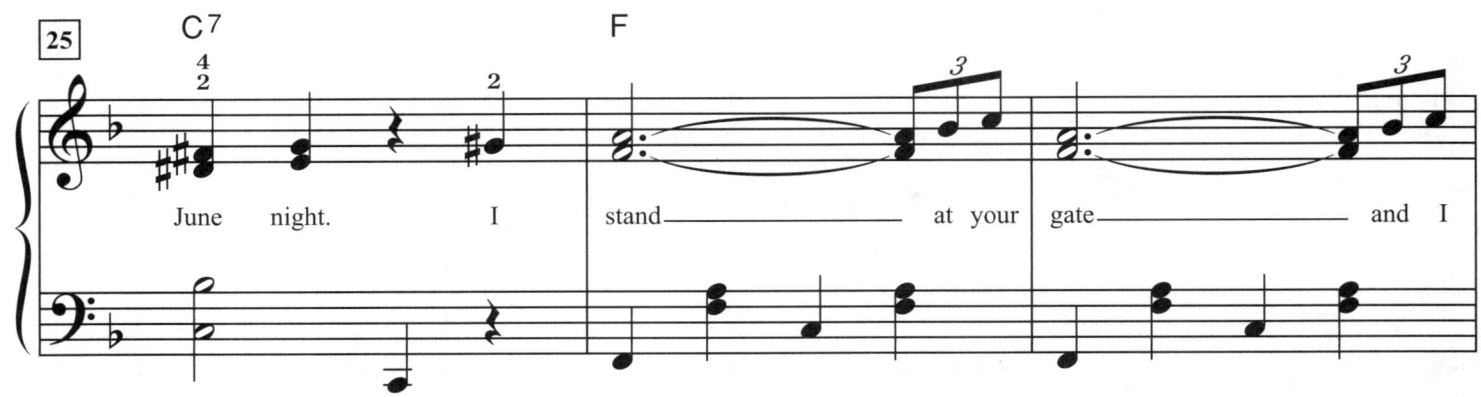
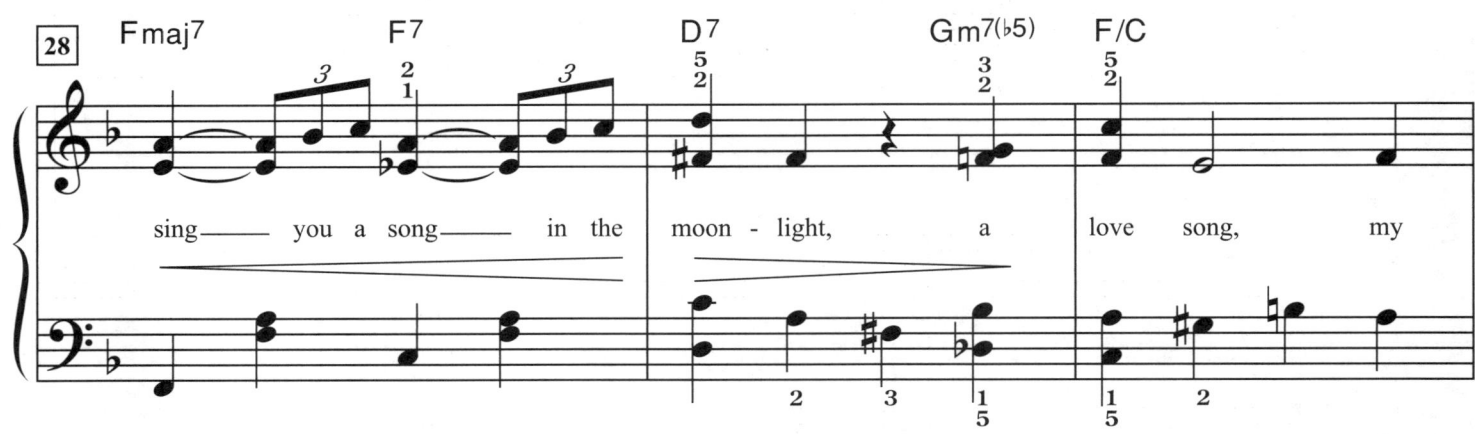
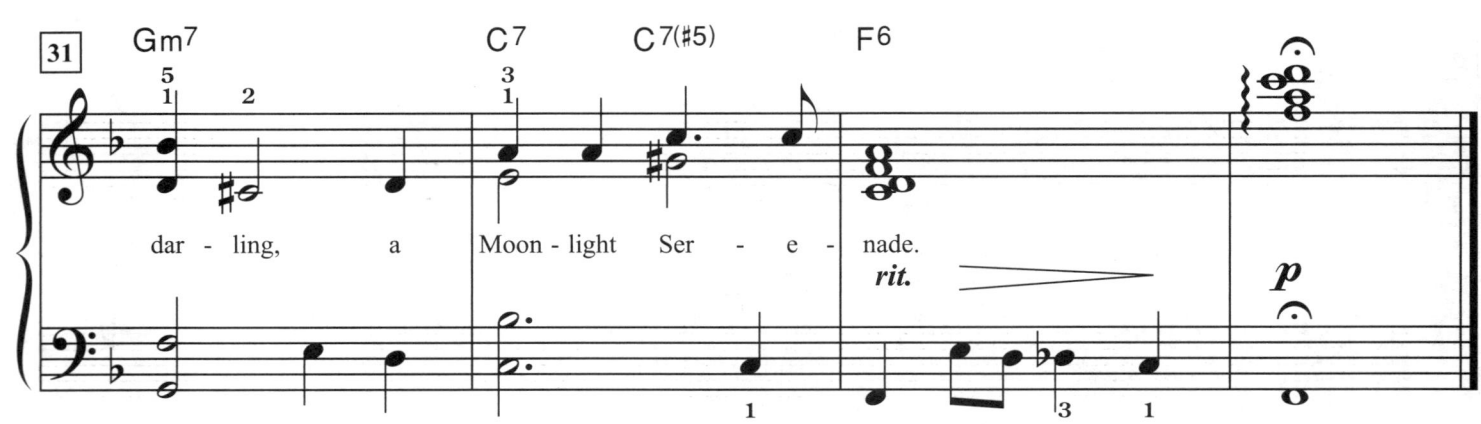

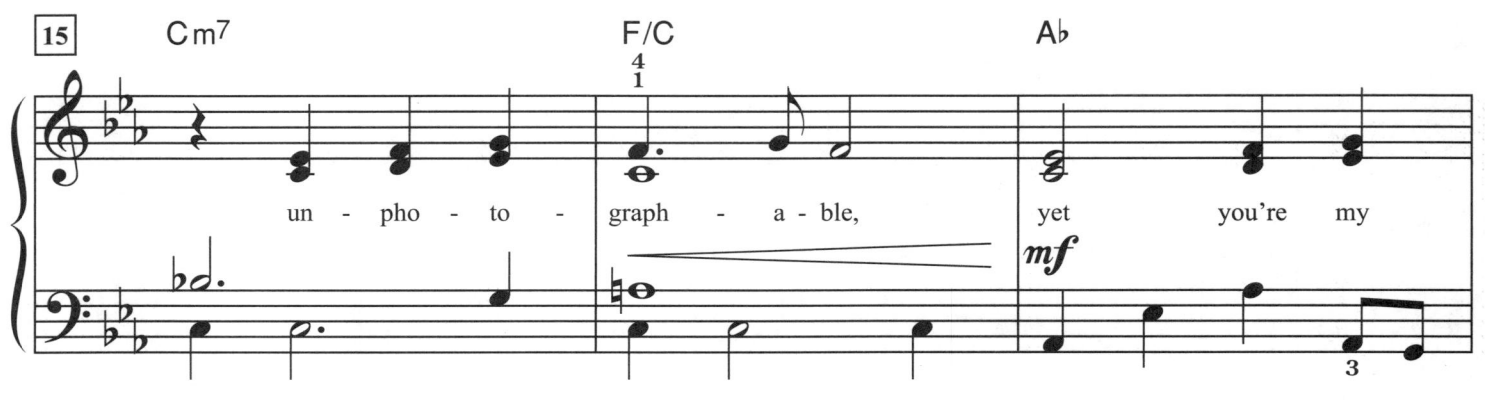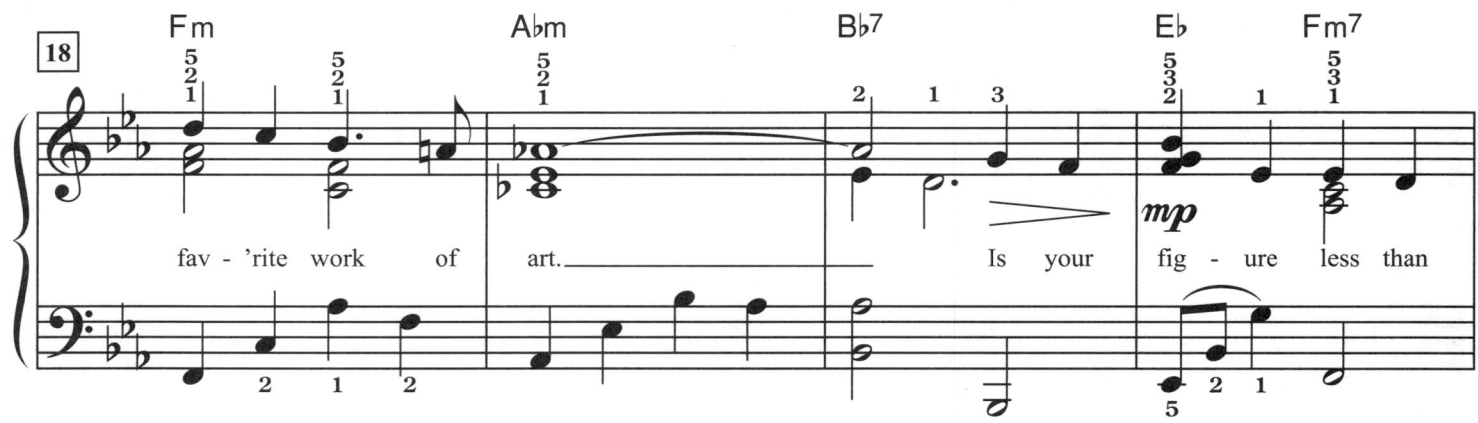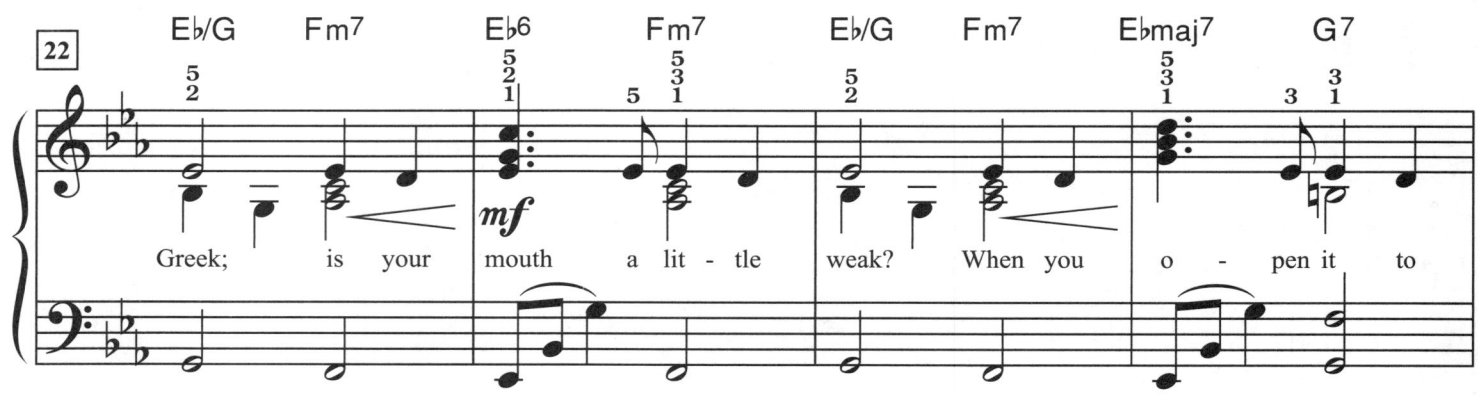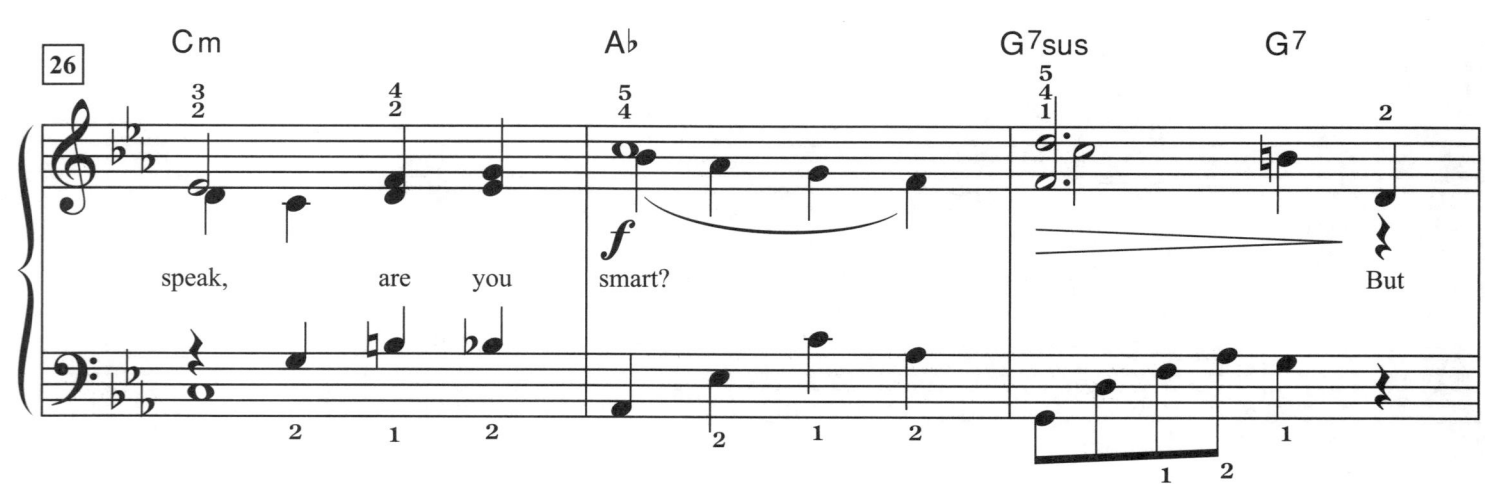

THE PRAYER

Words and Music by
Carole Bayer Sager and David Foster
Italian Lyric by Alberto Testa and Tony Renis
Arranged by Dan Coates

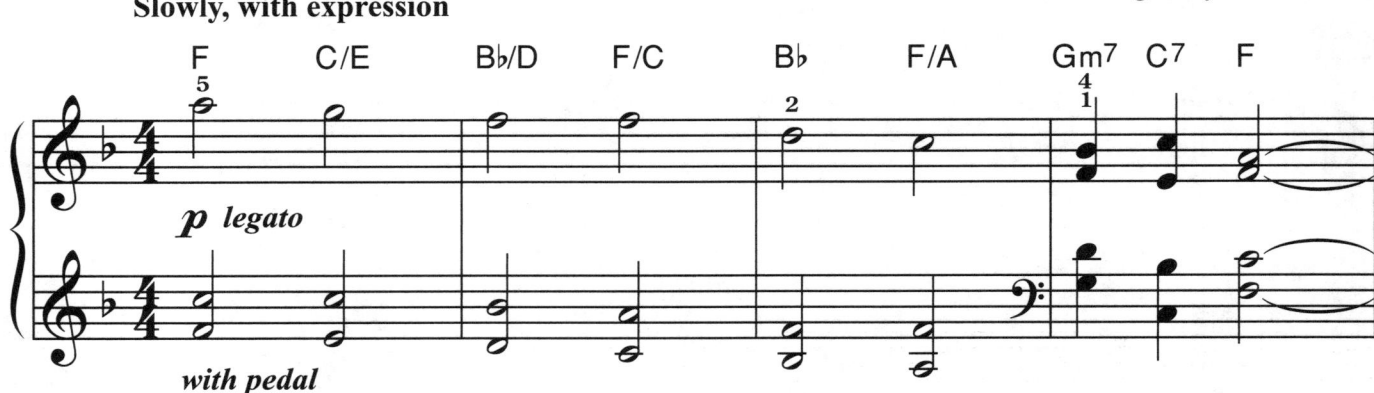

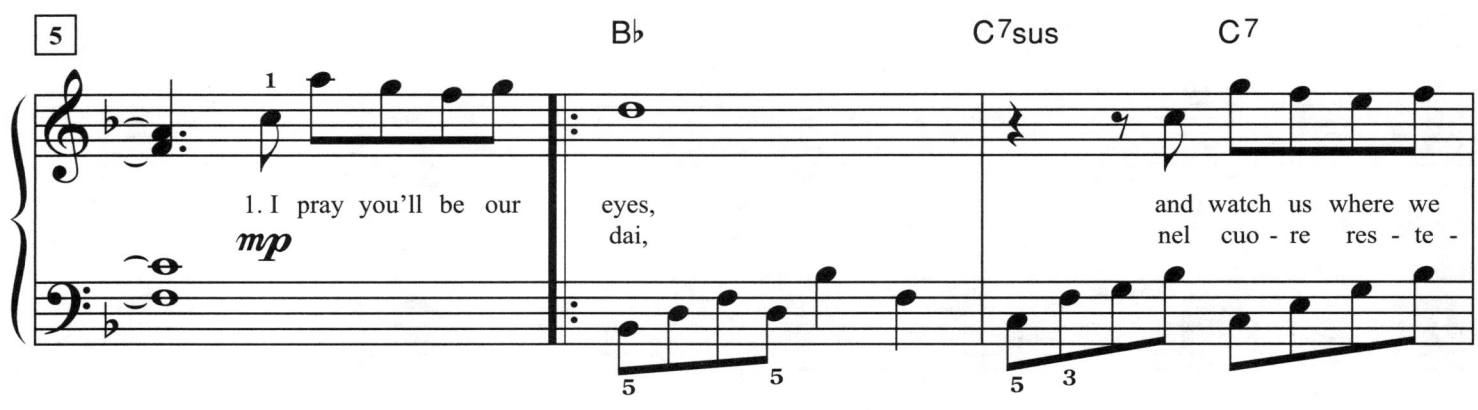

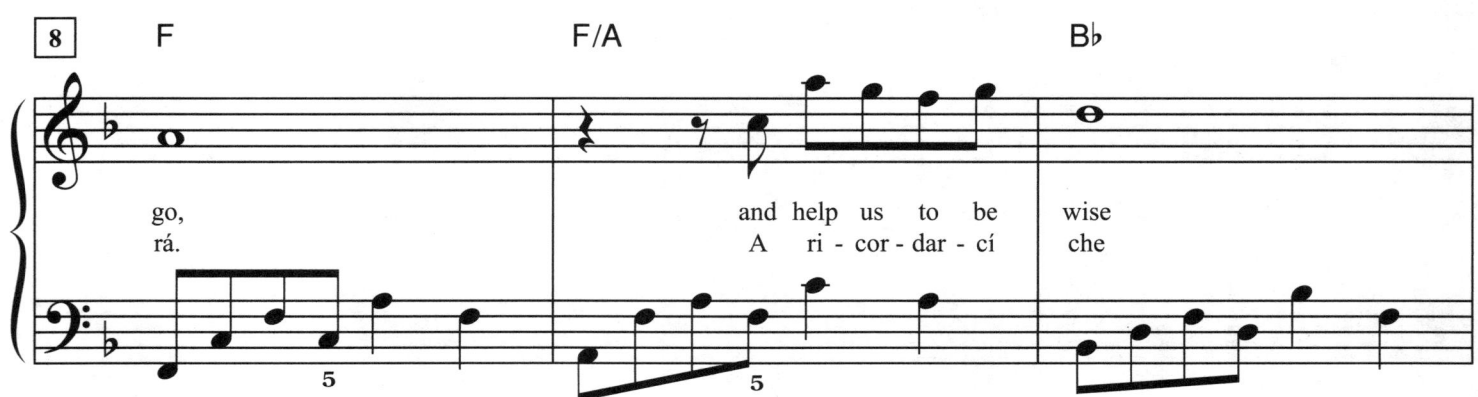

© 1998 WARNER-TAMERLANE PUBLISHING CORP.
All Rights Reserved

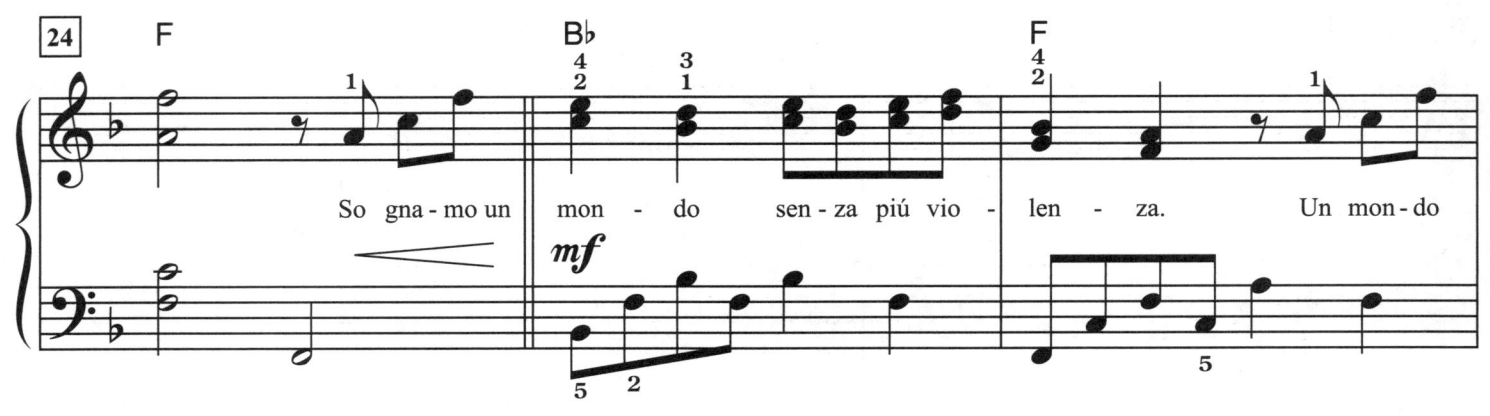
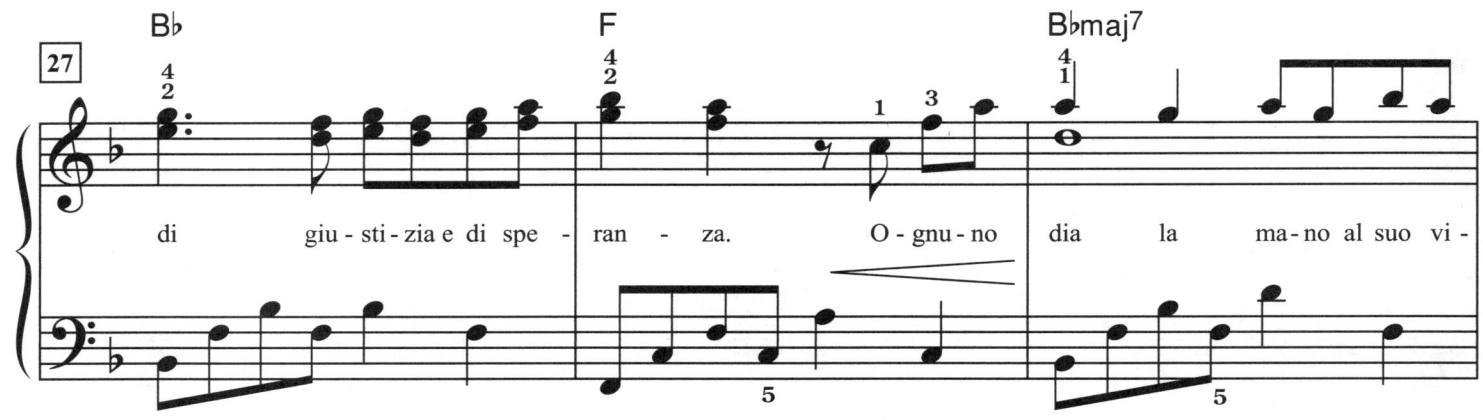
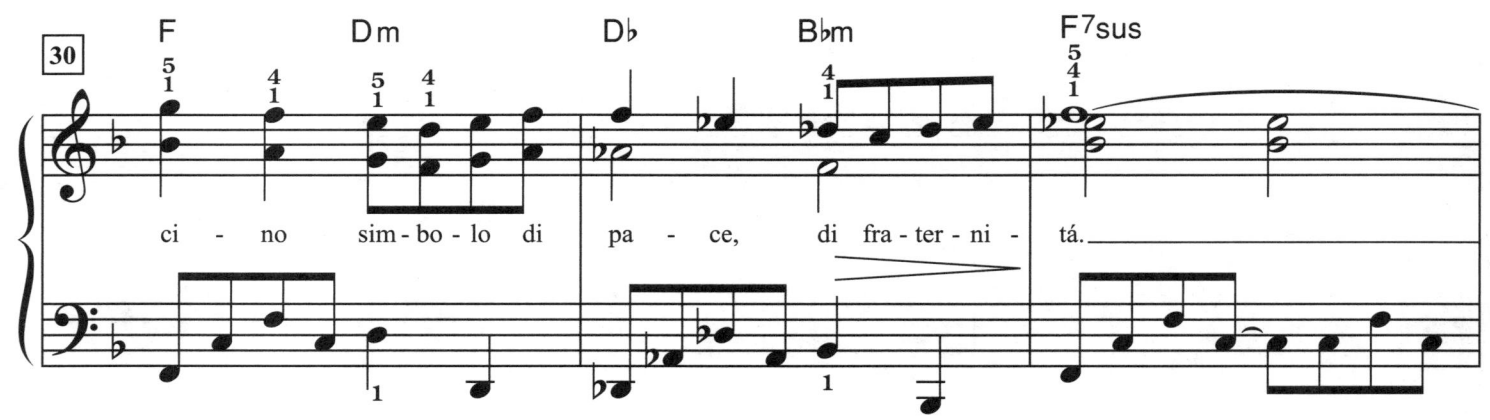
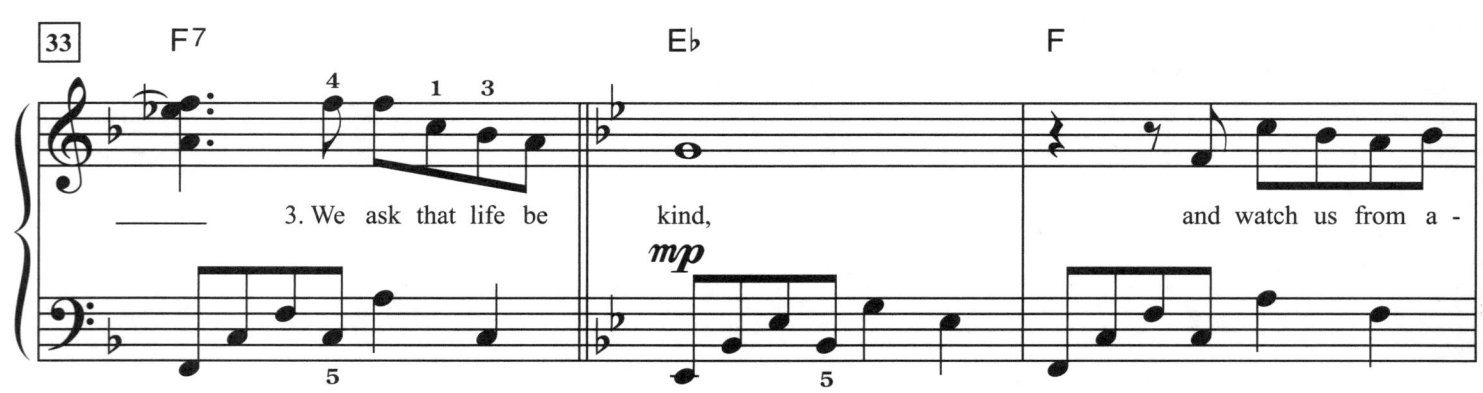

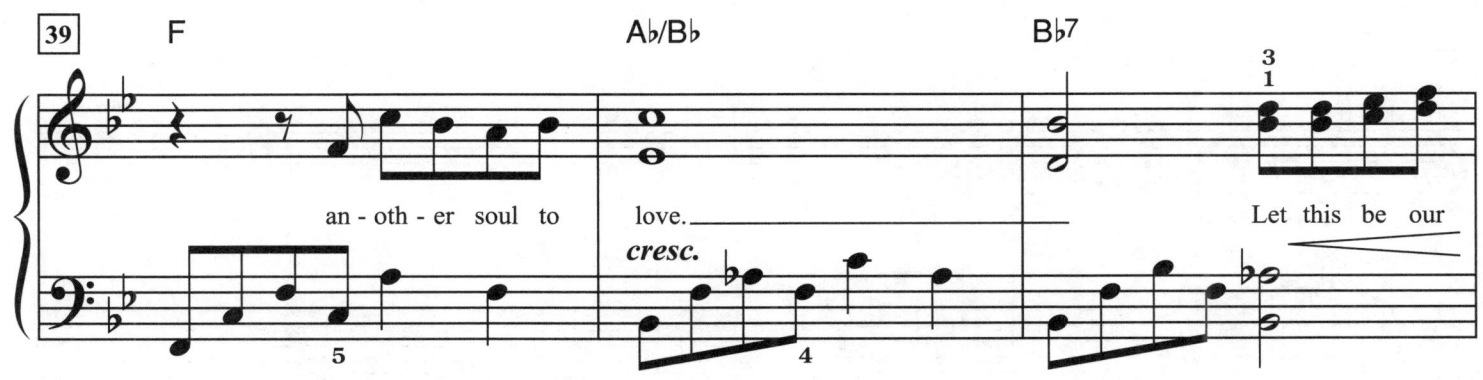
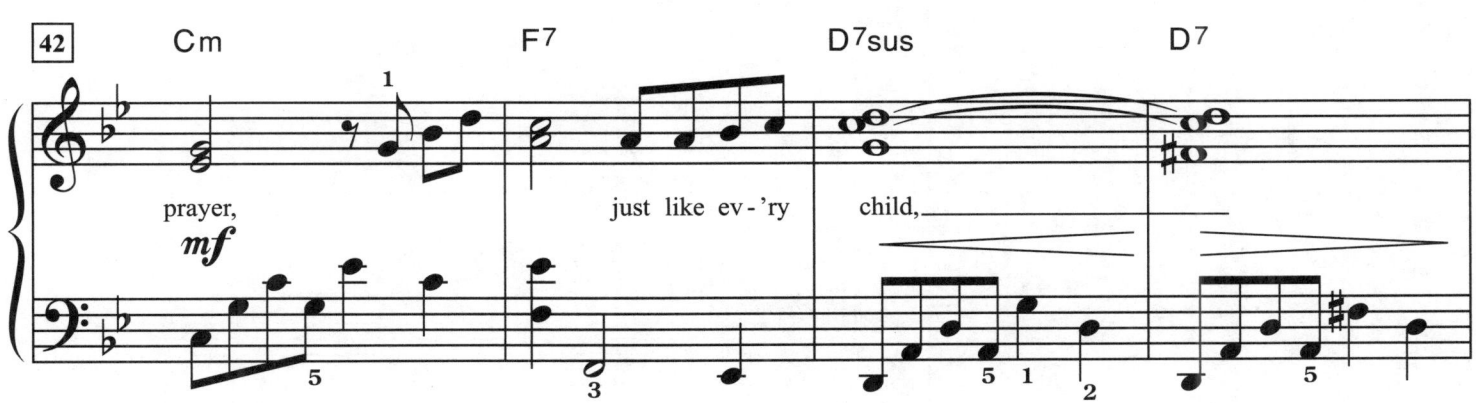
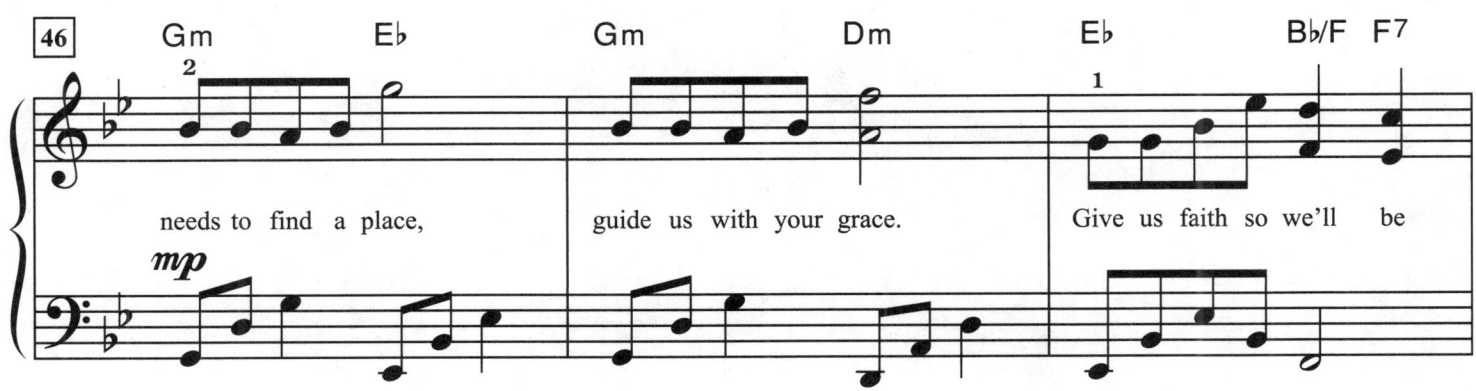

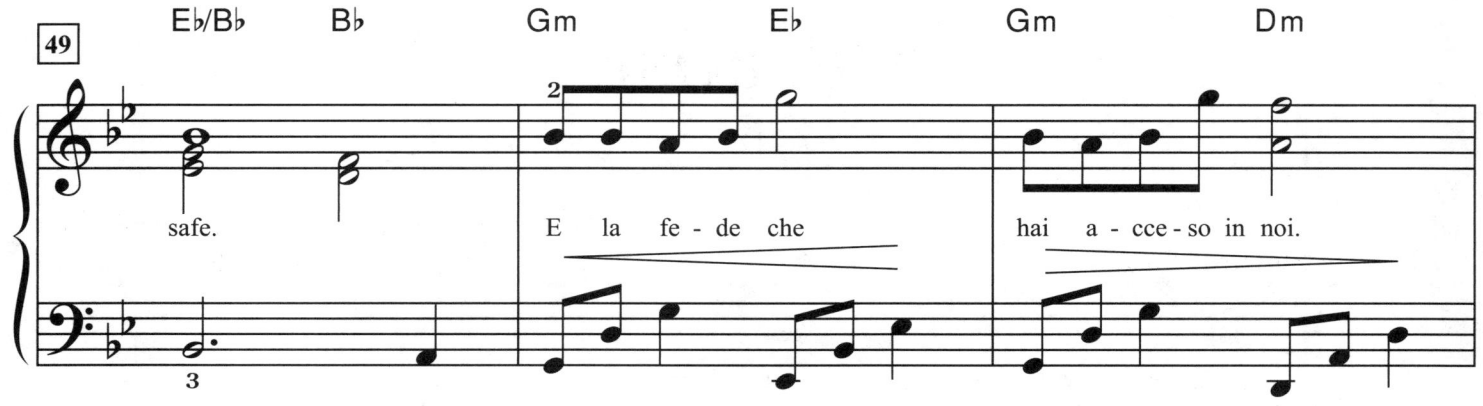
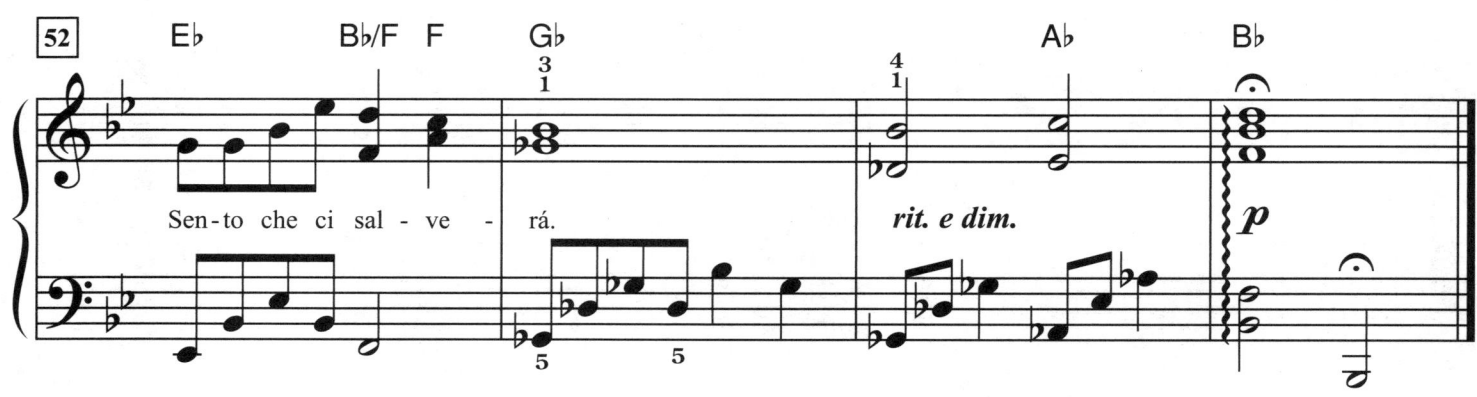

Verse 2 (English lyric):
I pray we'll find your light,
And hold it in our hearts
When stars go out each night.
Let this be our prayer,
When shadows fill our day.
Lead us to a place,
Guide us with your grace.
Give us faith so we'll be safe.

Verse 3 (Italian lyric):
La forza che ci dai
é il desiderio che.
Ognuno trovi amore
Intorno e dentro sé.

THE ROSE

Words and Music by Amanda McBroom
Arranged by Dan Coates

SOMEWHERE, MY LOVE

Music by Maurice Jarre
Lyric by Paul Francis Webster
Arranged by Dan Coates

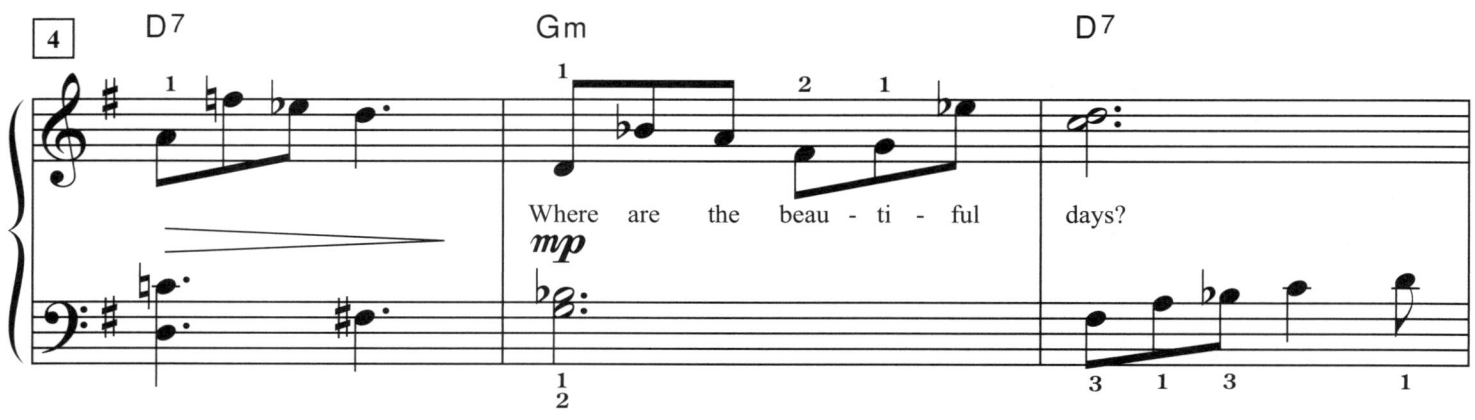
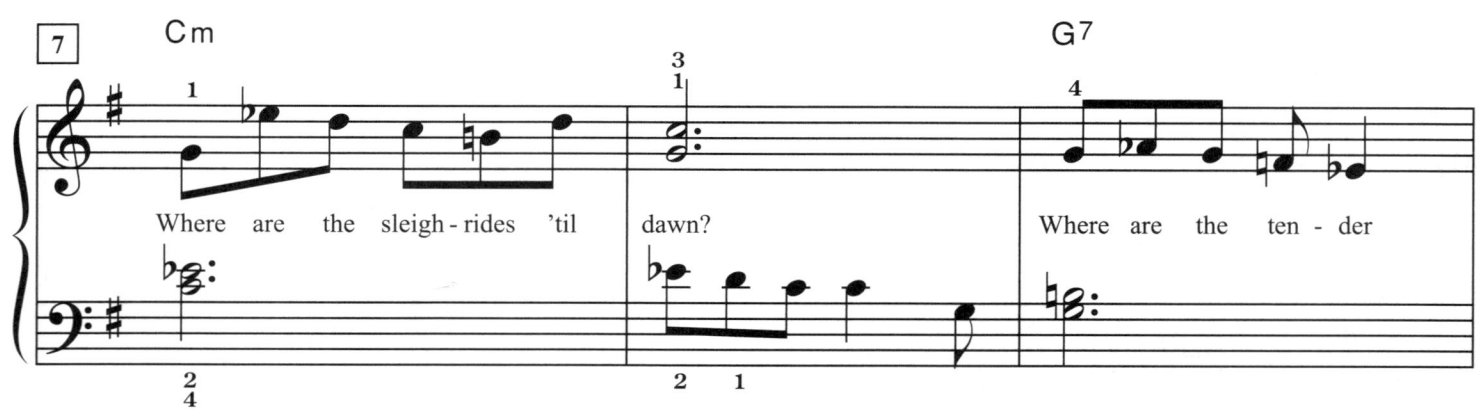

© 1965, 1966 METRO-GOLDWYN MAYER INC.
Copyrights Renewed and Assigned to EMI ROBBINS CATALOG INC.
All Rights Controlled by EMI ROBBINS CATALOG INC. (Publishing)
and ALFRED PUBLISHING CO., INC. (Print)
All Rights Reserved

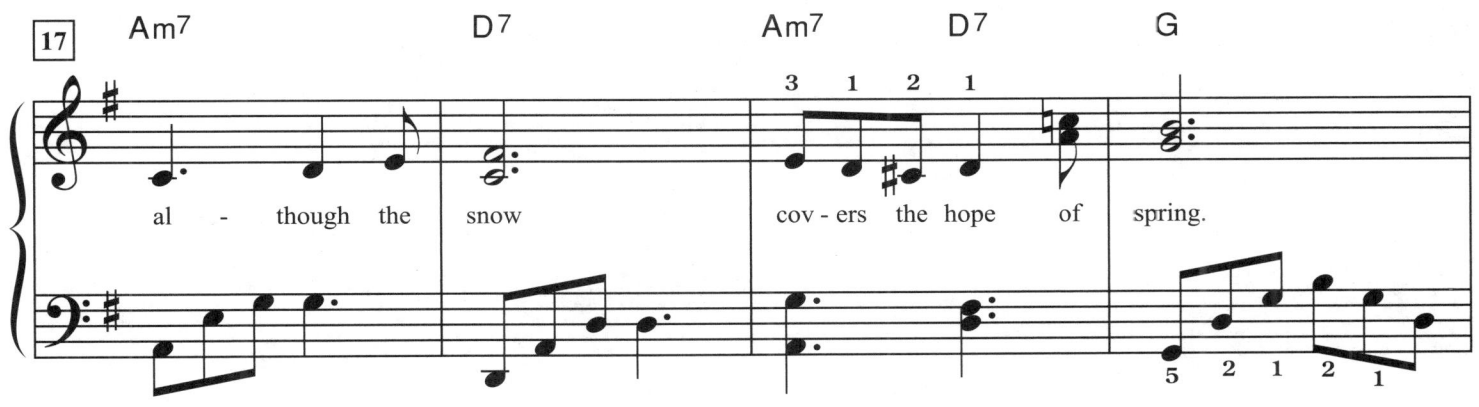

TAKE MY BREATH AWAY

Music by Giorgio Moroder
Words by Tom Whitlock
Arranged by Dan Coates

123

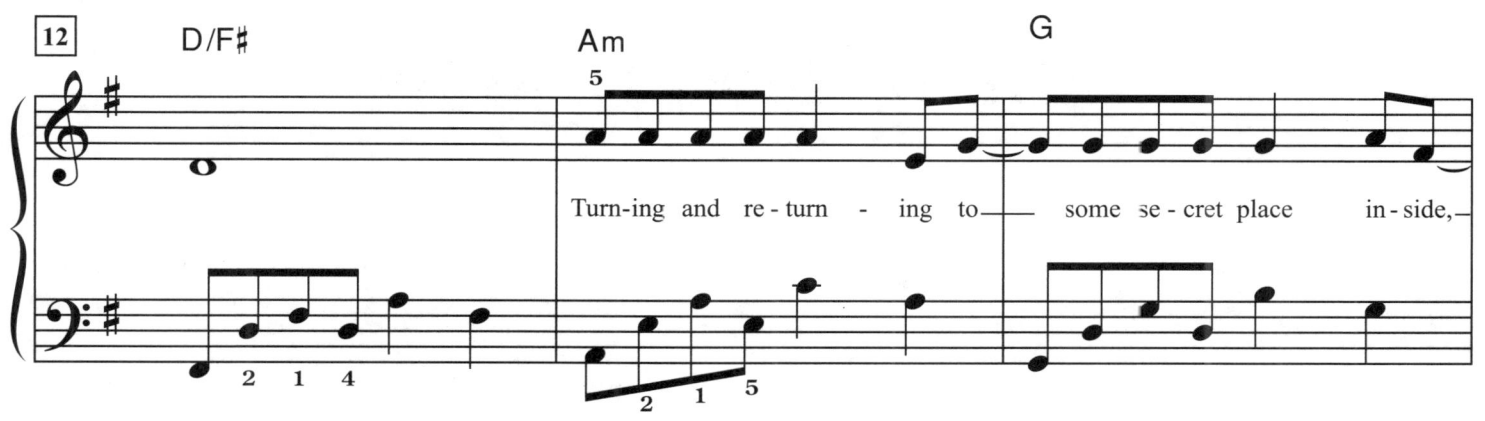
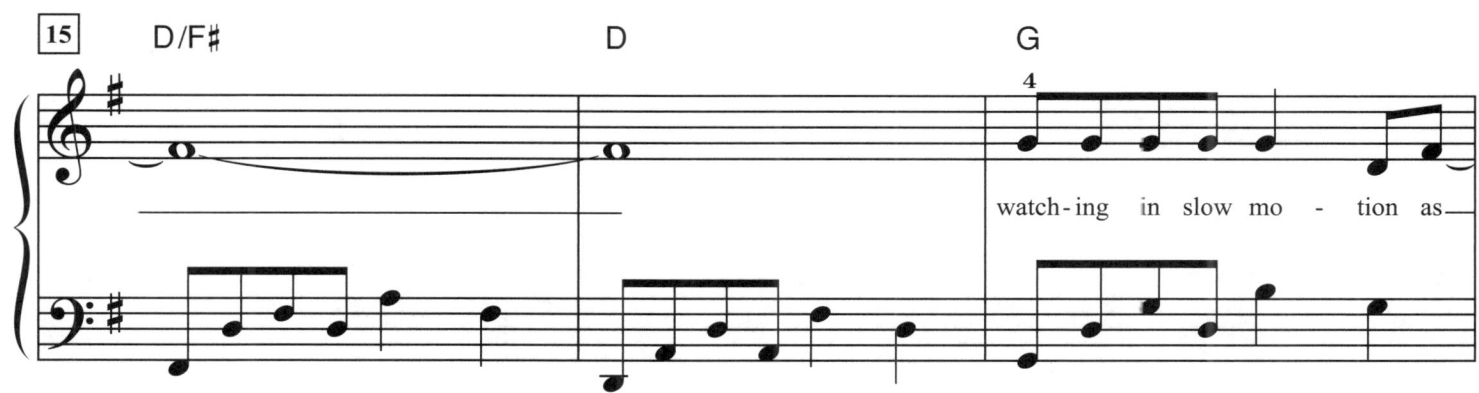
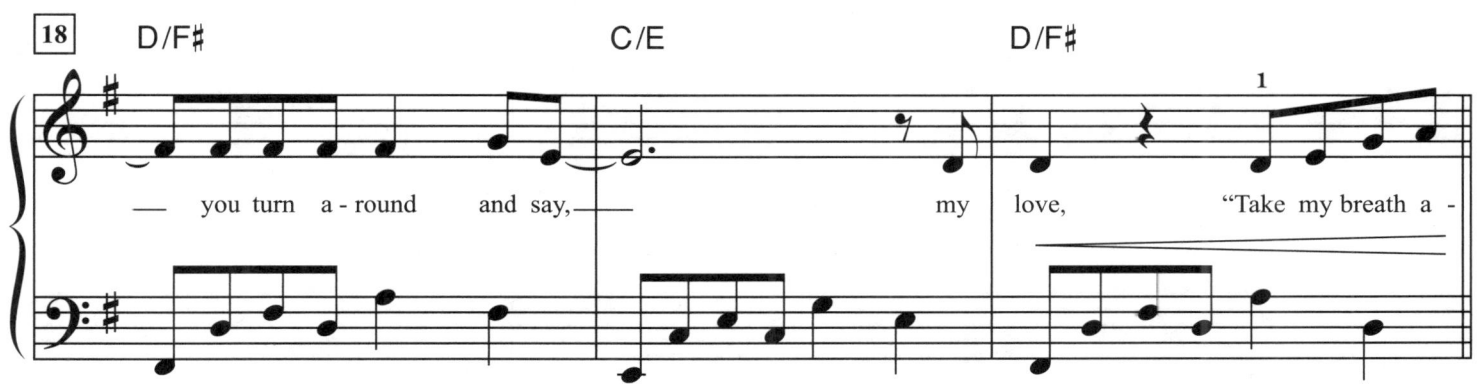
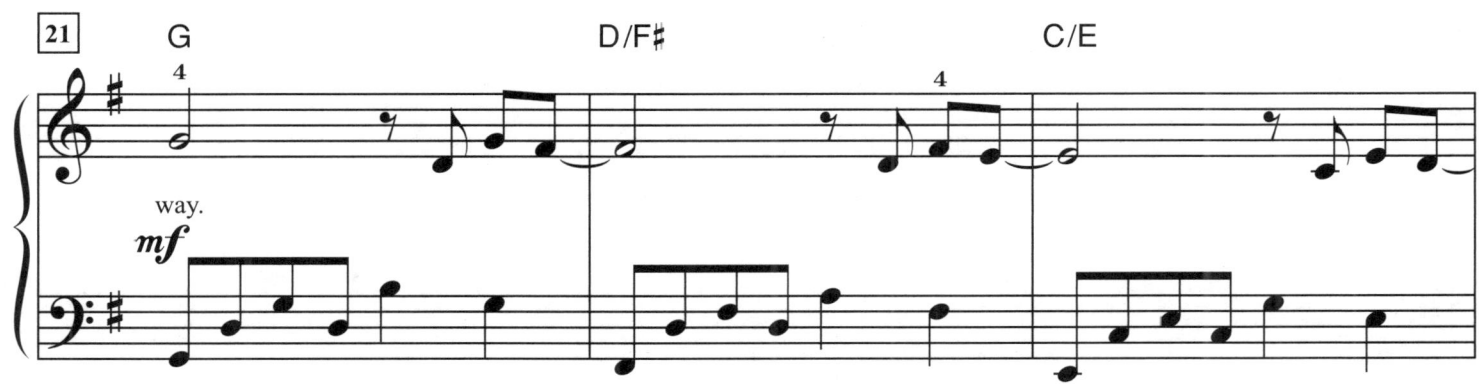

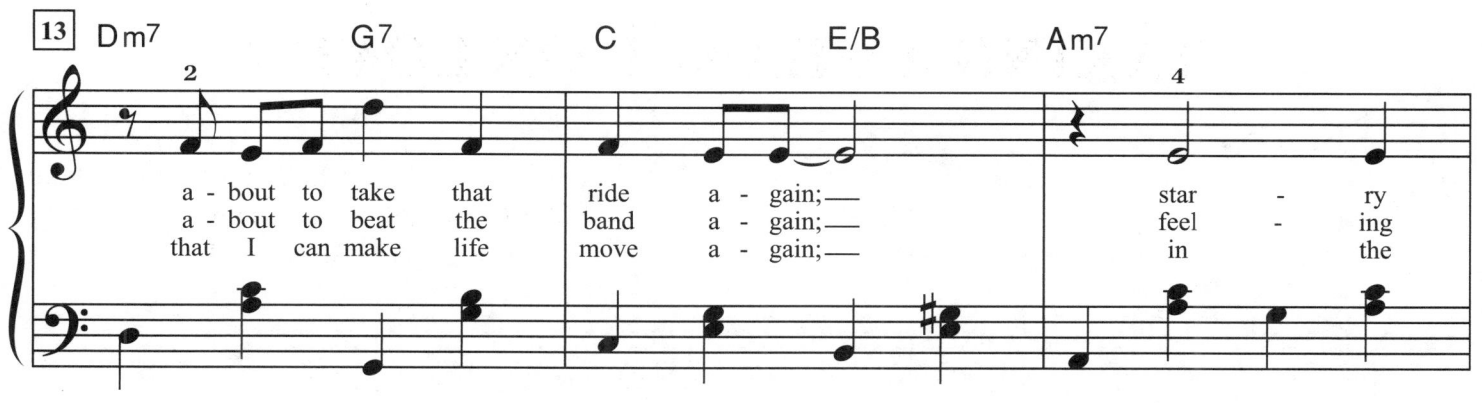
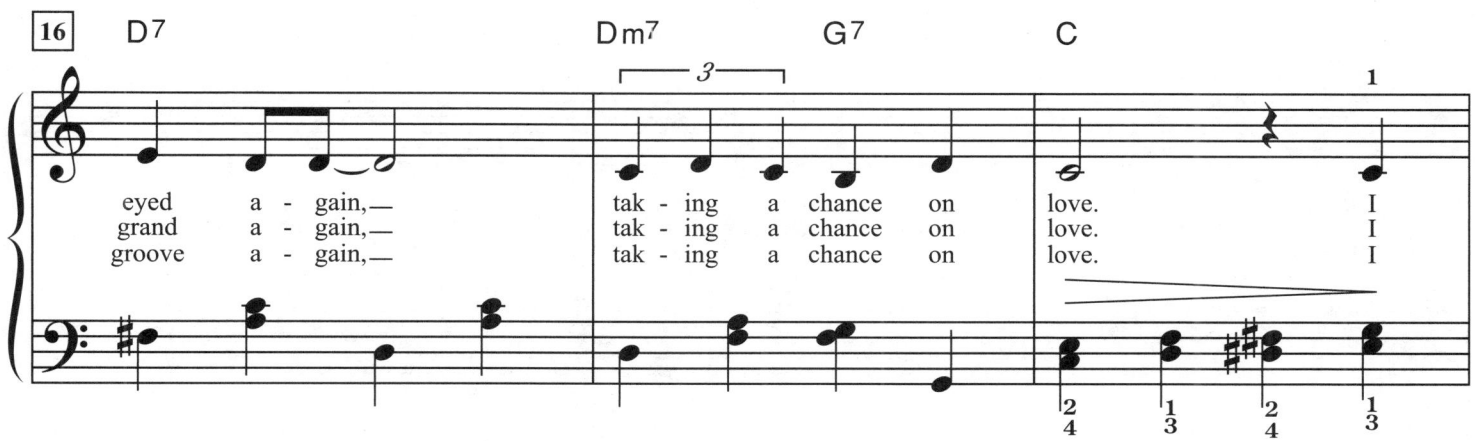

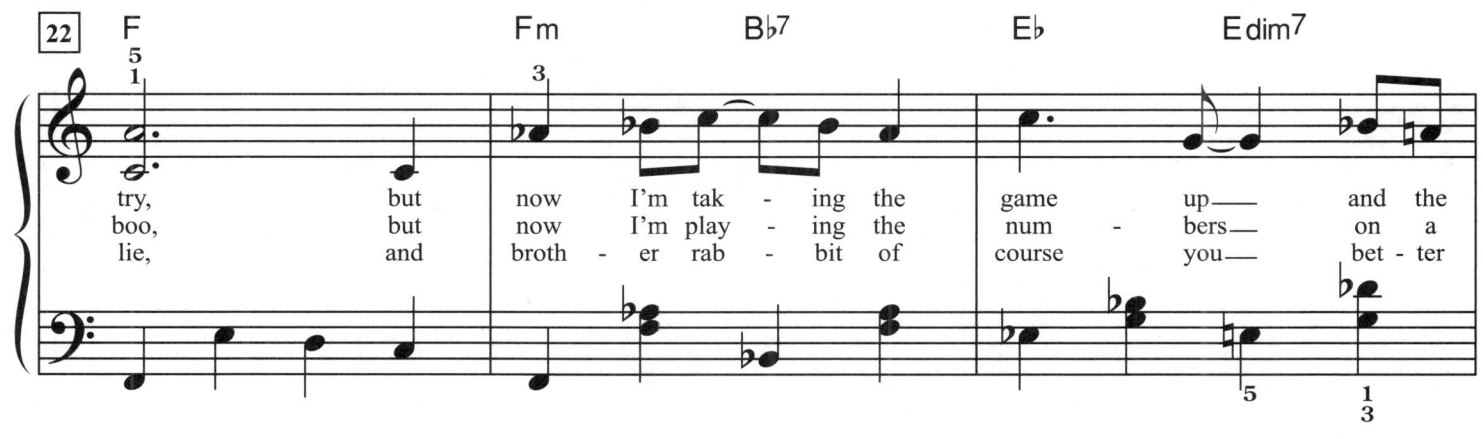

THIS I PROMISE YOU

Words and Music by Richard Marx
Arranged by Dan Coates

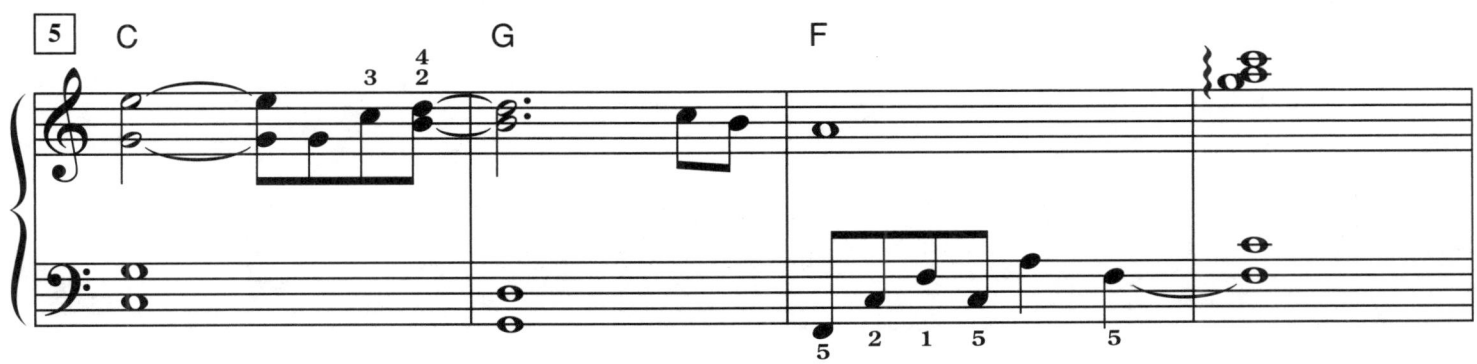

1. When the visions around you bring tears to your eyes,
2. I've loved you forever in lifetimes before.

© 2000 CHI-BOY MUSIC
All Rights outside the U.S. and Canada for CHI-BOY MUSIC Administered by WB MUSIC CORP.
All Rights Reserved

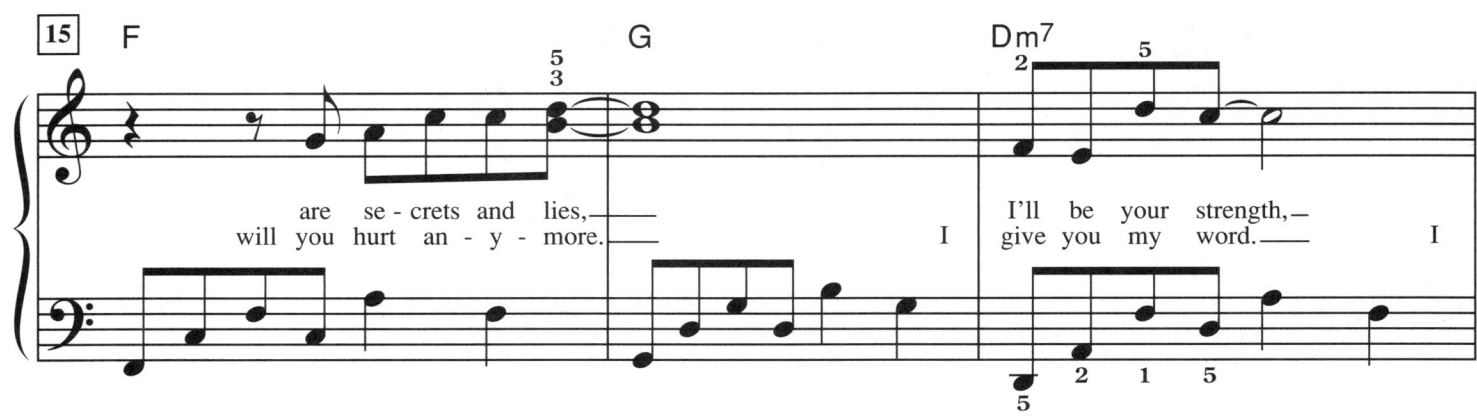
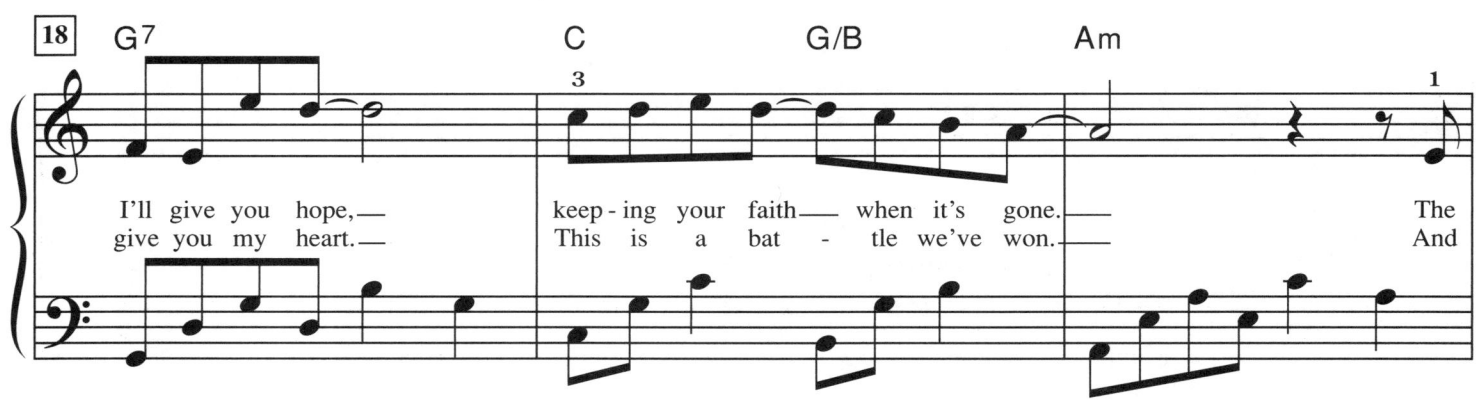
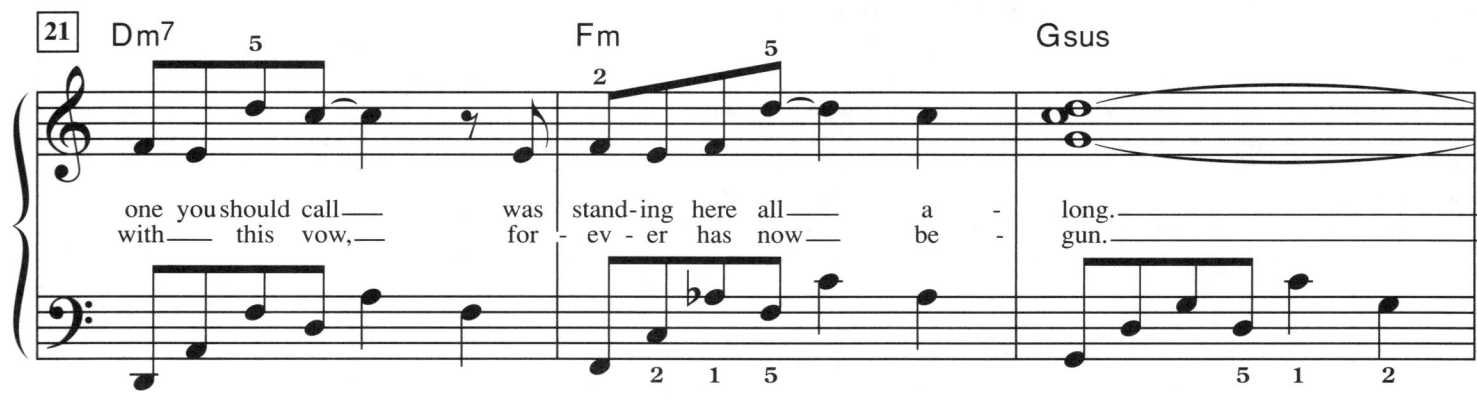

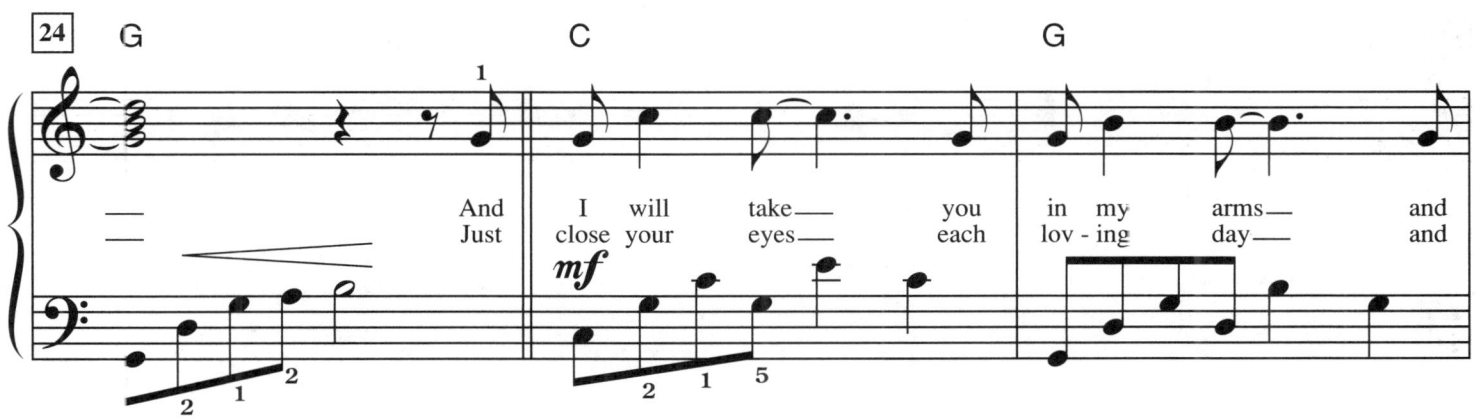
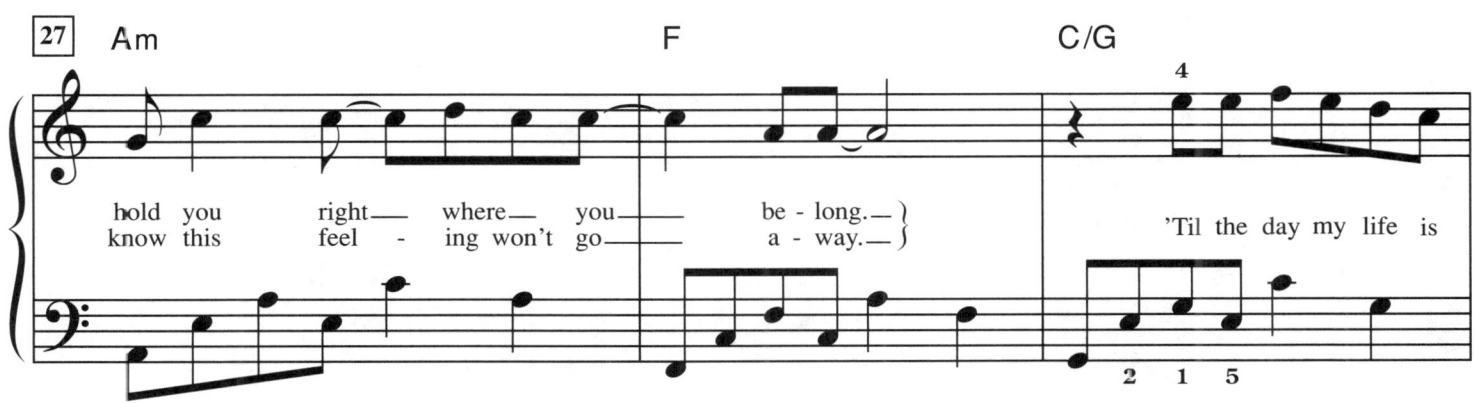

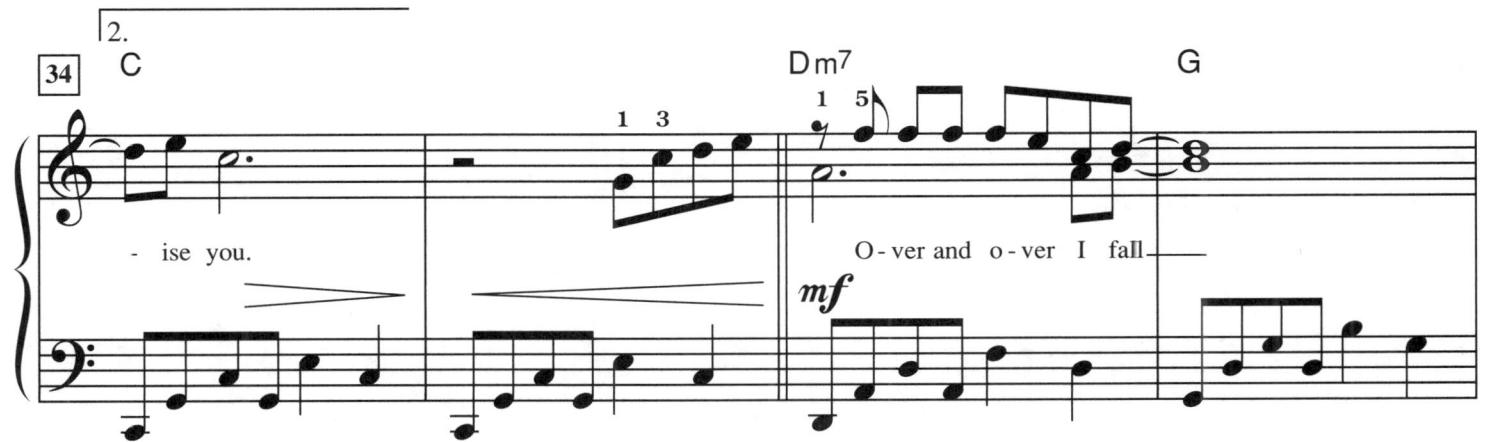

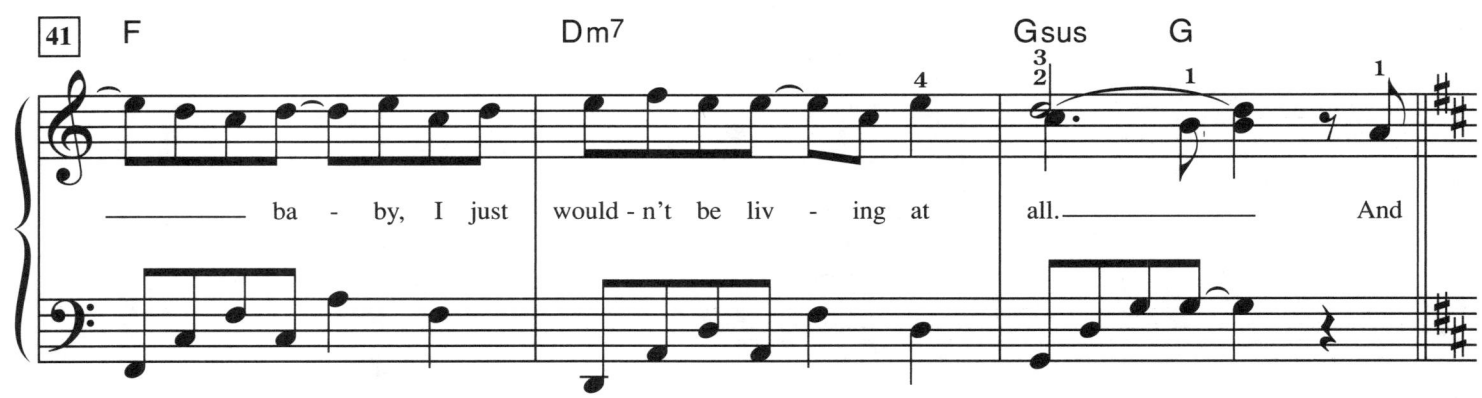

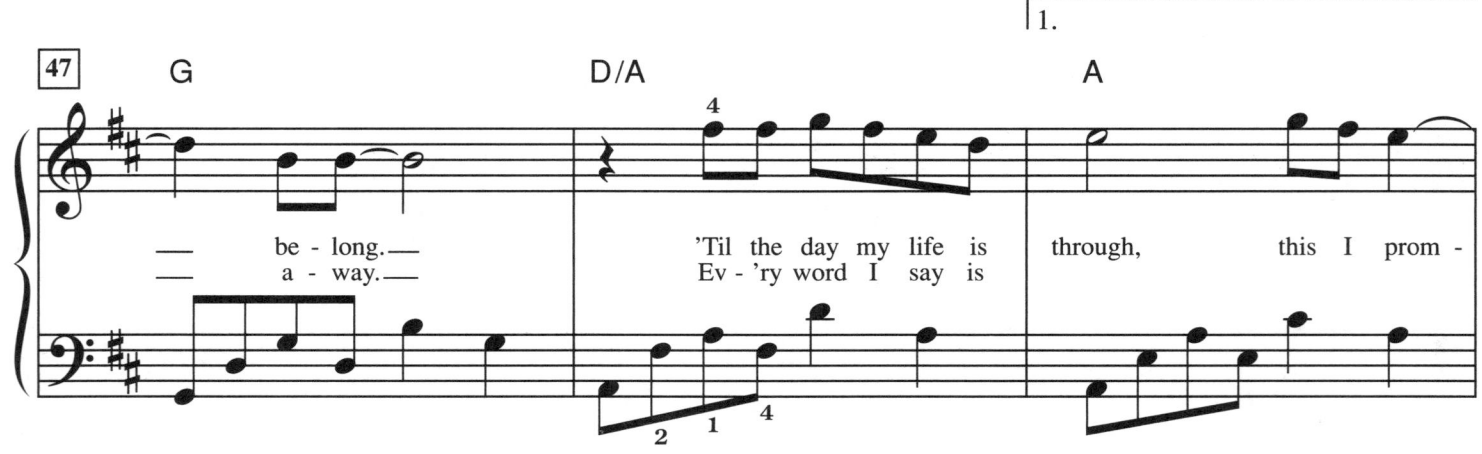

133

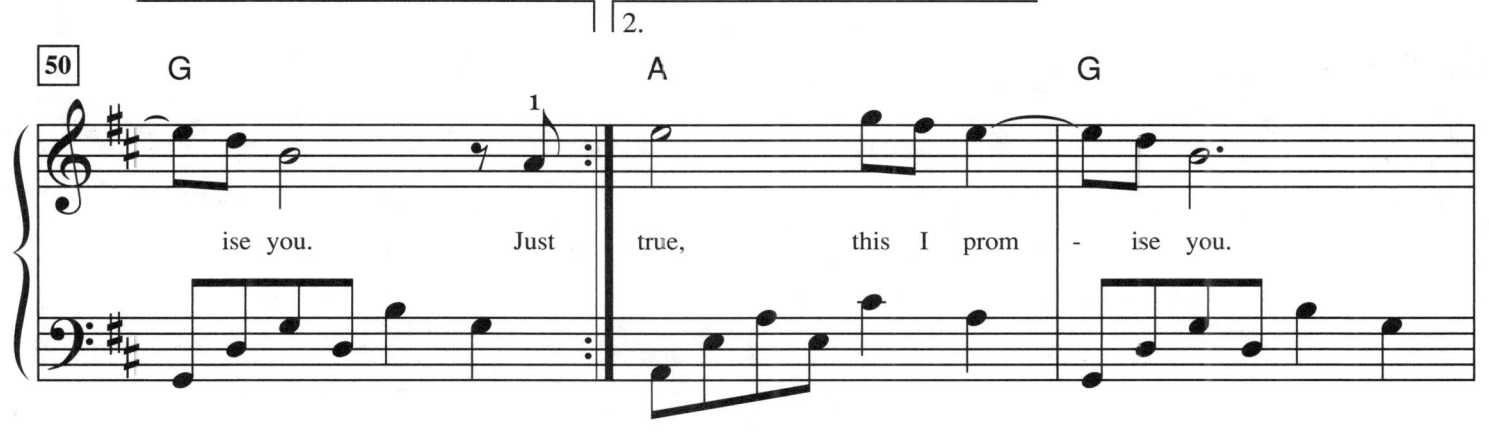
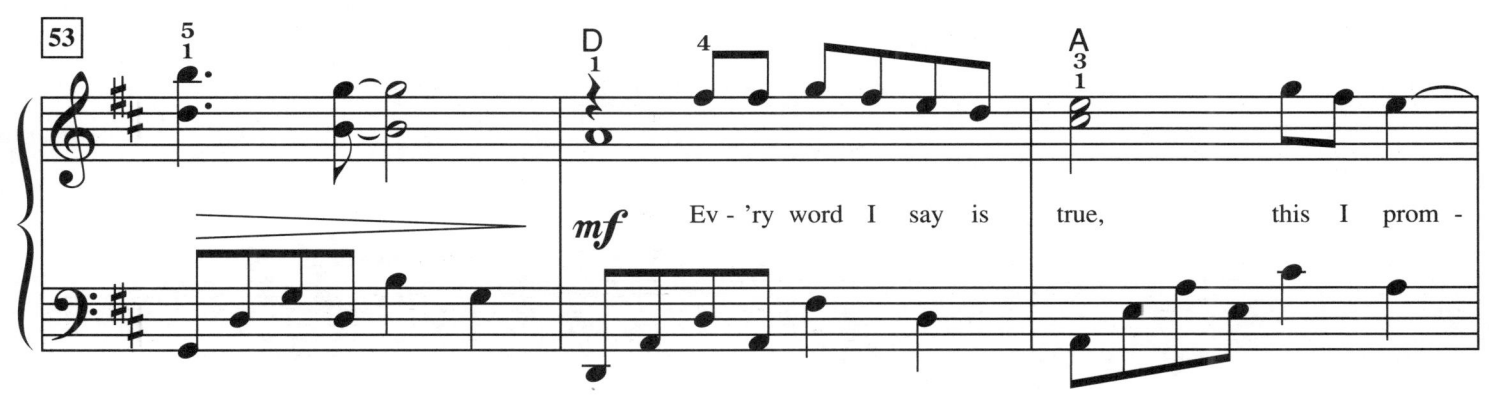

THIS KISS

Words and Music by Robin Lerner,
Annie Roboff and Beth Nielsen Chapman
Arranged by Dan Coates

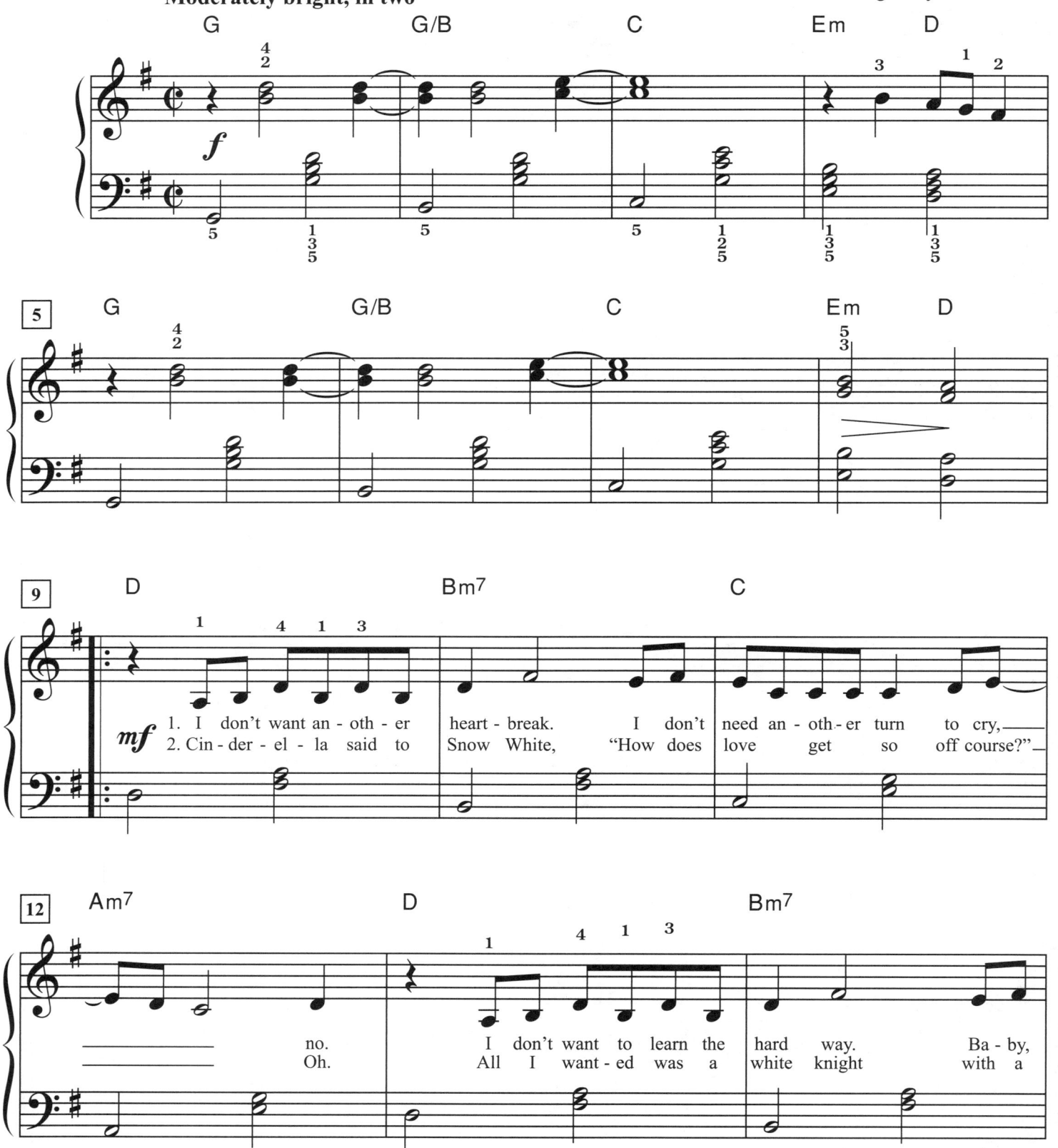

© 1998 WARNER-TAMERLANE PUBLISHING CORP., BUG MUSIC, INC., ALMO MUSIC CORP.,
BUGHOUSE MUSIC and R2M MUSIC LUX SARL
All Rights Reserved

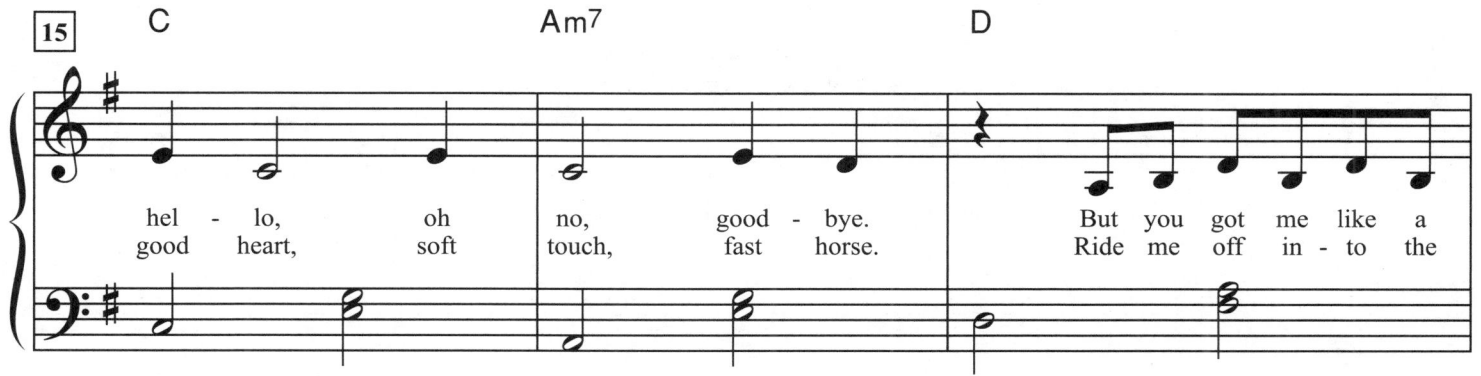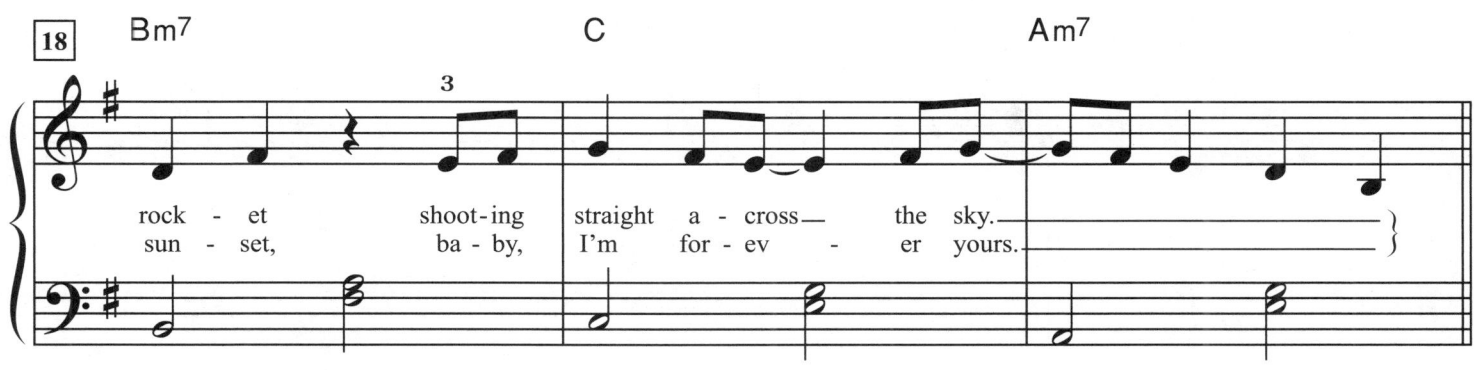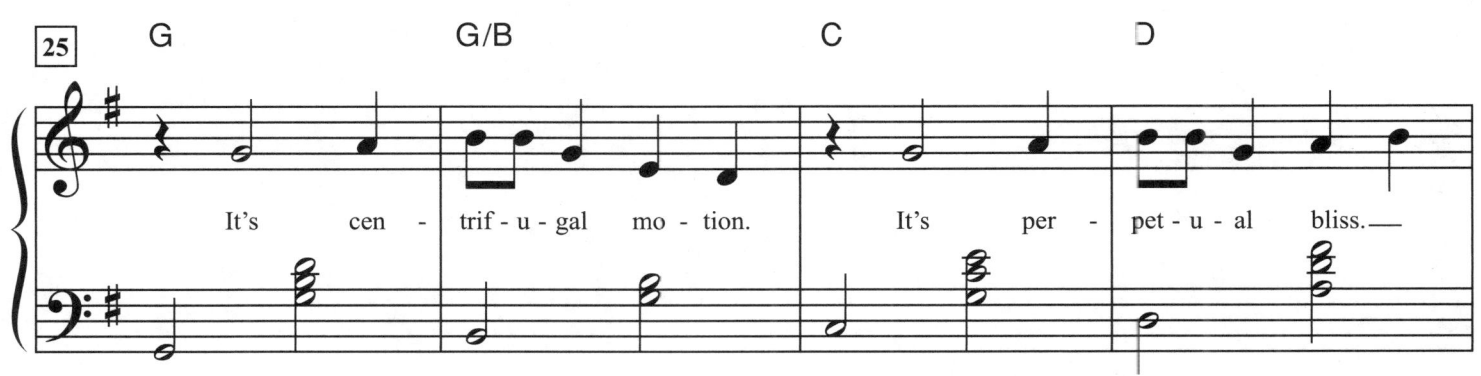

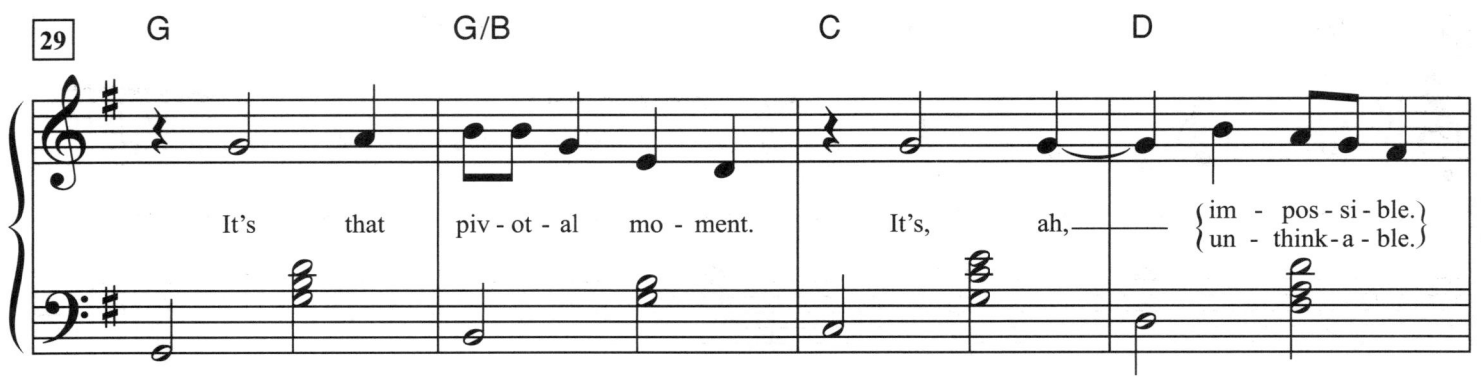
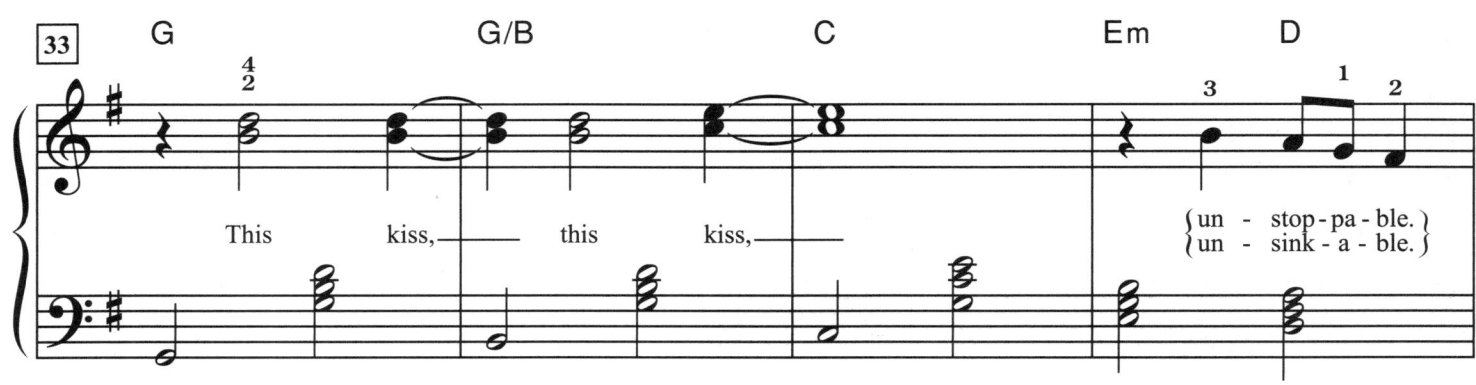
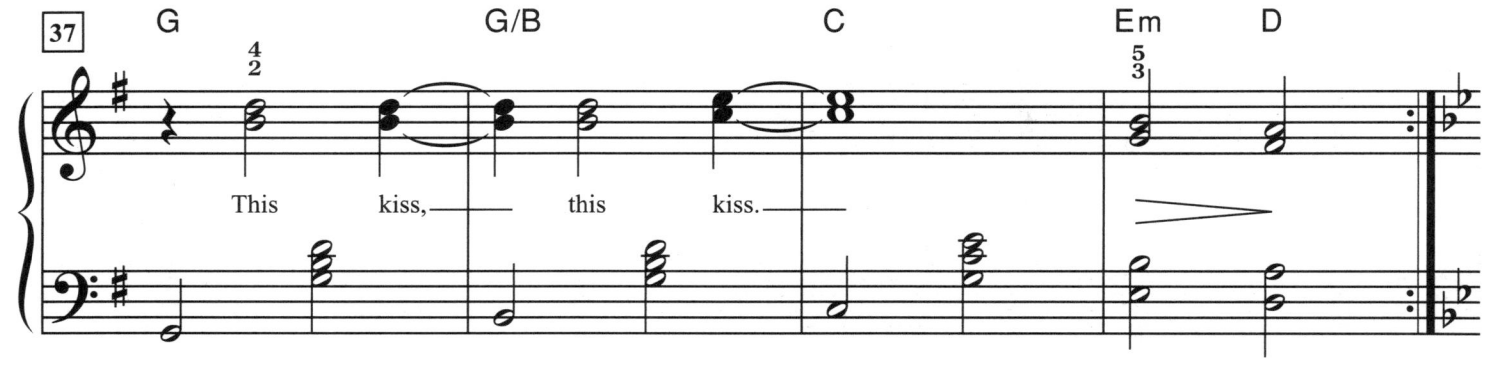
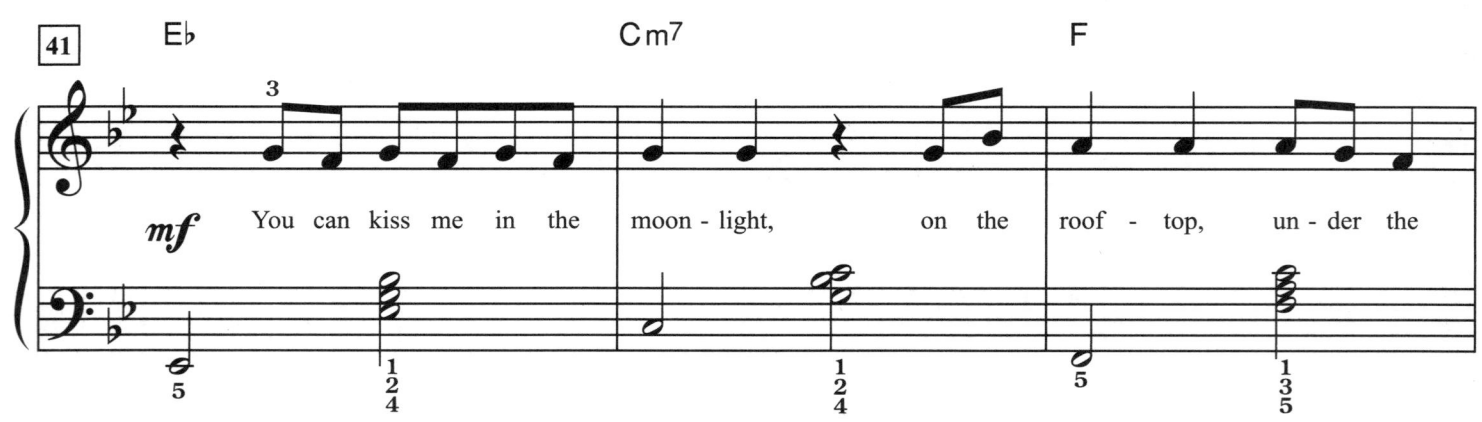

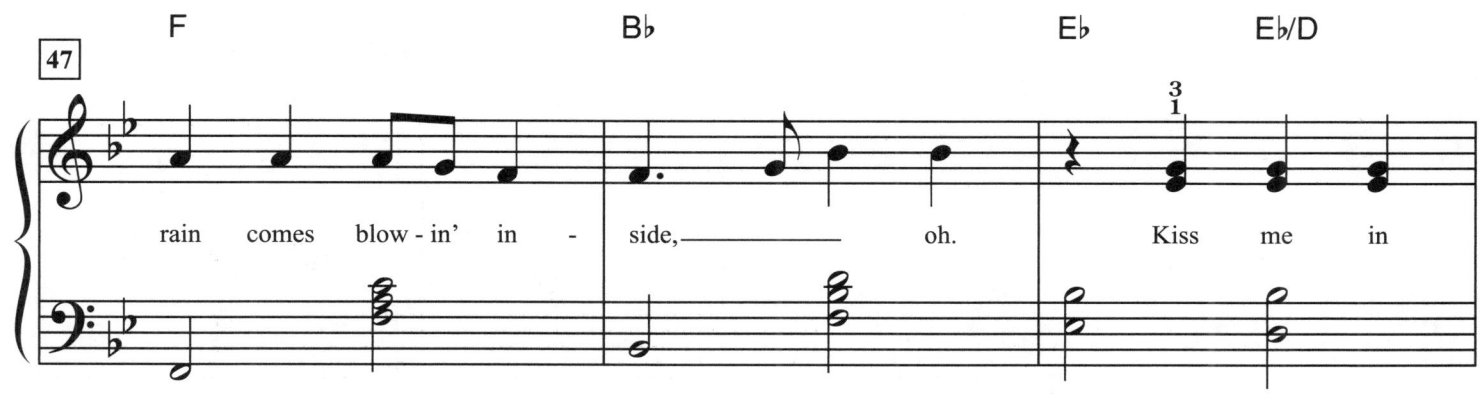
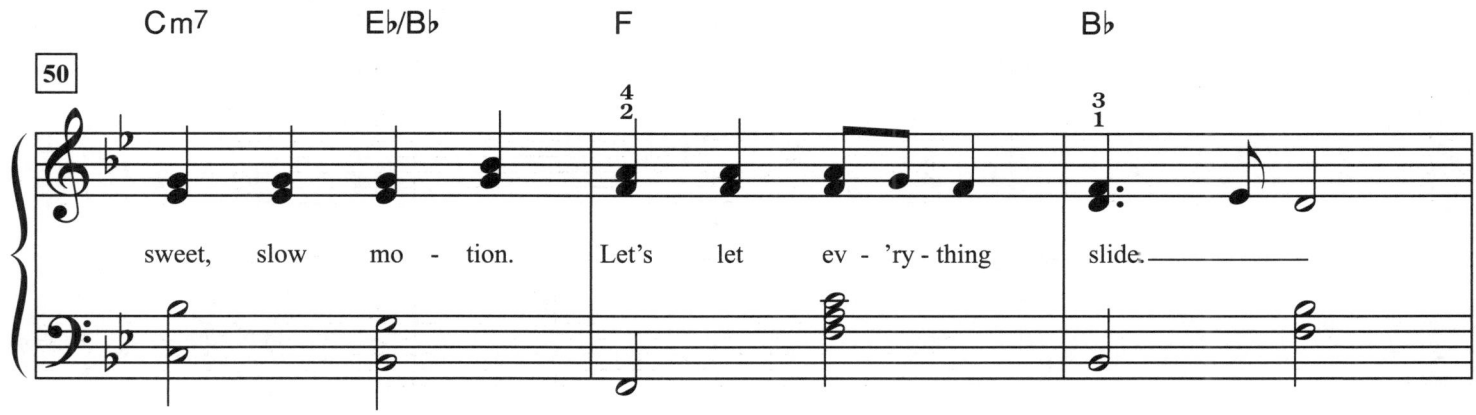
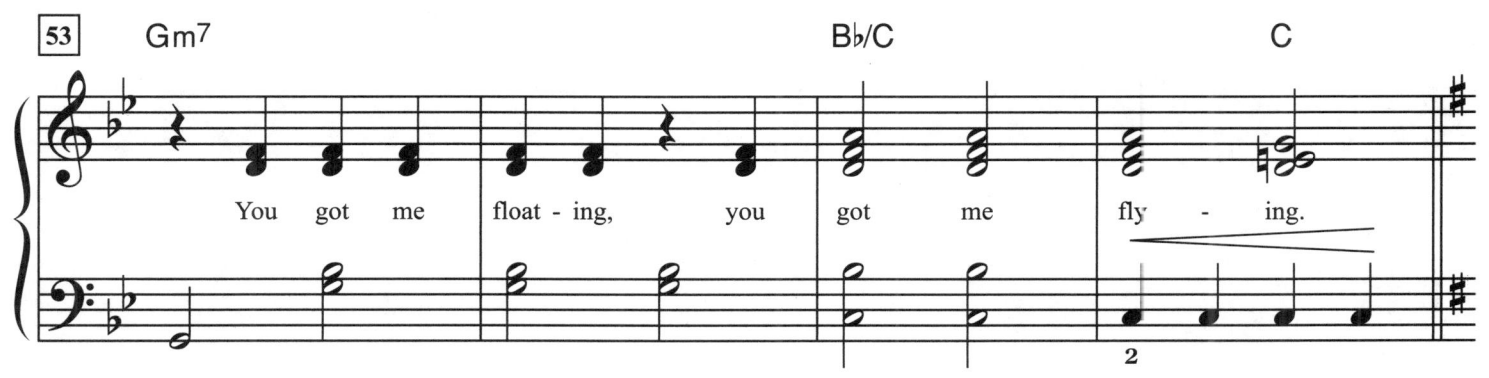

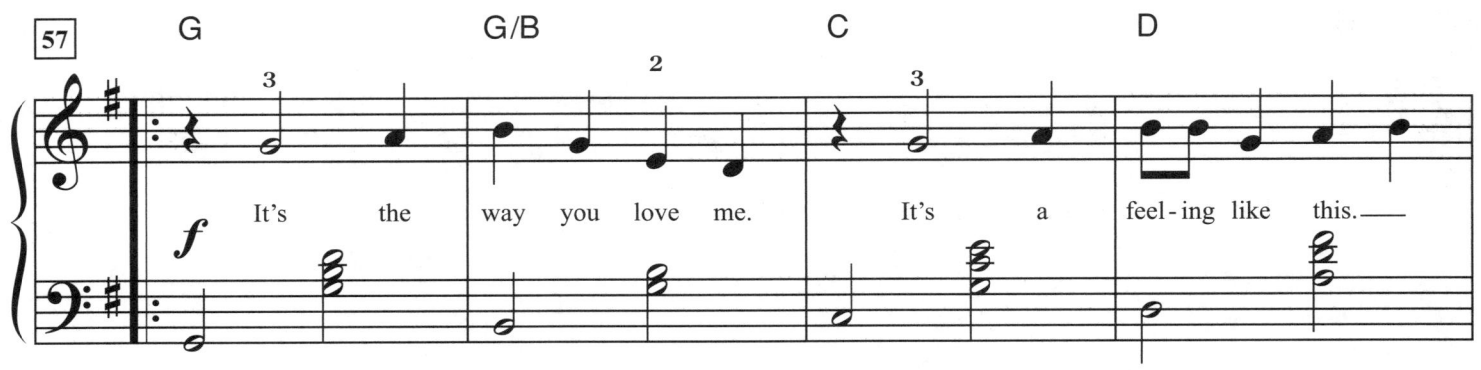
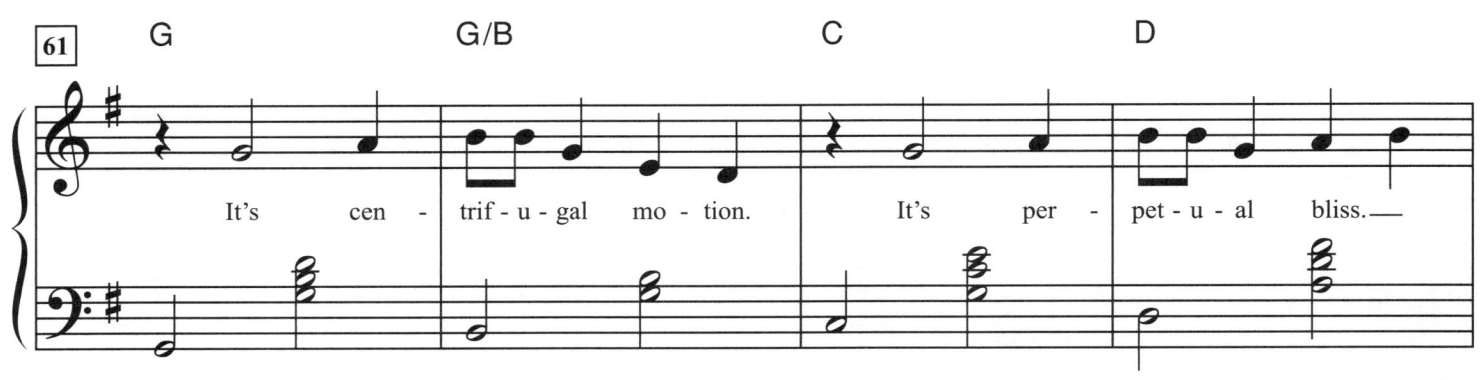
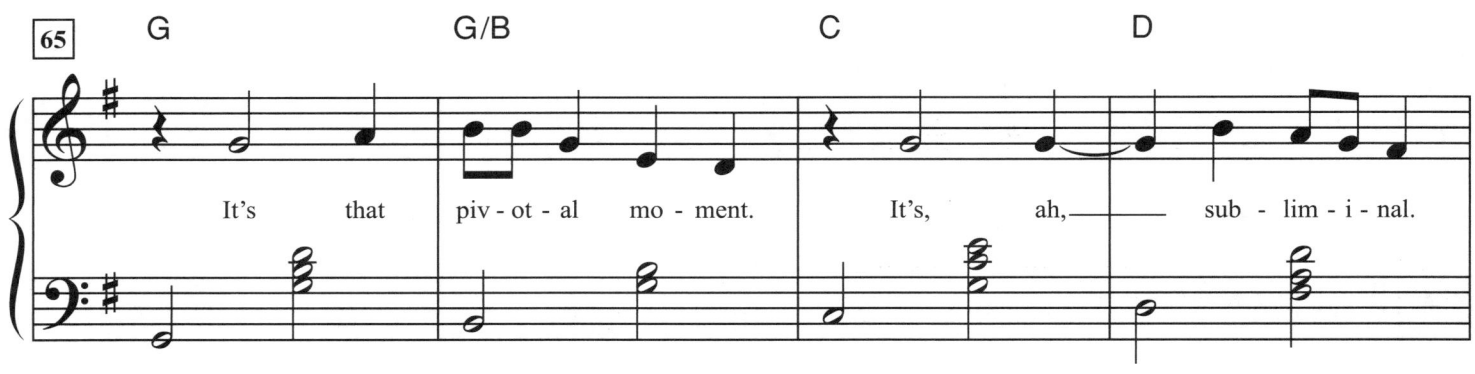
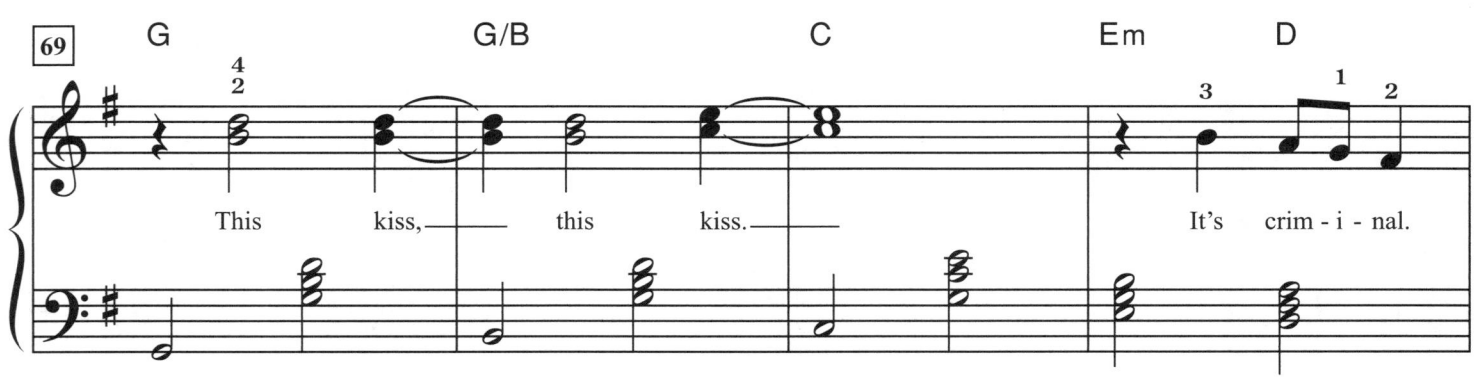

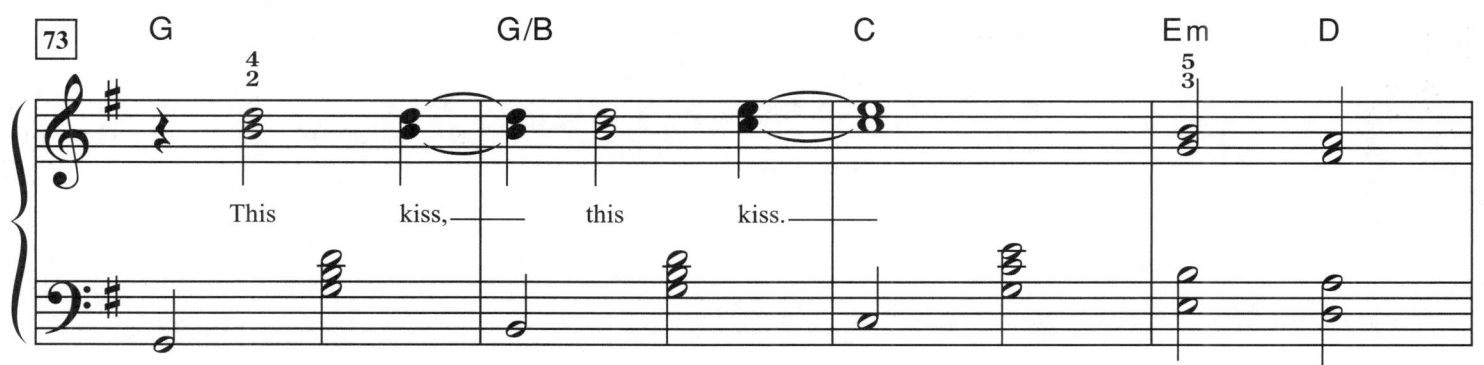
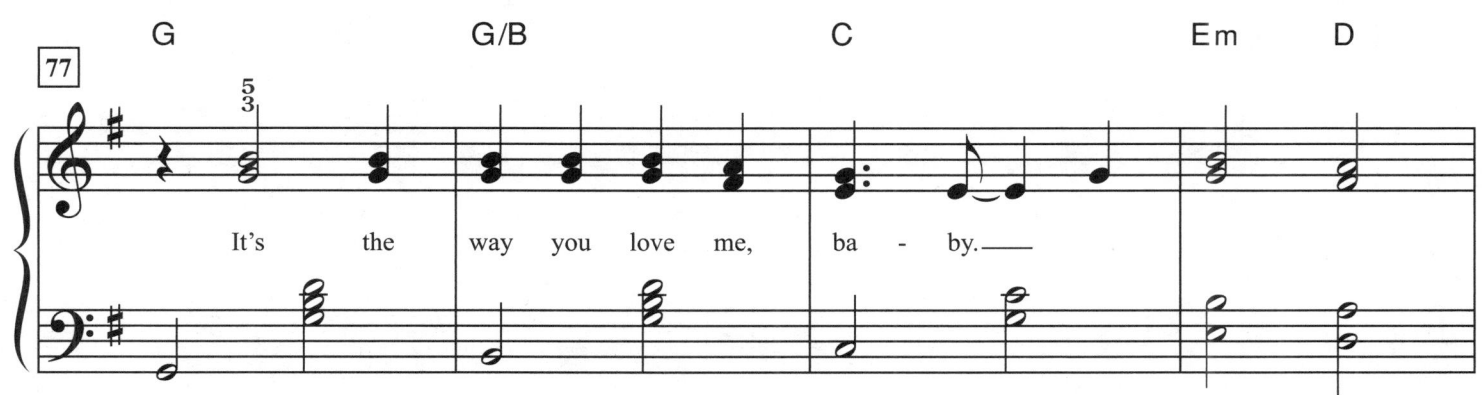
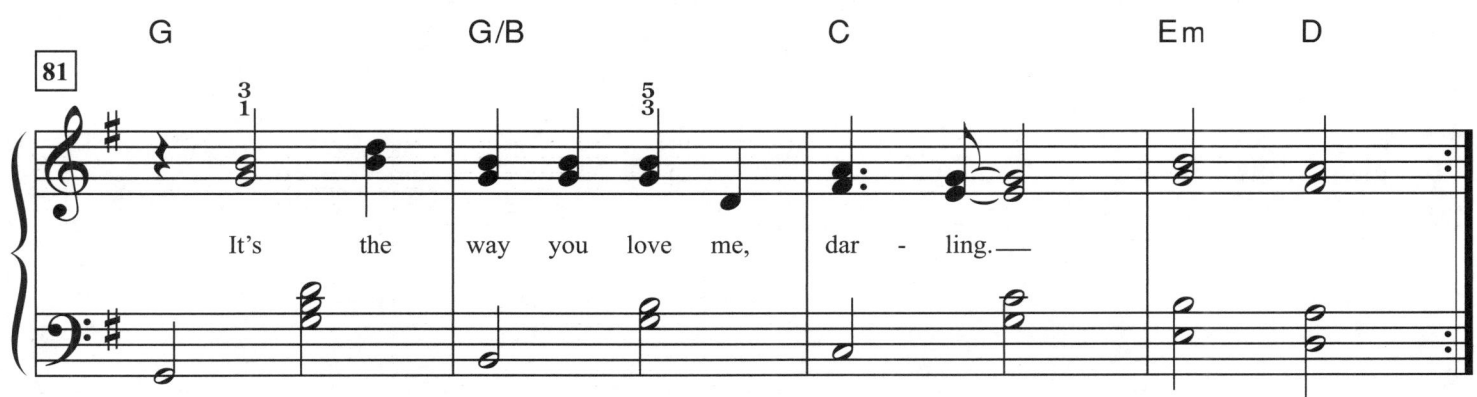
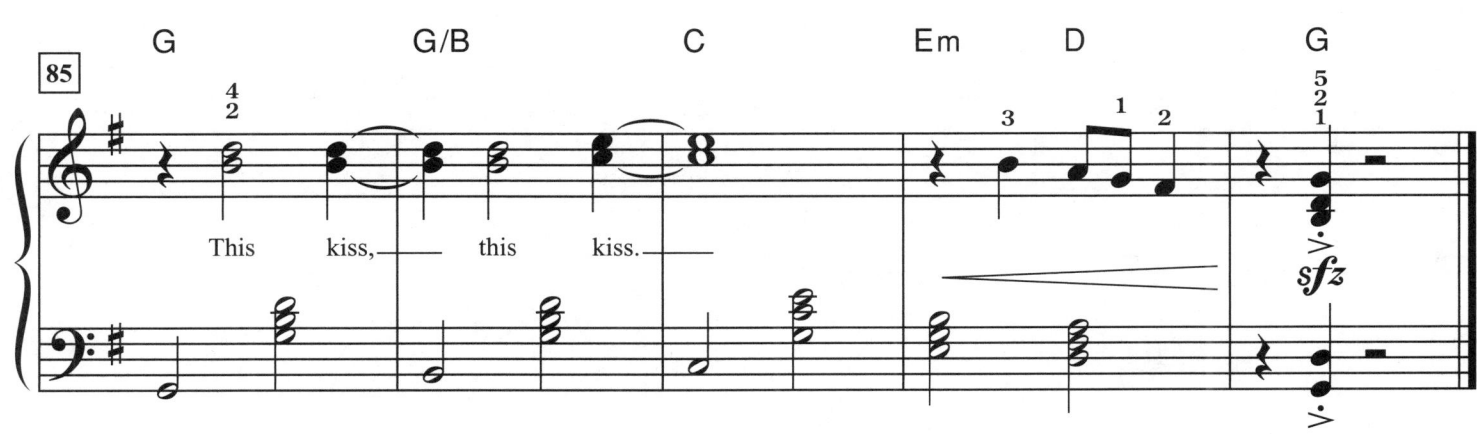

THIS MAGIC MOMENT

Words and Music by
Doc Pomus and Mort Shuman
Arranged by Dan Coates

© 1960 (Renewed) UNICHAPPELL MUSIC INC.
All Rights Reserved

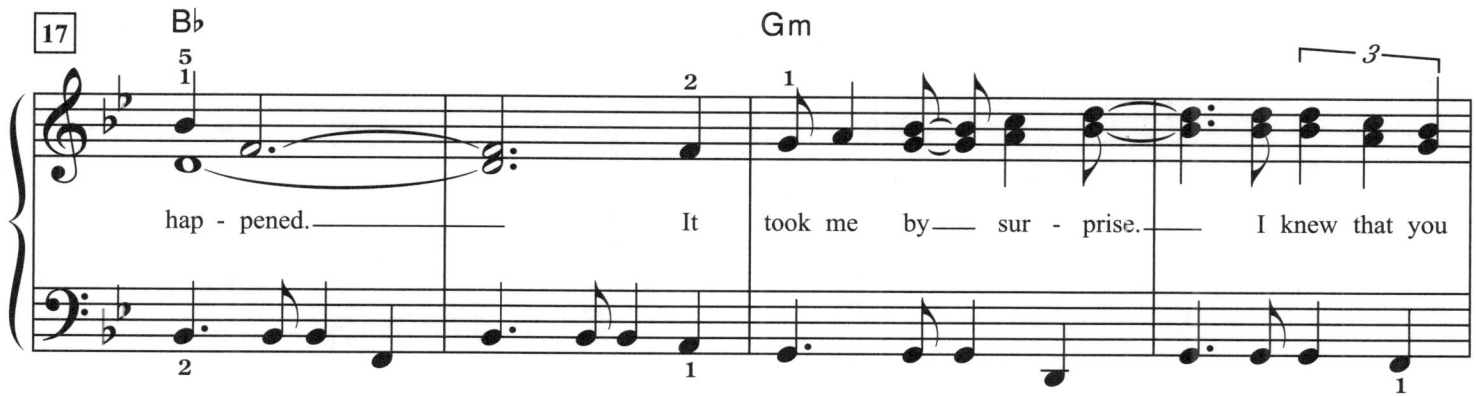

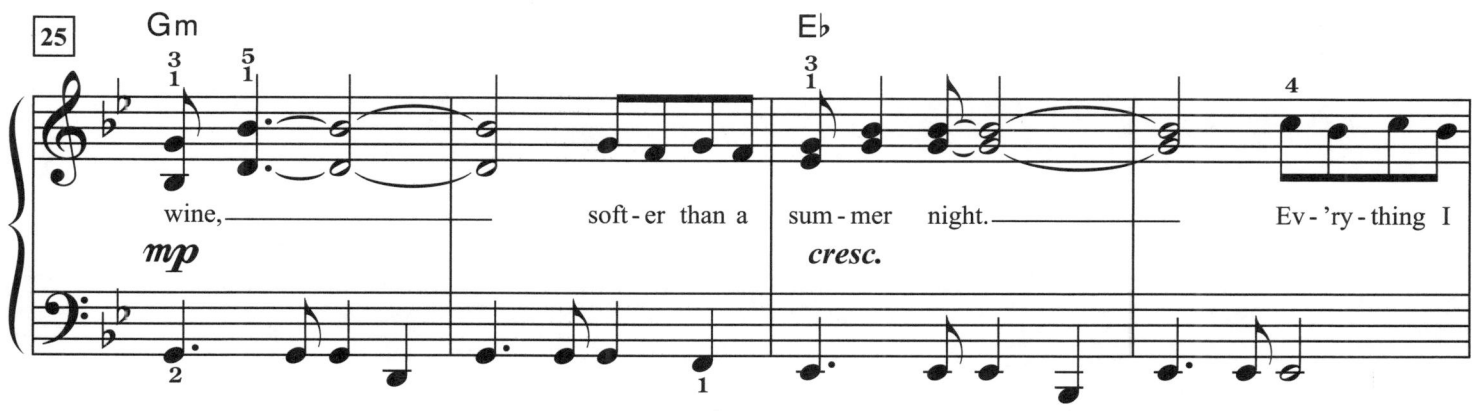
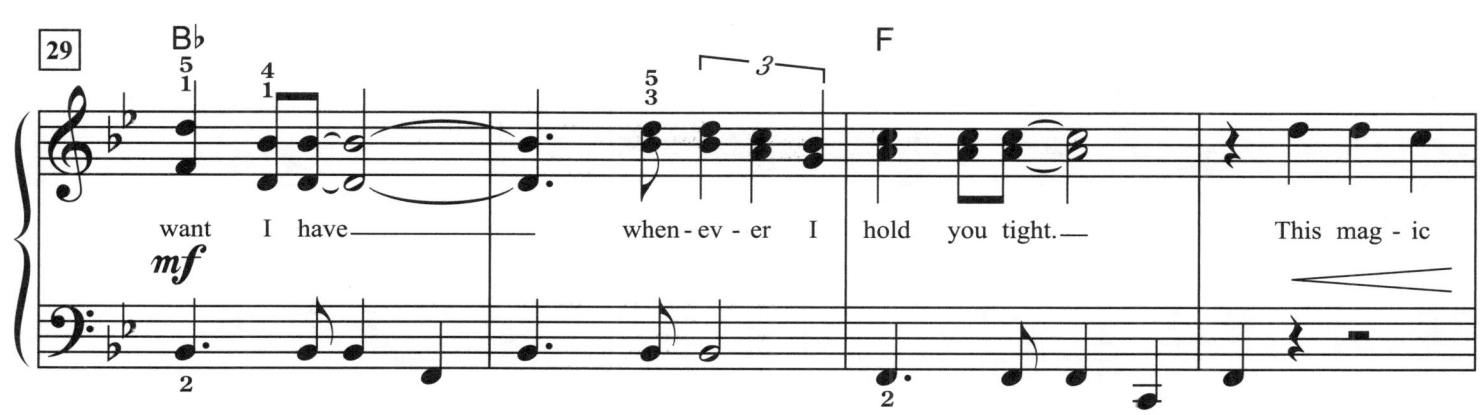

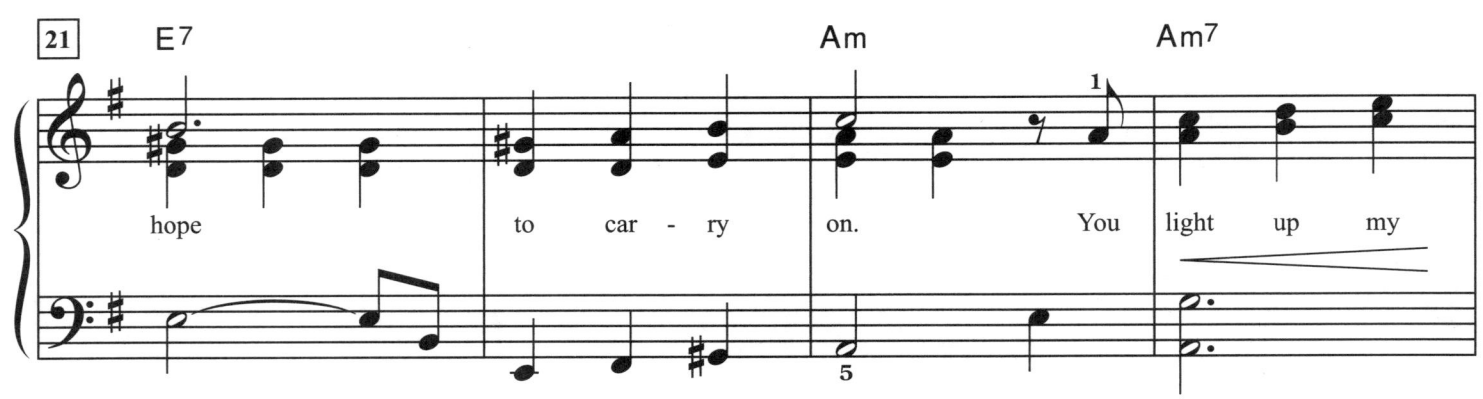
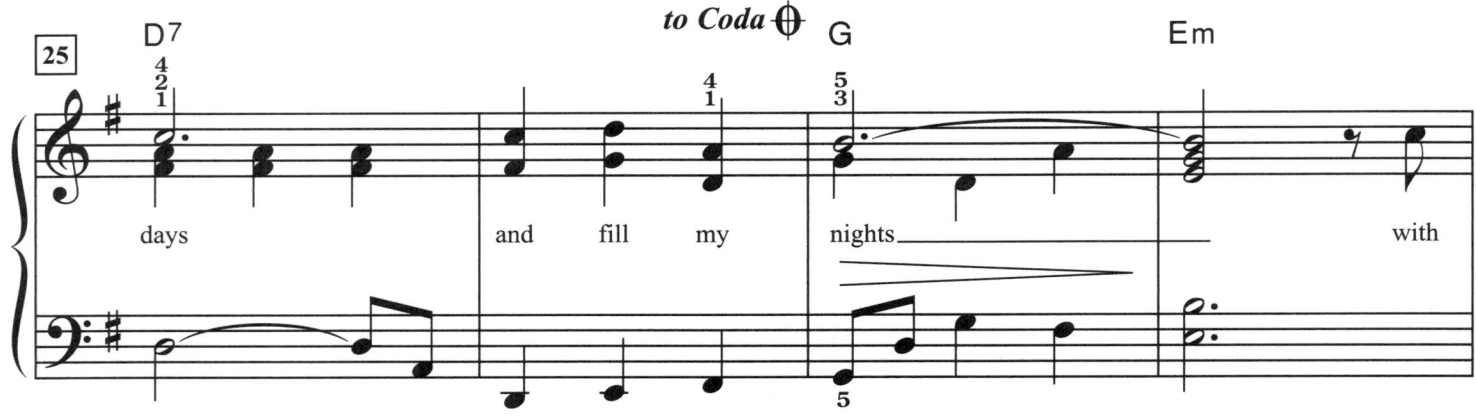
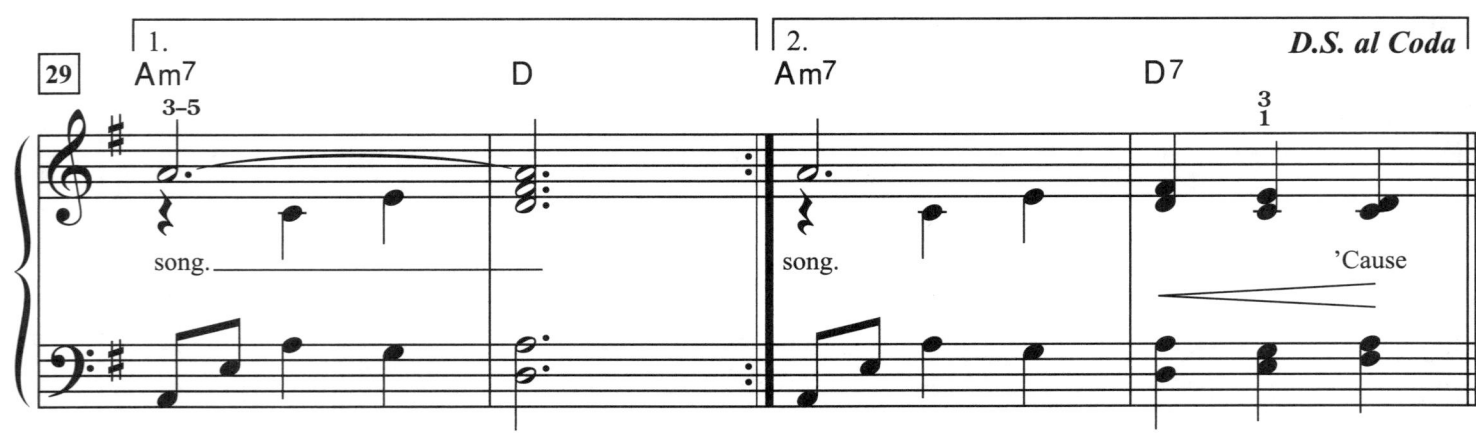

UP WHERE WE BELONG

Words by Will Jennings
Music by Jack Nitzsche and Buffy Sainte-Marie
Arranged by Dan Coates

© 1982 ENSIGN MUSIC CORP. and SONY/ATV HARMONY, 8 Music Square West, Nashville, TN 37203
All Rights Reserved

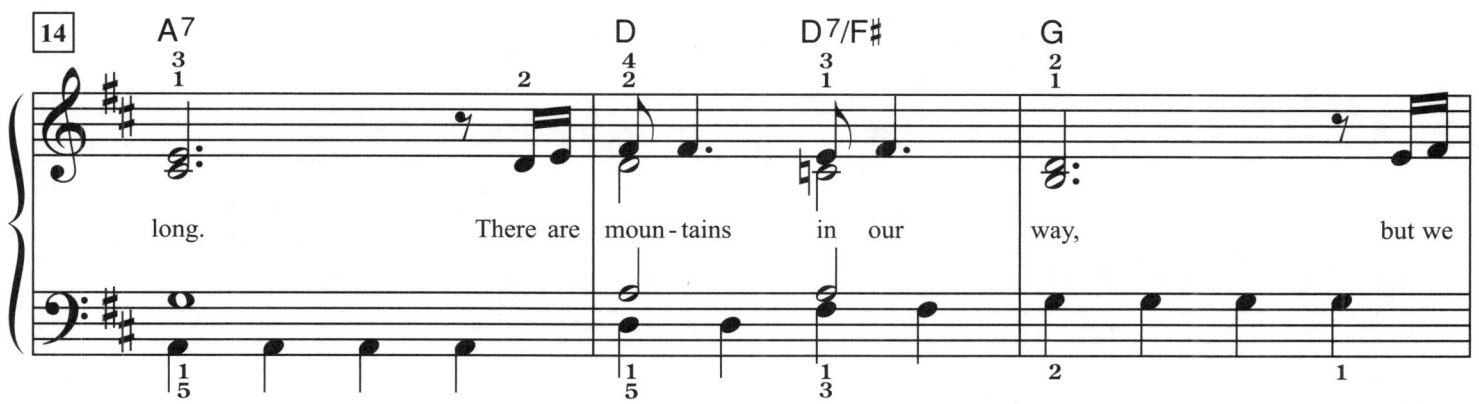
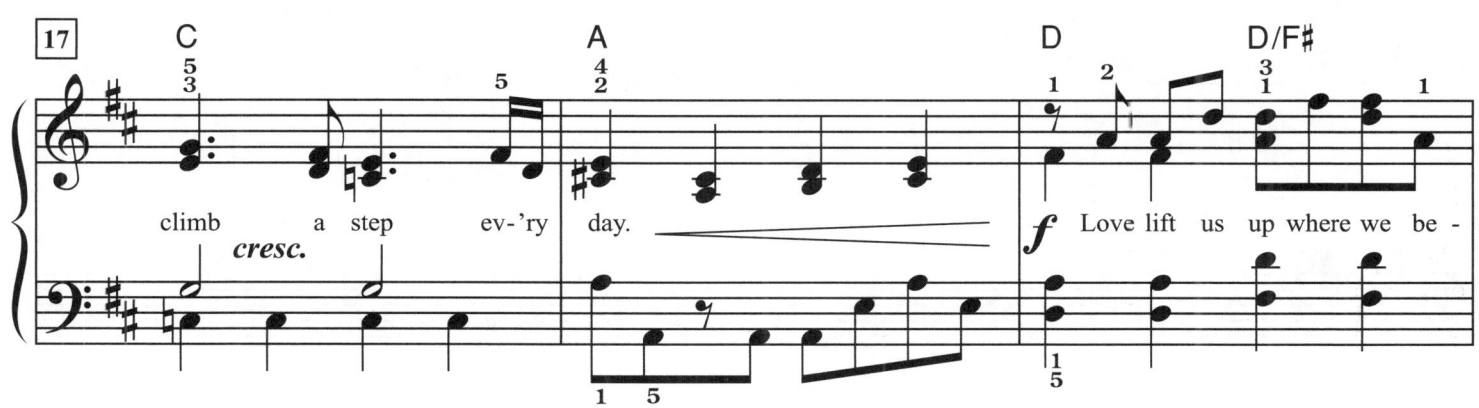
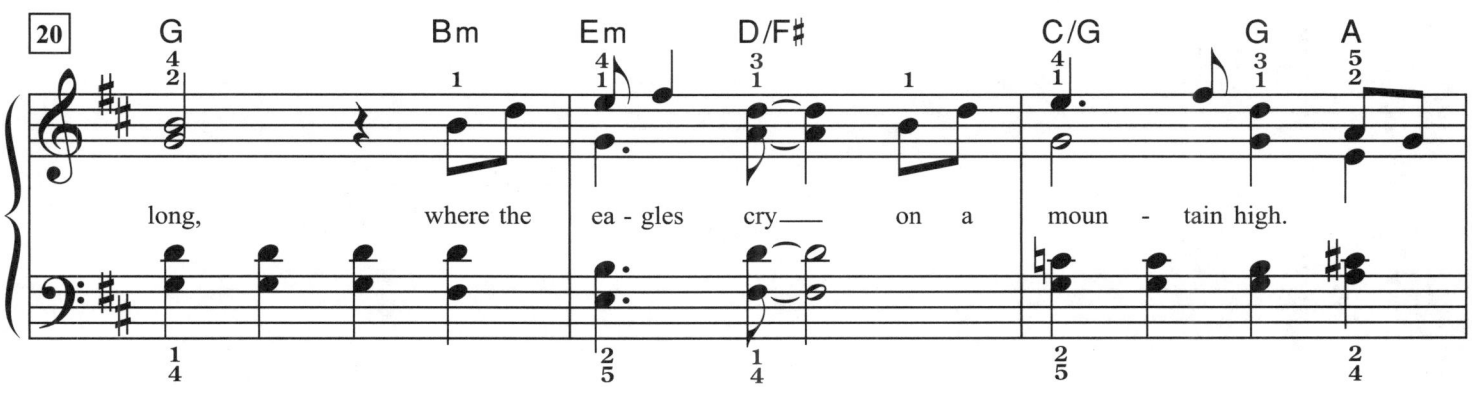
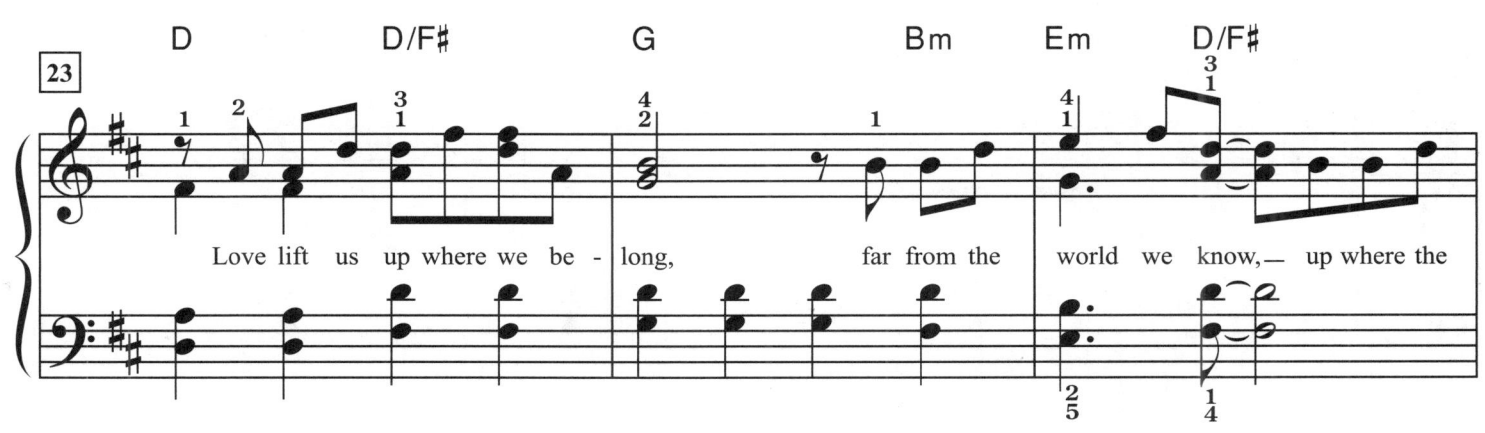

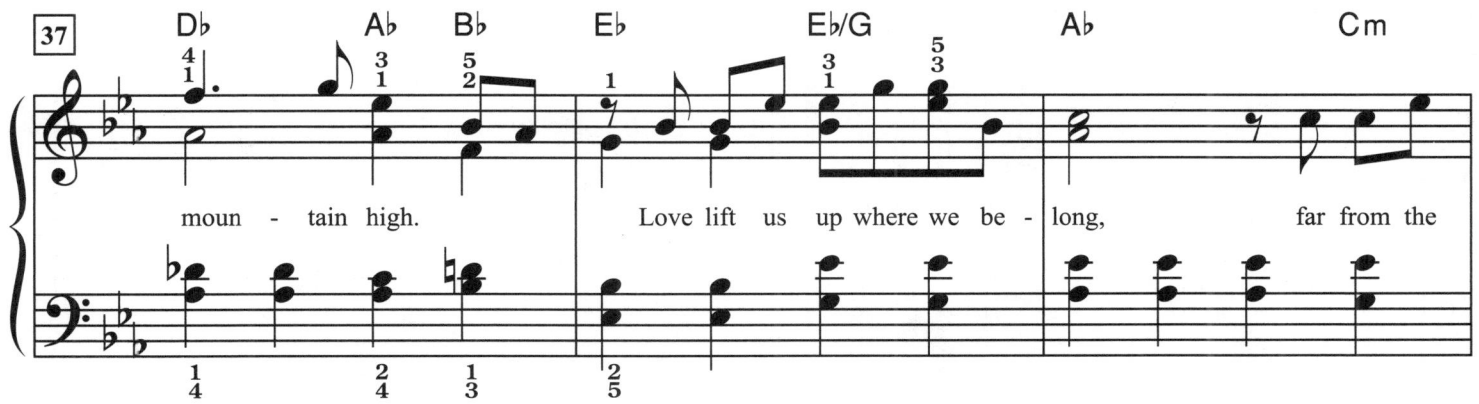
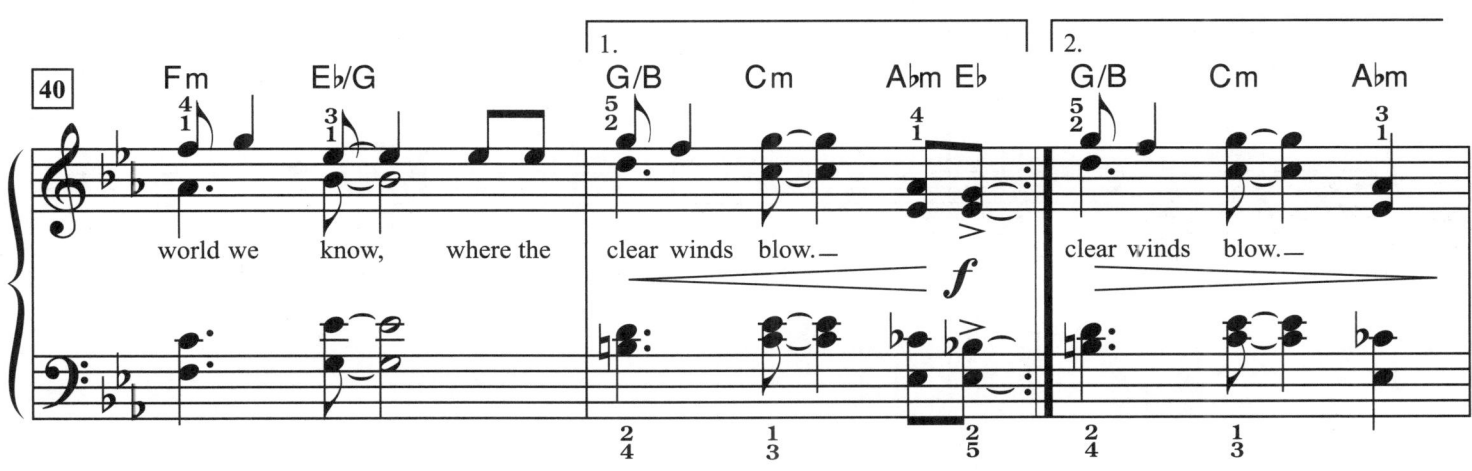
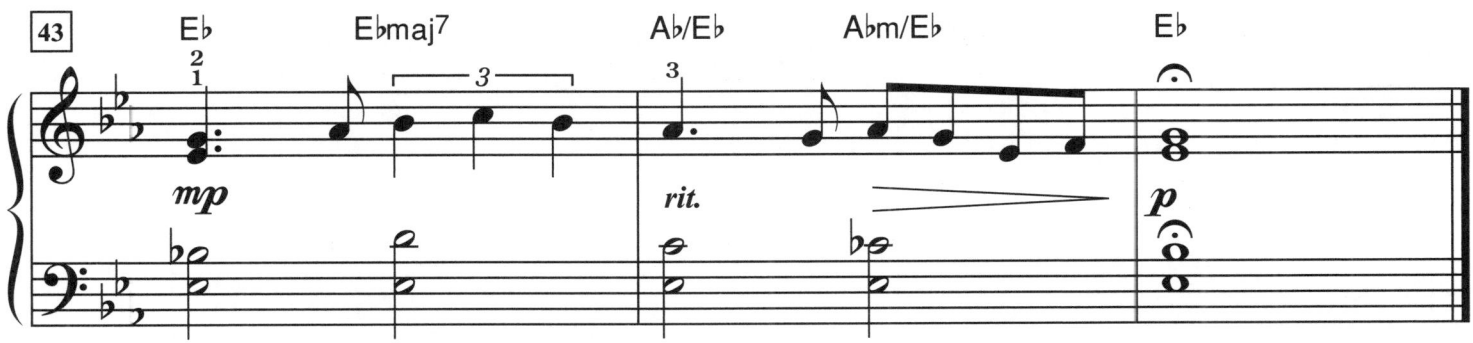

Verse 2:
Some hang on to "used-to-be,"
Live their lives looking behind.
All we have is here and now;
All our life, out there to find.
The road is long.
There are mountains in our way,
But we climb them a step every day.

VALENTINE

Words and Music by
Jim Brickman and Jack Kugell
Arranged by Dan Coates

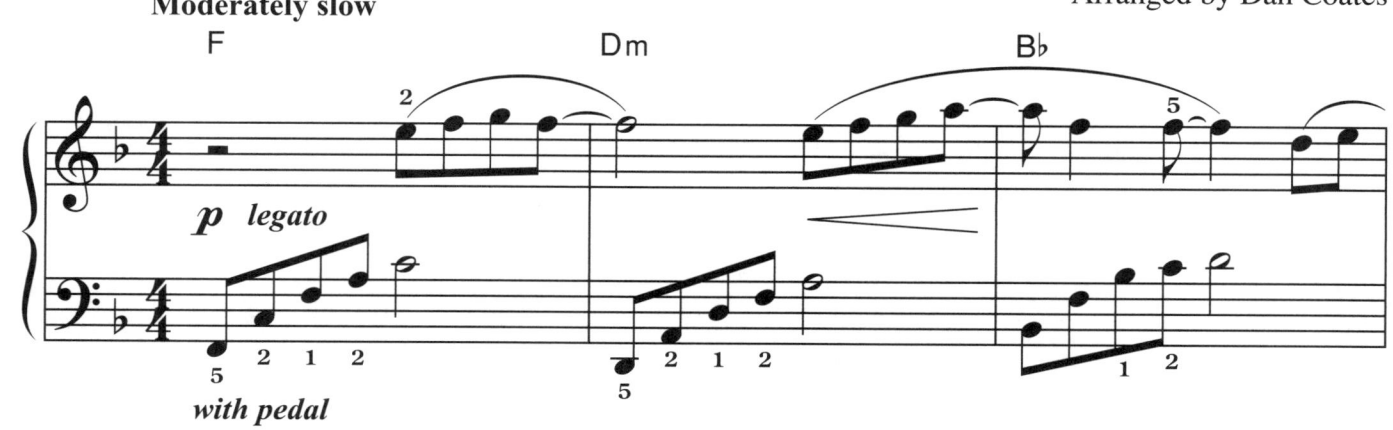

© 1996 BRICKMAN ARRANGEMENT and EMI APRIL MUSIC INC./DOXIE MUSIC
Print Rights for BRICKMAN ARRANGEMENT Administered Worldwide by
ALFRED PUBLISHING CO., INC.
All Rights Reserved

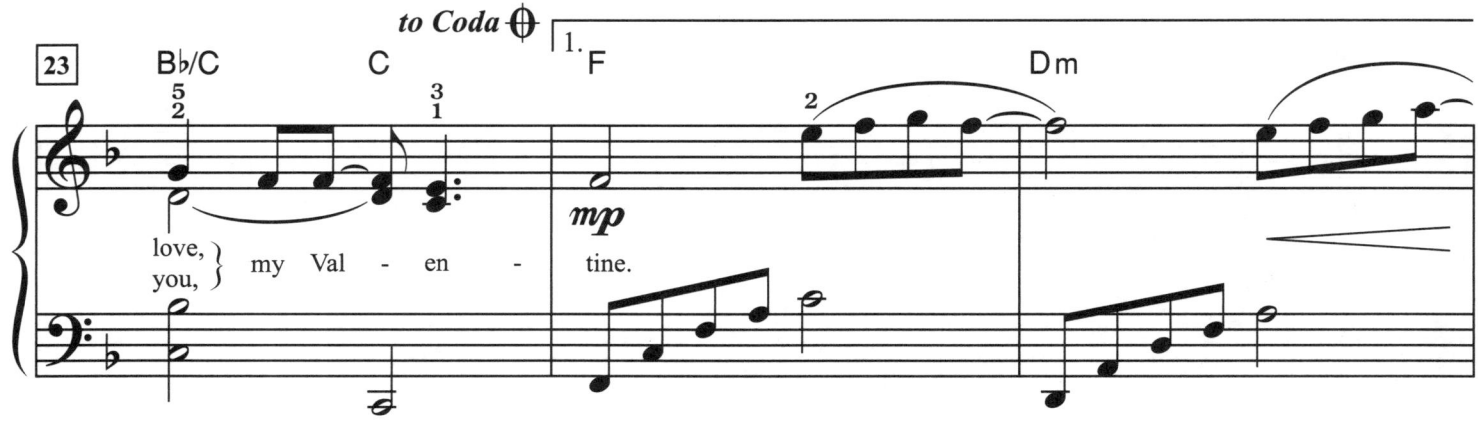
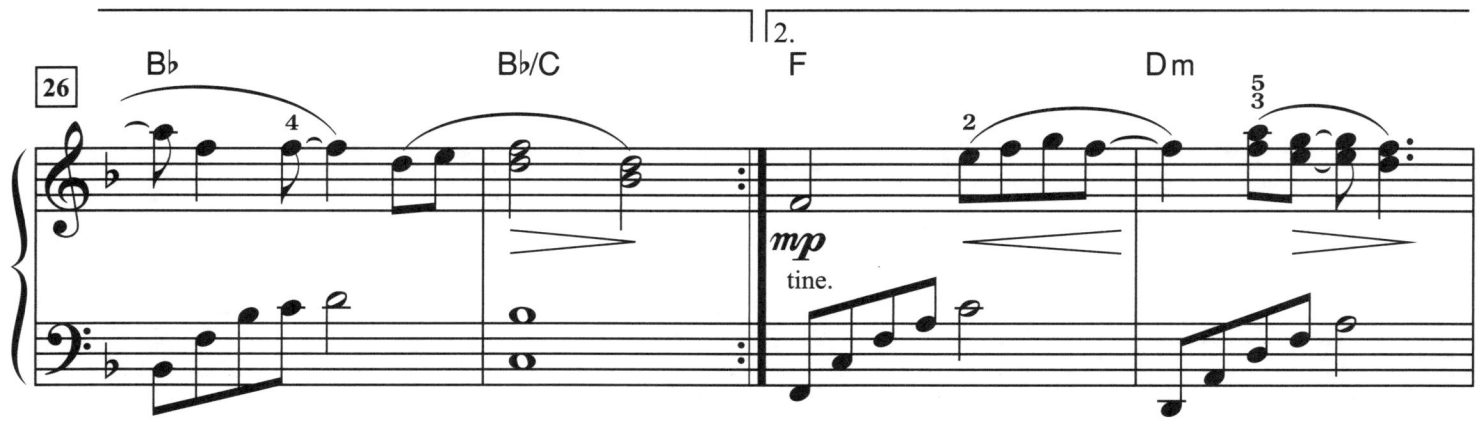
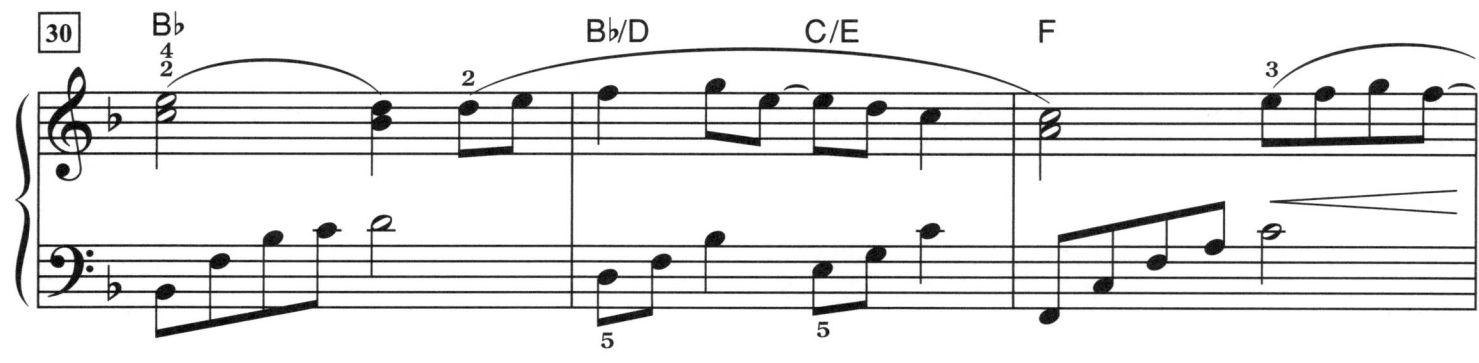
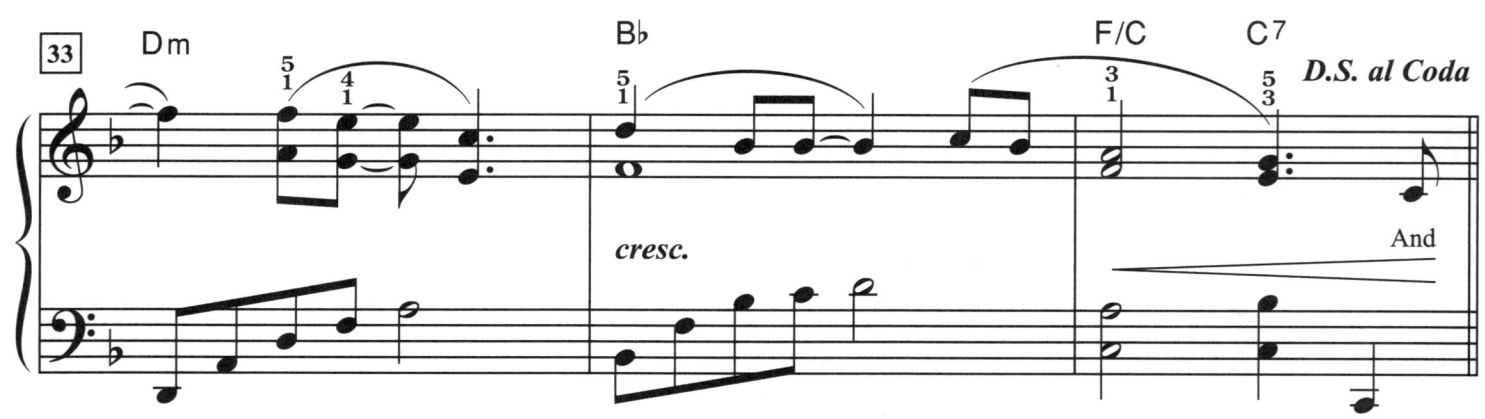

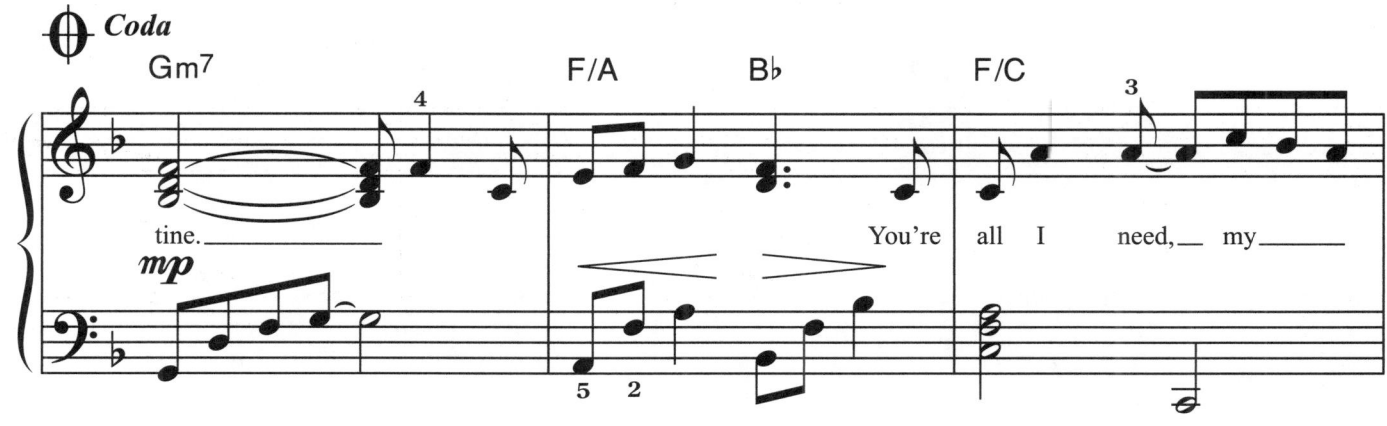
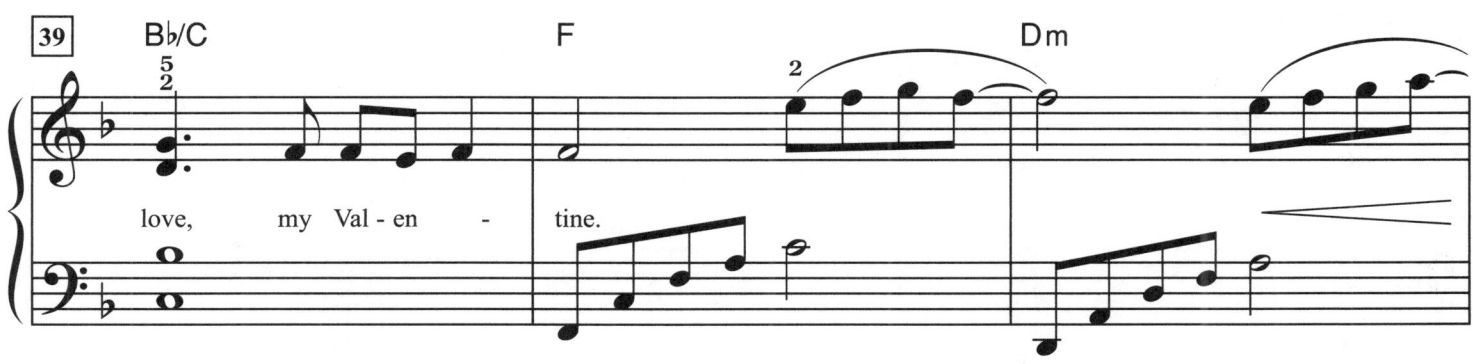
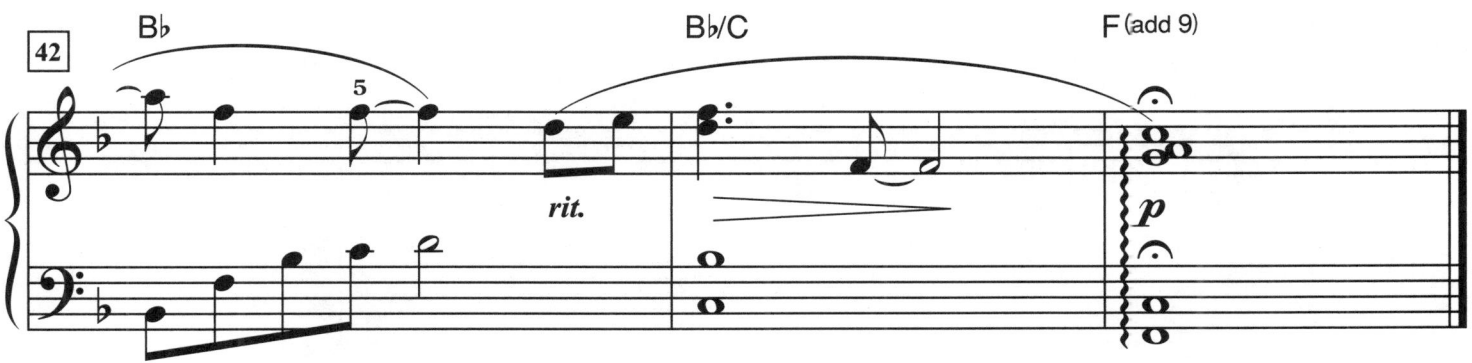

Verse 2:
All of my life,
I have been waiting for all you give to me.
You've opened my eyes
And shown me how to love unselfishly.
I've dreamed of this a thousand times before,
But in my dreams I couldn't love you more.
I will give you my heart until the end of time.
You're all I need, my love,
My Valentine.

WEEKEND IN NEW ENGLAND

Words and Music by Randy Edelman
Arranged by Dan Coates

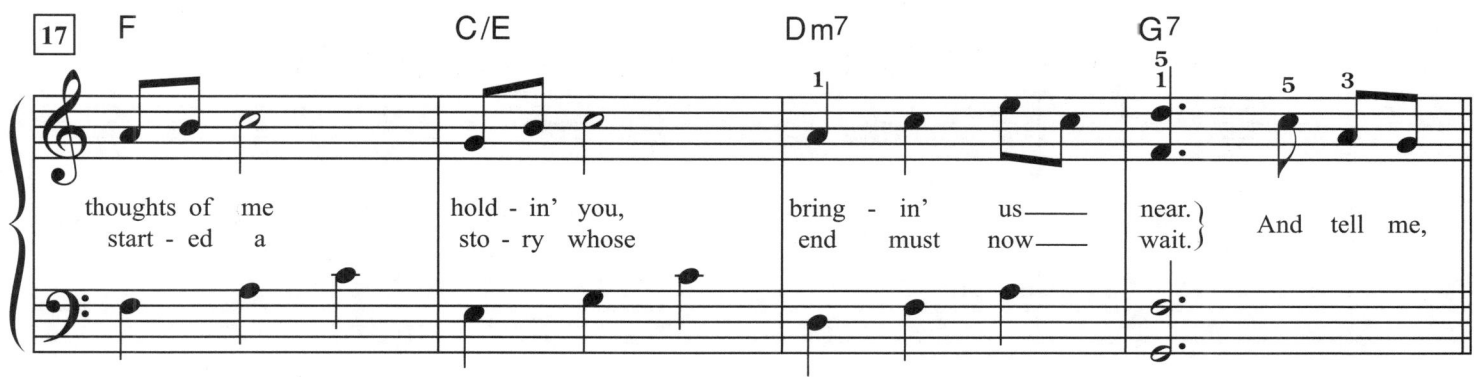
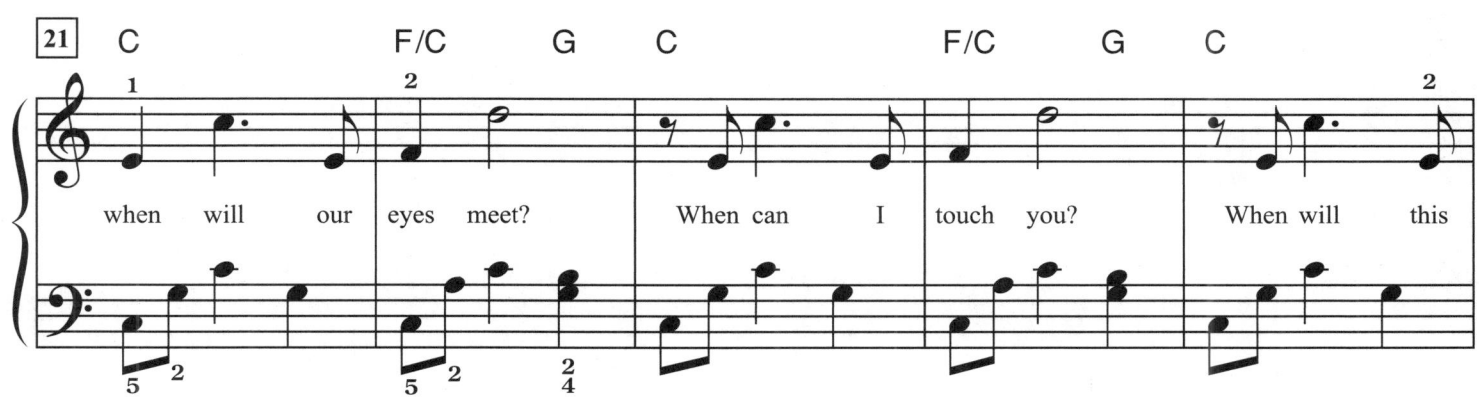
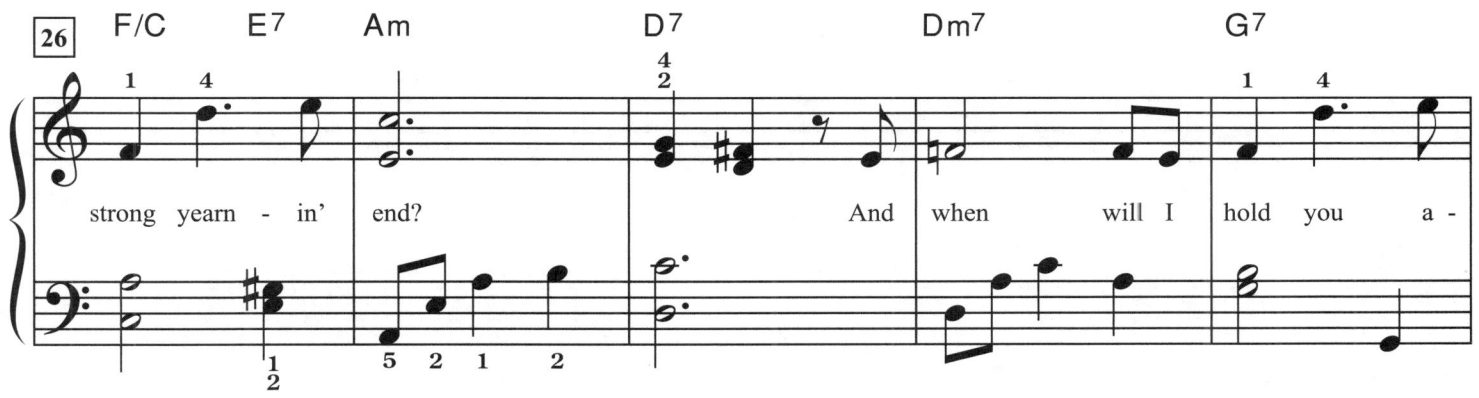
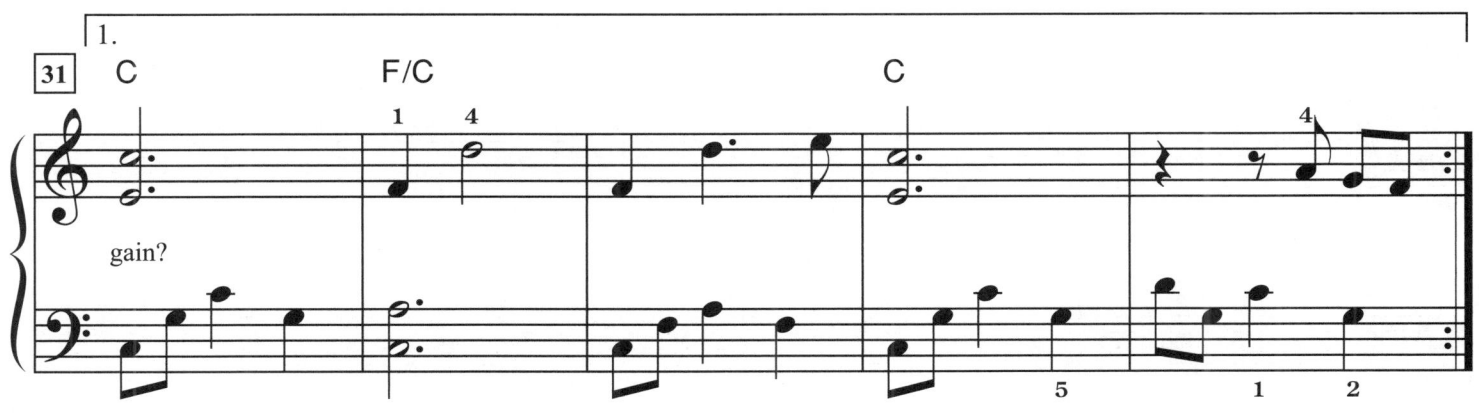

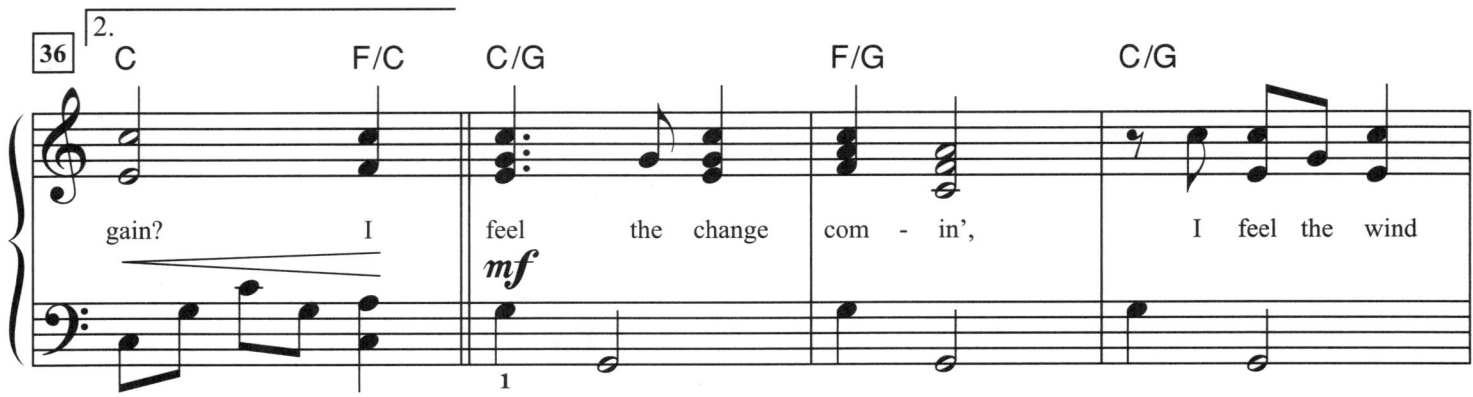
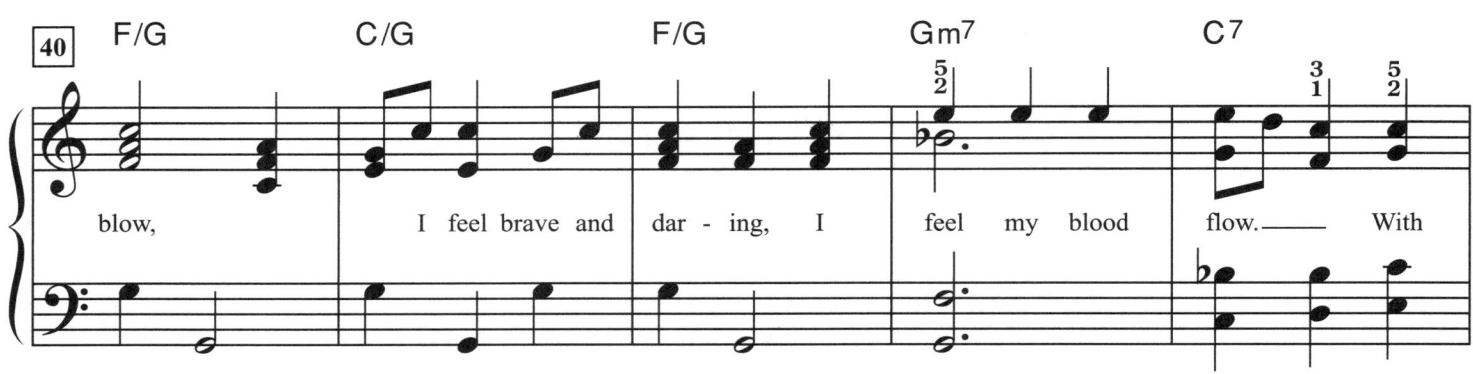
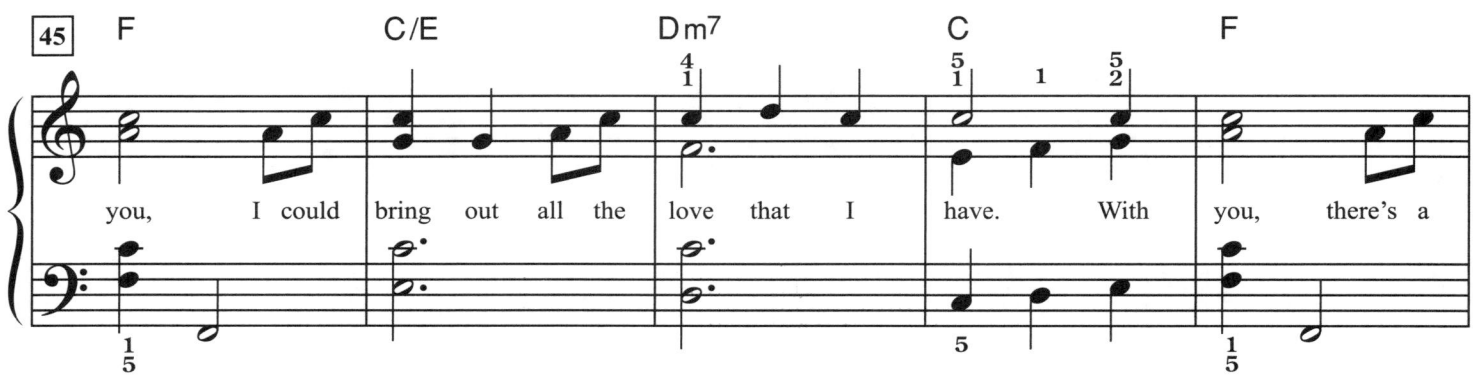
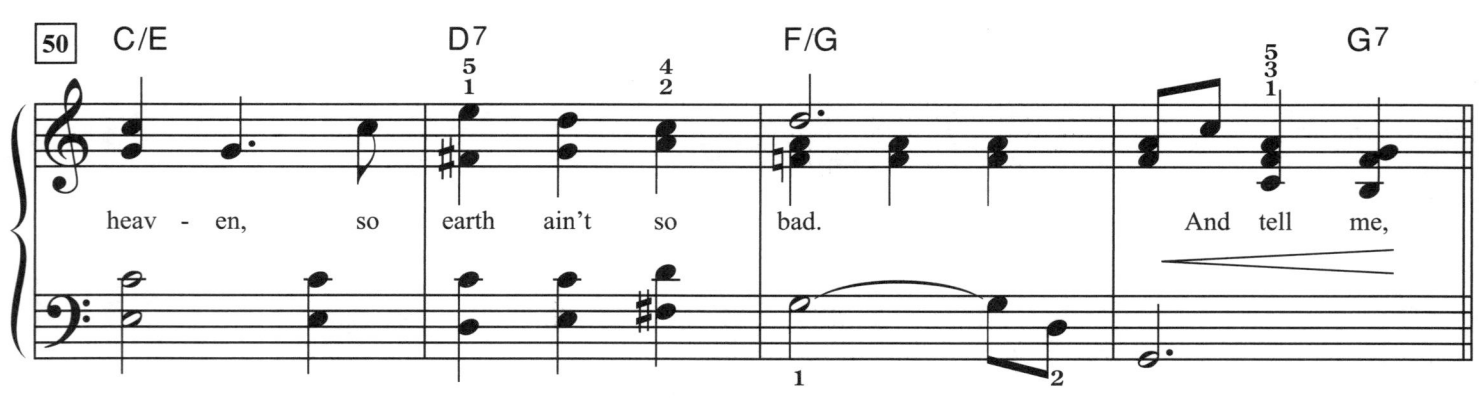

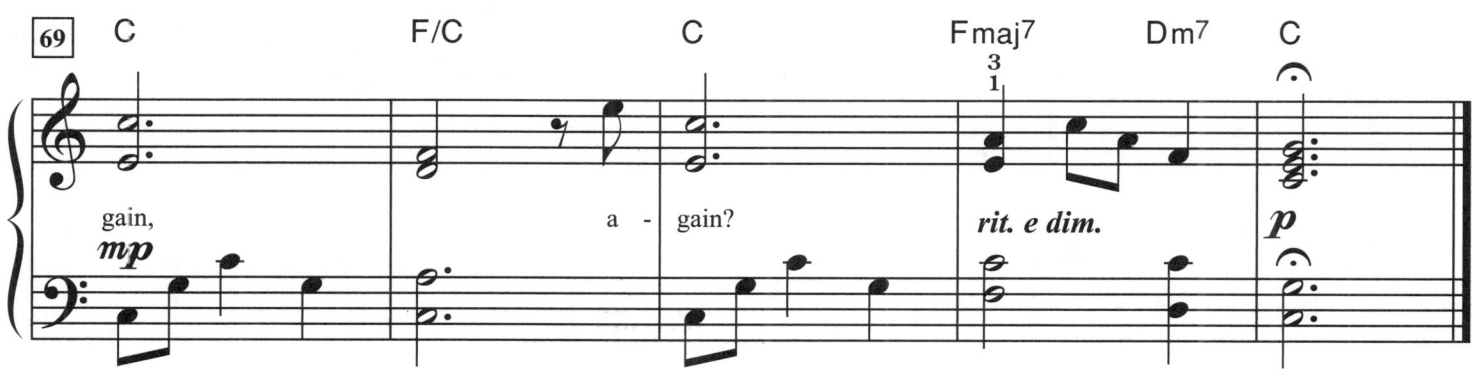

WHEN A MAN LOVES A WOMAN

Words and Music by
Calvin Lewis and Andrew Wright
Arranged by Dan Coates

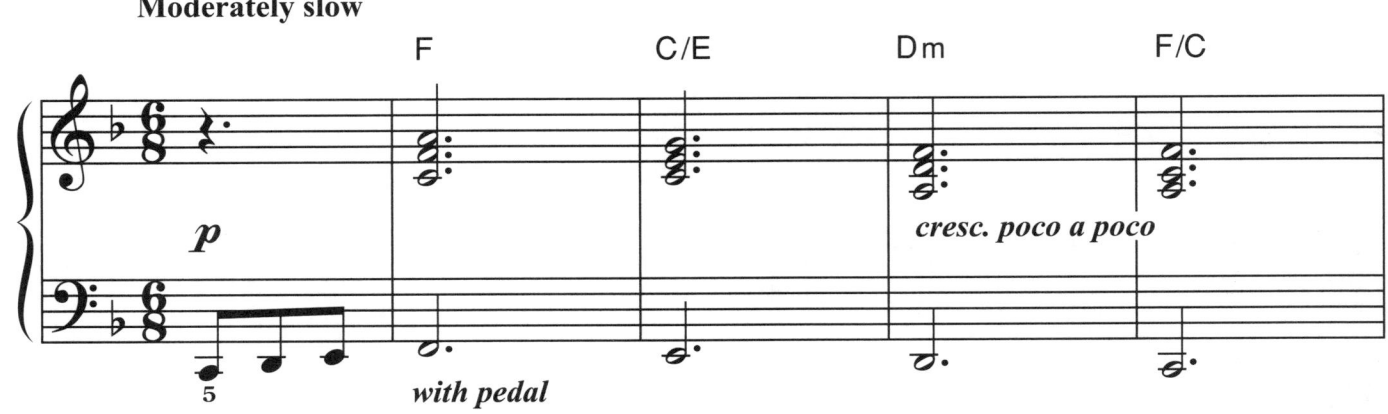

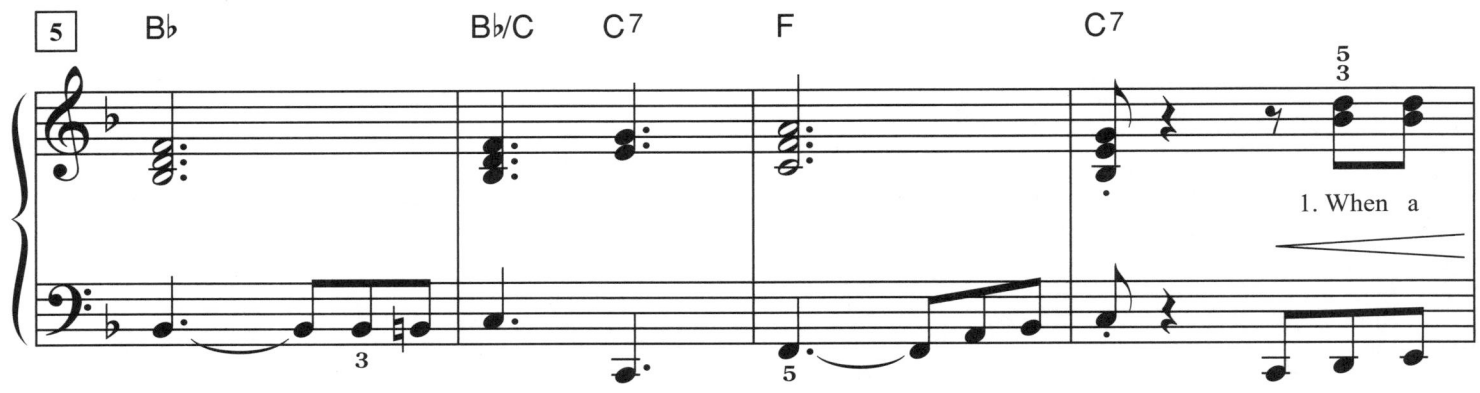

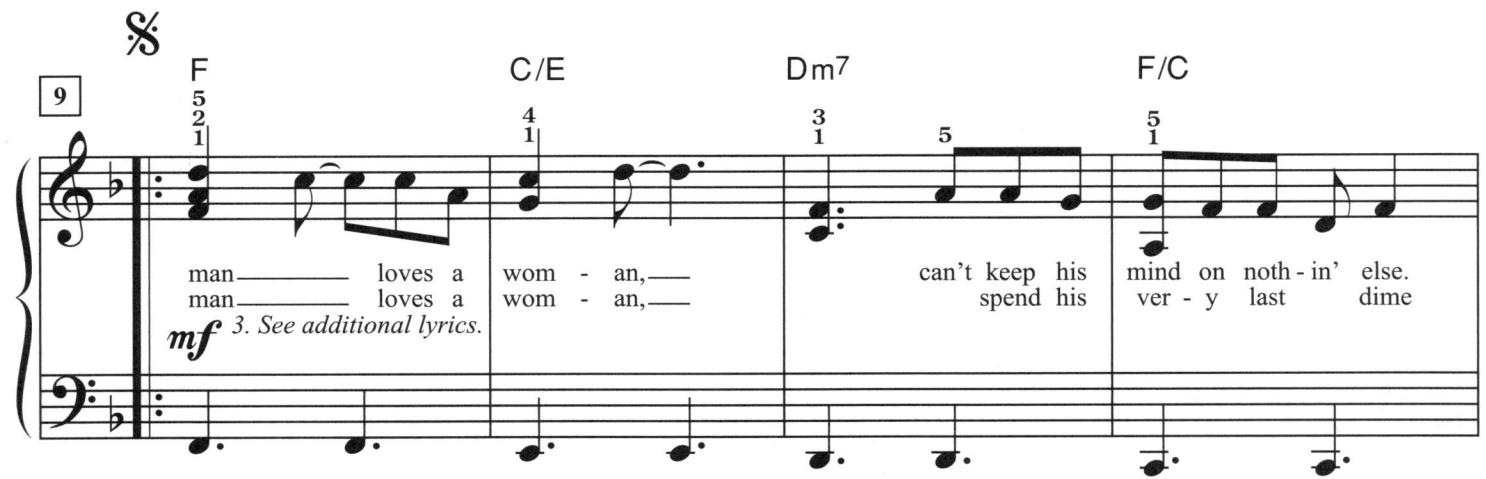

© 1966 (Renewed) PRONTO MUSIC, MIJAC MUSIC and QUINVY MUSIC PUBLISHING CO.
All Rights on behalf of itself and MIJAC MUSIC Administered by PRONTO MUSIC, INC.
All Rights for QUINVY MUSIC PUBLISHING CO. Administered by WARNER-TAMERLANE PUBLISHING CORP.
All Rights Reserved

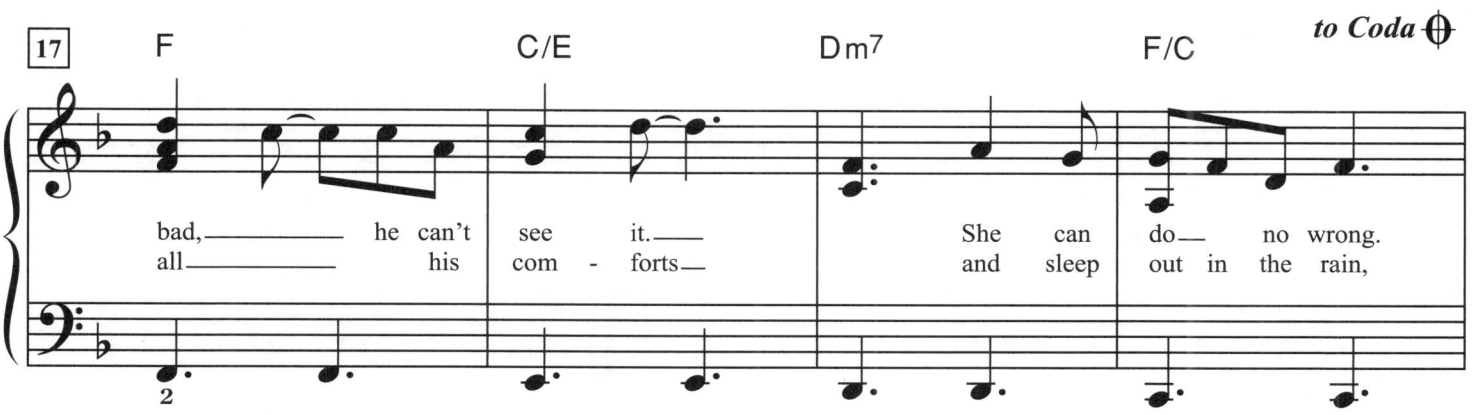
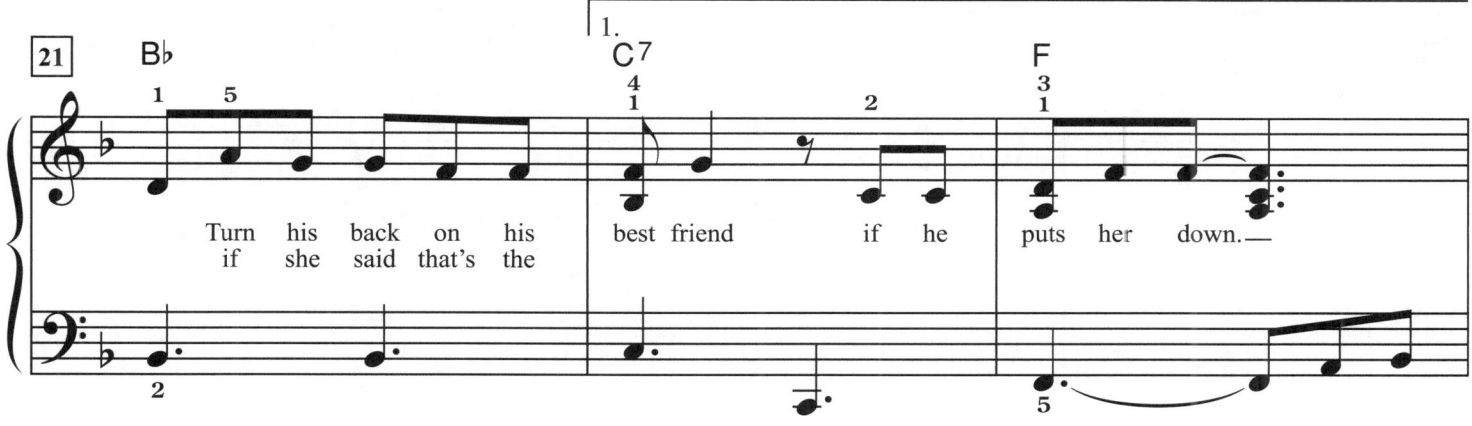
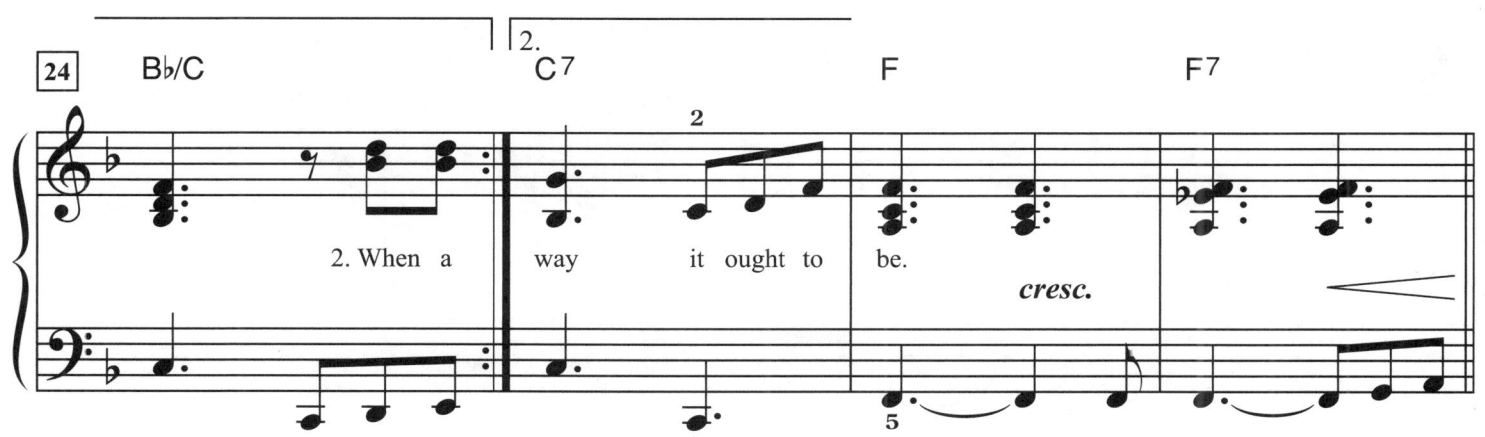

160

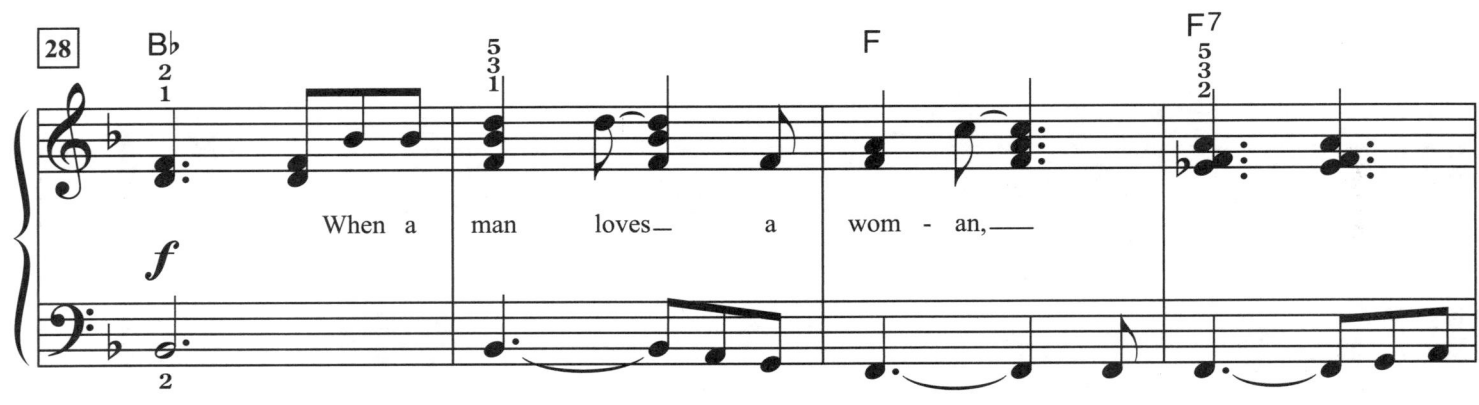

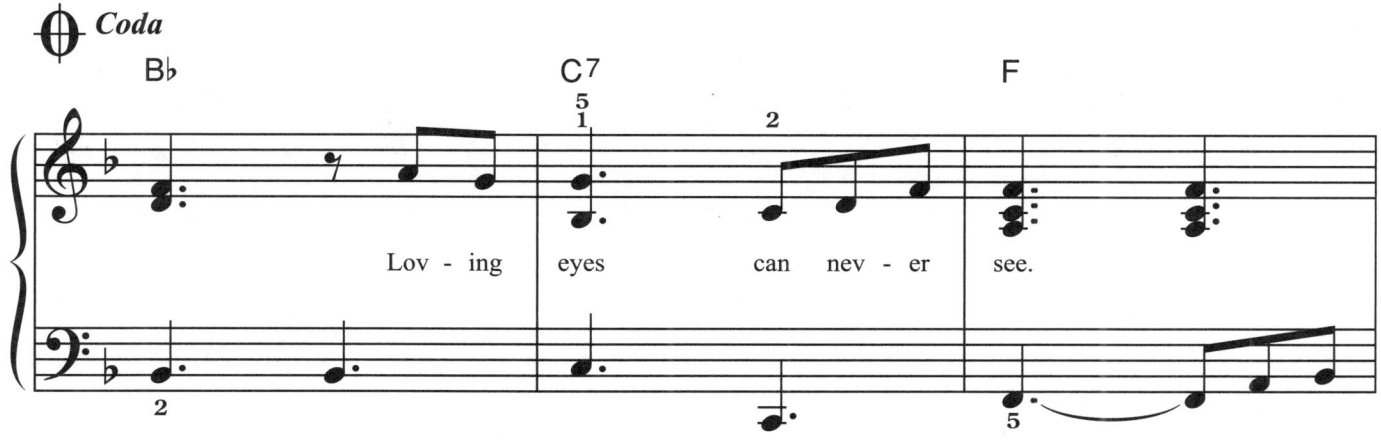
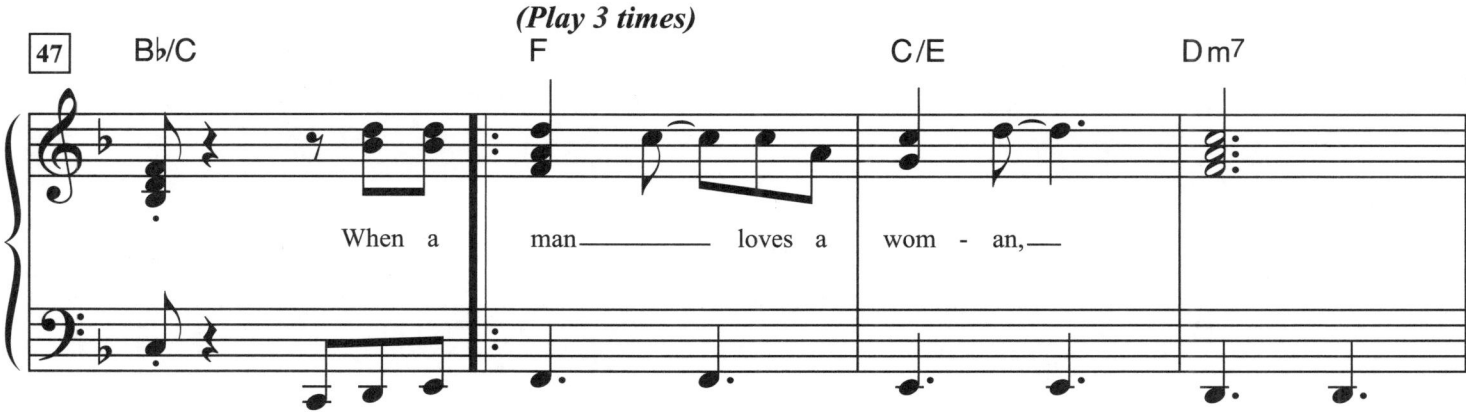
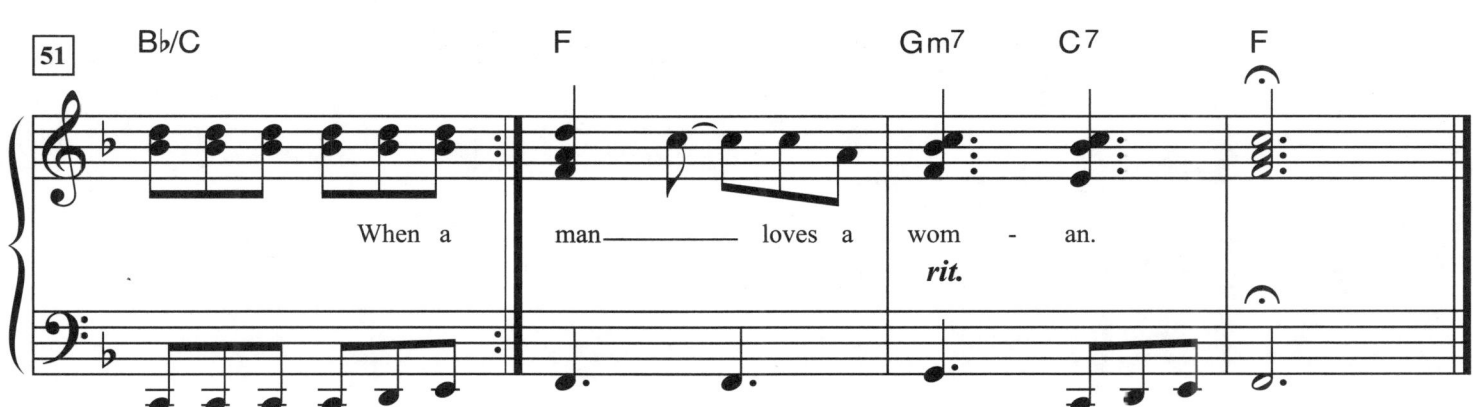

Verse 3:
When a man loves a woman,
Deep down in his soul,
She can bring him such misery.
If she is playing him for a fool,
He's the last one to know.
Loving eyes can never see.

WHERE OR WHEN

Words by Lorenz Hart
Music by Richard Rodgers
Arranged by Dan Coates

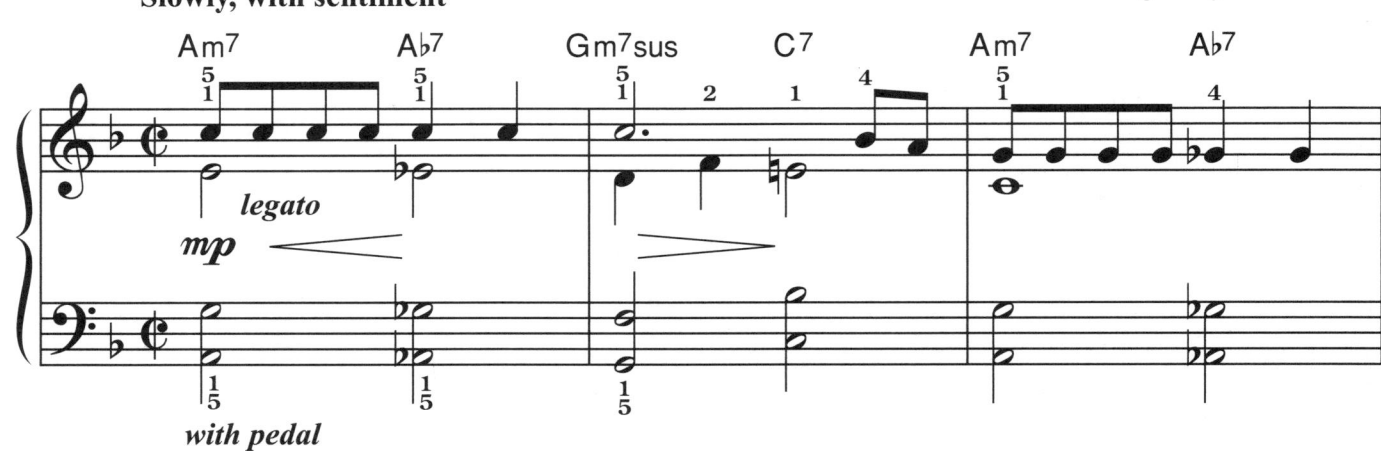

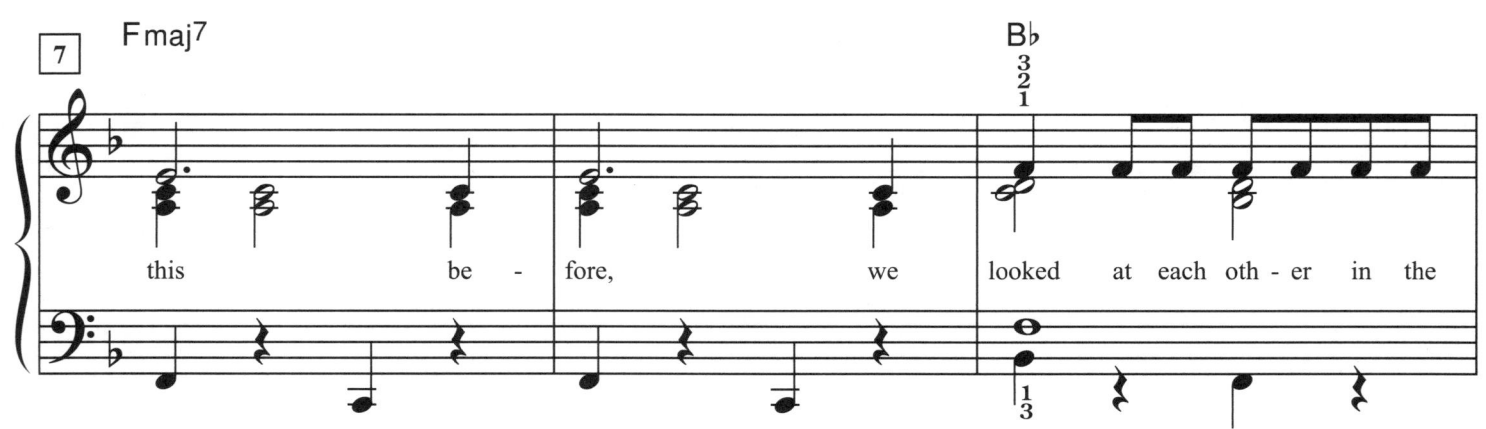

© 1937 (Renewed) by CHAPPELL & CO., INC.
Rights for the Extended Renewal Term in U.S. Controlled by WB MUSIC CORP. and WILLIAMSON MUSIC CO.
All Rights Reserved

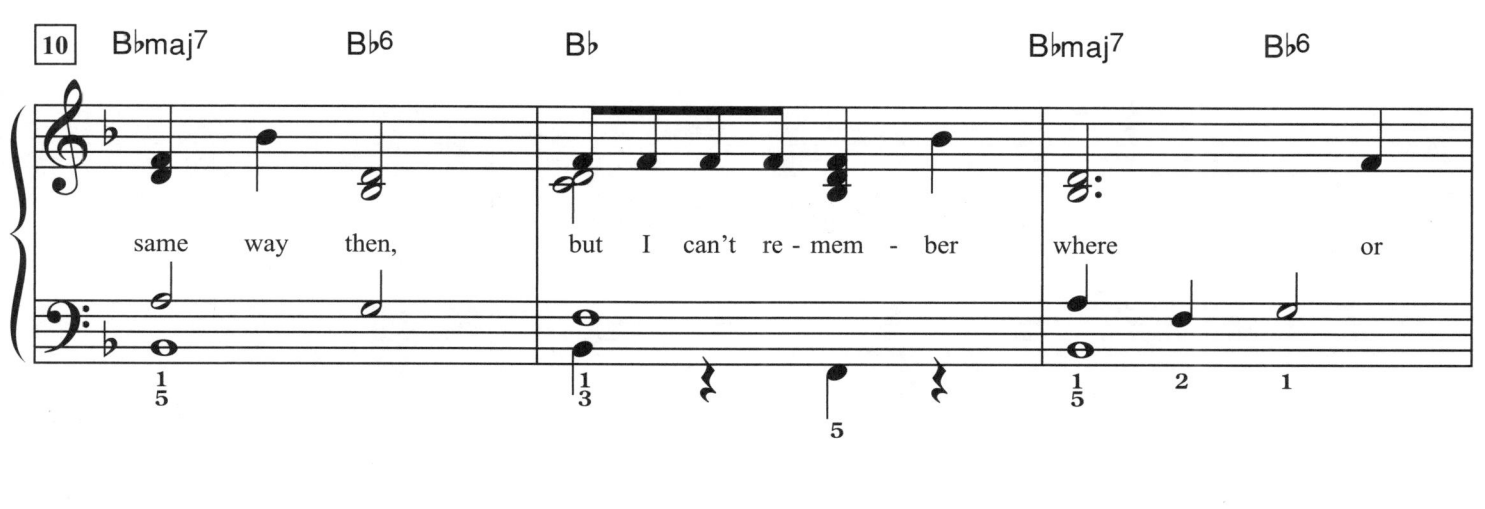
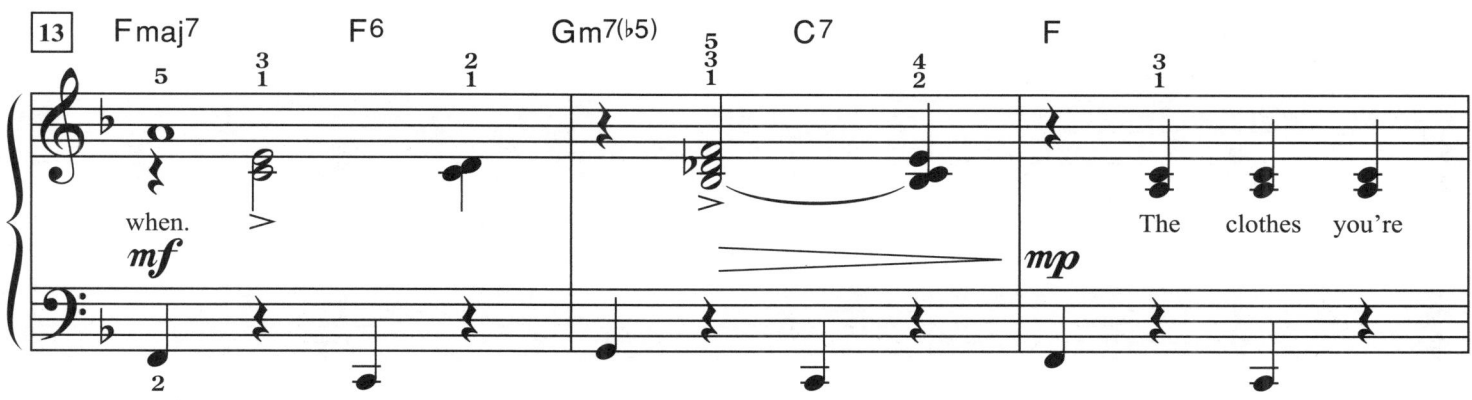
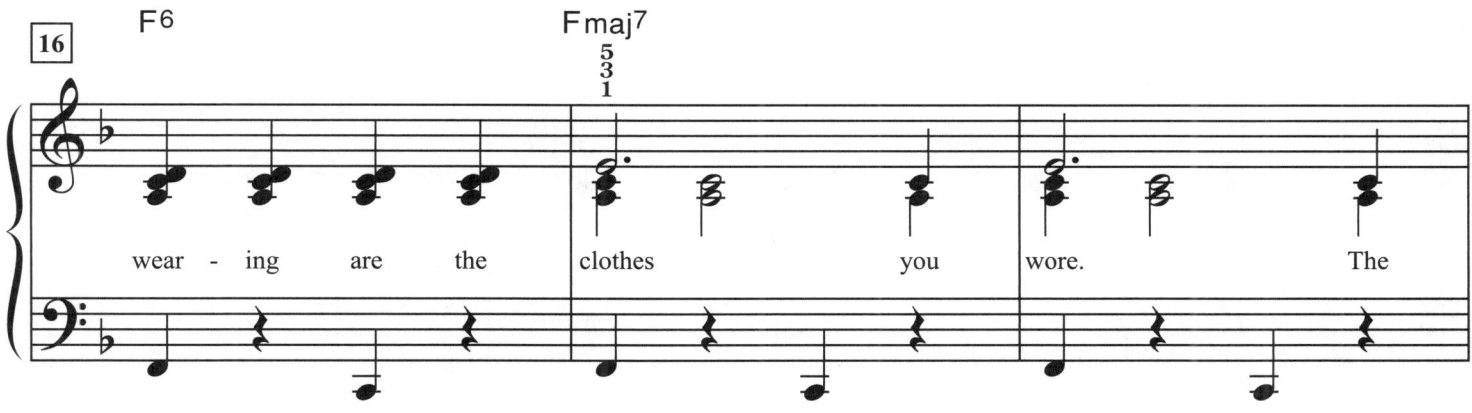
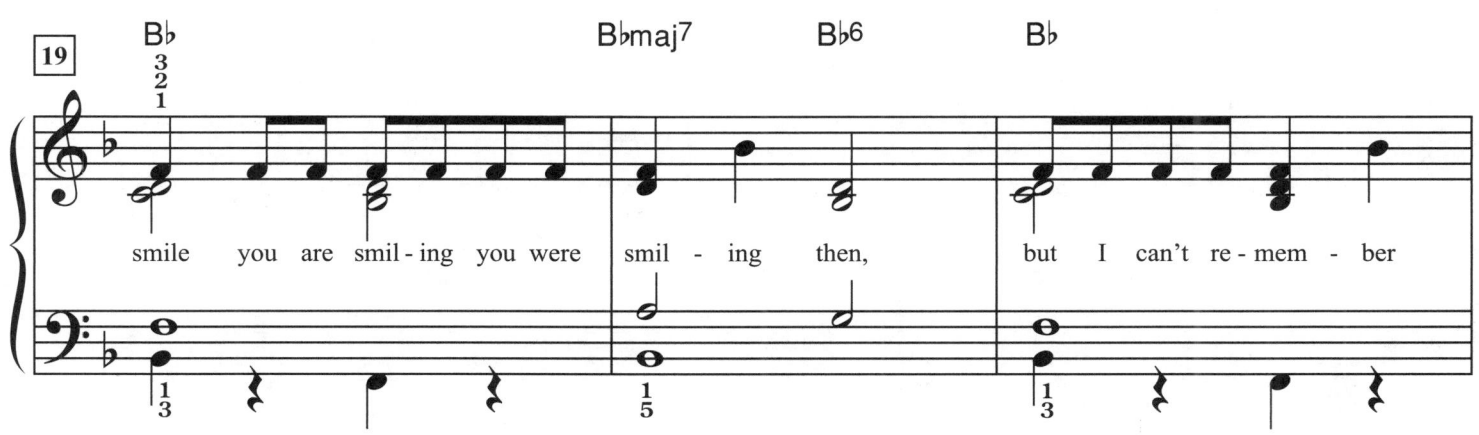

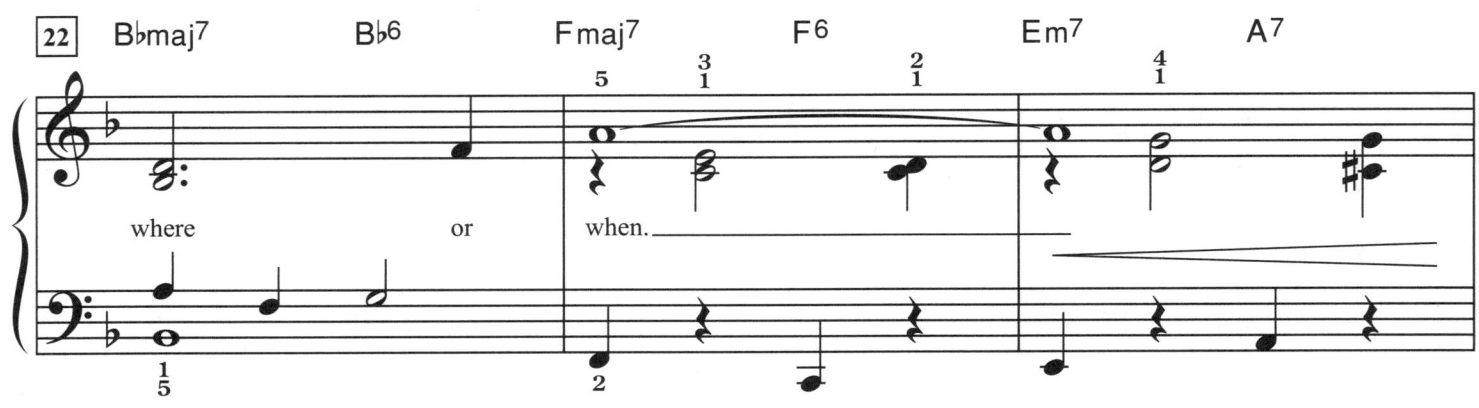
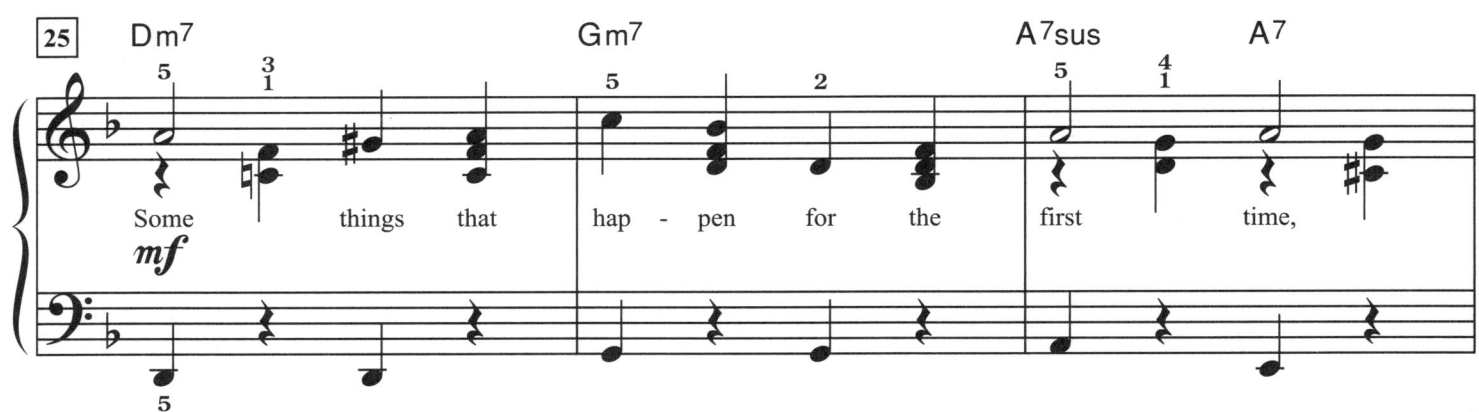
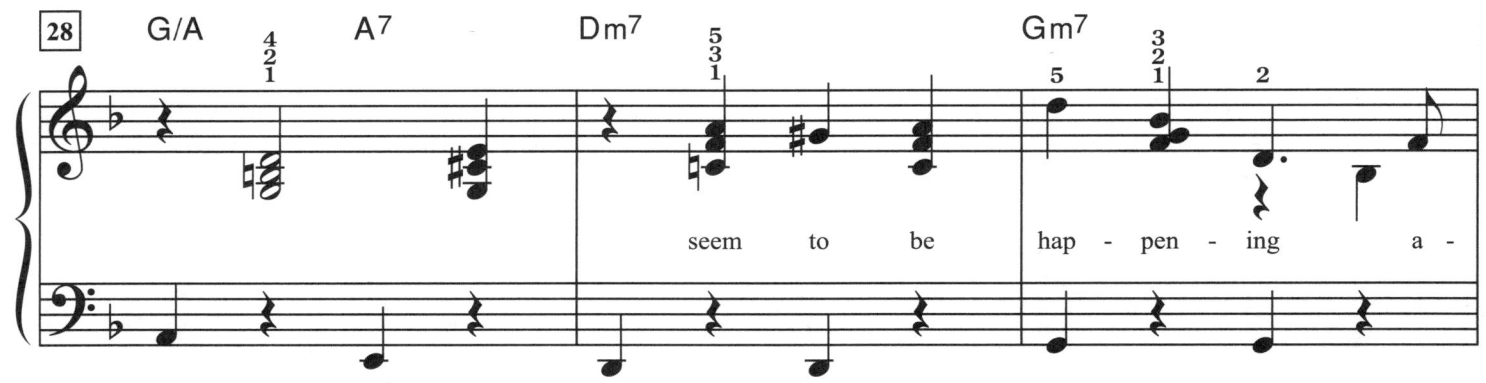
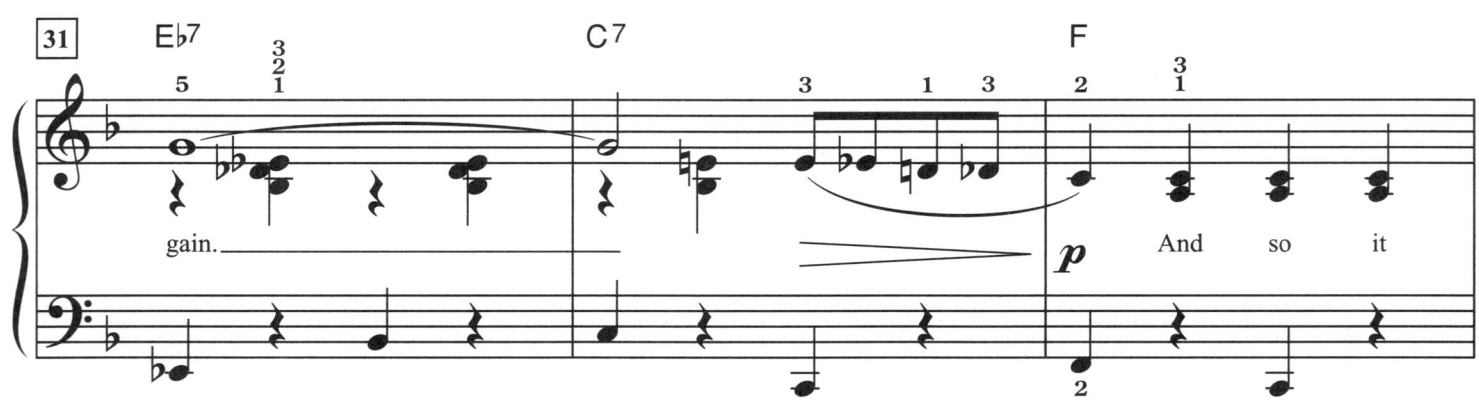

THE WIND BENEATH MY WINGS

Words and Music by
Larry Henley and Jeff Silbar
Arranged by Dan Coates

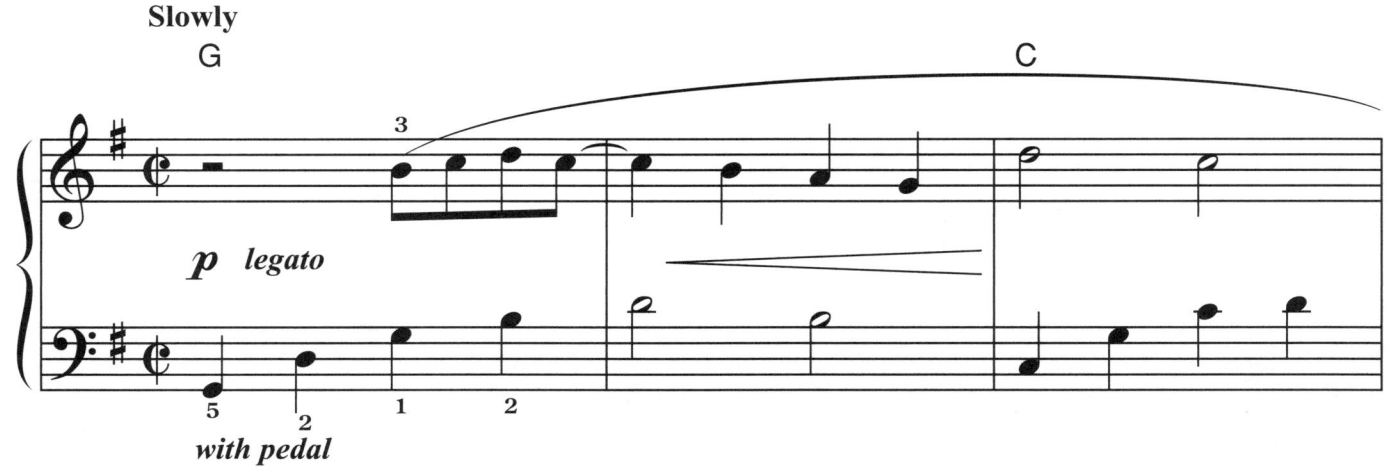

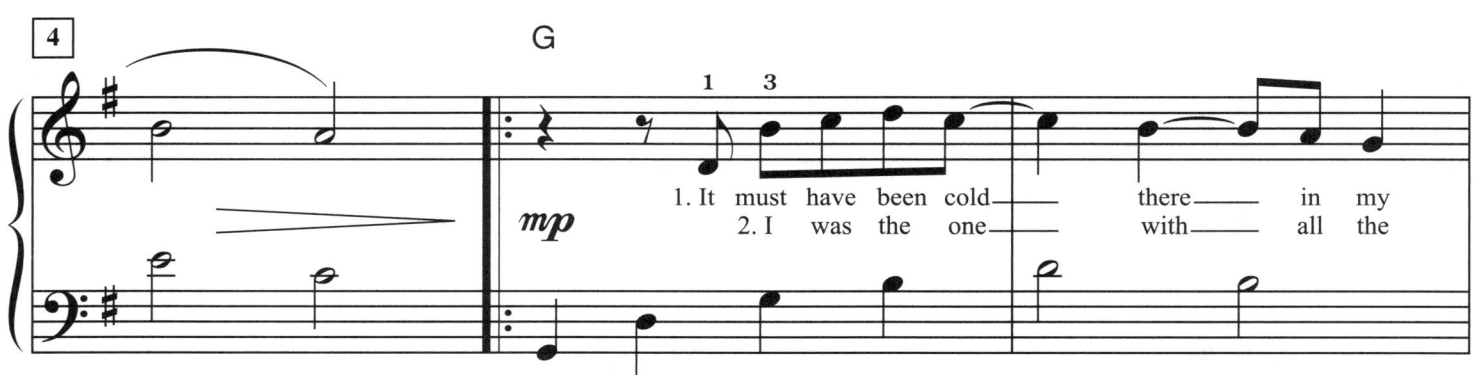

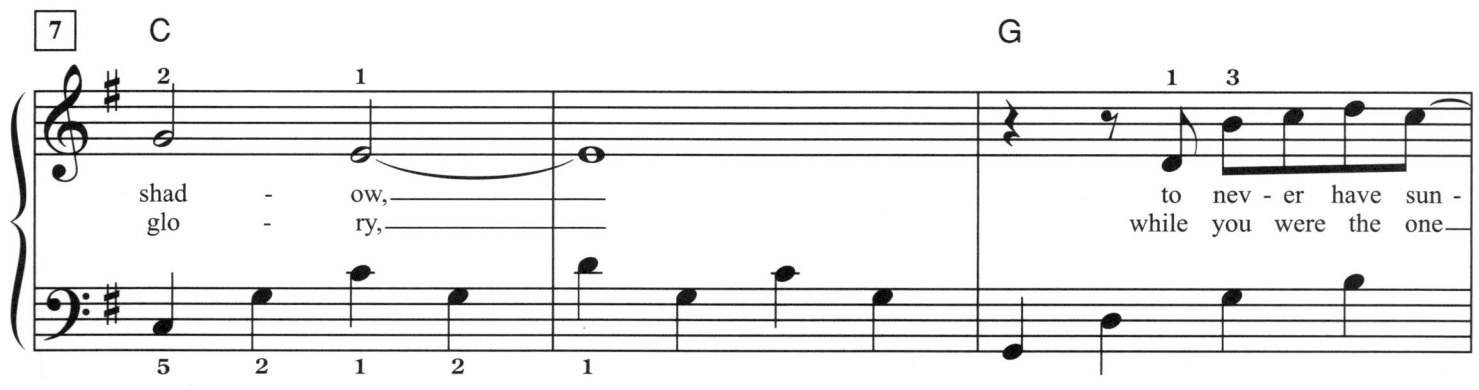

© 1982 WARNER HOUSE OF MUSIC and WB GOLD MUSIC CORP.
All Rights Reserved

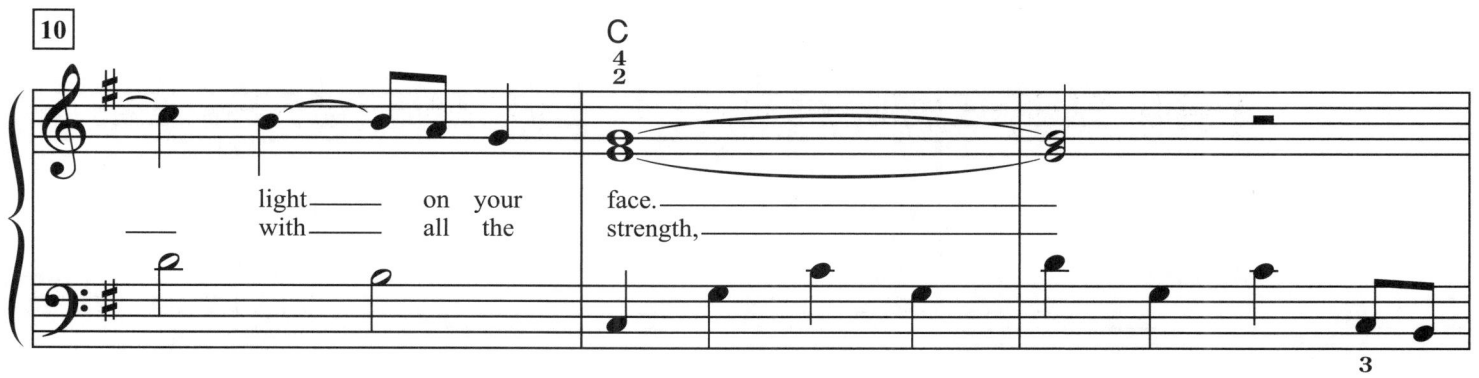
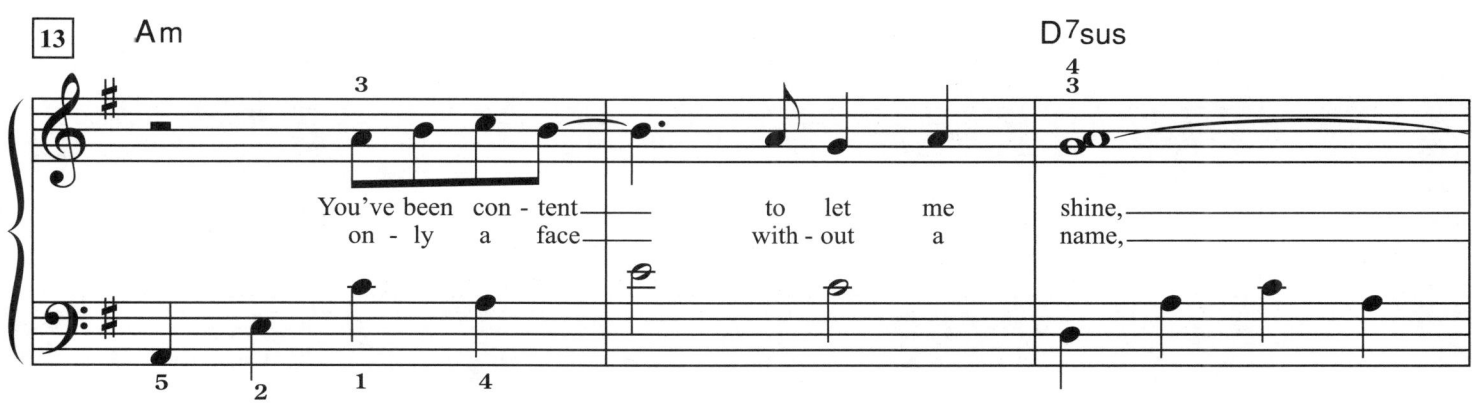

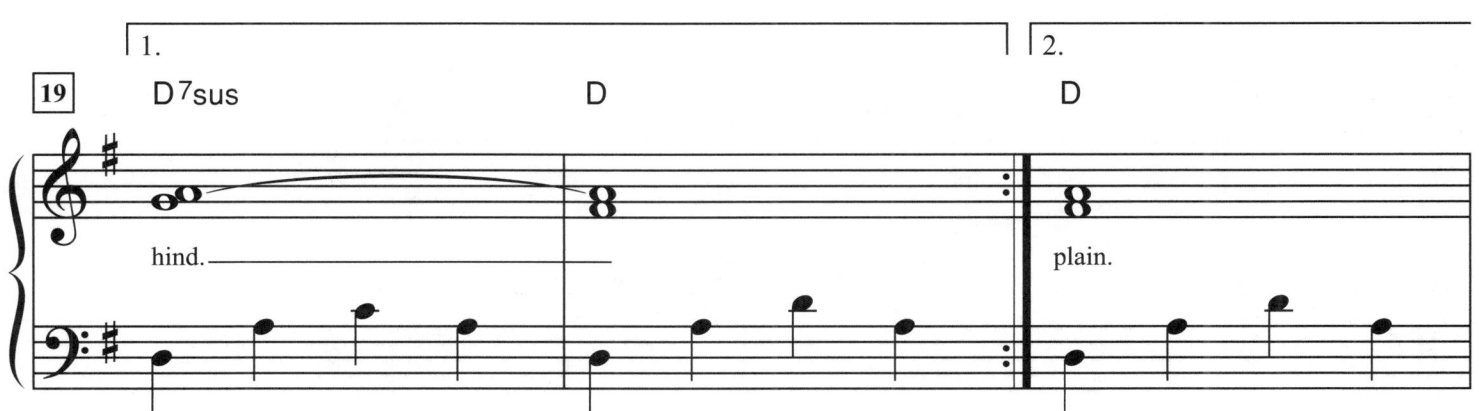

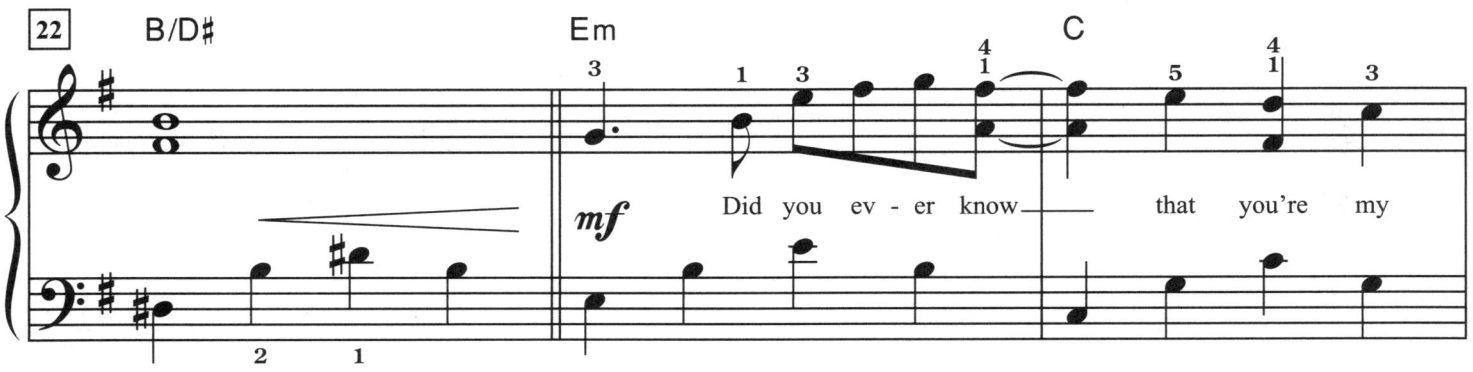
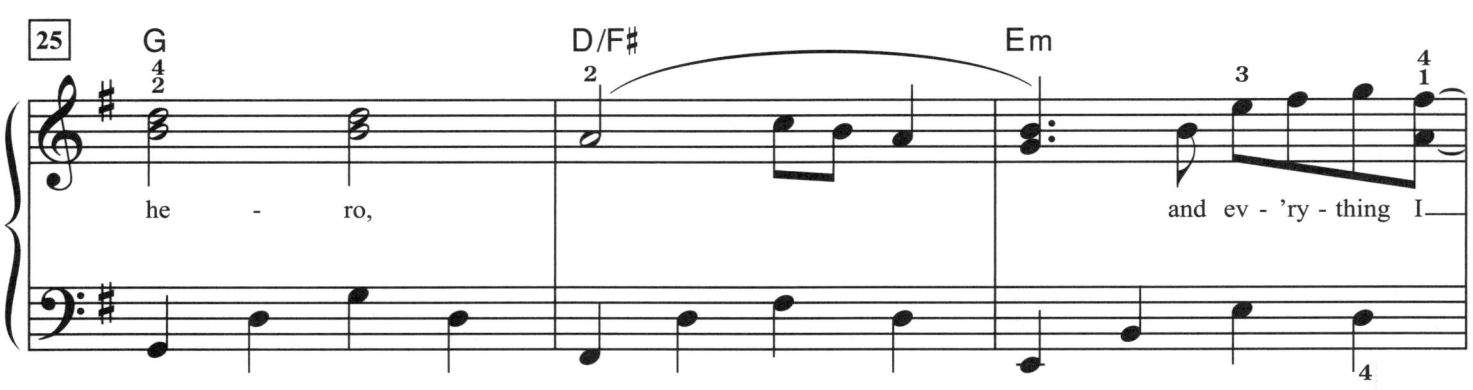
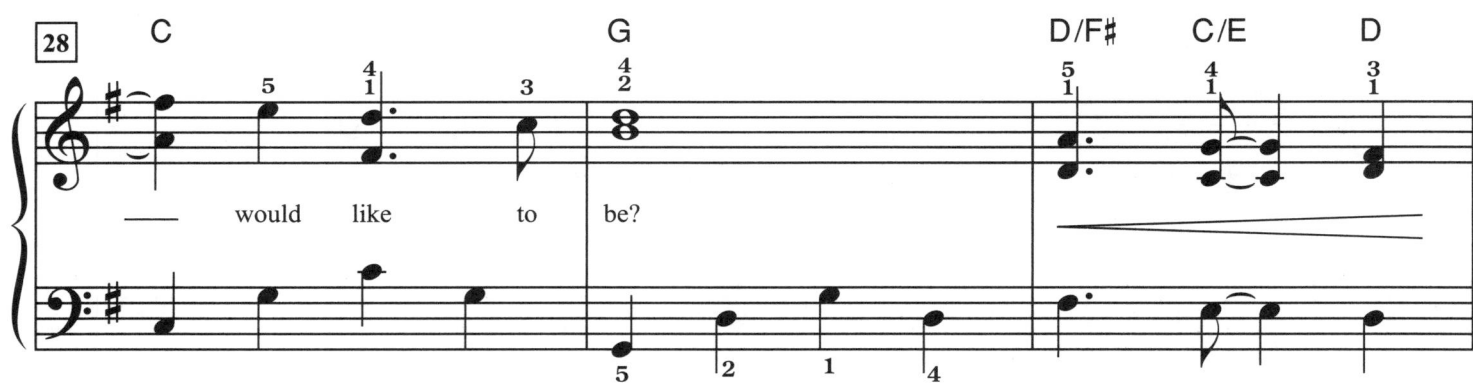
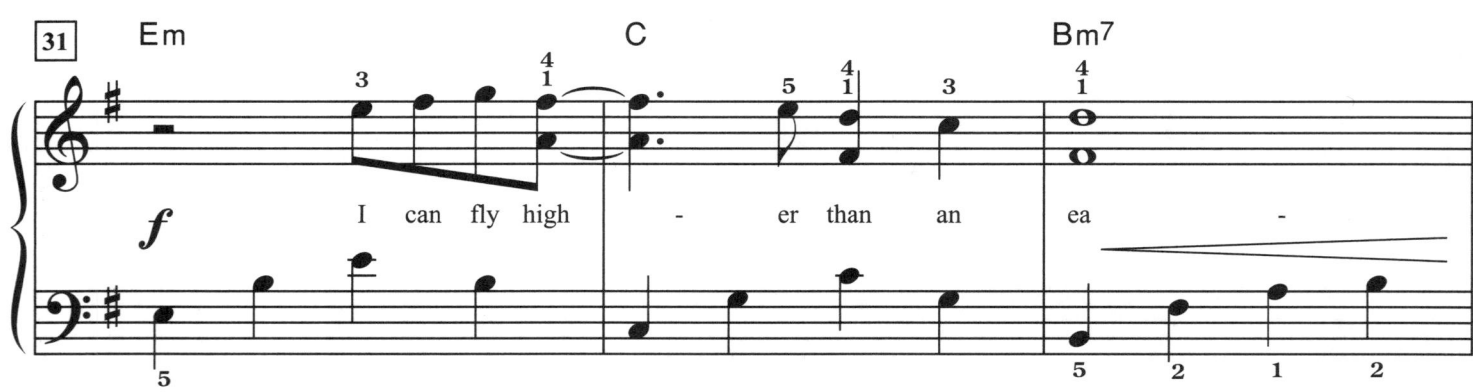

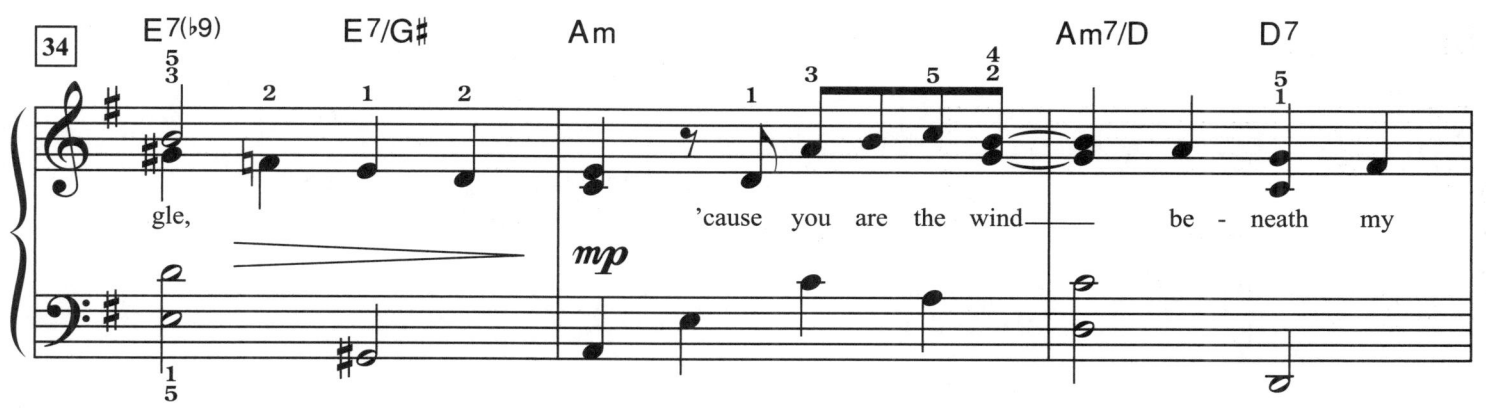
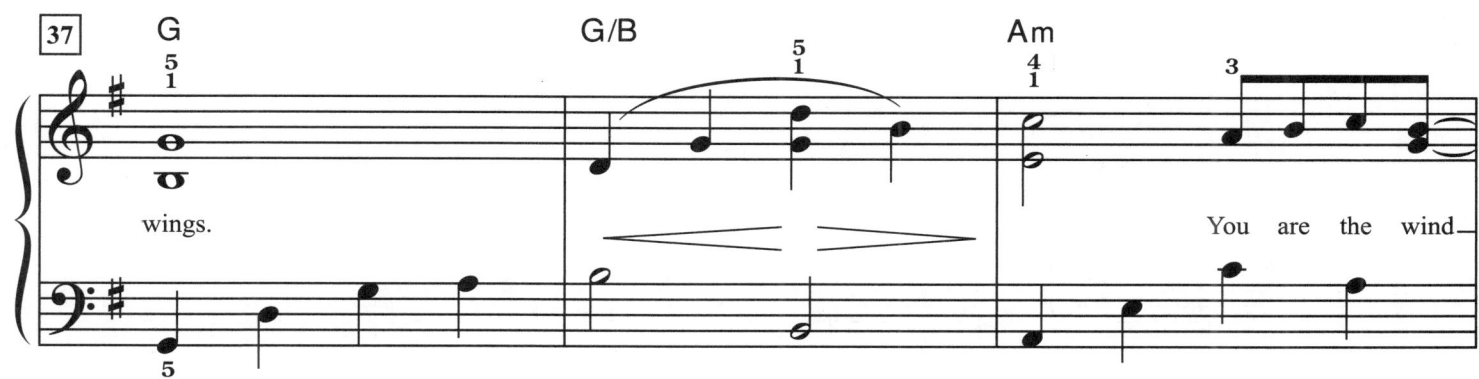
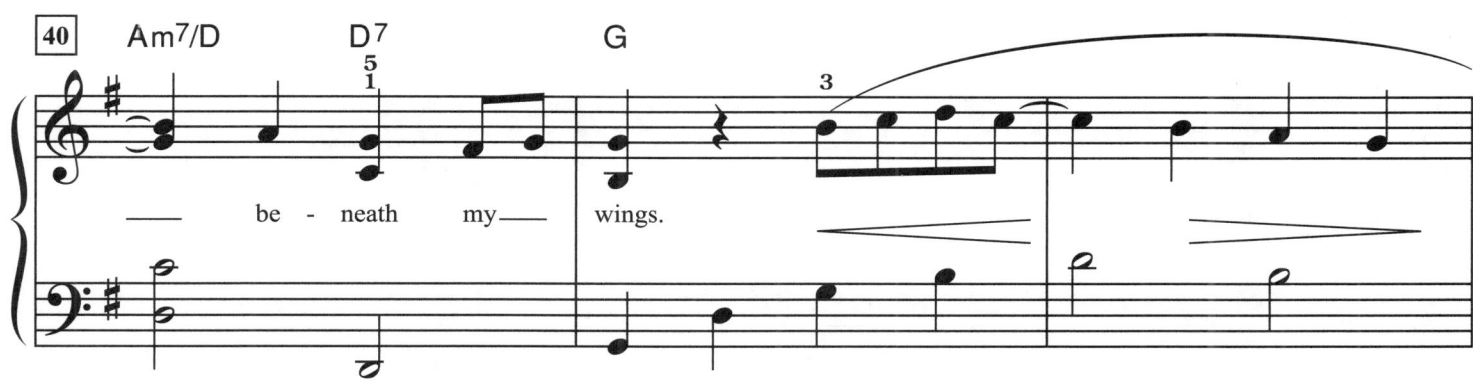
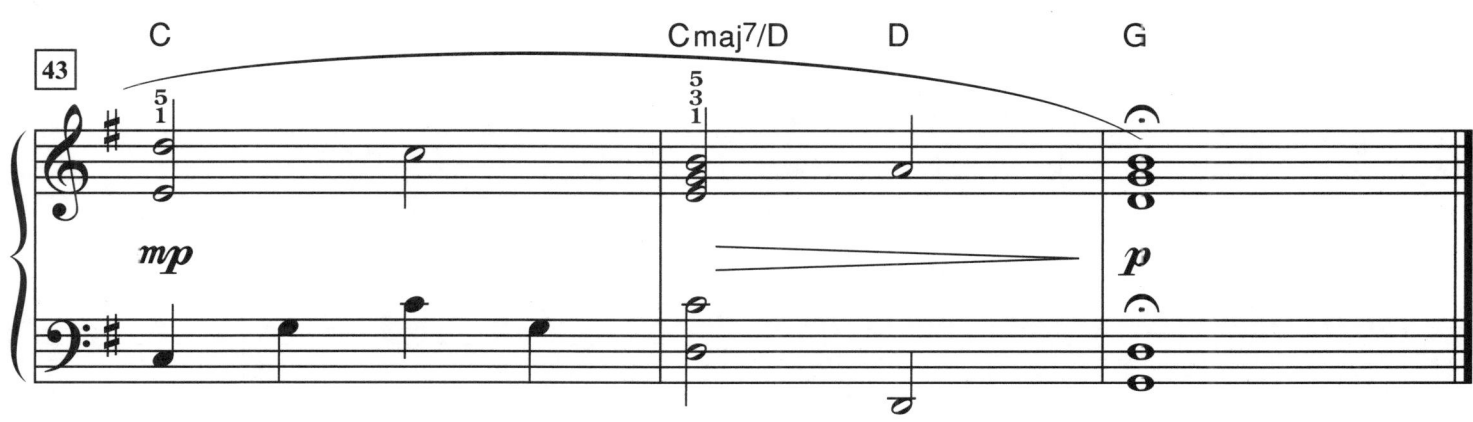

YOU MAKE ME FEEL SO YOUNG

Words by Mack Gordon
Music by Josef Myrow
Arranged by Dan Coates

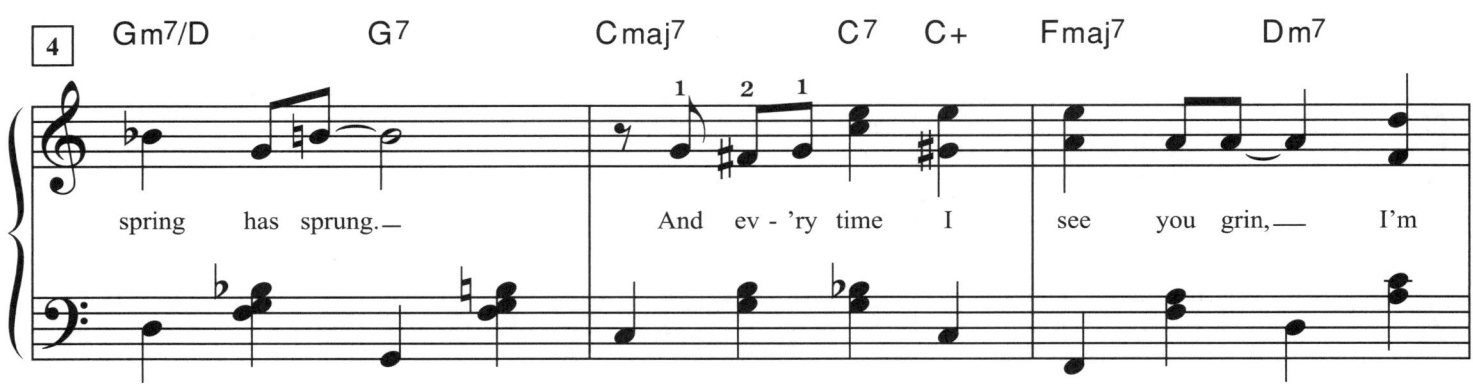

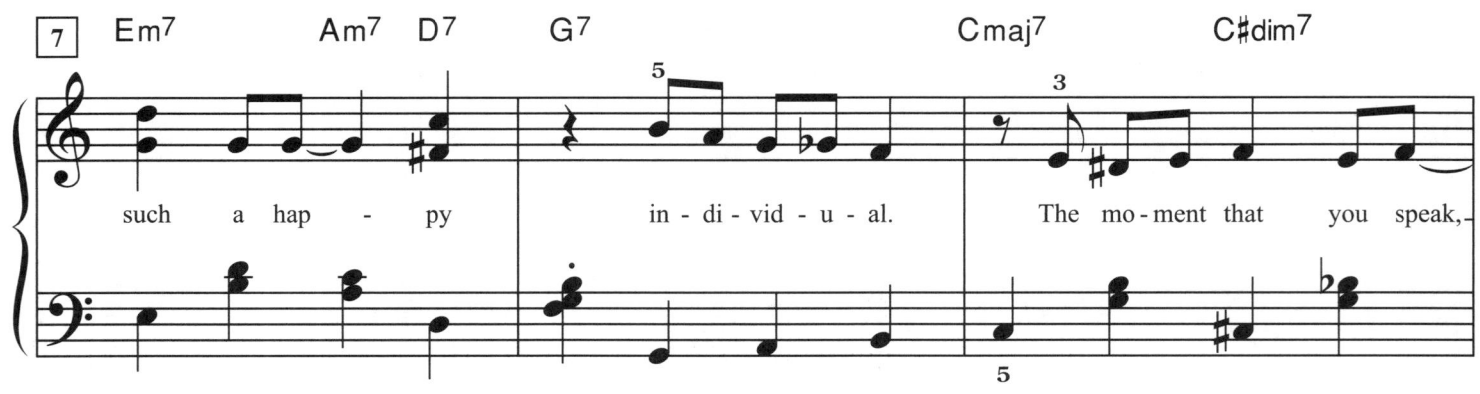

© 1946 (Renewed) WB MUSIC CORP.
All Rights Reserved

171

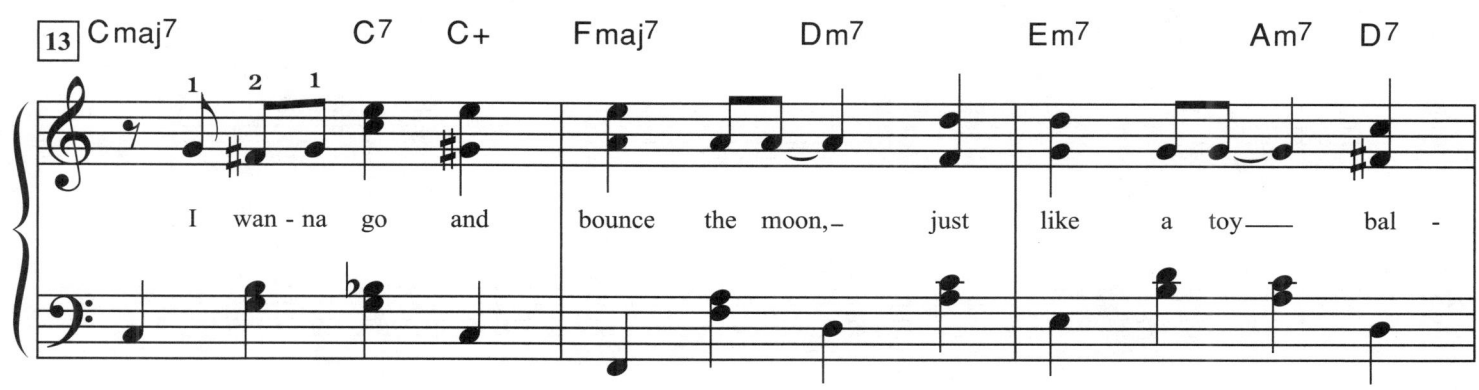

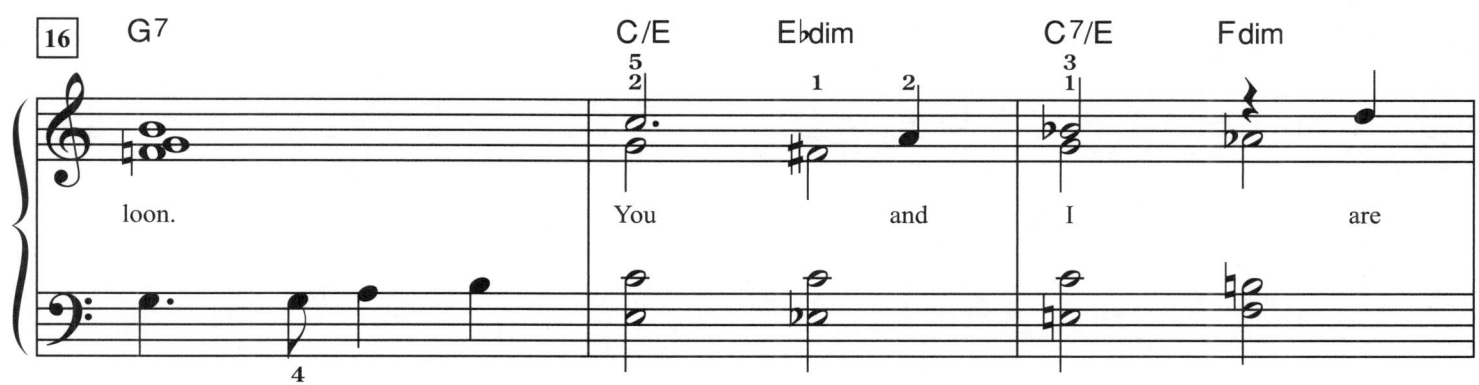

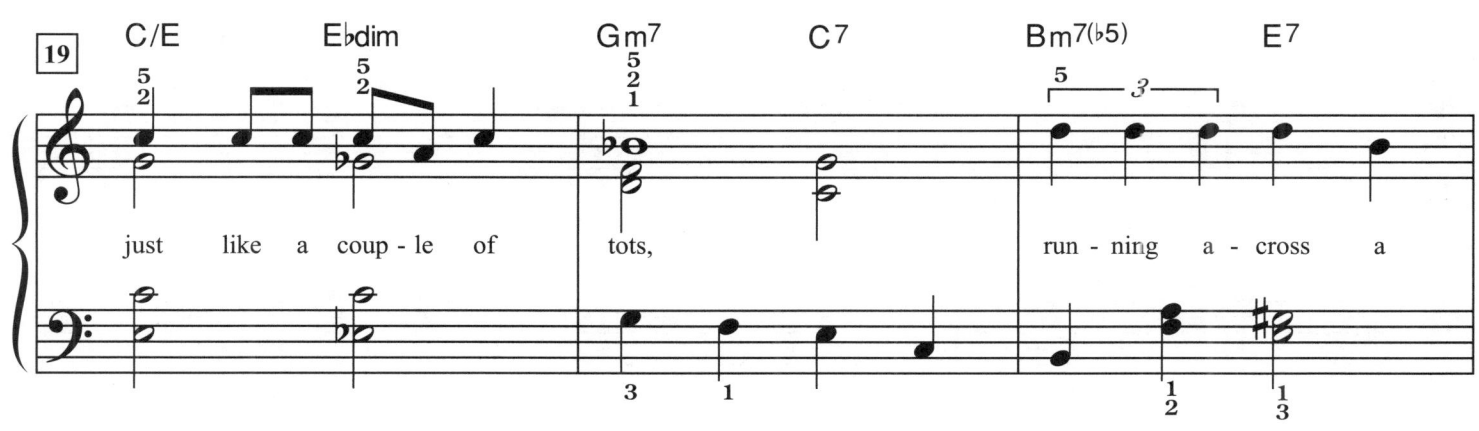

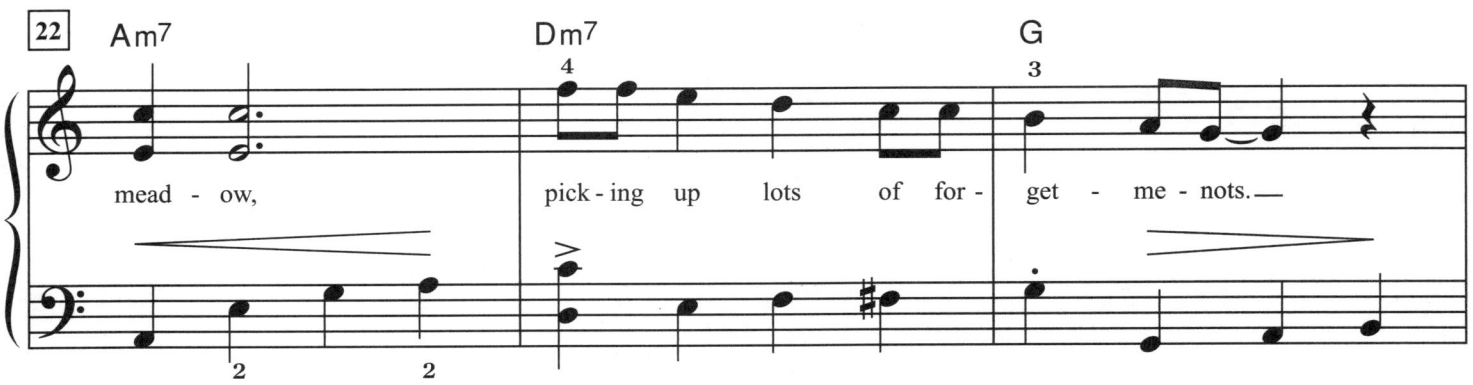
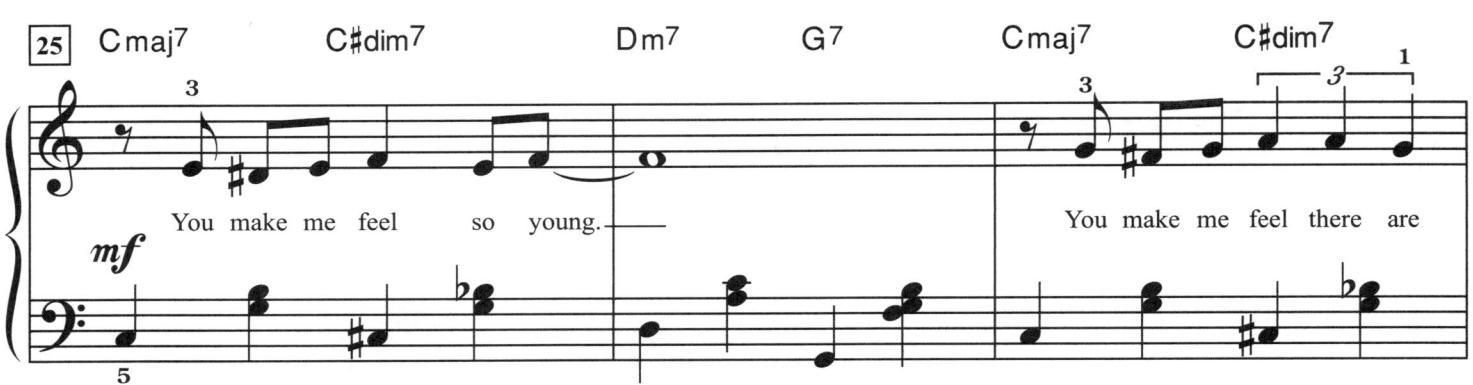
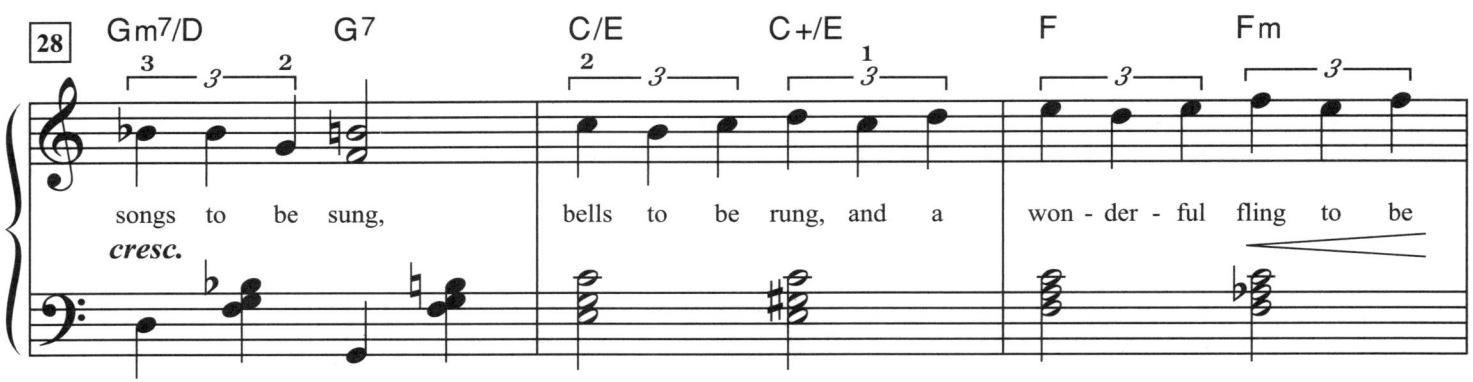

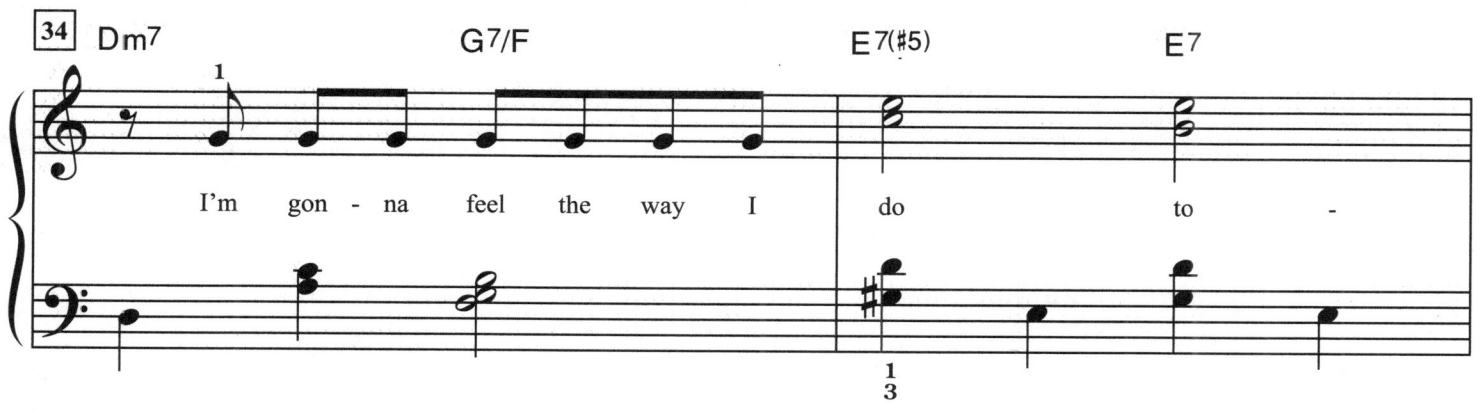
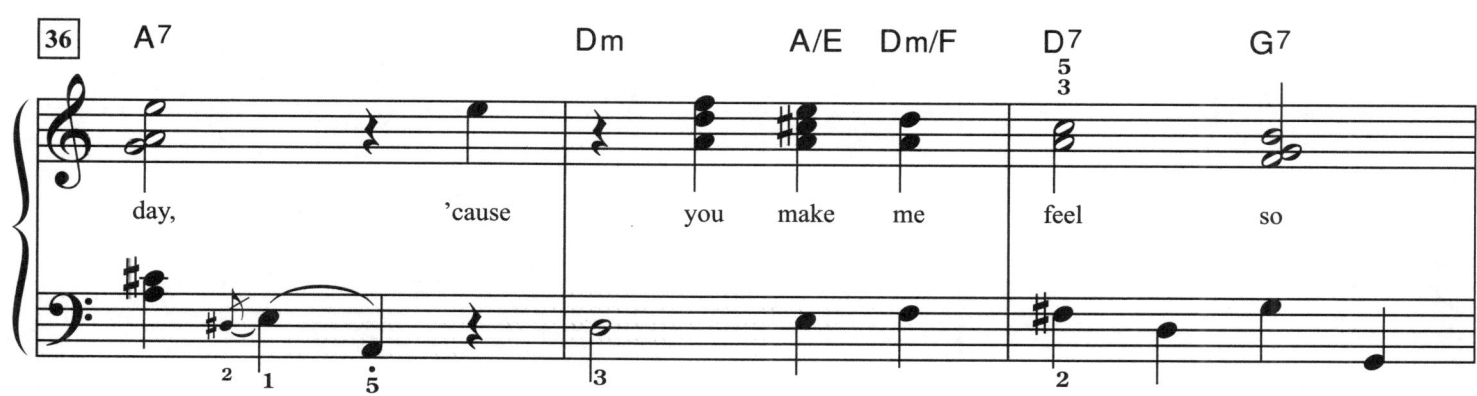
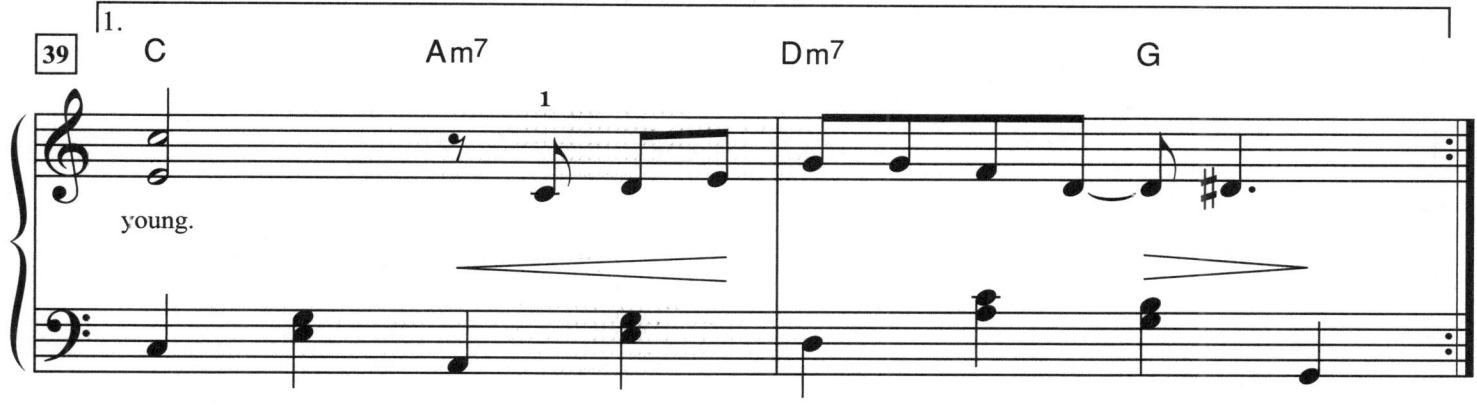

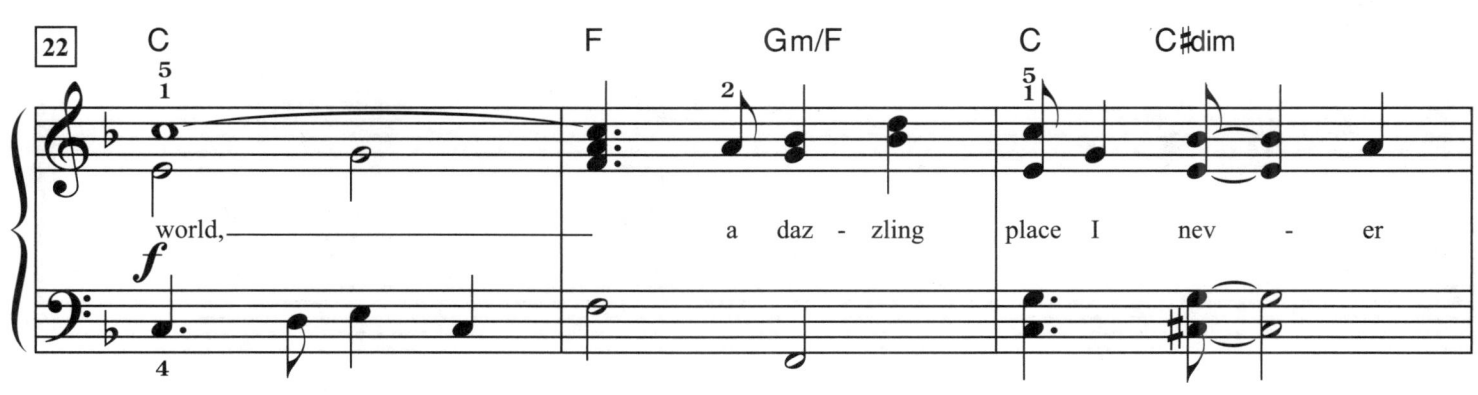

YOU RAISE ME UP

Words and Music by
Rolf Lovland and Brendan Graham
Arranged by Dan Coates

When I am down and oh, my soul, so

© 2002 UNIVERSAL MUSIC PUBLISHING, a division of UNIVERSAL MUSIC AS and PEERMUSIC (Ireland) Ltd.
All Rights for ROLF LOVLAND and UNIVERSAL MUSIC PUBLISHING Administered in the U.S. and Canada by
UNIVERSAL - POLYGRAM INTERNATIONAL PUBLISHING, INC. (Publishing) and ALFRED PUBLISHING CO., INC. (Print)
All Rights Reserved

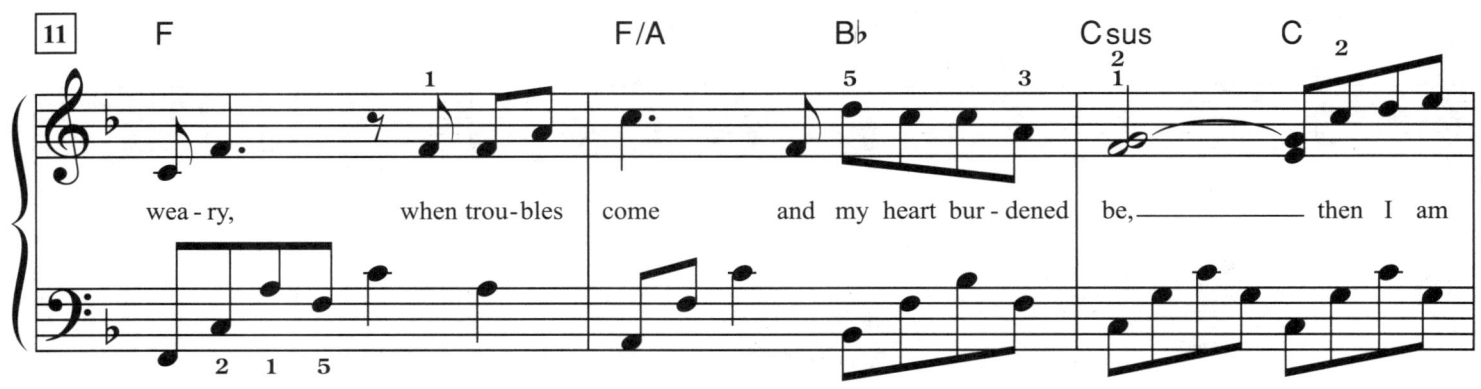
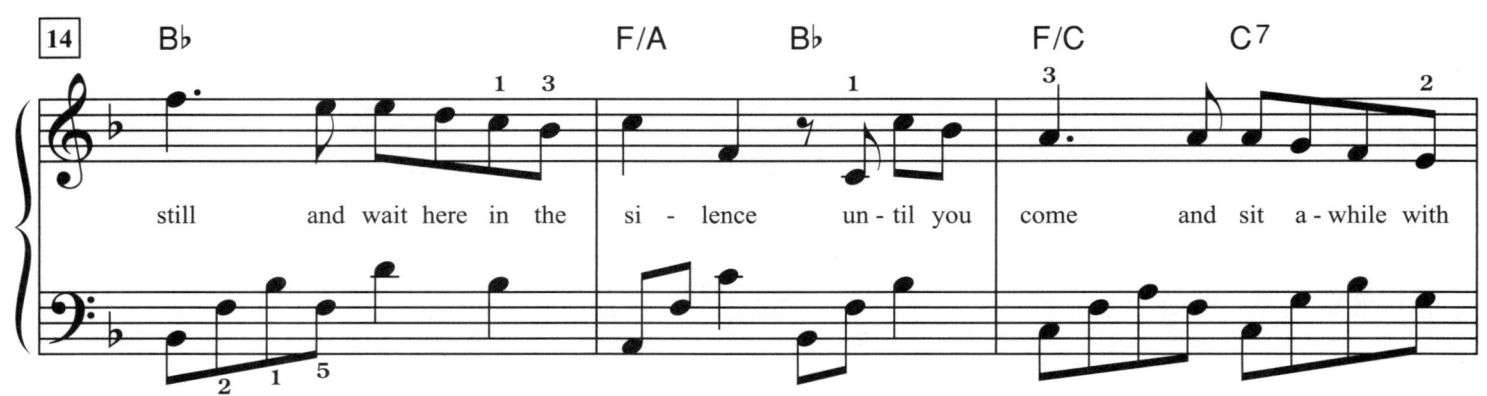
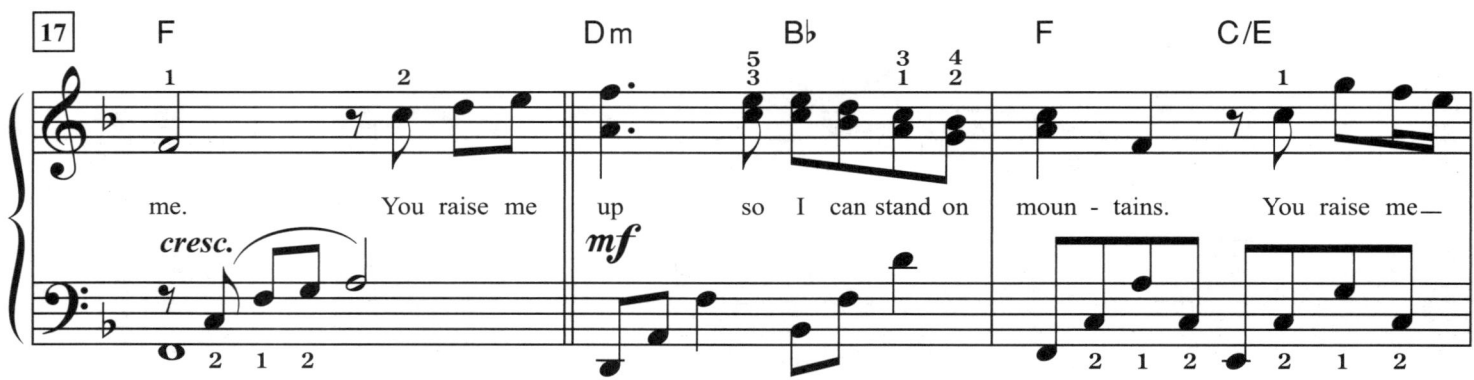
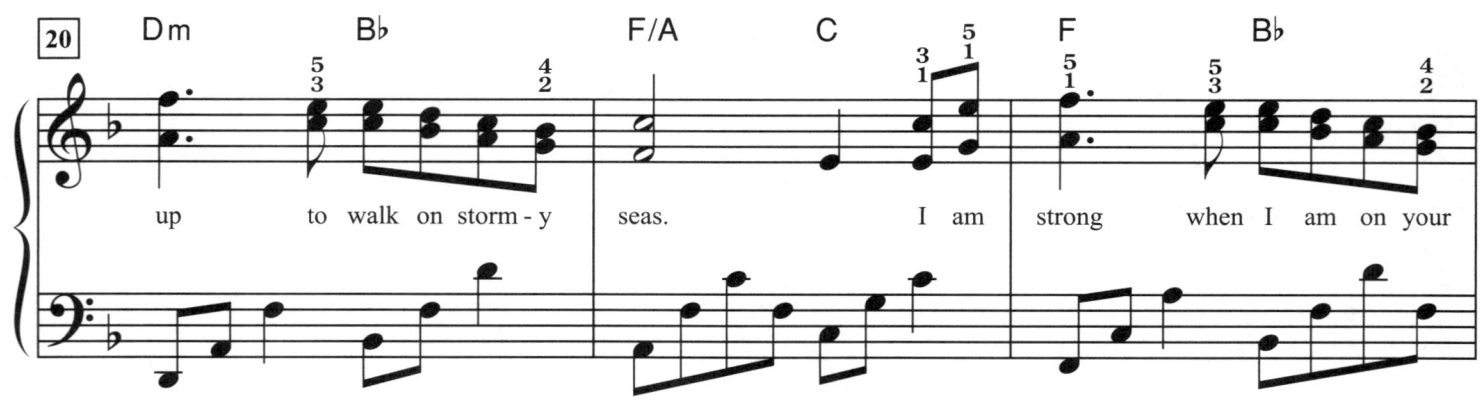

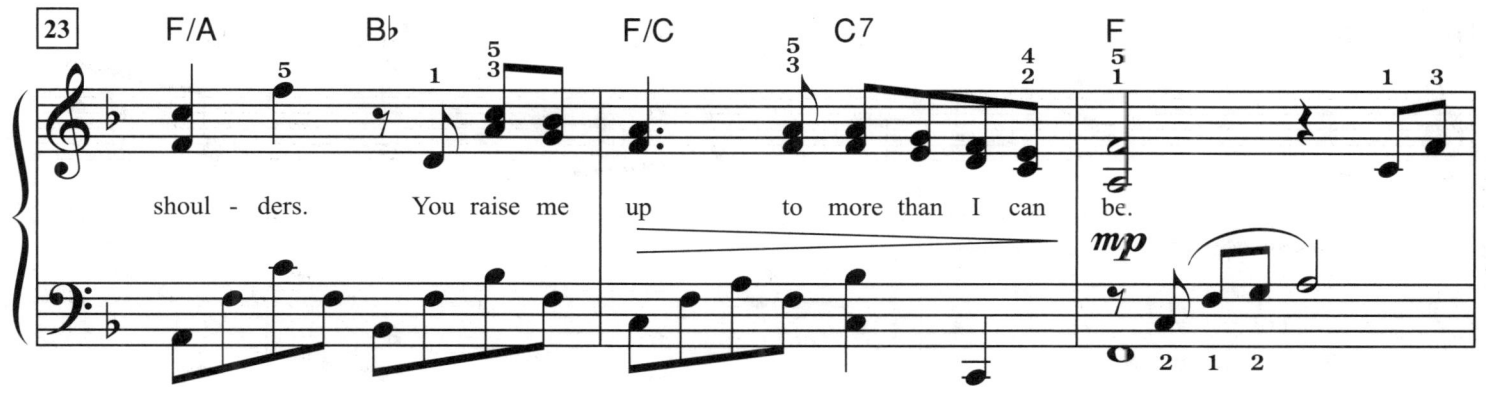
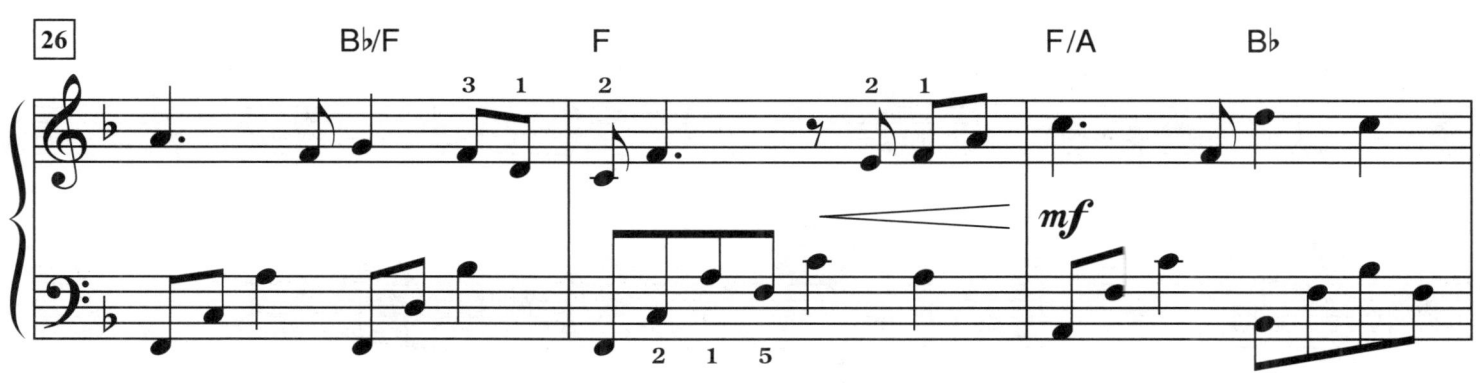
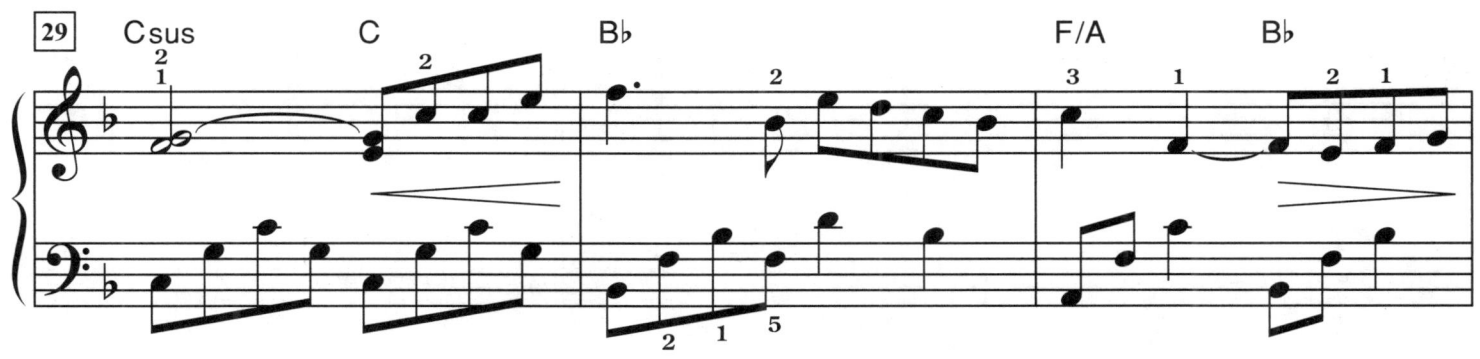
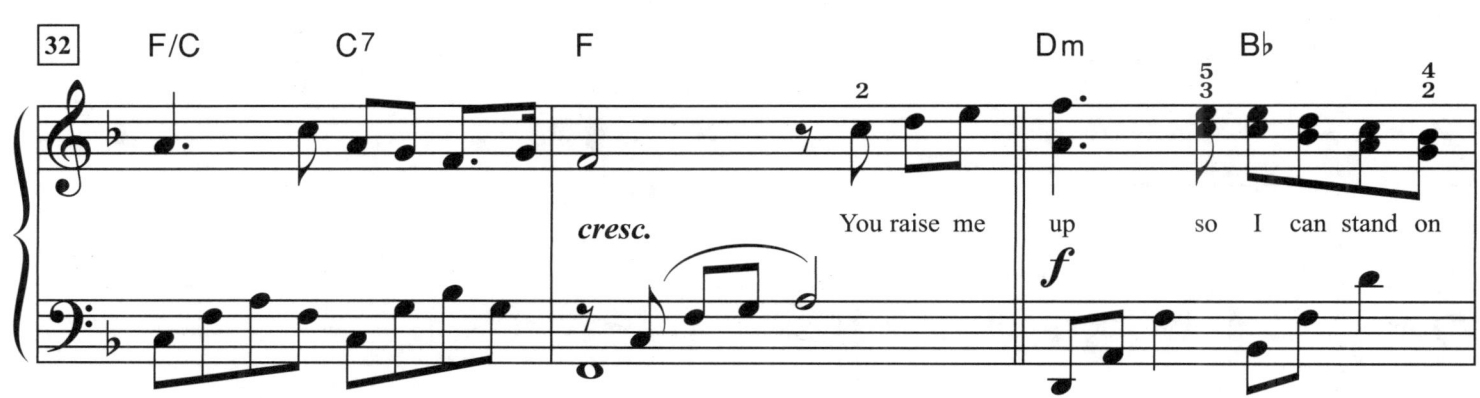

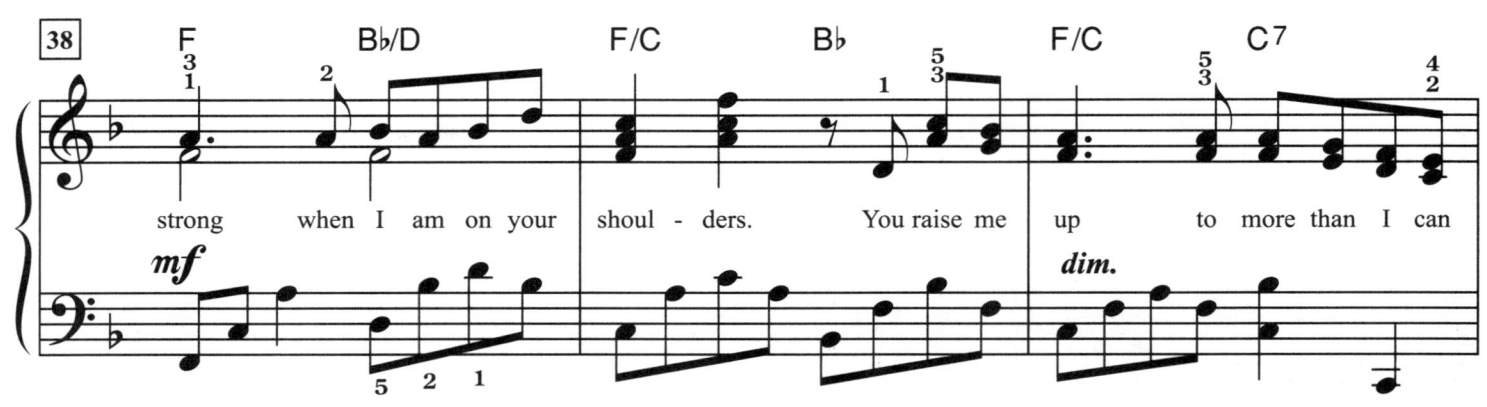

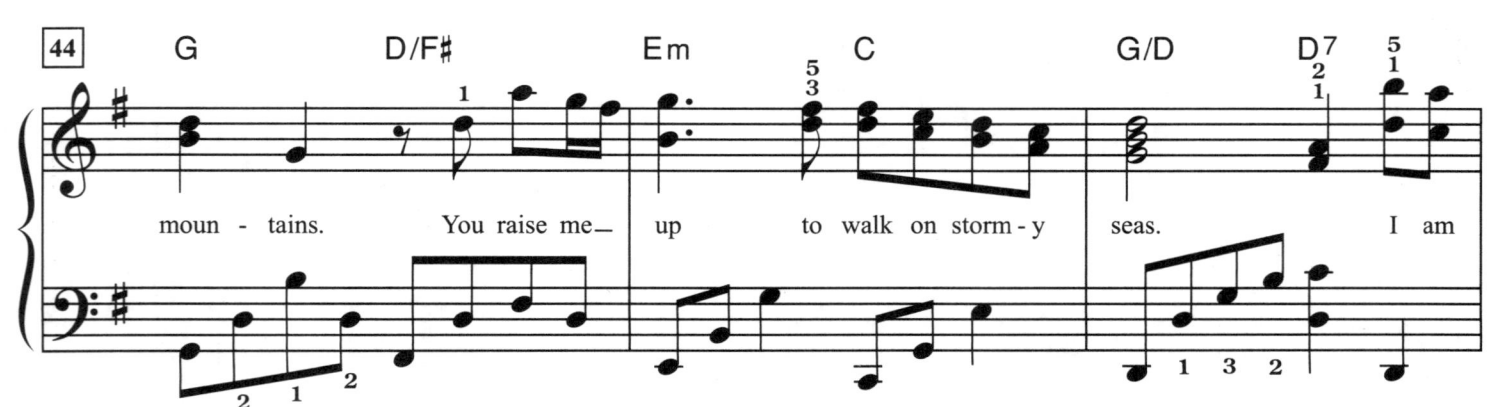

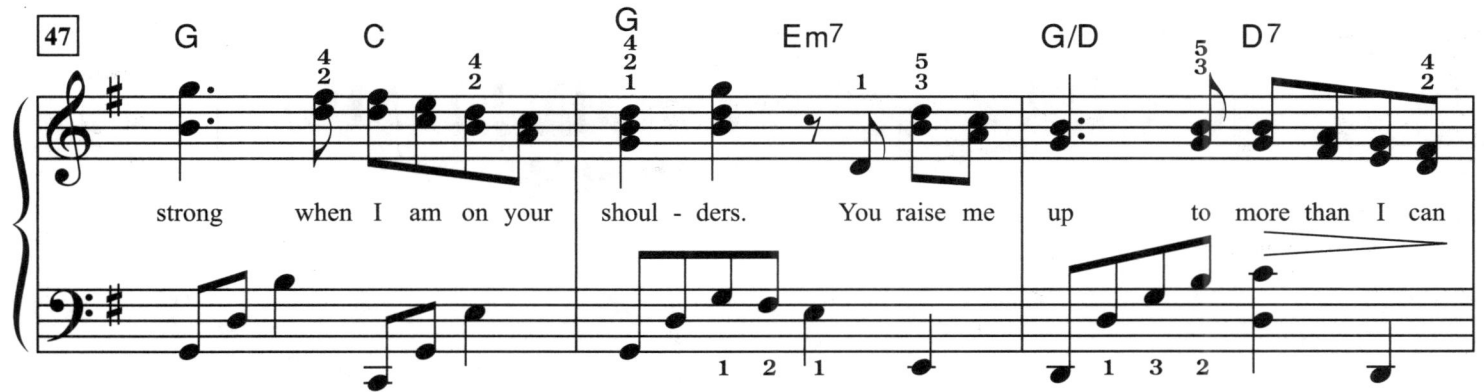
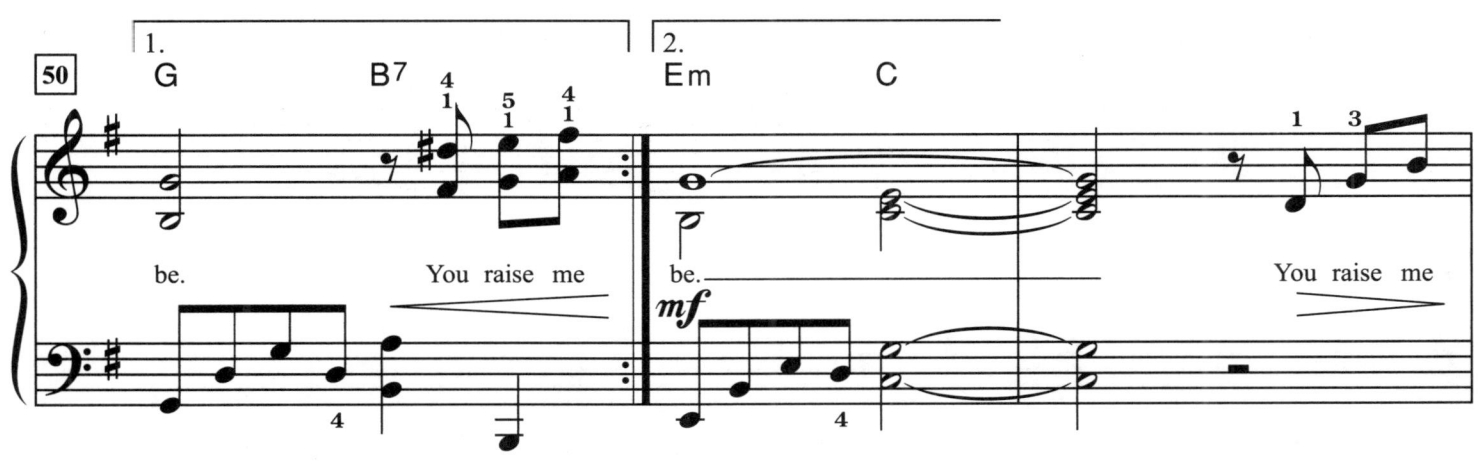

(YOUR LOVE HAS LIFTED ME) HIGHER AND HIGHER

Words and Music by
Gary Jackson, Carl Smith and Raynard Miner
Arranged by Dan Coates

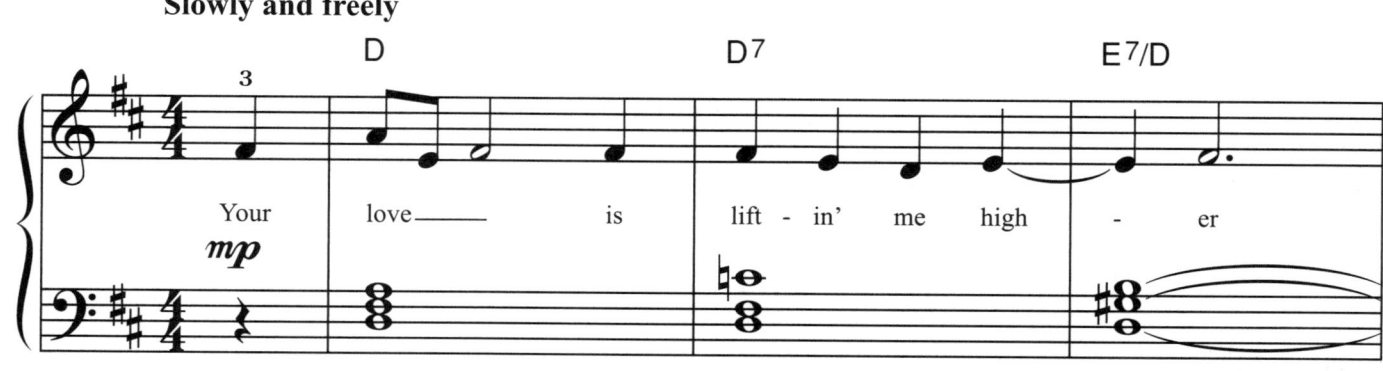

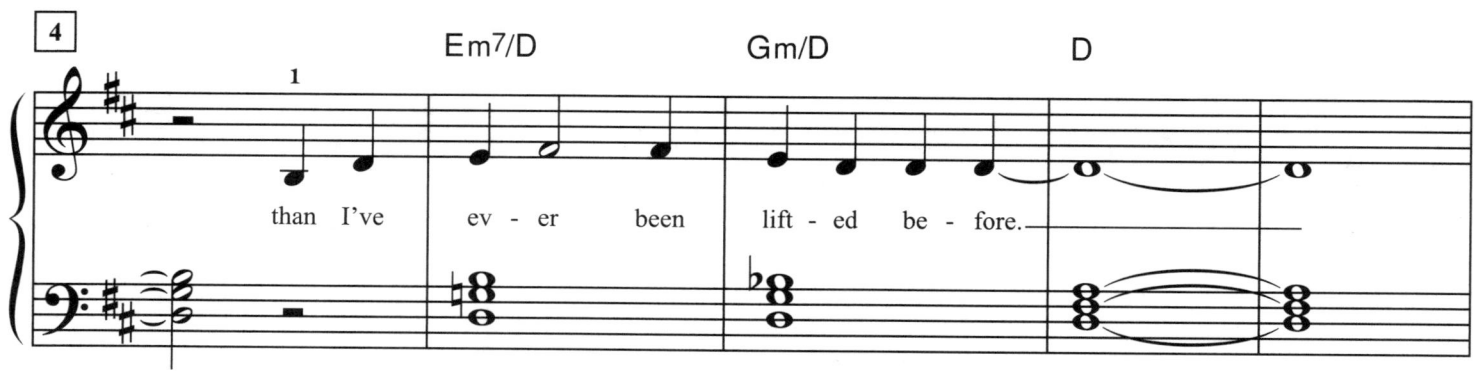

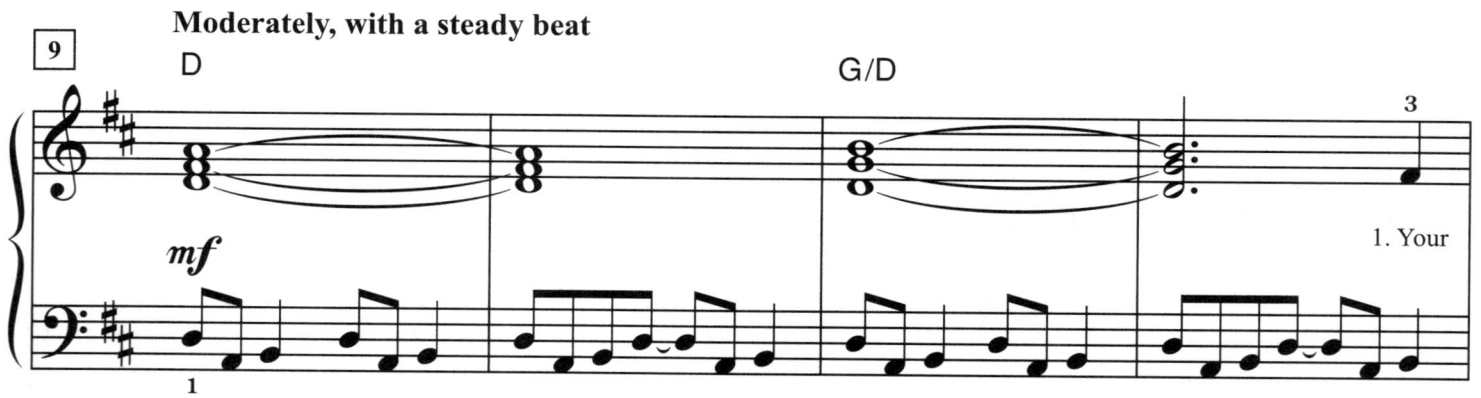

© 1967 (Renewed) UNICHAPPELL MUSIC INC., MIJAC MUSIC,
WARNER-TAMERLANE PUBLISHING CORP. and CHEVIS MUSIC, INC.
All Rights on behalf of itself, MIJAC MUSIC and UNICHAPPELL MUSIC INC.
Administered by WARNER-TAMERLANE PUBLISHING CORP.
All Rights Reserved

184

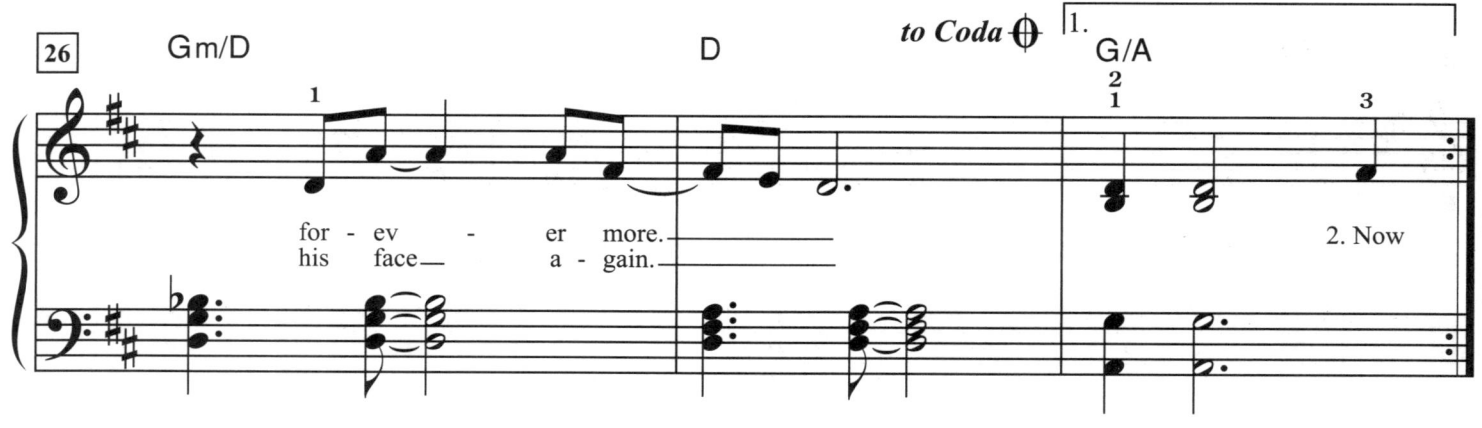
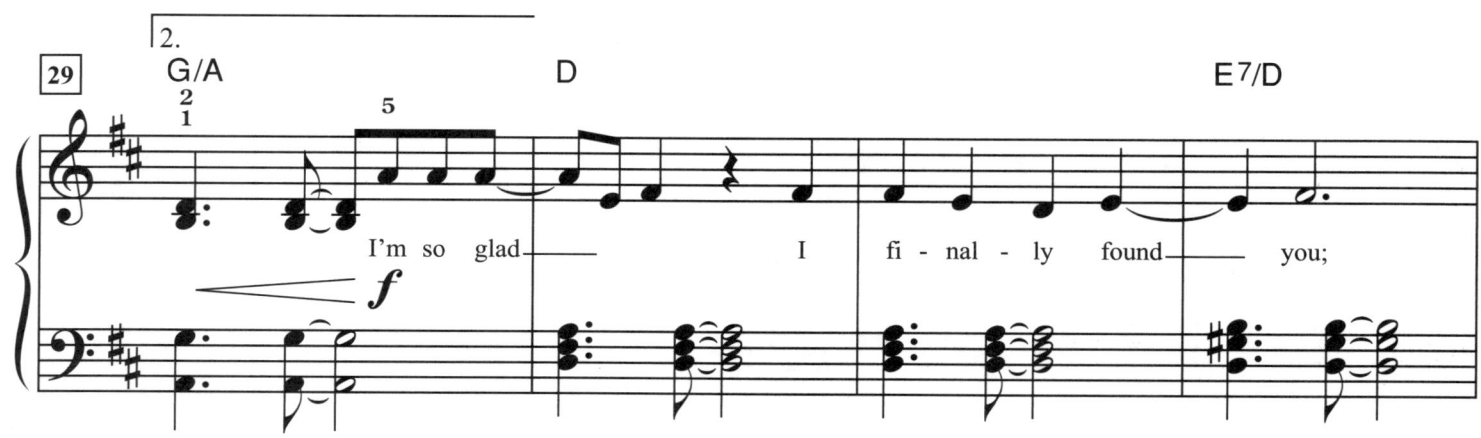

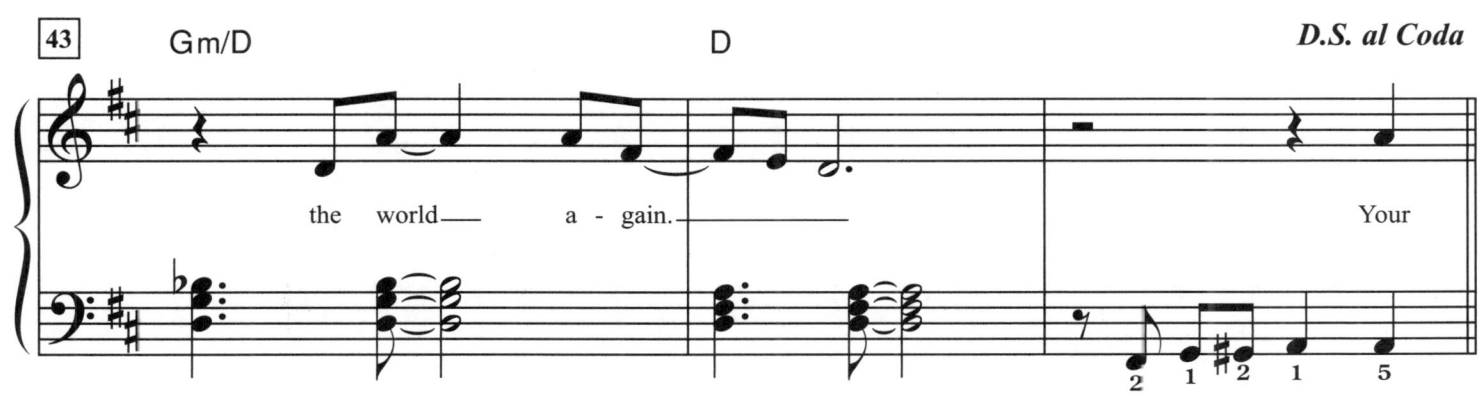
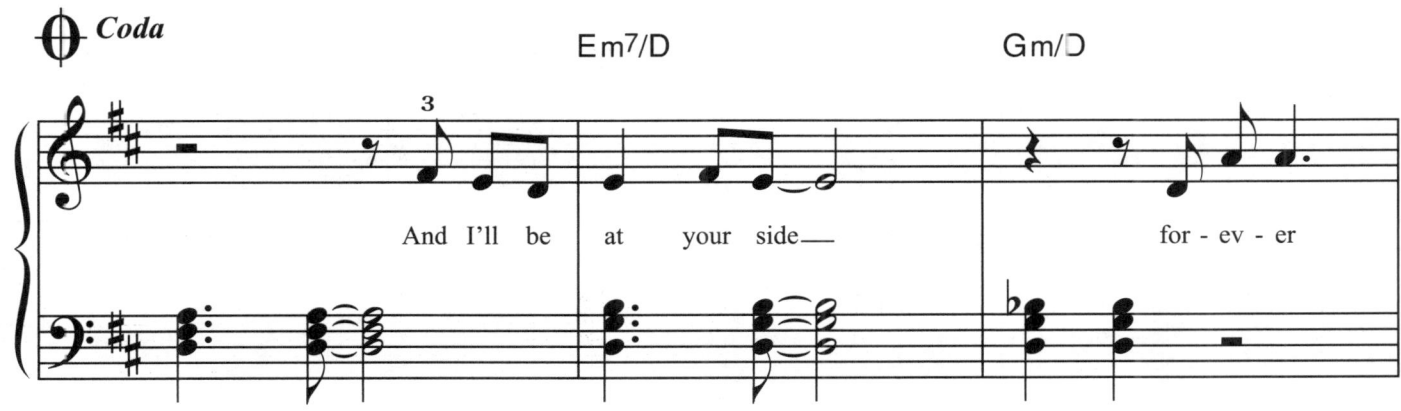

YOU'LL NEVER KNOW

Lyrics by Mack Gordon
Music by Harry Warren
Arranged by Dan Coates

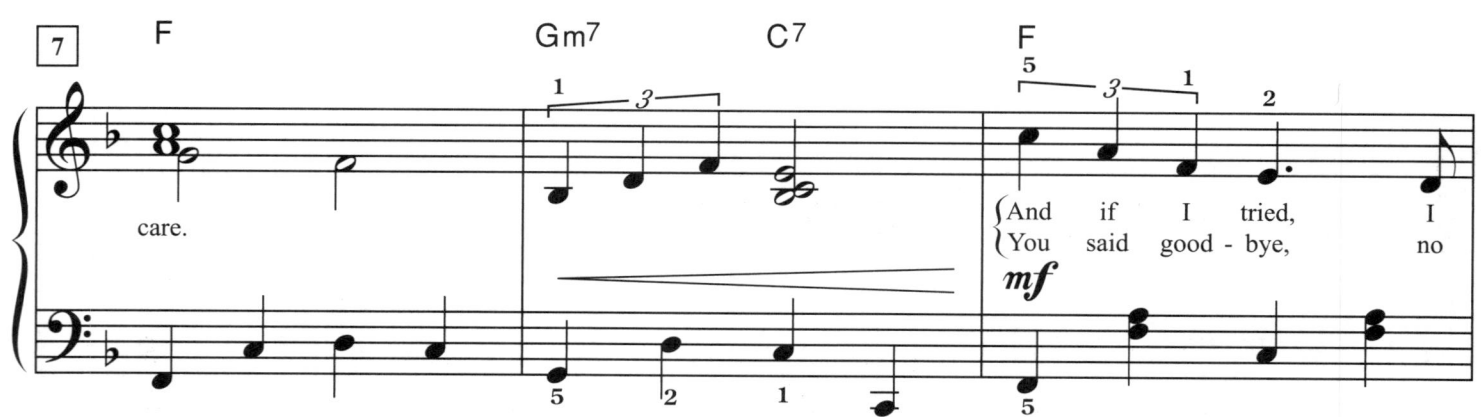

© 1943 (Renewed) WB MUSIC CORP.
All Rights Reserved

188